My name is DARWEN, a collection of letters in which I have reason to rejoice.

ANDREW is the patron saint of clowns. A WARDEN is a guardian, or keeper. ANDREW WARDEN, though he did not think of this when a "new" message to Hugh Darwen's object class gave birth to him, is a keeper of the Relational faith. He's also, I'm afraid, a bit of a clown at times.

Andrew Warden likes very much to WANDER in Relationland. We will do quite a bit of wandering in this lecture, but our feet will be firmly on the ground—we haven't time to climb the trees and look for birds' nests.

Don't be misled by Warden's vein. He's deadly serious. He just isn't solemn.* You have been WARNED.

And that's all the anagrams, unless we can contrive REDAWN for what would be a nice happening if only Relationlanders and Objectlanders could get together and make it happen, and END WAR.

Perhaps you already have the feeling that, in spite of the title of my lecture,† I prefer to be seen as a mediator, not a protagonist, in this Great Debate. I know I am not alone, among relational bigots, in that sense.

But I will not spoil my lecture by revealing its conclusion now. I will start with a very general observation about Relationland, and something nasty that happened to it. I'll make several important—at least, I think important—observations about Relationland and Objectland. My observations about Relationland are backed up by the 18 years since I first went there and the 12 years in which I have lived there. You may find my observations about Objectland a little naive in comparison—but, as I said, we're not climbing the trees. Somehow, I hope, these observations will cohere and be seen to lead to my conclusion.

Relationland was discovered, in 1970, by Ted Codd. Chris Date went there shortly afterwards, put down strong roots, and has been eloquently telling us all about it ever since.

Codd's seminal paper‡ precipitated much exciting work during the 1970s, as researchers and prototypers took his wisdom, and Date's tell-

---

*With thanks, via my friend Adrian Larner, to G. K. Chesterton.
†"OObservations of a Relational Bigot."
‡"A Relational Model of Data for Large Shared Data Banks," *Communications of the ACM* 13, No. 6 (June 1970); republished in *Communications of the ACM* 26, No. 1 (January 1983).

ing of it, as their common foundation. Suddenly, people knew how to talk about: database design; data independence; data integrity; query languages; query optimization; storage and access strategies; data security; transactions; data recovery; distributed data.

And even where they had been able to talk about these things before, they found they could now talk so much *better* about them.

The timeless bard, William Shakespeare, saw this Wisdom. So much so that his 122nd sonnet, it has recently been discovered, was written not to some Dark Lady, not to the Earl of Southampton, but to Codd himself. I reproduce it here, making one tiny orthographical correction—a matter of a capital letter.

> Thy gift, thy tables, are within my brain
> Full charactered with lasting memory,
> Which shall above that idle rank remain
> Beyond all Date, even to eternity;
> Or at the least so long as brain and heart
> Have faculty by nature to subsist,
> Till each to razed oblivion yield his part
> Of thee, thy record never can be missed.
> That poor retention could not so much hold,
> Nor need I tallies thy dear love to score;
> Therefore to give them from me was I bold,
> To trust those tables that receive thee more.
> > To keep an adjunct to remember thee
> > Were to import forgetfulness in me.

Here is my picture of Relationland (Fig. 1). Do you see its green fields, its trees and rolling countryside, not unlike that of Warwickshire (Shakespeare's county) where I live?

Now, when I wander around Relationland, in my Barbour coat and *black* wellies,* binoculars hanging from my neck and my dog at my heels, I wear this hat. Let me put it on and show you. Do you see how it encapsulates what I prefer to keep hidden? Do you see how versatile it is, when I pull down the flaps and tie them under my chin? Do you see how that not only keeps me warm and comfortable, but also keeps the hat in place in the wind? And do you see how, when I just want to be carefree and let it all hang out, I can untie the flaps and let them blow?

---

*Barbour coats and *green* wellington boots were trendy countrywear in England at the time of writing.

Fig. 1 Relationland (with thanks to the artist, Harold Hambrose)

This is my **relational hat.**

But do you also see that wall? Round about 1980, somebody built that wall around Relationland. This frightened the people who were already there, and kept out those honest citizens whom might well have otherwise wandered in. Many insiders rushed to the wall and trapped themselves in its cavernous interior; and many outsiders, failing to climb the wall, stayed inside it too.

Though it's a stout wall, and strong, it is strangely unorthogonal and higgledy-piggledy in its construction, and I call it the **Askew Wall**.

So many good people being trapped inside the Askew Wall made further research, in the 1980s, much more difficult than it should have been, and thus we had the *Dark Ages*. Worst of all, many participants in the Great Debate have even been comparing Objectland with the Askew Wall, mistakenly thinking they are comparing Objectland with Relationland.* But I live in the real Relationland, and I ask: Could some unification—that great destroyer of walls—of Objectland and Relationland bring about the end of the Dark Ages—a Renaissance?

In the body of the lecture I tried to develop the idea of unification of the best ideas from the two lands. Inevitably, this entailed modifying or discarding *none* of the Relationland wisdom and culture (except for a possible compromise concerning First Normal Form), but ignoring *some* of what Objectland has to offer—for example, I could not and still cannot see the sense in the Objectlanders' notion of sending messages to objects, and I asked "What problem, that I never knew I had, does this solve?" For most of the Objectlandish terminology I accepted, I found reasonable parallels somewhere in Relationland, and I concluded, desperately seeing this unification as our only hope of destroying the Wall (which has now been ennobled to the status of International Standard):

> And now, if Objectland will just accept the few small compromises I have asked for, we are surely there, and can bring in the bulldozers!

> I'll just briefly, if I may, put my relational hat back on, and stand firmly on the floor of this stage. Firm under my feet I have the 1970 vision of Ted Codd. Just under that I have the rock-solid First Order Predicate Calculus, and all those great logicians of the nineteenth century and early twentieth. Lurking in the wings is Bertrand Russell, with his dread warning about sets that are members of themselves. It's all right, Bert, I promise to be careful when I talk in set talk. And there's Wittgenstein, reminding me that all logical differences are Big Differences. I'll not forget that, Witty!

> And there's the likes of Shakespeare and Molière to help with the metaphors. And somewhere down there there's Aristotle. You can see why I find my relational hat so comfortable.

---

*Just as some Relationlanders, including me, have mistakenly taken Smalltalktown to be the whole of Objectland.

But the software development laboratory I work for is starting to move to Objectland. I need a new hat, if only to be sure of keeping my job! What shall it be? A bowler? A trilby? A cloth cap?

Everybody knows Juliet's lovely lines, and the warring between the Montagues and Capulets that made her say them. Now we have a new war, just as silly, and I say them again:

> What's in a name? That which we call a rose
> By any other name would smell as sweet.

So here is my Object Oriented hat—look: just a new deerstalker.

And here I still stand.

In spite of the valiant efforts of the international standardization community* (of which I now count myself a member), I do not think the Askew Wall can ever really be straightened. Having become the industry standard, it is now shackled by compatibility—no new version will ever be permitted to be without all of the undesirable features of its predecessors.

In "Adventures in Relationland" (in this volume's predecessor) I included the following complaints about SQL:

- *The Naming of Columns* describes the nasty consequences of "anonymous columns" in the results of query expressions. In SQL2 it is now possible to give names to derived columns, but for reasons of compatibility it is not compulsory to do so.

- *In Praise of Marriage* discusses further problems with column names in query expressions, along with the simple and elegant remedy that was shown to us by one of the very earliest relational prototypes, PRTV. Something like 20 years later, the first implementation of SQL2 will include this remedy, *natural join,* though duplicate column names will still be permitted (for compatibility reasons again).

- *The Keys of the Kingdom* bemoaned SQL's failure to honor the relational dictum that every relation has at least one candidate key, let alone the recommendation that every relation has exactly one *primary* key. This failure persists in SQL2.

- *Chivalry* explored some of the good things that are notably lacking in SQL as a consequence of those of its fatal flaws that I have chosen to write about. None of these are in SQL2, and I see little hope of them appearing in SQL3.

---

*I refer to the new, noticeably less askew version of SQL known informally as SQL2 and, at the time of writing, a Draft International Standard subject to public review, and to the efforts already under way to produce, yes, a third sequel (SQL2 was the second sequel, as we already had SQL/89 as a sequel to SQL/86).

- *A Constant Friend* dwells on one particular little act of chivalry (also absent from SQL2) that has more use than is apparent on first inspection.

- *Table_Dee and Table_Dum,* tables with no columns at all, though occurring naturally (albeit as rarities) in Relationland, would be quite out of their environment in SQL and would have no chance of surviving.

- In *Into the Unknown* I join in the attack on nulls.

In the present volume I have added:

- *Without CHECK Option,* in which I find serious problems in SQL's support for "updating through views" (such as it is).

- *The Role of Functional Dependence in Query Decomposition,* in which I show that SQL's lack of awareness of *functional dependencies* (FDs) causes it to behave in a number of user-hostile ways.

- *The Duplicity of Duplicate Rows.* I doubt whether I manage to add anything really novel in connexion with this, perhaps the most talked about of all of SQL's "fatal flaws," but I feel a duty to nail my colors clearly to the mast, using my own words.

Some of these problems will also be with us forever because of the compatibility shackle.

ACKNOWLEDGMENTS

The manager who sent me on that course in 1972 was **Colin Brown,** with whom I was associated for most of my career between 1969 and 1981, and to whom I owe very many debts of gratitude. All of my colleagues from the days of Terminal Business System and Business System 12 will know what I mean.

PART II

RELATIONAL DATABASE MANAGEMENT

4

What Is a Relation?

ABSTRACT

Despite the fact that the relational model has its foundations in mathematics, relations in the relational model and relations in mathematics are not the same thing. This paper discusses some of the differences between the two.

COMMENTS ON PUBLICATION

This book's predecessor *Relational Database Writings 1985–1989* included a paper with the title "What Is a Domain?" [6]. The present paper might be regarded as a logical companion to that earlier paper—especially since the earlier paper is referenced several times in what follows. In fact, the present paper clarifies and refines some of the ideas from that earlier paper.

1. INTRODUCTION

The title of this paper is slightly tongue in cheek: Every reader of this book will already have a pretty good idea of what a relation is, at least in the relational model sense. However, as the Abstract indicates, there are certain

---

Previously unpublished.

differences, some of them perhaps not widely appreciated, between relations as understood in mathematics and relations as understood in the relational model. The purpose of this paper is to spell out such differences in detail. Of course, it goes without saying—at least, I hope it does—that my objective is one of *clarification* merely: The paper is in no way intended as an attack on the relational model. (Nor is it intended as a defense! The relational model ideas discussed herein have all been very adequately defended elsewhere.)

For purposes of reference, let me begin with some definitions. First, here is a definition (taken from reference [4]) of "relation" as that term is understood in the relational model:

A *relation* (*R*, say) on a collection of domains *D1, D2, . . . , Dn* (not necessarily all distinct) consists of two parts, a *heading* and a *body*.

- The *heading* consists of a fixed set of distinct *attributes*

  { *A1, A2, . . . , An* },

  or more precisely attribute-domain pairs,

  { (*A1:D1*), (*A2:D2*), . . . , (*An:Dn*) }

  such that each attribute *Aj* corresponds to exactly one of the underlying domains *Dj* (*j* = 1, 2, . . . , *n*).

- The *body* consists of a time-varying set of *tuples,* where each tuple in turn consists of a set of attribute-value pairs

  { (*A1:vi1*), (*A2:vi2*), . . . , (*An:vin*) }

  (*i* = 1, 2, . . . , *m*, where *m* is the number of tuples in the set). In each such tuple, there is one such attribute-value pair (*Aj:vij*) for each attribute *Aj* in the heading. For any given attribute-value pair (*Aj:vij*), *vij* is a value from the unique domain *Dj* that is associated with the attribute *Aj*.

The values *m* and *n* are called the *cardinality* and the *degree*, respectively, of the relation *R*. The cardinality changes with time, whereas the degree does not.

By contrast, here is the mathematical definition (taken from reference [9]):

An *n*-ary relation is a set of ordered *n*-tuples.

(In this definition, an ordered *n*-tuple is taken to be simply an ordered list of *n* values.)

The mathematical definition is somewhat simpler!—and in the remainder of this paper, we will see why this is so. However, there are a couple of preliminary matters that we need to get out of the way first before we can go on to discuss some of the more substantive differences between the two definitions.

- First, the emphasis in most mathematics texts is generally (though not exclusively) on *binary* relations, and the unqualified term "relation" is usually taken in such contexts to mean a binary relation specifically. The "ordered *n*-tuples" of such a relation are of course simply ordered *pairs*.

- Second, the nature of the underlying domains is usually left quite unspecified in mathematical contexts; indeed, the term "domain" (in the relational model sense) does not seem to be used very much, if at all. In the particular case of binary relations, in fact, the term "domain" is often reserved to mean the first domain specifically, and the second domain is then referred to as the "range." (Note that it makes sense in the mathematical case to refer to "first" and "second" in this way, because a mathematical [binary] relation is a set of *ordered* pairs.)

2. RELATIONS IN THE RELATIONAL MODEL VS. RELATIONS IN MATHEMATICS

Fig. 1 is a table summarizing the major points of difference between relations in the relational model and relations in mathematics. (*Note:* A similar but not identical table of differences is given by Codd in reference [3].) Each of the points in the table is discussed in detail in the subsequent text.

Normalization

Note: A certain amount of care is needed in discussing this first point of difference—the distinction between "relational model relations" and mathematical relations with respect to normalization is perhaps more apparent

	Relational model	Mathematics
1.	Must be normalized	Need not be
2.	"Time-varying"	Not
3.	Heading an unordered set of attribute : domain pairs	Heading an ordered list of domains
4.	*n*-ary relational algebra operators exist	. . . see text . . .

Fig. 1 Relations in the relational model vs. relations in mathematics (summary)

*than real (or, rather, the concept of normalization is perhaps not as gener-
ally well understood as it ought to be!). For further explanation, read on.*

It is of course well known that relations in the relational model are
required to be normalized, whereas relations in mathematics are not. "Normalized" here means *first normal form*—i.e., the underlying domains contain simple values only, or in other words "all attribute values are atomic"
[4] (this is the well known "no repeating groups" requirement). "Atomic,"
in turn, means that the value in question "cannot be decomposed into
smaller pieces *by the DBMS*" [2; emphasis added]. But, of course, it does
not mean that the value in question cannot be decomposed at all. Indeed,
I have argued elsewhere [6] that a domain is basically nothing more nor less
than a data type, potentially (even probably) user-defined and thus potentially of arbitrary complexity, and hence that an attribute value that is
drawn from such a domain can certainly be "nonatomic." The point is,
however, that attribute values are always atomic, and relations are always
normalized, *from the DBMS's point of view.*

Now, I have stated elsewhere [4] that the domains of a normalized relation cannot be relation-valued—i.e., the values in those domains cannot
themselves be relations. In the light of the preceding paragraph, this statement obviously requires some clarification. Clearly it would be possible to
specify a domain (user-defined data type) whose values were relations, and
hence to construct a relation with a relation-valued domain. But, to repeat,
values from that domain would still be atomic from the DBMS's point of
view. Decomposing those values into "smaller pieces" would not be done
by the DBMS per se; instead, it would be done by invoking the user-defined
functions provided along with the specification of the user-defined data
type for precisely that purpose. (The situation is exactly the same as that
existing today in connexion with *all* "nonrelational" operators—comparison operators, arithmetic operators, etc. The DBMS per se does not know
what it means, for example, to add two numbers together, but it does know
how to invoke a builtin function called " + " that can perform that operation on its behalf.)

> *Aside:* Observe the difference between a system that supports the capa-
> bility just described and one that supports "NF squared relations."
> "NF squared" (NFNF) stands for *non first normal form* [8]; an NF
> squared relation is a relation whose domains are (possibly) relation-
> valued (and, of course, the relations in those domains can in turn be
> NF squared relations, and so on, recursively, to any depth). The differ-
> ence—and it is a crucial one—between an "NF squared relation"
> DBMS and one that supports the capability described above is that the
> NF squared relation DBMS *knows that the relation-valued domains*

are relation-valued, and decomposing individual values into "smaller pieces" is done by the DBMS, not by a user-supplied function. (And the DBMS is thus probably more complex than a pure relational DBMS.) *End of aside.*

Furthermore, I have also discussed (reference [4] again and elsewhere) the point that the relational model does permit *composite* domains and attributes, where a composite domain is basically just a named combination of simple domains, and a composite attribute is an attribute defined on a composite domain. These points also require some clarification. In fact, I would like to argue now that composite domains and attributes per se are not quite what is needed after all. Consider the following example, which is based on one first given in reference [6]. (We assume for the sake of this example that the system does not provide a builtin DATE data type.)

Example (expressed in pseudoSQL):

```
CREATE DOMAIN MONTH CHAR(2) ;
CREATE DOMAIN DAY   CHAR(2) ;
CREATE DOMAIN YEAR  CHAR(4) ;

CREATE DOMAIN DATE  ( MON DOMAIN ( MONTH ),
                      DAY DOMAIN ( DAY ),
                      YR  DOMAIN ( YEAR ) ) ;
```

The composite domain DATE here has three components MON, DAY, and YR, defined on the simple domains MONTH, DAY, and YEAR, respectively. Here is a sample relation definition using this composite domain:

```
CREATE TABLE EMP
     ( EMP#      DOMAIN ( EMP# ),
       ..... ,
       HIREDATE DOMAIN ( DATE ),
       ..... ,
       PRIMARY KEY ( EMP# ) ) ;
```

HIREDATE here is a composite attribute. And here are some sample queries against this relation:

```
SELECT ...
FROM    EMP
WHERE   EMP.HIREDATE = '01011984' ;

SELECT ...
FROM    EMP
WHERE   YR ( EMP.HIREDATE ) < '1984' ;
```

The first query here makes reference to the HIREDATE attribute in its entirety. The second makes reference to the YR component only, using the name YR as a *component selector function* (but see below).

End of example.

Let me now point out that, if we can agree (as we surely must) that the relational model should include proper support for user-defined data types, then there would be no need for (explicit) composite domains per se at all, and hence (of course) no need for (explicit) composite attributes either. In the example above, for instance, DATE could easily be defined as a user-defined data type; it might be defined in terms of "component" data types MONTH, DAY, and YEAR, or it might be defined in some quite different way, e.g., as a decimal integer representing the number of days since some defined origin point. Either way, it makes no matter; the data type *user* (as opposed to the data type definer) does not know and does not care what the internal representation of dates is; all such a user needs to know is that (a) certain functions called MON, DAY, and YR exist (they are provided by the data type definer), and (b) those functions return, respectively, the appropriate month, day, and year values for a given date.

> *Aside:* There would still be a need for *sets* of attributes, of course—e.g., in the definition of "candidate key" (a candidate key would be defined as a set of attributes [of the relation in question] that possesses the necessary uniqueness and minimality properties [4]). And we might agree to refer to such a set of attributes as a composite attribute. But there would be no need to provide a distinct mechanism, separate from the user-defined data type mechanism, by which users could group attributes together and give such a group a name. *End of aside.*

It follows from the foregoing discussion, by the way, that the term "component selector function," which I introduced above to refer to functions such as MON, DAY, and YR, is not really very apt. The reason is, of course, that those functions might not actually be selecting components at all. We might agree to continue to use the term informally, but we should understand that such usage is indeed informal, and possibly inaccurate.

Incidentally, this view of a "composite domain" as a special case of a user-defined data type shows clearly why access to the individual components of a "composite attribute" should be by means of appropriate functions, *not* by means of multiple dot qualifiers. For example, referring to the YR "component" of EMP.HIREDATE as "YR (EMP.HIREDATE)" is reasonable; referring to it as "EMP.HIREDATE.YR" is not. Why not? Because the two dot separators in this latter expression are *two different operators*. The first is being used to select an attribute of a relation, and is clearly an operator that must be understood by the DBMS; the second is being used to select a *"component"* of an attribute, and is *not* understood by the DBMS. In other words, HIREDATE is *not* a composite attribute, and YR is *not* a simple attribute within a composite attribute, so far as the DBMS is concerned.

Of course, most relational DBMSs today already support DATE (and other "composite domains," such as TIME and MONEY) as builtin data types. And those DBMSs typically do provide a set of "component selector functions" for those data types. The foregoing discussion shows why (conceptually, at least) those functions should be regarded, not as part of the DBMS per se, but rather as "external" functions that (a) are provided by some "user" (actually by the DBMS vendor), (b) can be invoked by the DBMS, but (c) in principle, at least, are not "understood" by the DBMS.*

To conclude this discussion of normalization as a difference between relations in mathematics and relations in the relational model, I return to the point that the emphasis in mathematics tends to be on binary relations specifically, whereas the emphasis in the relational model is on *n*-ary relations for arbitrary nonnegative integer *n*. *The whole field of what is now usually called dependency theory*—the large body of theorems and techniques concerning such matters as functional dependence, multivalued dependence, join dependence, higher normal forms, etc.—*is crucially dependent on this difference in emphasis.* For example, the concept of third normal form (3NF) is relevant only to relations of degree three or more, because *all* (well, almost all [7]) relations of degree less than three are necessarily in 3NF[†]). In fact, the entire field of dependency theory can be regarded as a new branch of mathematics, one that was brought into being by the special requirements of a theory of data and a theory of *n*-ary relations (as opposed to a theory of binary relations merely).

Time-Varying Relations

When we say that a relation is "time-varying" in the relational model, we mean that, as time progresses, we can insert, delete, and modify tuples of the relation. This notion accords well with our intuitive understanding of a relation as an abstraction of a file. But it has no meaning in mathematics. There is no notion in mathematics of (for example) inserting an element into a set. If A is the set $\{1,2,3\}$ and we somehow construct the set $B = \{1,2,3,4\}$—i.e., we somehow "insert" the element 4 into set A, speaking *very* loosely—the resulting set B is *a different set*.

In fact, of course, a "time-varying relation" is not really a relation at

---

*I find myself slightly at odds with Codd here. Here again is the quote from Codd's book regarding the meaning of "atomic," now given in its entirety: "Atomic data cannot be decomposed into smaller pieces by the DBMS (*excluding certain special functions*)" [3; emphasis added]. This quote seems to suggest that, in Codd's opinion, the "special" (i.e., "component selector") functions should indeed be considered to be part of the DBMS.

[†]Of course, this remark should not be construed to mean that the discipline of further normalization would be unnecessary if we dealt in binary relations only.

all in the mathematical sense. Certainly the *value* of a "time-varying relation" at any given time is a relation, but its value is *different relations at
different times* (in general). A relation per se (in the mathematical sense)
and a "time-varying relation" are thus very different things.

So where does this leave us? Well, a much better way to look at the
situation is as follows. A relation is basically just a *variable,* in the traditional programming language sense (see reference [5]). As such, it has a
type and it has a *value;* the value changes with time, of course, whereas the
type does not. In more conventional (relational model) terms, the type is
the *heading* of the relation and the value is the *body* (and, of course, the
body at any given time *is* basically a relation in the mathematical sense).

Incidentally, this interpretation of a "time-varying relation" as a variable shows why the term "time-varying" is really not a very good one. If
I say for example—

```
DECLARE QTY INTEGER ... ;
```

—I do not call QTY a "time-varying integer," I call it an *integer variable.*
Likewise, if I say—

```
CREATE TABLE EMP ... ;
```

—I should surely call EMP a *relation* (or table) *variable* and have done with
it. This is why, whenever I use the term "time-varying," I always at least
mentally put it in quotes.

To return to my main theme: It is important to understand that certain
critical aspects of the relational model—in particular, all aspects having to
do with *data integrity*—make sense only because of the "time-varying" nature of relations within the model. The general point is that integrity constraints (or most integrity constraints, anyway) are required by definition
to apply "for all time"—i.e., to every possible value of the relation body.
In particular, the concepts of *candidate key, primary key, alternate key,* and
foreign key [4]—all of which are essentially integrity-related constructs—
all have meaning only within the context of "time-varying relations." Thus,
these are all concepts that apply to relations in the relational model but not
to relations in mathematics.

In a like manner, the higher normal forms and associated dependencies
(functional dependence, multivalued dependence, etc.)—although usually
considered part of a separate theory that builds on top of the relational
model, rather than part of the relational model per se—are also concepts
that apply to "time-varying relations" but not (except in a rather trivial
sense) to relations in mathematics.

Relation Headings

We saw above that the concept of a "relation heading" really applies only to the relational model, not to mathematics—or at least, the concept is much more significant in the relational model than it is in mathematics. However, there is arguably *some* (perhaps rather weak) analog of the concept in mathematics. In the present subsection, we compare and contrast the relational model and mathematical versions of the concept.

The overriding point is that in the relational model, every attribute has a name that is unique within its containing relation,* and furthermore that name is independent of the relative left-to-right position of the attribute within that relation. (In fact, of course, there *is* no left-to-right ordering of attributes within a relation, so far as the relational model is concerned.) The heading of a relation thus consists of a *set* (unordered by definition) of attribute-name/domain-name pairs (refer back to the definition in Section 1 of this paper).

In mathematics, by contrast, there is no true notion of "attribute" at all, and hence (a fortiori) no notion of "attribute name" either. The heading of a relation (inasmuch as such a concept may be said to exist at all) is nothing more than an *ordered list* of domain names (in which, of course, a given domain name may appear any number of times).

It follows from the foregoing that a tuple in the relational model has no left-to-right ordering for its components; instead, each component (conceptually) carries the relevant attribute name along with it (again, refer back to the definition in Section 1). In mathematics, by contrast, a tuple consists of an ordered list of components, each component being associated with the relevant "attribute" by its ordinal position merely.

> *Aside:* In Codd's original paper on the relational model [2], we find the following: ". . . we propose that users deal, not with relations which are domain-ordered, but with *relationships* which are their domain-unordered counterparts . . . [Users] should interact with a relational model of the data consisting of a collection of time-varying relationships (rather than relations)." In other words, the domains (and hence attributes) of a relation *were* originally considered to have a left-to-right ordering, but the relational model was concerned with "relationships" instead of relations. In almost all subsequent work, how-

---

*I assume here a version of the model that is properly closed with respect to attribute naming, so that this remark applies to *all* relations, derived as well as base. See references [4] and [11] for further discussion of this important point.

ever, Codd has used the term "relation" to mean what he originally called a relationship. *End of aside.*

One final (and very tiny) point: Given that a tuple in the relational model has no left-to-right ordering for its components, the term "tuple" is perhaps not terribly appropriate!—since it is short for n-tuple, and "n-tuple" in mathematics is usually taken to mean an *ordered* n-tuple. (After all, if it were not ordered, then it would be indistinguishable from a set of cardinality at most n.)

Relational Algebra

Very little work seems to have been done in mathematics on general n-ary relational operators, presumably because of the historical emphasis already noted on binary relations specifically. For example, reference [10] gives a definition of an operator called *relative product:* If R(A,B) and S(B,C) are two binary relations, then their relative product T(A,C) is the binary relation consisting of all pairs (a,c) such that, for some b, the pair (a,b) appears in R and the pair (b,c) appears in S. In relational model terms, this is the projection over (A,C) of the natural join of R and S over B. But notice how the operation is specifically defined to produce a binary relation as its result; the ternary relation that is the intermediate result—the join—is never explicitly mentioned.

Thus, although operators such as natural join (and all of the other operators of the relational algebra) are clearly *applicable* to relations in the mathematical sense, it is fair to say that they were *first defined* (for the most part) in the context of relations in the relational model sense. Indeed, the theory of such operators (including the laws of expression transformation, the associated principles of optimization, etc.)—like the theory of functional dependencies (etc.) mentioned above—can reasonably be regarded as a new branch of mathematics; and, just like that other theory, the theory in question is one that arose specifically as part of the development of the relational approach to the problem of database management.

3. KINDS OF RELATIONS

Another difference between relations in mathematics and relations in the relational model is that it is convenient—indeed, necessary—in the relational model to categorize relations into a variety of different kinds. This (regrettably enough) is another area in which a certain amount of confusion reigns at the time of writing. Codd's original paper [2] included a section entitled "Expressible, Named, and Stored Relations," and the concepts introduced in that section bear repeating here. *Note:* I am not quoting Codd's paper verbatim, however, and I must accept responsibility for any distortion of his intended meaning. But the point is worth emphasizing that he was very definitely using the term "relation" to mean a relation *variable* (or "time-varying relation") specifically, and I shall do the same in what follows.

- First, a *named* relation is simply a relation that has been declared to the DBMS by some suitably authorized user; the declaration will include a relation name, of course. In current systems, the named relations are the base relations and the views (and we might want to add further kinds of relation—e.g., snapshots [1]—to this list at some future time).

- Second, an *expressible* relation is a relation that can be obtained from the set of named relations by means of an expression of the relational algebra (or whatever language is provided by the DBMS for writing relation-valued expressions). Of course, every named relation is an expressible relation, but the converse is not true. Base relations, views, snapshots, and query results are all expressible relations.

- Third, a *stored* relation is an expressible relation (*not* necessarily a named relation—see further discussion of this point below) that is supported by the DBMS in some "direct, efficient" manner (with appropriate definitions of "direct" and "efficient," of course—details beyond the scope of this paper).

- Reference [2] did not mention the term "base relation" (even though I used it a couple of times above), so let me give a definition of that term here, viz: A *base* relation is a named relation that is not expressible in terms of other named relations.

- It is also convenient to introduce the term "derived relation," which I define as follows: A *derived* relation is an expressible relation that is not a base relation.* Views—and snapshots—are thus named derived relations. Query results are unnamed derived relations. And a base relation is a named relation that is not a derived relation.

Naturally, the set of stored relations must be such that all named relations (and hence all expressible relations) can be derived from them. *Note carefully, however, that there is no requirement that all stored relations be base relations, nor that all base relations be stored relations* (a lack of understanding of this point is the principal source of the confusion referred to above). For example, we might store the join of two base relations (for

---

*Be warned, however, that other writers use "derived" to mean what I am here calling "expressible."

performance reasons); ORACLE does this today. Or we might store a base relation as two disjoint restrictions (again, for performance reasons); DB2 does this today. And there is no reason in principle why the differences between stored and base relations should not be much greater than these two rather simple illustrations suggest. Indeed, I venture to predict that we will see the potential for much greater differentiation as products evolve (especially in the direction of distributed database support).

> *Aside:* In most cases, of course, there does tend to be a one-to-one correspondence between stored and base relations, at least in those products on the market today, and no doubt this state of affairs accounts for the fact that many people do tend to confuse the two notions. Also, honesty compels me to confess that I might be partly responsible for the confusion: In several books (e.g. reference [4]) I have said that "a base [relation] . . . physically exists, in the sense that there exist physically stored records . . . that directly represent that [relation] in storage." My apologies to any reader who may have been led astray by such remarks in the past. Mea culpa. *End of aside.*

4. CONCLUSION

In this paper, I have tried to spell out some (not necessarily all, of course) of the differences between relations as understood in the relational model and relations in the mathematical sense. I hope the discussions have served to illustrate in part the true nature of Codd's contribution: Starting from the simple idea—obvious, after the fact!—of the *n*-ary relation as an abstraction of the intuitive notion of a file, he was able to lay the foundations for an extensive (and solid) theory of data and database management. Prior to his original paper [2], *n*-ary (as opposed to binary) relations had received comparatively little attention in the literature. Following Codd's pioneering work on their application to database management, however, *n*-ary relations have come to form the basis for certain branches of mathematics in their own right.

ACKNOWLEDGMENTS

I am grateful to Hugh Darwen and Adrian Larner for a great deal of correspondence and discussion regarding the matters addressed in this paper, and to Hugh again and Chris Loosley and David McGoveran for their careful and helpful reviews of earlier drafts.

REFERENCES AND BIBLIOGRAPHY

1. Michel E. Adiba, "Derived Relations: A Unified Mechanism for Views, Snapshots, and Distributed Data," IBM Research Report RJ2881 (July 1980).

2. E. F. Codd, "A Relational Model of Data for Large Shared Data Banks," *Communications of the ACM* 13, No. 6 (June 1970). Republished in *Communications of the ACM* 26, No. 1 (January 1983).

3. E. F. Codd, *The Relational Model For Database Management Version 2* (Reading, MA: Addison-Wesley, 1990).

4. C. J. Date, "The Relational Model," Part III of C. J. Date, *An Introduction to Database Systems: Volume I,* 5th edition (Reading, MA: Addison-Wesley, 1990).

5. C. J. Date, "What Is a Data Model?" in C. J. Date, *An Introduction to Database Systems: Volume II* (Reading, MA: Addison-Wesley, 1983).

6. C. J. Date, "What Is a Domain?" in C. J. Date, *Relational Database Writings 1985–1989* (Reading, MA: Addison-Wesley, 1990).

7. Hugh Darwen, "The Nullologist in Relationland" (in this volume).

8. Mark A. Roth, Henry F. Korth, and Abraham Silberschatz, "Extended Relational Algebra and Relational Calculus for Nested Relational Databases," *ACM Transactions on Database Systems* 13, No. 4 (December 1988).

9. Robert R. Stoll, *Sets, Logic, and Axiomatic Theories* (San Francisco, CA: W. H. Freeman and Company, 1961).

10. Patrick Suppes, *Introduction to Logic* (Princeton, NJ: Van Nostrand, 1957).

11. Andrew Warden, "The Naming of Columns," in C. J. Date, *Relational Database Writings 1985–1989* (Reading, MA: Addison-Wesley, 1990).

APPENDIX A:
A LOGICIAN'S VIEW

In the body of this paper, I gave the mathematician's view of a relation: "An *n*-ary relation is a set of ordered *n*-tuples." In this appendix, I would like to mention an alternative view very briefly—namely, the logician's view. In logic, an *n*-ary relation is simply that which is designated by an *n*-place *predicate* in what is called the *first order predicate calculus* [9]. For example, the expression "$>(a,b)$" is a 2-place predicate that designates the "greater than" relation, and "SP(S#,P#,QTY)" is a 3-place predicate that designates the "shipments" relation in the usual suppliers-and-parts database. In general, an *n*-place predicate can be thought of as a truth-valued function with *n* arguments; a given tuple appears in the corresponding relation if and only if the function evaluates to *true* for the argument values represented by that tuple.

One immediate consequence of this view of a relation is that the entire business of whether or not "duplicate tuples" should be allowed becomes completely irrelevant. For let $R(a,b, \ldots ,c)$ be an *n*-place predicate, and let $(a1,b1, \ldots ,c1)$ be an arbitrary assignment of specific values to the arguments a, b, $\ldots$, c. Then

```
R(a1,b1,...,c1)  AND  R(a1,b1,...,c1)  ≡  R(a1,b1,...,c1)
```

(this is the law of *idempotence*).

Another immediate consequence is that relations are *always* in "first normal form," because the logician has nothing whatever to say about any possible "internal structure" that a predicate's argument values might possess.

The operators of the relational algebra can easily be defined in terms of predicates, of course. For example, the union $U(a,b, \ldots ,c)$ of $R(a,b, \ldots ,c)$ and $S(a,b, \ldots ,c)$ is defined as follows:

```
U(a,b,...,c)  =def  R(a,b,...,c)  OR  S(a,b,...,c)
```

(using "=def" to mean "is defined as"). Similarly, the join $J(a,b,c)$ of $R(a,b)$ and $S(b,c)$ is defined as follows:

```
J(a,b,c)  =def  R(a,b)  AND  S(b,c)
```

And so on.

The point of all of the above is as follows, When we talk about the foundations of the relational model, we usually talk in terms of sets and set theory—a mathematical foundation, in fact. But the foregoing indicates that it is at least equally possible to talk in terms of a foundation in logic—specifically, in the first order predicate calculus—instead. And this alternative perception does have certain arguments in its favor, as the discussions above might suggest. In other words, some people would argue that the true foundation of the relational model is really the first order predicate calculus, not set theory, and moreover that there is no real need to invoke set-oriented ideas at all in developing or discussing the model.

APPENDIX B:
A NOTE ON REDUNDANCY

Codd's original paper [2] included some remarks on redundancy that are also relevant (perhaps somewhat tangentially) to the overall theme of this paper. To quote: "Redundancy in the set of named relations must be distinguished from redundancy in the set of stored relations" (paraphrasing slightly). This point is clearly correct, but I would like to elaborate on it slightly in this appendix.

First, redundancy in the set of named relations is important, because such redundancy very definitely affects the user's perception of the database. For consider, Any such redundancy is either controlled or uncontrolled (by "controlled," I mean that the DBMS assumes the responsibility for keeping the redundant data "in synch"). If it is controlled, the user has to know that certain updates will have side-effects. If it is not controlled, the user has to know that he or she is responsible for keeping things "in synch," and/or has to know that certain queries can produce inconsistencies or contradictions.

A concrete example of the foregoing is provided by views. As explained in the body of this paper, views are named relations that are derived from the base relations. The set of named relations is thus clearly redundant ("strongly redundant," to use the terminology of reference [2]); however, the redundancy is *controlled,* and the user has to understand that if he or she makes a change to some view, a corresponding change will automatically be made to the appropriate base data.

By contrast, redundancy in the set of *stored* relations is not important, at least not to the user. It is important to the DBMS, of course, and important for performance (presumably performance is the justification for there being such redundancy in the first place), but it is not important to the user, since it is not—I trust—visible in the named relations (unless of course it happens to *reflect* some redundancy in those named relations).

5

The Duplicity
of Duplicate Rows

ABSTRACT

Most commercial relational products permit tables to contain duplicate rows. This apparently tiny departure from the prescriptions of the relational model leads to a disproportionate degree of duplicitous behavior on the part of those products.

COMMENTS ON PUBLICATION

Duplicity is defined as "insincerity, double-dealing" (*Chambers Twentieth Century Dictionary*); "hypocritical cunning or deception" (*Webster's New World Dictionary*). Strong language, perhaps; the damage done to relational systems by duplicate row support is certainly serious, but presumably those who insisted on such support did not do so out of insincerity or hypocritical cunning. Anyway, I wrote a chapter myself in this book's predecessor entitled "Why Duplicate Rows Are Prohibited" [8], in which I presented as many arguments against duplicate rows as I could think of. In

---

Previously unpublished.

what follows, Hugh Darwen not only offers novel versions of some of those same arguments, he also manages to come up with some additional ones. In particular, he stresses the fundamental point that, in order to discuss (in any intelligent manner) the question of whether two objects are duplicates of each other, it is essential to have a clear *criterion of identity* for the class of objects under consideration. In other words, what does it mean for two objects, be they rows in a table or anything else, to be "the same"?

1. INTRODUCTION

It is difficult to find anything to say that has not already been said, particularly in view of reference [8], in support of the Relationlanders' position in the "duplicate rows" debate. On the other hand, it is also difficult to find anything that has been put in writing to oppose the Relationlanders' position by those who would permit duplicate rows, whom I will hereinafter refer to as "duplicaters" [sic]. (Reference [2] is the only attempt I am aware of, and I find the arguments presented therein unconvincing, and indeed self-contradictory.) Nevertheless, I know that duplicaters persist, particularly those who continue to defend the implementations to be found inside that Askew Wall they built around Relationland [6].

In reference [11] I came out as a firm opponent of duplicate rows, resting my case primarily on the impossibility of updating or deleting just one of a pair of duplicate rows without simultaneously doing exactly the same thing to the other. As a self-avowed "keeper of the relational faith," I could hardly do otherwise, but many duplicaters apparently remain unconvinced, not only by my arguments but also by those of the originator of the relational model in reference [3] (which have regrettably muddied the water by giving an example that many of us in the relational camp agree is spurious), and by the scholarly and in my view compelling treatment of reference [8].

On the other hand, I have further noticed that those I perceive as having no axe to grind find the arguments against duplicate rows so convincing that they wonder at the need to spell them out in such detail, and wonder too why there is any debate at all. They, like me, might feel entitled to a clear exposition of the duplicaters' view.

The arguments I present here are hardly novel, nor are any of the adverse consequences (e.g., for optimization) that I note. Nor do I give anything like the complete case against duplicate rows. I see the purposes of this chapter, rather, as:

▪ To present the relational argument again, in the manner of my own choosing, thereby to affirm my wholehearted support for those who have already taken the same trouble

- To describe a simple relational treatment of the problem that apparently underlies the "requirement" for duplicate rows

- To invite the duplicaters, should they remain unconvinced, to present their counterarguments *and* their counterproposals to my suggestion*

2. RELATIONS AND TUPLE-BAGS

My first question to the duplicaters is: "Do you want to be able to have duplicate rows in a relation?" Did anybody say "Yes"? Well, I'll agree to that on one condition, namely, that we agree on a *criterion of identity* for relations, such that, for instance, the following two tables represent the same relation:

UNITY1	N
	1

UNITY2	N
	1
	1

Loosely speaking, our criterion of identity will say that relations R1 and R2 are the same relation if and only if R1's heading is the same set of attributes as R2's heading, and R1's body is the same set of rows as R2's body. And we already agree, I'm sure, that sets S1 and S2 are the same set if and only if every member of S1 is a member of S2 and every member of S2 is a member of S1 (this is the criterion of identity for sets).

UNITY1 and UNITY2 meet the foregoing conditions, and so represent *the same relation.* The three depicted values for N are all *the same value,* namely 1, under the criterion of identity for integers (which again I'm sure we all understand). The three rows, one in UNITY1 and two in UNITY2, all represent *the same tuple,* under the criterion of identity for tuples (which is as follows: two tuples T1 and T2 are the same tuple if they comprise the same attributes and for each attribute T1 has the same value as T2).

Having squared things up, I hope, with the set theoreticians, I now try to do the same with the logicians. UNITY1 and UNITY2 are both tables representing the relation that represents the predicate: "The integer *n* is unity." The placeholder *n* corresponds to the attribute name N. If I replace *n* by the integer 1, I obtain the true proposition "1 is unity"; if I replace it by 2, I obtain the false proposition "2 is unity." UNITY2 says everything that UNITY1 says, and says nothing that UNITY1 does not say. Con-

---

*A similar (perhaps less demanding) challenge was recently issued by Codd: "Shoot down the following assertion using rational and technical arguments only—duplicate rows within a relation are not needed in database management" [4].

versely, UNITY1 says everything that UNITY2 says, and says nothing that UNITY2 does not say. UNITY1 says "1 is unity." UNITY2 says "1 is unity. Oh, and by the way, 1 is unity." The logician does not distinguish between what UNITY1 says and what UNITY2 says. Anything that can be derived (i.e., proved) from the proposition stated by UNITY1 can be derived from the (compound) proposition stated by UNITY2, and anything that can be derived from the proposition stated by UNITY2 can be derived from the proposition stated by UNITY1.

In case it bothers you that UNITY1 and UNITY2, the same relation, have different names, I merely observe that it is not at all uncommon for a thing to have several different names.

In Relationland we prohibit UNITY2 altogether, our justification being that redundancy such as that exhibited therein can *never* help, can *sometimes* confuse. If the answers to the following three questions are not all the same, then there's something nasty and counterintuitive in the woodshed:

1. How many numbers are unity?
2. How many 1-tuples are there in UNITY1?
3. How many 1-tuples are there in UNITY2?

(And by the way, if your answer to question 3 is not one but two, may I further enquire as to how you know?)

And yet the duplicaters still want somehow to distinguish UNITY1 and UNITY2. In that case I now ask them: "As UNITY1 and UNITY2 represent the same relation, and yet you want them somehow to be considered to contain different values, under what criterion of identity are those values different?" (for they are certainly not different under the criterion of identity for relations).

The duplicaters might reply that UNITY2 is different from UNITY1 because UNITY2 contains two rows, the *first* row and the *second* row. If they use such terms to distinguish the otherwise indistinguishable, they are very definitely far from Relationland. What we commonly call **lists** have a distinguished first element, and, as the first element (known as the "head") is followed by a list (the "tail"), we can indirectly identify the second and third elements and so on. The mathematics of lists has been worked out, but it is nothing much like the mathematics of relations. What we commonly call **arrays** have all their elements immediately distinguished by ordinal numbers, and the mathematics of arrays has been worked out and is not much like the mathematics of relations.

But actually, in my experience, the duplicaters do not often reply in terms of lists or arrays. They reply, rather, that UNITY2 is different from UNITY1 only in the sense that UNITY2 contains two rows (and the propositions represented by those two rows happen to be the same proposition), while UNITY1 contains just one row (that happens to represent the same proposition as both the rows of UNITY2). The mathematical term for a collection that can differ from another collection, even when the two collections represent the same set and are not ordered, is **bag** . As we are talking exclusively, here, about collections of tuples I use the more explicit term **tuple-bag** (the duplicaters, I know, prefer the term **multiset** , which I regard as dangerously alluring, as it seems to confer on tuple-bags an air of respectability that nobody has yet been able to show me is merited).

Of those duplicaters who espouse this notion of tuple-bags, I ask: "What are you going to give us for expressing queries against tuple-bags to replace the algebra and calculus that Ted Codd gave us for expressing queries against relations?"

Should the duplicaters offer some tuple-bag algebra or calculus (perhaps using operators such as those sketched in Appendix A), then I would further enquire if that algebra or calculus has its roots firmly planted in the First Order Predicate Calculus. And if the answer to that is "No," I want to know where their roots *are* planted.

Actually, I don't really want to know where their roots are planted, for I don't really *believe* in tuple-bags at all. But I do advise those who feel they might be interested in tuple-bags to ask such questions, and to keep on asking them until they get some satisfactory answers. For consider: A database is a set of *axioms*. The response to a query is a *theorem*. The process of deriving the theorem from the axioms is a *proof*. The proof is made by manipulating symbols according to agreed mathematical rules. The proof is as sound and consistent as the rules are. The First Order Predicate Calculus is sound and consistent.

Why don't I believe in tuple-bags? Because I live in terror of not being able to tell when I'm seeing double, and consequently not being able to count how many somethings there are. Which brings me back to **lists**.

3. RELATIONS AND LISTS

Let us suppose I see a group of birds on a feeding table, and I decide to write down the species of each individual bird:

   house sparrow

   blue tit

   great tit

   robin

   blue tit

   blue tit

I have constructed a **list**. Mathematicians have a good characterization of lists, just as they do of relations. A list is either no elements at all or an element, the *head,* followed by a list, the *tail,* and we happily leave "element" and "followed by" undefined (but intuitively appealing). One of the instances of "blue tit" in my list is the head of the tail of the list. Another is the head of the tail of the tail of the tail of the tail of the list. On the assumption that I was careful not to "count" the same individual bird twice, that means that those two blue tits are not the same bird.

The mathematicians have given me useful ways of operating on lists, but the operators certainly do not include things like *union, difference, project,* or *join.* So, how am I going to express queries against lists? One way is to be provided with a query language that operates on lists. In my case, that means I have to have two query languages, for I will not part with my relational one. Another way is to be able to derive relations from lists, without loss of information, and then to use relational queries. One way of deriving a relation from my list of birds is illustrated by ON_TABLE1 below:

ON_TABLE1	SPECIES	N
	great tit	3
	blue tit	2
	house sparrow	1
	blue tit	5
	robin	4
	blue tit	6

The predicate represented by ON_TABLE1 is: "The bird, on my bird table, that was the nth bird to be recorded in my list, was a *species*." The system-provided list-to-relation conversion function derived the correct value for N, in each case, by counting the number of times it had to say "of the tail" in identifying the element, and then adding one. Note that I have managed to represent the ordering that was inherent in my list, without in any way contravening the relational principle that order of rows is unimportant. The ordering is *my* interpretation of a relationship I have expressed. It is not the system's interpretation—the system has no interpretation.

Did I require the system to support lists, so that I could enter the data as such and then convert it to a relation? No. I declared the relation ON_TABLE1 at the outset, and I declared N to be a system-generated column representing arrival-time order (and, by the way, I further declared N to be the primary key of ON_TABLE1, hence the double underscoring in the figure). Thus, the list-to-relation conversion was done "on the fly."

Do you agree that any theorem that can be proved from my list can also be proved from ON_TABLE1?

Another method of deriving a relation from my list of birds—indeed, one that Codd expressly advocates in reference [5], where he proposes an operator for the purpose called "Control Duplicate Rows"—is illustrated by ON_TABLE2:

ON_TABLE2	SPECIES	COUNT
	house sparrow	1
	blue tit	3
	great tit	1
	robin	1

The predicate represented by ON_TABLE2 is: "I saw *count* instances of *species* on my bird table." Comparing ON_TABLE2 with ON_TABLE1, we can note the following:

1. Some of the information inherent in the original list is lost in ON_TABLE2. We can no longer tell, for instance, which was the first bird to be written down, which the second, and so on. ON_TABLE2 is thus not a faithful representation of the original list.

2. On the other hand, ON_TABLE2 will sometimes be more concise than ON_TABLE1, as it is, indeed, with my example list.

3. With ON_TABLE2 I have the opportunity, should I wish to avail myself of it, to record the fact that I saw no turkey vultures at all on my bird table. But this possibility raises rather awkward questions about when I should include rows such as (turkey vulture, 0) and when I should not.

It seems to me that ON_TABLE1 is more appropriate when the source of the data is as informative as a list can be, while ON_TABLE2 might be preferred when the source is no more informative than a tuple-bag can be. We can make my problematical turkey vulture go away by specifying integers greater than zero—the ones we sometimes call the **counting** numbers—as the domain of COUNT in ON_TABLE2.

4.   "SELECT ALL" AND "UNION ALL"

In the Askew Wall, as we know, they make no distinction between tuple-bags and relations, and that heinous crime is aggravated by the fact that they (attempt to) use *relational* operators to express queries against tuple-bags. They additionally provide a few nonrelational operators, such as SELECT ALL and UNION ALL—nonrelational in the sense that, although relations may be given as operands, these operators are not closed over relations (they are closed over tuple-bags instead). In this section, I examine some consequences of SELECT ALL and UNION ALL, in increasing order of absurdity.

1. SELECT ALL * FROM UNITY2 delivers a tuple-bag that appears to be the same as that in UNITY2. SELECT DISTINCT * FROM UNITY2, on the other hand, delivers a tuple-bag that appears to be the same as that in UNITY1. I deduce that the two rows in UNITY2 are **indistinguishable** under the criterion of identity used by DISTINCT. But clearly they are distinguishable under some criterion of identity, otherwise the duplicaters and I wouldn't be having this argument. I suggest that it is very unwise to have more than one criterion of identity, unless each such criterion is explicitly defined (and it is always 100 percent clear which one is being used, and moreover each one can be used in all contexts in which it makes sense). The criterion for the operator DISTINCT is explicitly defined (I suppose), but the criterion that, for instance, makes SELECT COUNT(*) FROM UNITY2 deliver 2, rather than 1, is not defined.

2. The UNION ALL of UNITY1 and UNITY2 is something that looks like this:

```
UNITY3 | N |
       |---|
       | 1 |
       | 1 |
       | 1 |
```

while the UNION of UNITY1 and UNITY2 looks very like UNITY1, as indeed does the UNION of UNITY2 with itself. I find the notion that the union of something with itself is not that very same thing, absurd. I find the consequence that the union of two collections can be smaller than both of them, surprising, counterintuitive.

3. The UNION ALL of UNITY2 with itself looks like this:

```
UNITY4 | N |
       |---|
       | 1 |
       | 1 |
       | 1 |
       | 1 |
```

Each of the somehow (we know not how) distinct rows of UNITY2 has been duplicated! Let us arbitrarily choose some row in UNITY2 and call it the *first* row, and let the other row be called the *second* row. UNITY2's *first* has somehow engendered no less than two distinct rows in UNITY4. Now, I have already noted that I don't really know what distinguishes *first* from *second,* and I am at least twice as puzzled about what distinguishes these two *first* clones from each other. And of course I can next take the UNION ALL of UNITY4 with itself, becoming twice as puzzled again, and so on, and so on. It seems 2^n times as difficult to distinguish two rows in the nth UNION ALL as it is in UNITY2.

4. Consider "the" natural join (see below) of these two tuple-bags:

UNITY2	N
	1
	1

SQRT	N	SQRT_N
	0	0
	4	2
	1	-1
	1	1
	4	-2

I could obtain this natural join—that is, the natural join I have in mind, for there seem to be several different natural joins of two tuple-bags— by means of the query

```
SELECT ALL  U.N, S.SQRT_N
FROM        UNITY2 U, SQRT S
WHERE       U.N = S.N ;
```

and the result would be

SQRT_U	N	SQRT_N
	1	1
	1	1
	1	-1
	1	-1

Now consider the two possible "projections" of this result over N, one using SELECT DISTINCT, the other using SELECT ALL:

DIS_PROJ	N
	1

ALL_PROJ	N
	1
	1
	1
	1

Note that neither DIS_PROJ nor ALL_PROJ contains the same tuple-bag as UNITY2. This is very unfortunate, for there is an important theorem concerning the *relational* algebra, saying that if R JOIN

S is nonloss with respect to R (that is, every tuple of R matches at least one tuple of S), then the projection of R JOIN S over the attributes of R is equal to R.

Now, the duplicaters often say to me: "If you don't like duplicate rows, don't use them—nobody is forcing them on you." True, but I object strongly to being deprived of some of the advantages that are claimed for really-and-truly relational systems, just so that the requirement expressed by the duplicaters—a requirement that I find to be demonstrably spurious—can be fulfilled. One advantage is that the relational query language has approximately one half the complexity of its tuple-bag counterpart—or would have, if the tuple-bag counterpart were complete.* Another advantage, and the loss of this one **particularly peeves** me, is the faster execution of queries, obtainable when the optimizer is able to take advantage of the various equivalence theorems that have been proved in connexion with the relational algebra.

For example, suppose the SQL query shown earlier is modified as follows:

```
SELECT S.N
FROM   UNITY2 U, SQRT S
WHERE  U.N = S.N ;
```

The result of this query, if UNITY2 were a relation rather than just a tuple-bag, would be the same as the *semijoin* of UNITY2 with SQRT. (The semijoin of relation A with relation B is equal to the join of A and B projected back on to the attributes of A.) When an optimizer detects a query that is equivalent to a semijoin, it can generate an executable form of the query that does not bother to search the right-hand operand of the semijoin more than once for each tuple of the left-hand operand. In this particular example the optimized query could be twice as fast as the unoptimized one. In other cases it could be very much more than twice as fast—ten times as fast, for instance, if there are on average ten matching right-hand-side tuples for each left-hand-side tuple.

As it happens, my own work in reference [7] gives a partial (but only partial!) counterargument to this possible complaint about loss of optimizability. In reference [7] I believe I have demonstrated that it is possible, by tracking functional dependencies during query decomposition, to distinguish true relations from mere tuple-bags. In that case

---

*SQL has the "DISTINCT or ALL" option on SELECT and UNION, but has forgotten to make it available in joins—you can "SELECT DISTINCT or ALL" from the join of A and B, but you cannot join "DISTINCT of A" with "ALL of B" or vice versa. This error (in implementation of an error!) is "corrected" in SQL2 [1].

the optimizer could implement the fast semijoin method for the relational users and make the others pay a penalty. But I say the others don't deserve a penalty, for they are likely to have been unwittingly beguiled into the unwise ways of tuple-bags. In any case, I would much prefer the DBMS implementers to be devoting their time to *really* important matters (like database integrity and query language orthogonality, to mention but two) than to the awkwardnesses and exceptions arising from tuple-bag support.

5. THE BILL-OF-MATERIALS EXAMPLE

Now, I do realize that there is a genuine requirement on relational systems, arising from this one that is so often expressed as the requirement for duplicate rows. In reference [11] I suggested a proper, relational method of meeting this requirement, involving system-generated key columns. I will now look at an example that some people have claimed to be a particularly compelling argument in favor of duplicate rows, and show how I would tackle that one in Relationland and why I don't find the case very compelling.

NEEDED	MAJOR_P#	MINOR_P#	QTY
	P1	P2	1
	P2	P4	3
	P1	P3	1
	P3	P4	3

The predicate expressed by NEEDED is: "You need *qty* of part *minor_ p#* to make one of part *major_ p#*." MAJOR_P# and MINOR_P# represent what are frequently referred to as "assembly" and "component," respectively.

Consider the manufacture of a P1. You'll need a P2 and a P3. To make a P2 you'll need 3 of P4. To make a P3 you'll need 3 of P4. The "bill of materials" for P1—the version thereof that the duplicaters would like to see—therefore (apparently) looks like this:

BOM_P1	P#	QTY
	P4	3
	P4	3

Thinking of the method suggested in reference [11] for handling the duplicate rows requirement, I ask why BOM_P1 doesn't show just one row, indicating that 6 of P4 are needed. The duplicaters reply that the interesting fact that you need 3 of P4 twice (for two different intermediate components) must be preserved. In that case I suggest a single row, with three columns, showing that 2 of 3 of P4 are needed. The duplicaters say they don't like that, as it requires an aggregating function to be used to generate the 2, and in any case they actually want to see the "3 of P4" fact twice—perhaps so they can allocate them to separate orders for separate delivery (I'm guessing, here).

We haven't reached the end of the dialog yet, but here I offer my reader a pause for breath, in which to consider the awesome prospect of losing the entire relational model over this issue, should the duplicaters win the day.

Now, to continue: I say that in that case some distinguishing data should be presented as an additional column in BOM_P1, so that BOM_P1 can be treated as a relation. They say it's very difficult to do that. Yes, in this oversimplified example we could include a column, MAJOR_P#, showing P2 and P3 to distinguish the two rows, but in real life the breakdown of a P1 might be much more complicated, such that we couldn't even say how many extra columns* would be needed to distinguish the duplicates by retaining their origins. I say, well, it jolly well shouldn't be so difficult—the system should be more helpful and provide a "keying" function to generate unique identifiers systematically. One not very difficult implementation of such a function would allow BOM_P1 to be represented *relationally* as:

BOM_P1	P#	QTY	KEY
	P4	3	2
	P4	3	1

I have deliberately written these two rows "in the wrong order," just in case anybody accuses me of violating the relational principle that relations are unordered sets. All I am doing, in order to distinguish n "duplicates," is to assign each of the natural numbers from 1 to n to exactly one of the duplicate rows, arbitrarily chosen (of course—how else?), and naming the column in which they appear. If those two instances of 3 of P4 are actually not the only things needed to make a P1, BOM_P1 might look something like this:

BOM_P1	P#	QTY	KEY
	P4	3	2
	P4	3	1
	P5	5	1
	P6	2	1
	P6	4	2

---

*For instance, P1 might also need a P7, made from a P8 and a P2, in which case the need for three P4s for a P2 would appear twice.

I have chosen to generate key values that are unique "within" part number. I might instead have chosen to generate key values that are unique within (P#,QTY), or unique over the whole of BOM_P1. My actual choice was psychological, based on the thought that the number of distinct sources of needs for each part might be of interest, and would be readily visible in a suitably ordered display or printout of the table, thanks to the choice of ordinal numbers as key values. In reference [11] I suggested timestamps as another way of supporting systematic generation of key values, workable so long as the system's timestamping granularity is fine enough to guarantee that no two rows can be recorded as having arrived simultaneously. (Of course, timestamps do inevitably carry some additional meaning compared with arbitrarily assigned numbers, and I would recommend this method only when that extra meaning is deemed to be useful.)

Now, in my theoretical discussion of the treatment of projection, join, and union of tuple-bags like UNITY2, I complained bitterly that the projection of R JOIN S over the columns of R is not, in Tuplebagland, the same as the semijoin of R with S, with consequent loss of optimizability. To show how this problem goes away with my treatment, I now propose to join (the most recent version of) BOM_P1 with the well-known table SP showing which suppliers supply which parts, in which quantities. You will agree, I hope, that this is a very realistic use of BOM_P1. For the purposes of the example, SP looks like this:

SP	S#	P#	SPQ
	S6	P4	500
	S6	P6	300
	S7	P4	400
	S7	P5	500
	S7	P6	300

(I have renamed the quantity column as SPQ in order to avoid naming conflicts when we do the join.) Here is the result:

SP_BOM_P1	P#	QTY	KEY	S#	SPQ
	P4	3	2	S6	500
	P4	3	2	S7	400
	P4	3	1	S6	500
	P4	3	1	S7	400
	P5	5	1	S7	500
	P6	2	1	S6	300
	P6	2	1	S7	300
	P6	4	2	S6	300
	P6	4	2	S7	300

Now, if I project SP_BOM_P1 over the columns of BOM_P1, namely P#, QTY, and KEY, I not only answer the possibly useful question "For which needs of P1 do I have at least one potential supplier?''—I also have something that is indeed identical to the semijoin of BOM_P1 with SP. And, when I take the difference of this with the original BOM_P1, I discover that the semijoin is the same relation as BOM_P1 itself (the difference is empty), and conclude that I do have potential suppliers for everything needed by P1.

I maintain that I am a very much happier user, in spite of this slightly intrusive KEY column, than the innocent but unfortunate user of the DBMS that delivers the "duplicate row" version of BOM_P1.

6. CONCLUSION

I have suggested a treatment of the duplicate row requirement that does not deviate in one iota from the principles of the relational model. By contrast, most of the current so-called relational systems, notably those based on SQL, have adopted the tuple-bag treatment instead (albeit somewhat half-heartedly). They support queries against tuple-bags using the same operators as for queries against relations, by implementing the same algorithms (for instance, the nested loop algorithm for joins) and by supplying some additional operators (such as SELECT ALL and UNION ALL) that are peculiar to tuple-bags. I have criticized this treatment for its lack of any well-known theoretical foundation, its sometimes puzzling and counterintuitive results, and its undermining of the simplicity and optimizability that we claim for truly relational implementations.

I invite counterargument and counterproposal, and I ask some specific questions of the counterarguers and counterproposers:

- Do you propose a model of data that embraces the notion of *list* or *array* instead of *relation?* If so, can you provide a nonnavigational, data-independent query language that is demonstrably as complete as the relational algebra or relational calculus? If you cannot provide such a query language, what query language *can* you provide, and can you argue that that language's deficiencies, with respect to the relational algebra or relational calculus, are compensated for by your "duplicate row" support?

- Do you propose a model of data that embraces the notion I have called *tuple-bag?* If so, can you define the semantics of tuple-bags, and can you provide a mathematics of tuple-bags—a tuple-bag algebra or a tuple-bag calculus, for instance? And can you then provide a nonnavigational, data-independent query language that is demonstrably as complete as the relational algebra or relational calculus? If you cannot provide such a query language, what query language *can* you provide, and can you argue that that language's deficiencies, with respect to the relational algebra or relational calculus, are compensated for by your "duplicate row" support?

- Do you propose a model of data that embraces a variety of types of collection, any or all of lists, arrays, tuple-bags, and relations, perhaps? If so . . . (same supplementary questions again), and if so, can you justify your deviation from that principle of the relational model that exhorts "just one structure"?

- Do you say that duplicate rows represent different propositions merely because there is some distinguishing fact, out there in the so-called Real World, that nobody has bothered to convert into data, so that tables with duplicate rows are merely relations with one or more "missing attributes"? If so, describe and justify your implementations of relational union and projection, and demonstrate that (a) they never give rise to puzzling or counterintuitive results, and (b) users who take the trouble always to avoid duplicate rows get all the benefits they might reasonably expect from being truly relational.

- Does none of the above satisfactorily approximate to your position? If so, please describe your position, your model of data, and your query language, in sufficient detail to enable comparison to be made with Relationland's equivalents.

Finally, whatever your position, please state what mechanism you have, if any, for distinguishing one member of a pair of duplicate rows from the other (so that, for instance, one may be deleted or updated without the same thing being done to the other).

REFERENCES AND BIBLIOGRAPHY

1. ANSI X3H2 / ISO/IEC JTC1 SC21 WG3 Data Base Languages: (*ISO working draft) Database Language SQL2,* Document X3H2-90-264 (July 1990).

2. David Beech, "New Life for SQL," *Datamation* (1st February 1989); "The Future of SQL," *Datamation* (15th February 1989).

3. E. F. Codd, "Fatal Flaws in SQL," Part 1, *Datamation* (15th August 1988); Part 2, *Datamation* (1st September 1988).

4. E. F. Codd, "Duplicate Rows Challenge: Prove a Need . . . Or Ban Them," *The Relational Journal for DB2 Users 2,* No. 2 (April/May 1990).

5. E. F. Codd, *The Relational Model for Database Management Version 2* (Reading, MA: Addison-Wesley, 1990).

6. Hugh Darwen, "The Askew Wall" (in this volume).

7. Hugh Darwen, "The Role of Functional Dependence in Query Decomposition" (in this volume).

8. C. J. Date, "Why Duplicate Rows Are Prohibited," in C. J. Date, *Relational Database Writings 1985–1989* (Reading, MA: Addison-Wesley, 1990).

9. C. J. Date, "A Logician's View," Appendix A to "What Is a Relation?" (in this volume).

10. Donald E. Knuth, *Seminumerical Algorithms,* 2nd edition (Volume 2 of *The Art of Computer Programming*) (Reading, MA: Addison-Wesley, 1981).

11. Andrew Warden, "The Keys of the Kingdom," in C. J. Date, *Relational Database Writings 1985–1989* (Reading, MA: Addison-Wesley, 1990).

APPENDIX A:
OPERATIONS ON TUPLE-BAGS

In this appendix I consider briefly what a "tuple-bag algebra" might look like (without, I hasten to add, necessarily endorsing such an idea). The following discussion is based in part on some suggestions from reference [10] (page 464).

- **Restriction** is similar to relational restriction. If a multiply-occurring tuple is included under the restriction condition, all of its occurrences are included, and if it is excluded, all of its occurrences are excluded. (Are we not missing something here, however—if tuple T3 occurs three times, how could we obtain a result in which T3 occurs just once, or twice?)

- **Extension** is similar to relational extension, using functions. There are as many tuples in the result as there are in the operand.

- **Union** comes in two varieties, union and union-plus. If a tuple, T, occurs m times in one operand and n times in the other, it occurs $MAX(m,n)$ times in the union and $m+n$ times in the union-plus. (Note, in the Askew Wall, they can do union-pluses of tuple-bags, but not unions!)

- In the **difference** of two tuple-bags, a tuple, T, occurring m times in the first operand and n times in the second occurs $MIN(0,m\text{-}n)$ times in the result.

- In the **intersection** of two tuple-bags, a tuple, T, occurring m times in the first operand and n times in the second occurs $MIN(m,n)$ times in the result.

- In something like the **extended Cartesian product** of two tuple-bags, if a tuple occurs m times in one operand, each of its m occurrences will be joined with every tuple in the other operand.

- In **summarize,** a tuple that occurs m times in the operand occurs m times in the only partition into which it is assigned by the grouping part of the operation.

And that just leaves **projection**. What about projection? I can see two choices, both bad. Either you can implement it like the Askew Wall's SELECT ALL, in which case you'll get nice (ha!) tuple-bags out of it, or you can implement it like the Askew Wall's SELECT DISTINCT, in which case it's very like relational projection—indeed, can be equated with the *existential quantification* of predicate calculus, with which projection is equated in Relationland—but, horror of horrors, if tuple-bag TB is thus projected over all of its columns, the result isn't the same tuple-bag as TB! This latter situation would be somewhat like having an arithmetic in which (e.g.) 1 multiplied by 1 was not equal to 1.

6

Relation-Valued Attributes
or
Will the Real
First Normal Form
Please Stand Up?

ABSTRACT

We investigate the true nature of first normal form, and argue that permitting attributes of relations to contain values that are in turn (encapsulated) relations themselves leads to a number of advantages.

COMMENTS ON PUBLICATION

This book's predecessor included a chapter by myself entitled "What Is a Domain?" [9], in which I contended that the domain concept of database management was basically identical to the *user-defined data type* concept

---

Previously unpublished.

of programming languages. And a companion paper in the present book, "What Is a Relation?" [10], goes on to point out that if the foregoing contention is accepted, then (among other things) it follows that it must be possible for the attributes of a relation to contain values that are relations themselves, in apparent contravention of the requirements of first normal form. In what follows, Hugh Darwen elaborates on this possibility.

Note: The version of the paper published here is really a joint production between Hugh and myself. However, Hugh wrote the first draft, and all references to the first person singular thus refer (at least primarily) to him! Also, I disclaim all responsibility for the alternative title, which Hugh chose as a parody of the title of another paper of my own [12].

1. INTRODUCTION

At first sight, the ideas propounded in this paper might seem somewhat heretical, especially coming as they do from a self-proclaimed relational bigot of many years' standing. But I hope to show that they are not really heretical at all, and moreover that they solve certain problems that the "orthodox" version of the relational model does have great difficulty with.

The basic idea, as the title of the paper suggests, is that *relations should be permitted to include other relations nested inside themselves,* or, more precisely, that an attribute of a relation should be permitted to have relations as its values in turn. Now, on the face of it, this idea is a clear violation of the requirements of first normal form, because the values in such an attribute are clearly not "atomic." I will argue, however, that this violation is more apparent than real. I will then go on to discuss some applications of relation-valued attributes, and show how conversions can be performed between relations that contain such attributes and relations that do not, making use of a generalized version of the relational algebra *extend* operator. I will also discuss the relationship between the foregoing ideas and the more familiar concept of "grouping," used in particular in the *summarize* operator of the relational algebra.

2. FIRST NORMAL FORM

It is well known that first normal form requires the data values that constitute a domain to be "atomic." In reference [2], Codd defines atomic values as "[values that] cannot be decomposed into smaller pieces by the DBMS (excluding certain special functions)." While there might be some debate as to whether values such as dates, times, and character strings can be said to be atomic in the foregoing sense,* it is commonly held that values that are *collections* (such as arrays, lists, sets, tuples, multisets, and relations) are certainly *not* atomic, and hence that first normal form does definitely preclude them.

Reference [9], however, argues that a domain is essentially nothing more nor less than a data type, possibly (even probably) user-defined, and thus potentially of arbitrary complexity. To quote from that paper: ". . . an attribute that is drawn from such a domain can [thus] certainly be nonatomic. The point is, however, that attribute values are always atomic . . . *from the DBMS's point of view.* . . . Decomposing [such] values into smaller pieces would not be done by the DBMS per se; instead, it would be done by invoking the user-defined functions provided along with the specification of the user-defined data type for precisely that purpose."

If the foregoing argument is accepted, then the attributes of a relation will certainly be allowed to contain such items as arrays, lists, sets, tuples, multisets, and in particular relations—but the DBMS will not be aware of the fact that these things are actually "nonatomic." To use the modern jargon, the values will be *encapsulated.* Indeed, let me now state my position without further ado: I see first normal form as the relational model's **Great Encapsulator,** and I therefore claim that there should be no further argument as to what is and is not "permitted" inside a relation. In what follows, however, I want to consider, specifically, the case of domains (and hence attributes) that contain values that are relations.

Now, this idea has been extensively researched (see, e.g., references [13], [14], and [16]) under such names as "nested relations" or "NFNF relations" (NFNF stands for "non first normal form," and is often further abbreviated to NF^2). However, I do not take the approach of references [13], [14], and [16], which add many new operators to the relational algebra and calculus to handle "nested relations," and thus definitely do breach first normal form (as the term "non first normal form" suggests). Rather, I propose a simple generalization of the relational algebra *extend* operator to permit (among other things) the use of relation-valued expressions to define attribute values. In this way, I stay within the spirit of the classical relational model, while still obtaining some of the benefits, such as they may be, of "nested relations."

Note: The reader should not infer from the foregoing that I deprecate the approach taken by references [13], [14], and [16]; rather, it is simply the case that I do not need that approach for the applications I wish to

---

*Dates and times are usually considered to consist of a combination of year, month, day, hour (etc.) components, and character strings are sequences of characters.

discuss in this chapter, and I would like to explore what is possible without the various additional operators—and complexities—of that approach.

3. AN EXAMPLE

Whether or not the real first normal form has now stood up for my readers (it has, for me), let us now explore some applications of relation-valued attributes. I will begin by considering the following example, based as usual on suppliers and parts (see Fig. 1). *Note:* Attribute names that are doubly underlined in my diagrams are components of the primary key of the relation that contains them.

S

S#	SNAME	STATUS	CITY
S1	Smith	20	London
S2	Jones	10	Paris
S3	Blake	30	Paris
S4	Clark	20	London
S5	Adams	30	Athens

SP

S#	P#	QTY
S1	P1	300
S1	P2	200
S1	P3	400
S1	P4	200
S1	P5	100
S1	P6	100
S2	P1	300
S2	P2	400
S3	P2	200
S4	P2	200
S4	P4	300
S4	P5	400

P

P#	PNAME	COLOR	WEIGHT	CITY
P1	Nut	Red	12	London
P2	Bolt	Green	17	Paris
P3	Screw	Blue	17	Rome
P4	Screw	Red	14	London
P5	Cam	Blue	12	Paris
P6	Cog	Red	19	London

Fig. 1 The suppliers-and-parts database

I will now use the relational operator *extend* to obtain an extension of relation S such that an additional attribute called SUPPLIED_PARTS shows the set of parts supplied by each supplier. (*Note:* The syntax used throughout this chapter for relational algebra operations is taken from reference [7]. For readers who may not be familiar with *extend,* here is a brief definition: The expression "EXTEND relation ADD expression AS attribute" adds a new attribute, with the specified name, to the specified relation, with values as defined by the specified expression. For further discussion, see reference [7].)

```
T       :=  SP RENAME S# AS TS# ;

S_SP    :=  EXTEND S
            ADD ( T WHERE TS# = S# ) [ P#, QTY ]
            AS SUPPLIED_PARTS ;
```

Explanation: The first step here (the assignment to T) merely produces a relation T that is identical to relation SP, except that its supplier number attribute is named TS# instead of S#. The purpose of this step is merely to avoid a naming clash in the second step, which constructs the desired result. In that second step, the expression specifying the computation of values for the attribute SUPPLIED_PARTS is a *relational* expression. In general, any expression of the relational algebra could appear in this position. In the particular case at hand, the expression includes a reference to what might be thought of as a *parameter* to the expression, namely S#, referring to the supplier number value in the particular tuple of relation S that is currently being extended. For a given tuple of S, therefore, the subexpression "T WHERE TS# = S#" evaluates to the set of T tuples having the same supplier number value as that S tuple. (That set of T tuples is then projected over the attributes P# and QTY.) The overall result can be represented pictorially as shown in Fig. 2.

S_SP	S#	SNAME	STATUS	CITY	SUPPLIED_PARTS	
	S1	Smith	20	London	P#	QTY
					P1	300
					P2	200
					P3	400
					P4	200
					P5	100
					P6	100
	S2	Jones	10	Paris	P#	QTY
					P1	300
					P2	400
	S3	Blake	30	Paris	P#	QTY
					P2	200
	S4	Clark	20	London	P#	QTY
					P2	200
					P4	300
					P5	400
	S5	Adams	30	Athens	P#	QTY

Fig. 2 Relation S_SP

Points to note about this result:

- The degree is 5, one more than that of S: It has the same attributes as S, plus one additional attribute called SUPPLIED_PARTS. SUPPLIED_PARTS is a *relation-valued attribute.*

- The cardinality is the same as the cardinality of S, as is to be expected with *extend.* Note in particular that there is a tuple for supplier S5, in which the SUPPLIED_PARTS value is *an empty relation.*

- The information imparted by S_SP is exactly the same as the information that (it is usually claimed) is imparted by the **left outer natural join** of S and SP (relation S_LONJ_SP in Fig. 3). Note, however, that I have argued elsewhere [5] that the particular kind of outer join represented by S_LONJ_SP is somewhat suspect (because it is one-to-many). I will have more to say about S_LONJ_SP below.

- The relations "nested" within the SUPPLIED_PARTS attribute all have exactly the same heading, as is implied by the relational expression from which they result.

- SUPPLIED_PARTS is functionally dependent on S#. As S# is a candidate key of S, it is therefore also a candidate key of S_SP.

- My diagrammatic notation is carefully chosen, and contrasts with that of references [13], [14], and [16], which use a single, structured column heading where I have a simple column heading, SUPPLIED_PARTS, plus a set of subheadings (showing P# and QTY repeated) in each row of S_SP. My notation emphasizes the encapsulation I seek. It should definitely not be taken as condoning the possibility that relations with different headings can be members of the same domain (I do not altogether rule out such a possibility, but I do not explore it in this chapter).

S_LONJ_SP	S#	SNAME	STATUS	CITY	P#	QTY
	S1	Smith	20	London	P1	300
	S1	Smith	20	London	P2	200
	S1	Smith	20	London	P3	400
	S1	Smith	20	London	P4	200
	S1	Smith	20	London	P5	100
	S1	Smith	20	London	P6	100
	S2	Jones	10	Paris	P1	300
	S2	Jones	10	Paris	P2	400
	S3	Blake	30	Paris	P2	200
	S4	Clark	20	London	P2	200
	S4	Clark	20	London	P4	300
	S4	Clark	20	London	P5	400
	S5	Adams	30	Athens	null	null

Fig. 3 The left outer join of relations S and SP

- As others have observed, S_SP looks very much like a hierarchy, as indeed it is, if you look inside the SUPPLIED_PARTS values at the same time as looking at the other attributes of S_SP. The point is, however, that it is the result of a **relational query** against a flat (i.e., nonhierarchic) representation of the same information, and, furthermore, any other hierarchic representation (such as that showing the set of suppliers for each part) could equally well have been expressed. This situation is to be contrasted with traditional implementations of the Hierarchic Model of Data, in which one has to commit to a particular hierarchy at database design time, and alternative hierarchies are not so easy to derive.

Contrasting Fig. 3 with Fig. 2, we can note the following:

- The degree of S_LONJ_SP is 6 (the sum of the degrees of S and SP, minus the number of common columns involved in the join).

- The cardinality of S_LONJ_SP is greater than the cardinality of S, because some tuples in S match several tuples in SP (under the joining condition). Note in particular that the contribution of an S tuple with no matching SP tuples at all is the same as the contribution of an S tuple that matches exactly one SP tuple—they both contribute exactly one tuple to S_LONJ_SP.

- The information that supplier S5 (Adams) supplies no parts is represented by *nulls* for the P# and QTY attributes, rather than by the empty relation shown for the SUPPLIED_PART attribute in S_SP.

- The lack of any double underlining of attribute names in Fig. 3 reflects my inability to discover a primary key for S_LONJ_SP.* (Were it not for supplier S5's tuple, with its null part number, the combination {S#,P#} could be chosen as a composite primary key.)

What is good and what is not good about S_SP and S_LONJ_SP may be subject to opinion and taste. Personally, I find much to admire in S_SP,[†] and offer the following observations to counter what I imagine to be its most likely criticisms.

- S_SP *is* in first normal form, insofar as each tuple has exactly one value for each attribute—despite the fact that, in the case of attribute SUPPLIED_PARTS, that value is itself a relation (and therefore composite, having internal structure). By contrast, whether or not

---

*Nullologists [4] can note, with pleasure, that "relations" such as S_LONJ_SP even ruin my notation for showing primary keys—the lack of double underlining *ought* to mean that the empty set is the primary key!

[†]My profound distaste for S_LONJ_SP is articulated in reference [5].

S_LONJ_SP has exactly one value for the P# and QTY attributes in the tuple for supplier S5 is a moot point.

- Although SUPPLIED_PARTS values admittedly do have internal structure, that structure is at least one that is known and understood. And note carefully that by "known and understood" here, I mean, specifically, known and understood *by the user,* not by the DBMS. Furthermore, the expressions by which relations within a relation-valued attribute such as SUPPLIED_PARTS are defined are exactly the familiar expressions of the relational algebra. Thus, a user who has learned the relational model of data (including the relational algebra) has almost nothing extra to learn in order to define and understand a relation like S_SP.

- For reasons already explained, I do not regard SUPPLIED_PARTS values as any more "decomposable by the DBMS" than values in any other attribute.

4.   WHY RELATION-VALUED ATTRIBUTES ARE USEFUL

The discussion at the end of the previous section (contrasting S_SP and S_LONJ_SP) shows one concrete example of a situation in which relation-valued attributes are genuinely useful. To be specific, such attributes permit *a more accurate representation* of certain real-world problems (for surely it is more accurate to represent an empty set by an empty set, not by some peculiar, poorly understood "null"). In this section, I will consider some further applications of the relation-valued attributes idea.

Relational Comparisons

Reference [11] proposes that a relational system should support a set of relational comparison operators ("equals," "subset of," etc.) by means of which the values of two union-compatible relations can be compared. Of course, the relations in question can be specified by means of arbitrary relational expressions, in general. Here I point out that such operators apply to (relations within) relation-valued attributes just as much as they do to "DBMS-understood" relations, and I give some examples of the usefulness of such a capability. In particular, I show that such operators provide a new and sometimes more intuitive approach to certain queries, an approach that overcomes some of the difficulties mentioned in reference [6] with respect to universal quantification and the *divide* operator. For example, supplier numbers of suppliers who supply every part can now be expressed like this:

```
T1   :=   SP RENAME S# AS T1S# ;
T2   :=   EXTEND S ADD ( T1 WHERE T1S# = S# ) [ P# ] AS S_P ;
ANS  :=   ( T2 WHERE S_P = P [ P# ] ) [ S# ] ;
```

The intermediate result T2 is similar to S_SP (see Section 3), except that I have chosen a short name, S_P, for the added, relation-valued attribute, and the values in S_P are relations of degree one (just the part numbers), rather than the binary relations in attribute SUPPLIED_PARTS of relation S_SP. The final step (the assignment to ANS) uses the relational equality comparison operator "=" to compare values in S_P with the unary relation obtained by projecting the parts relation P over its part number attribute P# (note the union-compatibility of this relation and each of the S_P values).

Observe in particular that the foregoing solution works correctly even if there are no parts at all (an example of the kind of situation in which *divide* fails [6]).

The relation T2 defined above could also be useful in queries such as: "Find all pairs of supplier numbers, Sx and Sy say, such that Sx and Sy supply exactly the same set of parts each" (this is Exercise 13.14 from reference [7]). Reference [7] shows that this query is quite difficult to express in "classical" relational algebra. However, the following solution is comparatively straightforward:

```
T3   :=   ( T2 RENAME S# AS SX ) [ SX, S_P ] ;
T4   :=   ( T2 RENAME S# AS SY ) [ SY, S_P ] ;
T5   :=   ( T3 JOIN T4 ) [ SX, SY ] ;
ANS  :=   T5 WHERE SY > SX ;
```

The third step here (the assignment to T5) is the one that does the work of finding the required pairs of supplier numbers. It uses a *natural join* over a relation-valued attribute! Under this join, a T3 tuple and a T4 tuple are joined only when their S_P values are exactly the same (i.e., the same relation). The final step removes redundant pairs of supplier numbers that are implied by the reflexivity and symmetry of the relation "supplies exactly the same parts as."*

Relation-Valued Attributes in Base Relations

So far, all of the examples we have seen of relations containing relation-valued attributes have been *derived* relations. Needless to say, however, it would be very undesirable to have to limit the appearance of such attributes

---

Reflexivity implies that the pair (x, x) will appear for all supplier numbers x. Symmetry implies that if the pair (x, y) appears, the pair (y, x) will appear as well.

to derived relations only, i.e., to prohibit them from appearing in base relations; indeed, the usual requirement of *orthogonality* militates strongly against such a prohibition. And it is certainly possible—though perhaps not very easy—to think of examples where including a relation-valued attribute in a base relation seems to be exactly the right thing to do. The following illustration is based on a real-world problem that arose in connexion with some work I was doing myself on functional dependencies [3].

First, a little bit of background. A functional dependency (FD) is a truth-valued statement involving two sets of attributes of some given relation. For example, the FD

$$\{ \text{ S\#, P\# } \} \quad \rightarrow \quad \{ \text{ S\#, P\#, QTY } \}$$

holds true in relation SP. The operator "→" represents the relation "determines," and we can further note that this relation holds true in SP between {S#,P#} and any subset of {S#,P#,QTY}. In general, of course, given any relation R and any two subsets A and B of the attributes of R, it may or may not be the case that the FD "$A \rightarrow B$" holds in R.

The requirement is to design a (base) relation to represent the FDs that hold in an arbitrary relation R.

The obvious design involves a binary relation, FDS_IN_R say, in which the attributes are both relation-valued and both defined on the domain of unary relations with single attribute ATTR, where those unary relations in turn represent sets of attribute names. For example, Fig. 4 shows the relation FDS_IN_SP, representing the FDs in relation SP of the suppliers-and-parts database. The attribute DET (determinant) represents the left-hand side of a functional dependency in SP, the attribute DEP (dependant) represents the right-hand side. FDS_IN_SP represents the predicate "the FD DET → DEP holds true in relation SP." (It so happens that

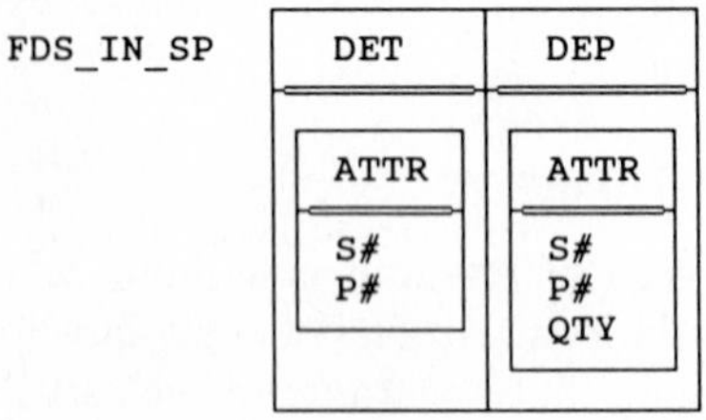

Fig. 4 Relation FDS_IN_SP

the relation in Fig. 4 contains just one tuple, but of course such a relation might contain any number of tuples, in general.)

Note, incidentally, that the primary key of relation FDS_IN_SP is not only composite, involving two attributes,* but those attributes are relation-valued! I have already shown (in connexion with relation S_SP in Section 3) that it is possible to have a relation-valued attribute as the *dependant* in a functional dependency: In that relation, we have the functional dependency S# → SUPPLIED_PARTS. The present example, by contrast, shows (albeit in a very simple, degenerate kind of way) that such an attribute can also appear as the *determinant* in such a dependency.

To return to the main thread of the discussion: I could equally well have represented the information contained in relation FDS_IN_SP by another relation, DEP_UNNESTED say, in which attribute DET is still relation-valued but attribute DEP is not (refer to Fig. 5). *Note:* Later I will show how DEP_UNNESTED might be systematically derived from FDS_IN_SP. See Section 5.

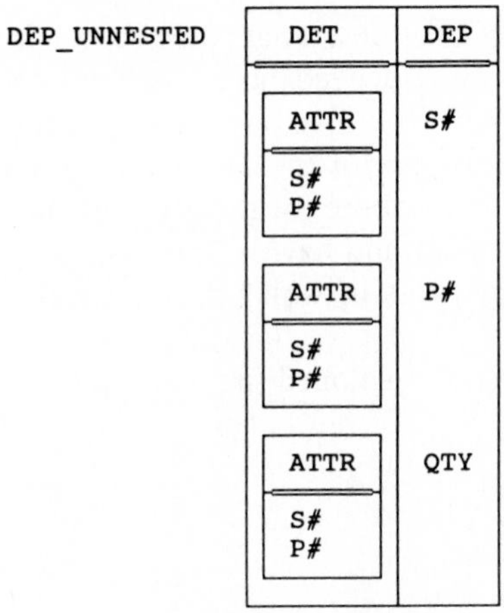

Fig. 5 Relation DEP_UNNESTED (equivalent to relation FDS_IN_SP)

---

*I am assuming here that FDS_IN_SP is allowed to include redundant rows (i.e., rows that are strictly unnecessary because they are implied by others). For example, it might include the rows ({S#,P#},{S#}) and ({S#,P#},{P#}), both of which are implied (using the familiar rules of inference for FDs) by the single row shown in Fig. 4. If instead we decided—for reasons of good database design, possibly!—that FDS_IN_SP should include only "maximal" FDs (i.e., it should contain just one row for each DET value, giving the set of *all* dependants as the corresponding DEP value), then clearly DET by itself would be the primary key.

The relation depicted by DEP_UNNESTED is still "determines," for of course it is true that the FD {S#,P#} → {S#,P#,QTY} holds if and only if the FDs

```
{S#,P#} → {S#}
{S#,P#} → {P#}
{S#,P#} → {QTY}
```

each hold individually, and we can surely agree to drop the braces enclosing a set of attribute names if that set contains just one member (thereby writing, e.g., S# for {S#}).

Note very carefully, however, that if we start with FDS_IN_SP and "unnest" attribute DET instead of DEP, we cannot make the same kinds of remarks at all. Relation DET_UNNESTED (see Fig. 6) certainly does *not* represent the same information as relation FDS_IN_SP—it is not the case, for example, that {S#} → {QTY}, nor is it the case that {P#} → {QTY}. All we can infer from relation DET_UNNESTED is that S# is a component of some determinant of {S#,P#,QTY} (and hence of some determinant of QTY specifically), and similarly for P#.

Bearing in mind the foregoing observations, what is the recommended design for a relation to record functional dependencies? Is it possible to avoid relation-valued attributes entirely? Well, we have seen that it is not absolutely necessary to use such an attribute for the dependants; however, the only way I can see to avoid such an attribute for the determinants is to assign a distinct name to each determinant and have a "member of" relation to record which attributes are members of which determinants, as in Fig. 7.

This design does adhere strictly to old-fashioned first normal form, but

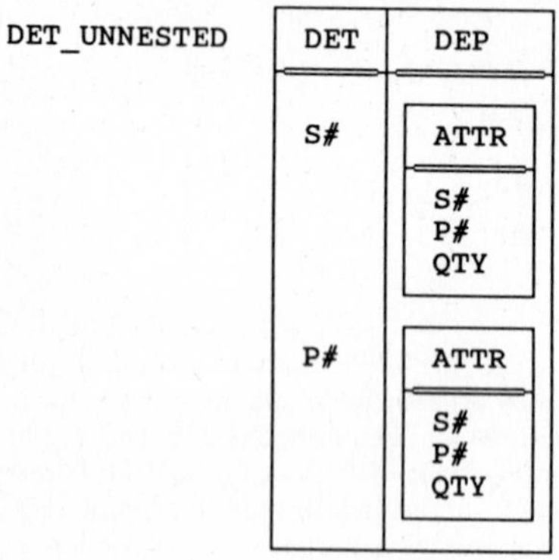

Fig. 6 Relation DET—UNNESTED (not equivalent to relation FDS_IN_SP)

DET_MEMBER

DET	ATTR
D1	S#
D1	P#

FDS_IN_1NF

DET	DEP
D1	S#
D1	P#
D1	QTY

Fig. 7 "FDS_IN_SP," avoiding relation-valued attributes

it looks much more difficult to manage than the one with relation-valued attributes for the determinants. For one thing, we now have to invent a distinct name for each distinct determinant. We also have to guard against the possibility of the same determinant being recorded more than once; that is, we must ensure that there do not exist two distinct values of DET, say *d1* and *d2,* such that the row (*d1,a*) appears in DET_MEMBER for every row (*d2,a*) appearing in DET_MEMBER. This integrity constraint looks like it might be rather difficult to enforce. Furthermore, devising suitable relational queries for deriving new FDs from the given ones also looks like it might prove rather difficult, whereas it is not nearly so difficult given the design of Fig. 4.*

We see, therefore, that there may well be occasional situations in which base relations with relation-valued attributes are useful. But as a general rule it does seem as if such base relations should be avoided, or at least treated with considerable circumspection. In order to see why this is so, let us return to (derived) relation S_SP of Section 3, with attributes S#, SNAME, STATUS, CITY, and SUPPLIED_PARTS (the last of which is relation-valued, containing relations with attributes P# and QTY in turn). What would be the consequences of making S_SP a base relation?

Well, it is certainly true that the information imparted by relation S_SP is exactly the same as that imparted by the existing base relations S and SP. Furthermore, relation S_SP does not involve any redundancy: Each (S#,P#,QTY) triple of relation SP corresponds to exactly one (P#,QTY) pair in exactly one tuple of relation S_SP.[†]

What is more, the S_SP design has the advantage that deleting a sup-

---

*In connexion with this example, it is interesting to note that Codd himself, in his original paper on the relational model [1], remarked that he "knew of no application that would require a primary key to have a [relation-valued] component." The case under discussion does seem like a good example of a situation where such a primary key might be desirable.

[†]Of course, I am making use here of the semantic constraint that every shipment does have a corresponding supplier. If it were possible for a shipment (SP tuple) to exist without a corresponding supplier (S tuple), the S_SP design would be a nonstarter, because it could not represent such a shipment.

plier will automatically delete all shipments for that supplier, and there is
no need to resort to complex multitable operations such as DELETE
CASCADES.

On the other hand, of course, there are numerous disadvantages too.
Since (as pointed out in Section 3) S_SP is basically a hierarchic representation, all of the old familiar arguments against hierarchies apply. It is not
worth repeating them all in detail here. I will therefore content myself by
just mentioning some of the most significant ones:

- The design is asymmetric. It is biased in favor of certain applications
  at the expense of others. Problems—even ones involving retrieval
  only—that have a symmetric formulation in the real world have asymmetric solutions in the system.

- Inserting an individual shipment is more difficult than it would be with
  the symmetric design, and probably requires a new kind of INSERT
  operator.

- Updating an individual shipment is more difficult than it would be with
  the symmetric design, and probably requires a new kind of UPDATE
  operator.

- Deleting an individual shipment is more difficult than it would be with
  the symmetric design, and probably requires a new kind of DELETE
  operator.

- Deleting an individual part is more difficult than it would be with the
  symmetric design, and probably requires some kind of support for
  DELETE CASCADES after all, in fact of a more complex nature than
  would otherwise be necessary.

- The criteria for choosing the S_SP hierarchy as a basis for the design
  in favor over the alternative "P_SP" hierarchy are far from clear, to
  say the least. To quote Polya [15]: "Try to treat symmetrically what is
  symmetrical, and do not destroy wantonly any natural symmetry."

Thus, it does seem as if the traditional first normal form design remains
the one to be recommended in most situations. But note that in current
products, it is not merely recommended, it is enforced. In the (comparatively rare?) cases where base relations with relation-valued attributes do
seem to be genuinely useful, this fact might be a trifle unfortunate.

5. NESTING AND UNNESTING

Consider relation S_SP once again (Fig. 2). If, for every tuple of S_SP,
we form zero or more new tuples by joining that tuple with every tuple
in its own SUPPLIED_PARTS value, and if we then discard the
SUPPLIED_PARTS attribute, we will have "unnested S_SP along"

SUPPLIED_PARTS.* "Unnesting along" is the term used in reference [16], which proposes a new operator for the purpose, *unnest,* in the relational algebra. But such an operator clearly exposes the structure of SUPPLIED_PARTS values to the DBMS. It might be said to violate encapsulation. In what follows, I counterpropose an approach that, I argue, retains the encapsulation that I see as concomitant to first normal form, and requires no genuine extension to the relational algebra.

Generalizing the EXTEND Operator

My approach involves taking a new look at the relational *extend* operator. I propose certain generalizations of this operator, and to do so I temporarily abandon suppliers and parts for a much simpler example: **square roots of numbers.** Suppose we are given the relation NUMBER shown in Fig. 8. With the usual *extend* operator, and a SQRT function that returns the nonnegative square root of its argument, I can write the expression:

```
SQRT1   :=   EXTEND NUMBER ADD SQRT ( N ) AS SQRT_N ;
```

and thus obtain the binary relation SQRT1 also shown in Fig. 8.

Suppose now that SQRT(N) is not required to be a function, but instead returns *every* square root of its argument as a result. Suppose too that relation NUMBER includes the value -1 in addition to 1, 0, 4, and 9 (see Fig. 9). Then SQRT returns two values for N = 1, 4, and 9, one for N = 0, and none at all for N = -1 (because "square root" is undefined for negative arguments). Hence the assignment

```
SQRT2   :=   EXTEND NUMBER ADD SQRT ( N ) AS SQRT_N ;
```

yields the relation SQRT2 (again, see Fig. 9). *Note:* I am assuming here that if the expression in the ADD clause returns n distinct values, then the overall result contains n corresponding rows.

Note that SQRT2 is exactly what we would obtain from the *natural join* of NUMBER with some binary relation, R, mapping numbers to their

NUMBER	N		SQRT1	N	SQRT_N
	1			1	1
	0			0	0
	4			4	2
	9			9	3

Fig. 8 Relations NUMBER and SQRT1

---

*The result is identical to the natural join of relations S and SP, of course.

NUMBER	N
	1
	0
	4
	9
	-1

SQRT2	N	SQRT_N
	1	1
	1	-1
	0	0
	4	2
	4	-2
	9	3
	9	-3

Fig. 9 Relations NUMBER (revised) and SQRT2

square roots, so long as *R* includes all mappings for all numbers in NUMBER. In the case of N = −1, there are no mappings at all, so there is no corresponding tuple in SQRT2. I make this astoundingly trivial observation merely to emphasize the point that I find nothing perverse in this generalization of *extend* to support nonfunctional mappings; on the contrary, it seems utterly natural. I call it the **vertical** generalization of *extend*.

The **horizontal** generalization considers the values returned by the ADD expression to be *tuples*. The tuples are 1-tuples in the case of SQRT1 and SQRT2, but in general they might be of any degree. Suppose, for example, that the function SQRT is (re)defined to return an ordered pair (PR,NR) of square roots of its argument N, such that PR is nonnegative and NR = −PR. Then there are—arguably—two distinct ways in which

SQRT3	N	SQRT_N	
	1	PR	NR
		1	-1
	0	PR	NR
		0	0
	4	PR	NR
		2	-2
	9	PR	NR
		3	-3

SQRT4	N	PR	NR
	1	1	-1
	0	0	0
	4	2	-2
	9	3	-3

Fig. 10 Relations SQRT3 and SQRT4

NUMBER, extended with SQRT(N), might be represented, SQRT3 and SQRT4 (see Fig. 10).

The difference between these two representations is as follows. In SQRT3 (a binary relation), the 2-tuple values returned by SQRT(N) remain encapsulated. The domain of SQRT_N is "pairs of numbers." My pictorial representation of such 2-tuple values is (questionably) identical to my pictorial representation of relations, but note that if they were misunderstood to be relations, the lack of double underlining could correctly be interpreted as announcing the empty set to be the primary key (thereby constraining the "relations" to a maximum of one tuple each, though actually they are constrained, by *being* tuples, to *exactly* one tuple each).

In SQRT4 (a ternary relation), by contrast, the 2-tuples returned by SQRT(N) are joined directly to the tuples of NUMBER from which they were derived. In this case the syntax

```
EXTEND NUMBER ADD SQRT ( N ) AS SQRT_N
```

is clearly inappropriate, because the result does *not* have an attribute called SQRT_N, and it *does* have two attributes (PR and NR) whose names are somehow extracted from the definition of the SQRT operator. It does not seem to be a good idea (as a general principle) for attribute names in the result of an *extend* to be taken from the definition of a function or operator in the ADD clause, for those names might clash with names already appearing in the relation being extended, and in any case such a rule might once again be regarded as violating encapsulation. *Note:* The *rename* operator might be used to get around such difficulties, but it would still be the case that the user would have to know rather more about the SQRT operator than is customary in order to be sure of avoiding problems.

However, the difficulties of SQRT4 can be overcome if we regard SQRT3 as an intermediate step. Let ATTR(t,a), where t is a tuple and a is an attribute of t, be the function that delivers the value of a in t. Then we can obtain SQRT4 from SQRT3 by using ATTR to obtain the PR and NR values from SQRT_N and then discarding SQRT_N:

```
SQRT4   :=   ( EXTEND SQRT3 ADD ATTR ( SQRT_N, PR ) AS PR,
                            ATTR ( SQRT_N, NR ) AS NR )
                                        [ N, PR, NR ] ;
```

(It would be more convenient, of course, to be able to specify the attributes to be discarded, rather than those to be retained, in the final projection, but I am concerned here only with demonstrating the "conceptual purity" of what I am doing. I realize that all sorts of syntactic shorthands might be considered, and desirable.)

Although I opened the present discussion by talking about a "horizontal generalization" of *extend,* I have now shown that it is not strictly necessary: SQRT3 is derived from NUMBER by means of a function that returns an encapsulated 2–tuple as a single value, and SQRT4 is derived from SQRT3 by means of a conventional *extend* operation that uses a perfectly straightforward scalar function (ATTR). But I do definitely need the "vertical" generalization; and in the next subsection below I will show how the vertical and horizontal generalizations can be used together to perform an "unnesting" operation.

Unnesting

I now return to suppliers and parts, and show how we can "unnest" relation S_SP (Fig. 2) along the attribute SUPPLIED_PARTS.

First, let EACHTUPLE(*R*), where *R* is a relation of cardinality *n,* be an operator that delivers *n* results (all distinct), each one being a tuple of *R*. Then:

```
T    :=     EXTEND S_SP
            ADD EACHTUPLE ( SUPPLIED_PARTS ) AS P#_QTY ;

S_UNNEST_SP
     :=    ( EXTEND T ADD ATTR ( P#_QTY, P# ) AS P#,
                           ATTR ( P#_QTY, QTY ) AS QTY )
                      [ S#, SNAME, STATUS, CITY, P#, QTY ] ;
```

The result, S_UNNEST_SP, is very nearly the same relation as S_LONJ_SP (refer back to Fig. 3). The difference is that S_UNNEST_SP contains no tuples at all for supplier S5 (Adams), whereas S_LONJ_SP contains one (suspect) tuple for S5. The expression EACHTUPLE (SUPPLIED_PARTS) returns six tuples for supplier S1, two for S2, one for S3, three for S4, and none at all for S5. Is this not reminiscent of how SQRT(N) (in one of its incarnations!) returned two values for positive values of N, one for N = 0, and none at all for negative values of N?

Now, I hope—indeed, I am confident—that many of my readers will have noticed by now that S_UNNEST_SP is exactly the same as the (inner) *natural join* of S and SP.* Of course, I do not propose to dispense with the natural join operator, nor with the syntax we use for it in this book (which would be simply S JOIN SP, in the case at hand); I am merely noting that, whereas it is well known that natural join can be defined as a projection of a restriction of a Cartesian product, there is in fact an alternative way of expressing it, using extension and projection.

By contrast, I do not bother to investigate ways of deriving the *outer* join S_LONJ_SP from S_SP, because I really don't want S_LONJ_SP at all, on account of those highly suspect nulls. S_SP is my replacement

---

*Indeed, this point was made in an earlier footnote.

for S_LONJ_SP; relation-valued attributes are my replacement for outer joins.*

Nesting

References [13], [14], and [16] propose another new operator in the relational algebra, *nest,* as well as the *unnest* I have already mentioned. If *R* is a relation and *A* is a subset of the attributes of *R,* then *R* can be *nested along A.* The result, *T* say, has a single, relation-valued attribute in place of *A,* and unnesting *T* along this relation-valued attribute takes us back to *R.* For example, Fig. 11 shows the shipments relation SP of Fig. 1 nested along the attributes P# and QTY.

Note that if we join SP_NESTED with S (over S#) we obtain a relation that is identical to S_SP, except that the tuple for supplier S5 is excluded.

SP_NESTED	S#	SUPPLIED_PARTS	
	S1	**P#**	**QTY**
		P1	300
		P2	200
		P3	400
		P4	200
		P5	100
		P6	100
	S2	**P#**	**QTY**
		P1	300
		P2	400
	S3	**P#**	**QTY**
		P2	200
	S4	**P#**	**QTY**
		P2	200
		P4	300
		P5	400

Fig. 11 Relation SP_NESTED

---

*Elsewhere in this book [5], I show how certain "respectable" (null-avoiding) versions of outer join might be cleanly handled, but I remark here that outer join per se would not be needed *at all* if the proposals of the present chapter were adopted.

It should by now be apparent to the reader that SP_NESTED can be obtained by using *extend* and *project*, and there is no need to resort to an additional operator in the relational algebra:

```
T   :=  SP RENAME S# AS TS# ;

SP_NESTED
    :=  ( EXTEND SP
          ADD ( T WHERE TS# = S# ) [ P#, QTY ]
          AS SUPPLIED_PARTS ) [ S#, SUPPLIED_PARTS ] ;
```

Note that SP_NESTED can very reasonably be thought of as that mysterious intermediate result delivered by the *group by* component of the relational algebra *summarize* operator (or by SQL's GROUP BY clause, for that matter)—except that, strictly speaking, we should include an S# attribute in the relations nested inside SUPPLIED_PARTS, because *summarize* does not prohibit aggregation over the "grouping columns" themselves. I will return to this topic in Section 6, later.

Reversibility

I have already remarked that if we nest relation *R* along a set of attributes *A* to give relation *T*, there is an inverse unnesting that allows *R* to be reconstructed from *T*. This point is made in reference [13], which also discusses the circumstances in which an unnesting can be reversed by a corresponding nesting.

If some tuple of *R* has an empty relation as the value of some relation-valued attribute *RV*, then that tuple is "lost" irretrievably when we unnest *R* along *RV* to give *T*, and *R* cannot possibly be reconstructed from *T* alone. But even if there are no empty values of *RV* in *R*, *R* still cannot necessarily be reconstructed from *T*. Consider the example shown in Fig. 12. If we start with TWO_ROWS and unnest it along RV, we obtain THREE_ROWS.

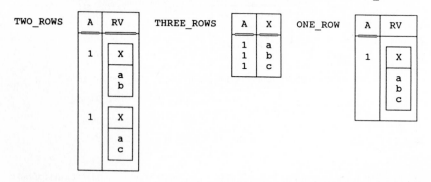

Fig. 12 Unnesting is not always reversible

But if we now nest THREE_ROWS along X (and name the resulting relation-valued attribute RV once again), we obtain not TWO_ROWS but ONE_ROW.

Note that in ONE_ROW, RV is (necessarily) functionally dependent on A, which is thus a candidate key for ONE_ROW. If we now unnest ONE_ROW along RV, we return to THREE_ROWS, and we have already seen that THREE_ROWS can be nested to give ONE_ROW; thus, the nest and unnest operations are indeed inverses of one another for this particular pair of relations. As reference [13] remarks, it is the functional dependency that is crucial in determining whether or not a given unnesting is reversible. In general, if RV is a relation-valued attribute of a relation R, then R is reversibly unnestable along RV if and only if both of the following are true:

- No tuple of R has an empty relation as its RV value.

- RV is functionally dependent on the set consisting of all the other attributes of R. An alternative way of expressing the same thing is to say that there must be some candidate key of R that does not include RV as a component.

6. GROUPING AND SUMMARIZING

Let me now return to the SP_NESTED example (Fig. 12). I have already pointed out that relation SP_NESTED (or, rather, a version of SP_NESTED in which the relation-valued attribute SUPPLIED_PARTS includes an additional attribute, namely S#) can be regarded as the intermediate result produced by the *group by* component* of the expression

```
SUMMARIZE SP GROUPBY ( S# )
        ADD  aggregate-computation  AS  attribute
```

The other component of *summarize*—the one that computes the values of aggregate functions over the partitions defined by the grouping—can also be expressed in terms of extension and projection. Consider the following example, in which we wish to obtain the count of parts supplied by each supplier:

```
P_COUNT  :=  SUMMARIZE SP GROUPBY ( S# ) ADD COUNT AS P_CT ;
```

The following statement clearly produces the same result:

```
P_COUNT  :=  ( EXTEND SP_NESTED
                ADD CARD ( SUPPLIED_PARTS ) AS P_CT )
                                        [ S#, P_CT ] ;
```

---

*It is worth pointing out that if we partition the attributes of relation R into two disjoint subsets A and B, then nesting R along B is equivalent to grouping R by A.

I have assumed the existence of a function CARD(*R*) that returns the cardinality of its argument relation *R*.

Now, we would hardly want to give up our useful *summarize* operator just because we have discovered a way of expressing it using *extend, project,* and relation-valued attributes. But at least the foregoing might help in the teaching and understanding of *summarize,* and in explaining the functional dependencies that hold (admittedly fairly obviously) in its result [3]. Furthermore, if we are permitted to use relation-valued attributes in the manner suggested above, we can overcome that problem for which *summarize* is so often derided, where the zero counts and sums that would arise from aggregation over empty sets cannot be obtained. For instance, relation P_COUNT as defined above does not show that supplier S5 supplies zero parts. All is well, however, if we start with relation S_SP (Fig. 2) instead of SP_NESTED:*

```
P_COUNT  :=  ( EXTEND S_SP
               ADD CARD ( SUPPLIED_PARTS ) AS P_CT )
                                         [ S#, P_CT ] ;
```

Note, however, that the foregoing discussion does show that *summarize* needs to be treated with a certain degree of caution, just as *divide* does [6], and for essentially the same reason.

7. CONCLUDING REMARKS

The study of the data types on which domains might be defined is orthogonal to the study of relations. We are already well accustomed to those data types (numbers, character strings, dates and times, etc.) typically supported by today's relational, pseudorelational, and nonrelational database management systems. We are not yet accustomed to *collective* data types, such as sets, arrays, lists, and multisets, as a basis for relational domains, but there is much talk of such things in connexion with the growing interest in Object-Oriented systems. In this chapter I have studied one such data type, namely relations, that I perceive to be receiving less attention than the others. I think that relations deserve *more* attention in this context than sets, arrays, lists, and multisets, because:

- We need relations anyway, as our primary database objects; we don't know how to do nonnavigational queries without them. And if we need them on the "outside," we have to understand them anyway, and we have to know how to perform relational operations and relational com-

---

*Reference [5] (mentioned in a previous footnote) shows how this same result can be achieved by means of a comparatively respectable version of a left outer join.

parisons (etc.) anyway. Thus, if we need any kind of collective data type at all on the "inside," then surely relations will be the one requiring the minimum of extra learning.

- And the minimum amount of extra syntax in our DBMS's query language.

- And the minimum number of extra pages in the documentation.

- And so on.

- Furthermore, sets, arrays, lists, and multisets can all be mapped into relations. Therefore, if we need collections at all, all such needs can be satisfied with relations. True, relations might sometimes not be quite the "best fit" for the purpose at hand—but is the extra effort of implementing, teaching, and learning all the other kinds of collection really justified? We would be better placed to answer this question if we had practical experience of relation-valued attributes to go on. Since we do not have that experience at this time, I am strongly tempted to invoke The Principle of Cautious Design [8] and vote for supporting relations as the *only* collective data type, until further notice.

By favoring the term "relation-valued attribute" (also used in references [13] and [14]) over "nested relation," I have suggested an approach that (I claim) adheres as much to the letter of first normal form as do number-valued attributes, character-string-valued attributes, date-valued attributes, and time-valued attributes, if not to the spirit of that part of first normal form, *nondecomposability,* that I am in any case unable to pin down. In place of the *nest* and *unnest* operators proposed by other researchers, I have suggested a generalization of relational *extend* to perform the necessary conversions between relations that include relation-valued attributes and relations that do not. I have also shown that this generalization provides a new way of looking at the *natural join* and *summarize* operators.

Finally, I have discovered that relation-valued attributes do offer straightforward and intuitive approaches to some problems that have proved difficult within the confines of traditional first normal form. That makes me quite keen on the idea (and I commend it to all Objectlanders, but that's another story).

REFERENCES AND BIBLIOGRAPHY

1. E. F. Codd, "A Relational Model of Data for Large Shared Data Banks," *Communications of the ACM* 13, No. 6 (June 1970). Republished in *Communications of the ACM* 26, No. 1 (January 1983).

2. E. F. Codd, *The Relational Model for Database Management Version 2* (Reading, MA: Addison-Wesley, 1990).

3. Hugh Darwen, "The Role of Functional Dependence in Query Decomposition" (in this volume).

4. Hugh Darwen, "The Nullologist in Relationland" (in this volume).

5. Hugh Darwen, "Outer Join with No Nulls and Fewer Tears" (in this volume).

6. Hugh Darwen and C. J. Date, "Into the Great Divide" (in this volume).

7. C. J. Date, "Relational Algebra," Chapter 13 of C. J. Date, *An Introduction to Database Systems, Volume I,* 5th edition (Reading, MA: Addison-Wesley, 1990).

8. C. J. Date, "The Principle of Cautious Design" (in this volume).

9. C. J. Date, "What Is a Domain?" in C. J. Date, *Relational Database Writings 1985–1989* (Reading, MA: Addison-Wesley, 1990).

10. C. J. Date, "What Is a Relation?" (in this volume).

11. C. J. Date, "Notes Toward a Reconstituted Definition of the Relational Model Version 1 (RM/V1)" (in this volume).

12. C. J. Date, "Will the Real Fourth Normal Form Please Stand Up?" (in this volume).

13. G. Jaeschke, "Nonrecursive Algebra for Relations with Relation-Valued Attributes," IBM Technical Report 85.03.001, IBM Scientific Centre, Heidelberg, Germany (March 1985).

14. G. Jaeschke, "Recursive Algebra for Relations with Relation-Valued Attributes," IBM Technical Report 85.03.002, IBM Scientific Centre, Heidelberg, Germany (March 1985).

15. G. Polya, *How to Solve It,* 2nd edition (Princeton: Princeton University Press, 1971).

16. Mark A. Roth, Henry F. Korth, and Abraham Silberschatz, "Extended Relational Algebra and Relational Calculus for Nested Relational Databases," *ACM Transactions on Database Systems* 13, No. 4 (December 1988).

7

An Anomaly in Codd's Reduction Algorithm

ABSTRACT

We examine a logical anomaly in Codd's reduction algorithm [1], according to which relational calculus queries can occasionally produce somewhat surprising results.

COMMENTS ON REPUBLICATION

"Codd's reduction algorithm" is the algorithm, first presented by Codd in reference [1], for translating ("reducing") an arbitrary expression of the relational calculus to a semantically equivalent expression of the relational algebra. That algorithm can be taken as a basis for either (a) an implementation of a calculus-based language or (b) a formal definition of the semantics of such a language (or indeed both). However, I was surprised to discover in 1989 that the algorithm contains a minor anomaly (some would say a flaw), as a result of which certain calculus expressions have a rather

Originally published under the title "A Note on the Relational Calculus" in *ACM SIGMOD Record* 18, No. 4 (December 1989). Reprinted with permission.

counterintuitive interpretation. I wrote the paper that follows in order to document and explain that anomaly.

1. INTRODUCTION

We start by considering a simple example. Suppose we have a database containing three union-compatible relations X, Y, and Z, each with just one attribute called A. Suppose also that relations X and Y each contain just one tuple, each of which in turn contains the single scalar value "a", and relation Z contains no tuples at all (refer to Fig. 1).

Fig. 1 Sample data values

Now let *tx, ty,* and *tz* be tuple variables ranging over relations X, Y, and Z, respectively, and consider the following query (i.e., relational calculus expression):

```
tx.A   WHERE   EXISTS ty ( ty.A = tx.A )
       OR       EXISTS tz ( tz.A = tx.A )
```

The intuitive interpretation of this query is "Find those values in relation X that exist in either relation Y or relation Z (or both)." Given the sample data of Fig. 1, the result intuitively expected is "a"; or, more precisely, it is a relation of degree one, containing just one tuple, which in turn contains the single scalar value "a"—see Fig. 2, part (a). The result actually produced, however, is a relation of degree one containing no tuples at all!—see Fig. 2, part (b).

(a) Expected result: A / a   (b) Actual result: A

Fig. 2 (a) Result intuitively expected
      (b) Result actually produced

The reason for this somewhat surprising state of affairs is explained in the sections that follow.

Aside: For people unfamiliar with the relational calculus, we show a SQL version of the query also:

```
SELECT  TX.A
FROM    X TX
WHERE   EXISTS
      ( SELECT *
        FROM    Y TY
        WHERE   TY.A = TX.A )
OR      EXISTS
      ( SELECT *
        FROM    Z TZ
        WHERE   TZ.A = TX.A ) ;
```

Or, still more intuitively (using the SQL trick that allows the name of a relation to be used as an implicit tuple variable that ranges over the relation in question, together with SQL's rules for implicit name qualification):

```
SELECT  A
FROM    X
WHERE   EXISTS
      ( SELECT *
        FROM    Y
        WHERE   Y.A = X.A )
OR      EXISTS
      ( SELECT *
        FROM    Z
        WHERE   Z.A = X.A ) ;
```

Two points in connexion with this SQL version, however:

1. First, the SQL version may actually *not* be equivalent to the original calculus version, as will subsequently be made clear. Indeed, this fact is part of the overall message of this short paper.

2. Second, we are assuming (in both the SQL version and the original calculus version) that the system is supporting conventional two-valued logic. If instead it is supporting three-valued logic, then the SQL version is *definitely* not equivalent to the original calculus version, as has been amply demonstrated elsewhere [2].

End of aside.

2. RELATIONAL CALCULUS EXPRESSIONS

In order to explain what is happening in the example, it is first necessary to digress for a moment and elaborate on exactly what it is that constitutes a relational calculus expression. It is of course well known that relational calculus is an applied form of predicate calculus, tailored for use with relational databases. A relational calculus expression is really a special case of a *set definition*. It takes the general form

```
target  WHERE  qualification
```

where "target" identifies the relations and attributes from which the result set (more precisely, result *relation*) is to be constructed, and "qualification" identifies a condition to be satisfied by each tuple of that result relation. To be a little more specific:

1. "target" is a comma-separated list of elements, each of the form

   ```
   variable . attribute
   ```

   where "variable" is the name of a tuple variable and "attribute" is the name of an attribute of the corresponding relation;

2. "qualification" is a *well-formed formula* (abbreviated wff, pronounced "weff"), defined in accordance with the following production rule:

   ```
   wff ::=   term
             NOT wff
             term AND wff
             term OR  wff
             IF term THEN wff
             EXISTS variable ( wff )
             FORALL variable ( wff )
   ```

   Note: For present purposes, there is no need to define "term" any further; it can be regarded as essentially a simple comparison, such as "*ty*.A = *tx*.A", or else a wff in parentheses. Also, of course, there are several more rules governing the correct formulation of "targets" and "qualifications," and further rules that allow the dropping of redundant parentheses. We assume that these rules are basically well understood and omit the details here.

3.   PRENEX NORMAL FORM

Now, it is a fact that any wff of the *predicate* calculus (as opposed to the relational calculus) can always be converted into an equivalent wff in what is called *prenex normal form* ("equivalent" in that it has the same denotation or meaning). A wff is in prenex normal form if and only if all the quantifiers appear unnegated and at the left-hand end. For example, the predicate calculus wff

```
EXISTS x ( x > 5 ) OR EXISTS y ( y > 2 )
```

is equivalent to the prenex normal form wff

```
EXISTS x ( EXISTS y ( x > 5 OR y > 2 ) )
```

(*Note:* We are specifically interested in this paper in wffs of the form EXISTS . . . OR EXISTS. . . .) More generally, if

1. $p(x)$ is a wff in which y does not occur as a free variable, and

2. $q(y)$ is a wff in which x does not occur as a free variable

(where by "free variable" we mean a variable that is not bound, i.e., not quantified), then the wff

```
EXISTS x ( p(x) ) OR EXISTS y ( q(y) )
```

is equivalent to the prenex normal form wff

```
EXISTS x ( EXISTS y ( p(x) OR q(y) ) )
```

The validity of this assertion, and hence the validity of the transformation of the original wff into prenex normal form, is easily shown (see, e.g., reference [4]).

4. THE MEANING OF RELATIONAL CALCULUS EXPRESSIONS

We return now to the relational calculus per se. In reference [1], Codd gives a *reduction algorithm* by which any expression of the relational calculus can be transformed into an expression of the relational algebra. That transformation is then effectively used as a basis for defining the meaning of the original calculus expression (i.e., the meaning of the calculus expression is defined to be identical to that of the corresponding algebraic expression).

The very first step in Codd's reduction algorithm is as follows:

"Convert [the qualification part of the expression] to prenex normal form . . . *without expanding the range-coupled quantifiers*" [1; emphasis added].

In this step, according to Codd, "the range-coupled quantifiers behave just like ordinary quantifiers" [1].

As these two quotes suggest, the quantifiers of relational calculus are not identical to the quantifiers of ordinary predicate calculus. Instead, they are "range-coupled" quantifiers. Loosely speaking, a range-coupled quantifier is a quantifier that includes a definition of the range (i.e., set of permitted values) of its associated bound variable; in other words, it is shorthand for a predicate calculus wff of the form

```
Qx ( x ε X )
```

where Q is a normal quantifier, x is a bound variable, X is a relation, and "$x \in X$" is a term meaning "x is a member (i.e., tuple) of X." For example, the relational calculus wff

```
EXISTS x ( p(x) )
```

is really shorthand for the *predicate* calculus wff

```
EXISTS x ( x є X AND p(x) )
```

Let us examine once again the sample relational calculus expression from the beginning of this paper:

```
tx.A   WHERE   EXISTS ty ( ty.A = tx.A )
       OR      EXISTS tz ( tz.A = tx.A )
```

We concentrate on just the qualification part, namely the relational calculus wff

1. ```
   EXISTS ty ( ty.A = tx.A ) OR
   EXISTS tz ( tz.A = tx.A )
   ```

Let us agree to refer to this expression as "Expression 1." Expanding out the two range-coupled quantifiers to show the range definitions, we obtain the *predicate* calculus wff (Expression 2):

2. ```
   EXISTS ty ( ty є Y AND ty.A = tx.A ) OR
   EXISTS tz ( tz є Z AND tz.A = tx.A )
   ```

("EXISTS ty" and "EXISTS tz" are now genuine quantifiers, not range-coupled quantifiers.) The prenex normal form equivalent of this wff in predicate calculus is as follows (Expression 3):

3. ```
   EXISTS ty ( EXISTS tz (
               ( ty є Y AND ty.A = tx.A ) OR
               ( tz є Z AND tz.A = tx.A ) ) )
   ```

In *relational* calculus, however, since "range-coupled quantifiers behave just like ordinary quantifiers" in the conversion process, the prenex normal form "equivalent" of Expression 1 is Expression 4:

4. ```
   EXISTS ty ( EXISTS tz (
               ( ty.A = tx.A ) OR
               ( tz.A = tx.A ) ) )
   ```

Here the quantifiers are range-coupled. Expanding them out, we obtain Expression 5:

5. ```
   EXISTS ty ( ty є Y AND EXISTS tz ( tz є Z AND (
               ( ty.A = tx.A ) OR
               ( tz.A = tx.A ) ) ) )
   ```

which is obviously syntactically different from Expression 3. In fact, *it is semantically different also.* In particular, if relations X, Y, and Z are as shown in Fig. 1, then for the sole possible value of tuple variable *tx,* Expression 3 evaluates to *true* but Expression 5 evaluates to *false* (as the reader may easily confirm).

The first step in the reduction algorithm has thus changed the semantics
   ```

of the original expression!—and it is this fact that accounts for the counter-intuitive nature of the result of the original relational calculus query.

Of course, the anomaly just described is presumably due to a mere oversight in Codd's definition of the reduction algorithm. It looks as if Codd was making a tacit assumption that the (qualification) expression under consideration did not contain any "OR"s—especially since he goes on to form the Cartesian product of the ranges of all pertinent tuple variables, which is not appropriate in the presence of "OR"s. (To see why this is so, the reader is invited to consider the example addressed in the body of this paper once again. The Cartesian product of relations X, Y, and Z is clearly empty.)

ACKNOWLEDGMENTS

I would like to thank Charley Bontempo and Nat Goodman for several helpful discussions. I would also like to thank the vendor (RTI, as it then was) of the commercial INGRES product for giving me the opportunity to check the original example on INGRES (using QUEL), and Colin White for trying out the SQL version for me on ORACLE. For the record, INGRES/QUEL did indeed return an empty relation, and ORACLE/SQL returned a relation containing the single value "a"—which shows, if nothing else, that ORACLE's dialect of SQL is at least not just a syntactic variation on Codd's original relational calculus.

Note added in final version: After I had prepared the original version of this paper, I discovered that the error in the reduction algorithm had already been pointed out in an earlier paper by Klug [3]. Readers are referred to that paper for an alternative proof of the equivalence of the calculus and the algebra, one that avoids the error discussed in the present paper.

REFERENCES AND BIBLIOGRAPHY

1. E. F. Codd, "Relational Completeness of Data Base Sublanguages," in R. Rustin, ed., *Data Base Systems,* Courant Computer Science Symposia Series 6 (Englewood Cliffs, NJ: Prentice-Hall, 1972).

2. C. J. Date, "EXISTS Is Not "Exists"! (Some Logical Flaws in SQL)," in C. J. Date, *Relational Database Writings 1985–1989* (Reading, MA: Addison-Wesley, 1990).

3. Anthony Klug, "Equivalence of Relational Algebra and Relational Calculus Query Languages Having Aggregate Functions," *Journal of the ACM* 29, No. 3 (July 1982).

4. Zohar Manna and Richard Waldinger, *The Logical Basis for Computer Programming. Volume I: Deductive Reasoning* (Reading, MA: Addison-Wesley, 1985).

8

Why Quantifier Order Is Important

ABSTRACT

We review the relational calculus quantifiers EXISTS and FORALL and discuss some subtleties in dealing with them.

COMMENTS ON REPUBLICATION

From my experience in teaching seminars on the relational model, I have found that database professionals tend to be somewhat leery of the relational calculus in general, and of the quantifiers EXISTS and FORALL in particular. This is a pity, since the concepts involved are not really unfamiliar, nor are they very difficult to understand—and they *are* very powerful, and indeed fundamental. I wrote this paper in an attempt to improve the situation.

Originally published (in considerably edited form) under the title "Quantifiers and Ambiguity: Order Makes a Difference" in *The Relational Journal for DB2 Users* 2, No. 2 (April/May 1990). Reprinted with permission.

1.   INTRODUCTION

This paper is concerned with the quantifiers EXISTS and FORALL. EXISTS ("there exists") is the *existential* quantifier, FORALL ("for all") is the *universal* quantifier. EXISTS and FORALL are used in the construction of *truth-valued expressions,* and hence in the formulation of queries, view definitions, etc., in the relational model. Now, it is true that most relational systems do not directly support FORALL at the time of writing; however, they typically do support EXISTS, since EXISTS (or at least an approximation to it [2]) is included in the SQL standard, and I therefore assume that readers do have a basic familiarity with EXISTS at least. However, let me begin by briefly explaining both quantifiers.

Let x be a variable that ranges over some set X. For example, X might be the set of people that work for IBM; x would then represent some individual IBM employee. Now let $p(x)$ be a truth-valued expression involving x—for example, the expression "x is Albanian." Then:

1. The expression "EXISTS x $(p(x))$" is also a truth-valued expression, which evaluates to *true* if there exists at least one value of x such that $p(x)$ evaluates to *true,* and to *false* otherwise. In the example, "EXISTS x $(p(x))$" is *true* if IBM has at least one Albanian employee and *false* otherwise. (*Note:* Here and throughout this paper I am assuming two-valued logic only, not three-valued logic.)

2. Likewise, the expression "FORALL x $(p(x))$" is also a truth-valued expression, which evaluates to *true* if $p(x)$ evaluates to *true* for all values of x, and to *false* otherwise. In the example, "FORALL x $(p(x))$" is *false* if any IBM employee is not Albanian and *true* otherwise. (Note, incidentally, that the expression therefore evaluates to *true* if IBM has no employees at all!)

Of course, the foregoing explanations are recursive; that is, the truth-valued expression $p(x)$ might already involve one or more quantifiers. As a result, expressions of the form (e.g.)

```
EXISTS x ( FORALL y ( EXISTS z ( ... ) ) )
```

are perfectly legal, in general. In other words, quantified expressions can be nested to arbitrary depth.

2.   FORALL IS NOT STRICTLY NECESSARY

Having just introduced the two quantifiers, I must now explain that we don't really need both—either one can be defined in terms of the other, by virtue of the following identity:

```
FORALL x ( p ( x ) )  ≡  NOT EXISTS x ( NOT p ( x ) )
```

It follows that any expression involving FORALL can always be replaced by an equivalent expression involving EXISTS instead, and vice versa. For example, let x and y range over the set of integers. Then the (true) statement

```
FORALL x ( EXISTS y ( y > x ) )
```

("for all integers x, there exists an integer y such that $y > x$") is equivalent to the statement

```
NOT EXISTS x ( NOT EXISTS y ( y > x ) )
```

("there does not exist an integer x such that there does not exist an integer y such that $y > x$"). But it is usually easier to think in terms of FORALL than in terms of EXISTS and a double negative; in other words, query languages should ideally support both quantifiers. Certainly it is a criticism of SQL (which supports only EXISTS) that "FORALL-type" queries are not very easy to formulate, nor to understand. (What is more, extending SQL to provide direct support for FORALL would not be an easy thing to do. But that problem is not the topic of the present article. See reference [2] for further discussion.)

3. QUANTIFIER ORDER

Suppose now that we have an expression that involves a sequence of multiple quantifiers, all adjacent to one another. If the quantifiers are all of the same type (i.e., all existential or all universal), then the order in which they appear is irrelevant. For example, the expressions

```
EXISTS x ( EXISTS y ( q ( x, y ) ) )
```

and

```
EXISTS y ( EXISTS x ( q ( x, y ) ) )
```

are equivalent. If the quantifiers are not all of the same type, however, then the order matters. For instance, let x and y range over the set of integers, as before. Then (as already explained) the expression

```
FORALL x ( EXISTS y ( y > x ) )
```

("for all integers x, there exists an integer y such that $y > x$") is true. However, the expression

```
EXISTS y ( FORALL x ( y > x ) )
```

("there exists an integer y such that, for all integers x, y is greater than x"—i.e., there exists an integer greater than all others"), which is obtained from the first expression by simply inverting the order of the quantifiers, is *false*.

The foregoing example probably seems straightforward enough. However, matters can be a little more tricky in practice, especially if the query language at hand is one that uses *implicit* quantification. An example of such a language is Query-By-Example (QBE). Here is an example of a query expressed in QBE. *Note:* The dialect of QBE I am using here is essentially that proposed by Zloof in his original paper (reference [4]). It is *not* identical to the dialect used in the IBM product QMF [1]. See the further remarks on this point at the end of this section.

SALES	DEPT	ITEM
	P.	_ink

SUPPLY	ITEM	SUPPLIER
	_ink	¬ Smith

Here "Smith" is a *constant element* and "_ink" is an *example element* (a variable, in more conventional terms—indicated in QBE by a leading underscore character, as in the example); "−" means negation, and "P." stands for "Print" (meaning "Retrieve"). The intuitive—and correct—interpretation of this query is "Retrieve departments that sell some item (say ink) that is available from someone other than Smith." The row in the SUPPLY table is *implicitly* existentially quantified. The query is equivalent to the following relational calculus expression:

```
SALES.DEPT
WHERE EXISTS SUPPLY ( SUPPLY.ITEM = SALES.ITEM AND
                      SUPPLY.SUPPLIER ¬= 'Smith' )
```

(I am playing the usual punning trick here by which a table name can be used to refer to an implicitly declared variable that ranges over the table with the same name. For example, references in the WHERE clause to the name "SUPPLY" denote a variable that ranges over the table called SUPPLY.)

Here is a second example:

SALES	DEPT	ITEM
	P.	_ink

SUPPLY	ITEM	SUPPLIER
¬	_ink	Smith

The correct interpretation of this query is "Retrieve departments that sell some item (e.g., ink) that is not available from Smith." This time, the implicitly quantified row in the SUPPLY table is explicitly negated. The query is thus equivalent to the following relational calculus expression:

```
SALES.DEPT
WHERE NOT EXISTS SUPPLY ( SUPPLY.ITEM = SALES.ITEM AND
                          SUPPLY.SUPPLIER = 'Smith' )
```

or alternatively

```
SALES.DEPT
WHERE FORALL SUPPLY ( NOT ( SUPPLY.ITEM = SALES.ITEM AND
                            SUPPLY.SUPPLIER = 'Smith' ) )
```

So far, so good; each of the foregoing queries has involved only a single quantifier. But now consider the following example:

SALES	DEPT	ITEM
	P.	_ink

SUPPLY	ITEM	SUPPLIER
¬	_ink _ink	Smith

THIS ONE IS AMBIGUOUS! Its interpretation depends on the order in which the two rows in table SUPPLY are examined (note carefully that QBE does not specify any such order). If we take the negated row first, the query is equivalent to

```
SALES.DEPT
WHERE NOT EXISTS SUPPLY1
          ( EXISTS SUPPLY2 ( SUPPLY1.ITEM = SALES.ITEM AND
                             SUPPLY2.ITEM = SALES.ITEM AND
                             SUPPLY1.SUPPLIER = 'Smith' ) )
```

(Here SUPPLY1 and SUPPLY2 represent two separate variables, both ranging over the SUPPLY table.) Intuitive interpretation: "Retrieve departments that sell some item that is not available from Smith (and possibly not from anyone at all)."

On the other hand, if we take the nonnegated row first, the query is equivalent to

```
SALES.DEPT
WHERE EXISTS SUPPLY2
          ( NOT EXISTS SUPPLY1 ( SUPPLY1.ITEM = SALES.ITEM AND
                                SUPPLY2.ITEM = SALES.ITEM AND
                                SUPPLY1.SUPPLIER = 'Smith' ) )
```

Intuitive interpretation: "Retrieve departments that sell some item that *is* available from someone, but not from Smith."

So which of the two interpretations is correct? And how do we know? And whichever it is, how do we formulate the other?

An interesting sidelight on the foregoing is the following: In the paper from which I took the example [3], the author was actually trying to formulate a different query entirely!—namely, "Retrieve departments that do not sell anything available from Smith." A correct formulation of *this* query would be:

SALES	DEPT	ITEM
¬	P._d _d	_ink

SUPPLY	ITEM	SUPPLIER
	_ink	Smith

Relational calculus equivalent:

```
SALES1.DEPT
WHERE NOT EXISTS SALES2
         ( EXISTS SUPPLY ( SALES2.DEPT = SALES1.DEPT AND
                           SALES2.ITEM = SUPPLY.ITEM AND
                           SUPPLY.SUPPLIER = 'Smith' ) )
```

The author was trying to show that negation is troublesome in QBE, and he succeeded.

Here is an example for the reader to try. Given (a simplified form of) the usual suppliers-and-parts database, with definition as follows—

```
S    ( S#, CITY )
     PRIMARY KEY ( S# )

P    ( P#, CITY )
     PRIMARY KEY ( P# )

SP   ( S#, P# )
     PRIMARY KEY ( S#, P# )
     FOREIGN KEY ( S# ) REFERENCES S
     FOREIGN KEY ( P# ) REFERENCES P
```

—what are the possible interpretations of the following QBE query?

SP	S#	P#
	P._sx	_px

S	S#	CITY
	_sx	_cx

P	P#	CITY
¬	_px	_cx

Show the output produced by each interpretation, given the following sample data:

SP	S#	P#
	S1	P1
	S2	P2

S	S#	CITY
	S1	London

P	P#	CITY
	P2	Paris

Answers are given in Appendix A.

Note: Precisely because of the ambiguities discussed above, the ability to negate a row was omitted from the dialect of QBE implemented in the IBM product QMF (reference [1]). Thus, the foregoing problems do not exist in QMF. However, the effect of the omission is to make it impossible to formulate certain "FORALL-type" queries in QMF/QBE, and hence to make QMF/QBE strictly less powerful in expressive capability than QMF/SQL. Here, for instance, is an example of a QMF/SQL query—"Find cities of suppliers who do not supply any parts"—that cannot be formulated in QMF/QBE:

```
SELECT S.CITY
FROM   S
WHERE  NOT EXISTS
         ( SELECT *
           FROM   SP
           WHERE  SP.S# = S.S# ) ;
```

4. CONCLUSION

I hope that the examples and discussions of this paper have made it clear why it is important for both users and designers of formal query languages to have a good understanding of the EXISTS and FORALL quantifiers. While I realize that this state of affairs may be regarded as a little unfortunate by some people, I do not think it is as unfortunate as the alternative—which is WRONG ANSWERS from the database.

ACKNOWLEDGMENTS

I am grateful to Charley Bontempo and Hugh Darwen for numerous helpful discussions.

REFERENCES AND BIBLIOGRAPHY

1. IBM Corporation, *Query Management Facility General Information.* IBM Form No. GG26-4071.

2. C. J. Date, "EXISTS Is Not "Exists"! (Some Logical Flaws in SQL)," in C. J. Date, *Relational Database Writings 1985–1989* (Reading, MA: Addison-Wesley, 1990).

3. John Owlett, "A Theory of Database Schemata: Studies in Conceptual and Relational Schemata," doctoral dissertation, Wolfson College, Oxford, England (October 1979).

4. M. M. Zloof, "Query By Example," Proc. NCC 44 (May 1975).

APPENDIX A:
ANSWERS TO EXERCISES

Here are the answers to the two questions posed in the body of the paper. First, there are two possible interpretations of the query, as follows:

1. SP.S# WHERE EXISTS S (NOT EXISTS P (SP.S# = S.S# AND
                                          SP.P# = P.P# AND
                                          S.CITY = P.CITY))

("supplier numbers for suppliers who do supply at least one part, but not any parts that are stored in the supplier's own city").

2. SP.S# WHERE NOT EXISTS P (EXISTS S (SP.S# = S.S# AND
                                         SP.P# = P.P# AND
                                         S.CITY = P.CITY))

("supplier numbers for suppliers who do not supply any part that is stored in the supplier's own city").

Given the specified sample data, the first interpretation produces as output just the single supplier number S1; the second produces both S1 and S2.

9

Relational Calculus
As an Aid to
Effective Query Formulation

ABSTRACT

An approach to the construction of certain "complex" SQL queries is discussed. The approach makes use of an extended version of the relational calculus that includes aggregate functions.

COMMENTS ON PUBLICATION

I have been teaching the ideas and techniques described in this paper in live seminars and presentations for a number of years. I have also discussed at least some of those ideas and techniques in certain earlier books and papers. However, they have never been collected together in a single place before. It therefore seemed to me to be a good idea to bring them together in the present paper, for purposes of future reference if nothing else. Please note, however, that I make no claims for completeness of any kind—the tech-

Previously unpublished.

niques described, while useful, certainly do not constitute a panacea; some "complex" queries will always be complex.

My thesis essentially is that it is very difficult to construct "complex" queries directly in SQL: The language is so very unorthogonal, it suffers from so many functional deficiencies, it displays such a variety of counter-intuitive (arguably even incorrect) behavior, etc., etc. Thus, I believe a good approach to the construction of such "complex" queries in SQL is to formulate them in relational calculus first—relational calculus being a formalism that does not suffer from such SQL-style drawbacks—and then to go through the process (almost a mechanical process) of mapping the relational calculus version of the query into a SQL equivalent. The resulting SQL query will very likely be quite difficult to understand, but at least it will be *correct*. (At least, it should be! This point also is discussed in the paper that follows.)

Note: The paper might equally well have been included in Part VI of the book. I decided to include it here because of the direct relevance of the discussions of the previous chapter.

1. INTRODUCTION

It is a truism to say that almost all relational products on the market today are based on SQL, and hence almost all ad hoc queries—certainly those that are "too complex" for the frequently rather limited capabilities of the vendor's ad hoc query frontend—have to be expressed in SQL. At the same time, it is undeniable that SQL is a very difficult language: It suffers from such lack of orthogonality, such lack of functionality, such lack of predictability, etc., etc.—in a word, it is so ad hoc*—that those very same queries that are "too complex" for the ad hoc query frontend are often too complex to be formulated directly in SQL as well (at least with any confidence that the formulation in question is correct).

Needless to say, relational calculus stands in sharp contrast to the foregoing. Relational calculus is not ad hoc. Instead, it is sound, systematic, orthogonal, etc., etc. Moreover, relational calculus directly supports certain very useful concepts—e.g., the concept of the *universal quantifier* (FORALL)—that SQL does not directly support. "As a consequence, many queries—certainly any queries that are a little more complex than the usual bread-and-butter examples given in vendor manuals—are frequently most easily expressed in SQL by formulating them in relational calculus first and then converting that formulation, more or less mechanically, into

---

*I was sorely tempted to give this paper the subtitle "SQL: An Ad Hoc Language for Ad Hoc Queries."

its SQL equivalent" [2]. In this paper, we will explore such an approach to SQL query formulation in some detail.

Please note, incidentally, that I do not guarantee that the resulting SQL queries will be easy to understand; in many cases, in fact, the opposite will be true. Nor do I guarantee that those SQL queries will be the most efficient possible (but then I am much more interested in getting the right answer!— speed of response is irrelevant if the answer is wrong). And I certainly do not guarantee that all possible queries can be treated using the techniques of this paper. Nevertheless, I do think those techniques can be of genuine practical use in many situations.

Note: The reader is expected to be familiar with relational calculus at least to the elementary level described in reference [5], including the extensions sketched therein for dealing with aggregates such as COUNT and SUM (but those latter extensions are reviewed briefly in Section 4 of the present paper).

2. QUERIES INVOLVING UNIVERSAL QUANTIFICATION

Note: The base example for this section is taken from reference [7].

A universal quantification query is a query whose "natural" formulation involves the quantifier FORALL. Here is an example. We are given the usual suppliers-and-parts database, with definition as follows:

```
S    ( S#, SNAME, ... )
     PRIMARY KEY ( S# )

P    ( P#, PNAME, ... )
     PRIMARY KEY ( P# )

SP   ( S#, P#, QTY )
     PRIMARY KEY ( S#, P# )
     FOREIGN KEY ( S# ) REFERENCES S
     FOREIGN KEY ( P# ) REFERENCES P
```

The query is: "Find names of suppliers who supply all parts" (where "all parts" means all parts that exist, i.e., all parts represented in relation P). Here first is a "natural" relational calculus formulation of this query (2.1):

```
(2.1) SX.SNAME WHERE FORALL PX ( EXISTS SPX (
                              SPX.S# = SX.S# AND
                              SPX.P# = PX.P# ) )
```

("find names of suppliers SX such that, for all parts PX, there exists a shipment SPX saying that SX supplies PX"). SX, PX, and SPX here are tuple variables, ranging over relations S, P, and SP, respectively).

In order to transform this expression into valid SQL, I will make use of the following transformation rule: The truth-valued expression

```
FORALL x ( p )
```

can always be replaced by the logically equivalent expression

```
NOT ( EXISTS x ( NOT ( p ) ) )
```

For example, the statement "For all persons x, it is the case that x is mortal" is equivalent to the statement "There does not exist a person x such that it is not the case that x is mortal." (In colloquial English, the statements "Everybody is mortal" and "Nobody is immortal" say the same thing.)

Applying the foregoing transformation to (2.1), we obtain the following (2.2):

```
(2.2) SX.SNAME WHERE NOT ( EXISTS PX ( NOT ( EXISTS SPX (
                                      SPX.S# = SX.S# AND
                                      SPX.P# = PX.P# ) ) ) )
```

Now the expression involves only operators such as NOT and EXISTS that SQL does directly support. It can therefore be converted into SQL form (2.3):

```
(2.3) SELECT DISTINCT SX.SNAME
      FROM    S SX
      WHERE   NOT ( EXISTS
              ( SELECT DISTINCT PX.*
              FROM    P PX
              WHERE   NOT ( EXISTS
                      ( SELECT DISTINCT SPX.*
                      FROM    SP SPX
                      WHERE   SPX.S# = SX.S#
                      AND     SPX.P# = PX.P# ) ) ) ) ;
```

Note that an expression such as (e.g.) "EXISTS PX (. . .)" in the calculus formulation becomes "EXISTS (SELECT DISTINCT PX.* FROM P PX WHERE . . .)" in the SQL version. In other words, the "PX" in "EXISTS PX" becomes "(SELECT DISTINCT PX.* FROM P PX)," and the opening parenthesis immediately following that "EXISTS PX" becomes a WHERE.

Last, we can make a few purely cosmetic changes to arrive at the final SQL version (2.4):

```
(2.4) SELECT DISTINCT SNAME
      FROM    S
      WHERE   NOT EXISTS
              ( SELECT DISTINCT *
              FROM    P
              WHERE   NOT EXISTS
                      ( SELECT DISTINCT *
                      FROM    SP
                      WHERE   SP.S# = S.S#
                      AND     SP.P# = P.P# ) ) ;
```

I have made use of SQL's rules regarding implicit tuple variables to eliminate the variables SX, PX, and SPX. I have also eliminated two pairs of redundant parentheses. *Note:* The two inner DISTINCTs (but not the outermost one!) could be eliminated also, but I have argued elsewhere [2] that DISTINCT should *always* be specified, even in cases where it is logically unnecessary.

> *Caveat:* Unfortunately, there is a flaw in the foregoing example. The sad fact is that the EXISTS function in SQL is not a truly faithful implementation of the existential quantifier of relational calculus [3] (assuming the version of the calculus in question to be a version based on three-valued logic). To be precise, EXISTS in SQL will return the wrong answer—*false* instead of *unk* ("unknown")—if (a) the subquery that represents the EXISTS argument evaluates to an empty set and (b) the reason why the set is empty is that the relevant WHERE- or HAVING-condition evaluates to *unk* for every value that might otherwise be a member of the set. To avoid this problem, the user is urged to *avoid SQL-style nulls entirely* [2]. The transformation techniques discussed in the present section will then work correctly.

Purely for interest, I now show a different SQL formulation of the query, one that is based on a somewhat different perception of the problem to be solved. Clearly, if a given supplier supplies all parts, then the set of parts supplied by that supplier must be the same as the set of all parts. The following would thus appear to be at least plausible as an expression of the query (2.5):

```
(2.5) SELECT   DISTINCT SNAME        /*** Warning: INVALID !!! ***/
      FROM     S
      WHERE  ( SELECT DISTINCT P#
               FROM    SP
               WHERE   SP.S# = S.S# )
             =
             ( SELECT DISTINCT P#
               FROM    P ) ;
```

Unfortunately, most SQL dialects do not support comparisons between sets; the foregoing query would not be legal in most systems today. Note, however, that it follows from the semantics of the problem that the two sets will be identical if their *cardinalities* are identical. This fact suggests another plausible version of the query, one that replaces the set comparison by a simple scalar comparison (2.6):

```
(2.6) SELECT   DISTINCT SNAME        /*** Warning: INVALID !!! ***/
      FROM     S
      WHERE  ( SELECT COUNT ( DISTINCT P# )
               FROM    SP
               WHERE   SP.S# = S.S# )
             =
             ( SELECT COUNT ( DISTINCT P# )
               FROM    P ) ;
```

This query is unfortunately also illegal in most systems today, because most SQL dialects simply do not allow two subqueries to be compared, even if they are both scalar-valued. Yet the following query, logically equivalent to the previous one although conceptually and syntactically much more complex, *is* legal (2.7):

```
(2.7) SELECT   DISTINCT SNAME
      FROM     S
      WHERE    S# IN
             ( SELECT S#
               FROM   SP
               GROUP  BY S#
               HAVING COUNT (*) =
                    ( SELECT COUNT (*)
                      FROM   P ) ) ;
```

("find names of suppliers such that the relevant supplier number is in the set of supplier numbers for which the count of parts supplied is equal to the count of all parts that exist").

3. QUERIES INVOLVING LOGICAL IMPLICATION

Note: The base example for this section is taken from reference [2].

A logical implication query is a query whose "natural" formulation involves the logical connective IF . . . THEN. . . . Here is an example, based once again on suppliers-and-parts: "Find supplier names for suppliers who supply at least all those parts supplied by supplier S2," which might be expressed as follows in a kind of "pidgin" form of the calculus (3.1):

```
(3.1) SX.SNAME WHERE FORALL PX ( IF   S2 supplies PX
                                 THEN SX supplies PX )
```

("find names of suppliers SX such that, for all parts PX, if supplier S2 supplies part PX, then supplier SX supplies part PX also"). SX and PX here are tuple variables ranging over relations S and P, respectively.

The first thing to do is to tighten up the expressions "S2 supplies PX" and "SX supplies PX", giving (3.2):

```
(3.2) SX.SNAME WHERE FORALL PX
                    ( IF   EXISTS SPX ( SPX.S# = 'S2'
                                        AND
                                        SPX.P# = PX.P# )
                      THEN EXISTS SPY ( SPY.S# = SX.S#
                                        AND
                                        SPY.P# = PX.P# ) )
```

SPX and SPY here are tuple variables, both of which range over relation SP.

In order to transform this expression into valid SQL, I will make use of two transformation rules—the one introduced in Section 2 concerning FORALL, and a new one regarding IF . . . THEN . . . , as follows: The truth-valued expression

```
IF p THEN q
```

can always be replaced by the logically equivalent expression

```
NOT ( p ) OR ( q )
```

For example, the statement "If it is raining, then the streets are getting wet" is equivalent to the statement "Either it is not raining or the streets are getting wet (or both)." (In general, the expression "IF *p* THEN *q*" evaluates to *true* if *p* is *false* or *q* is *true;* it evaluates to *false* if *p* is *true* and *q* is *false;* and it evaluates to *unk* otherwise.)

Applying these two transformation rules to (3.2), we obtain the following (3.3):

```
(3.3) SX.SNAME WHERE NOT EXISTS PX ( NOT
                      ( NOT ( EXISTS SPX ( SPX.S# = 'S2'
                                          AND
                                          SPX.P# = PX.P# ) )
                    OR   ( EXISTS SPY ( SPY.S# = SX.S#
                                          AND
                                          SPY.P# = PX.P# ) ) )
```

Now the expression involves only operators such as NOT and EXISTS that SQL does directly support (with the proviso noted earlier regarding EXISTS). It can therefore be converted into SQL form (3.4):

```
(3.4) SELECT DISTINCT SX.SNAME
      FROM    S SX
      WHERE   NOT EXISTS
            ( SELECT DISTINCT PX.*
              FROM    P PX
              WHERE   NOT
                    ( NOT ( EXISTS
                          ( SELECT DISTINCT SPX.*
                            FROM    SP SPX
                            WHERE   SPX.S# = 'S2'
                            AND     SPX.P# = PX.P# ) )
                  OR  ( EXISTS
                          ( SELECT DISTINCT SPY.*
                            FROM    SP SPY
                            WHERE   SPY.S# = SX.S#
                            AND     SPY.P# = PX.P# ) ) ) ) ;
```

Finally, we can apply a variety of cosmetic improvements to yield (3.5):

```
(3.5) SELECT DISTINCT SX.SNAME
      FROM    S SX
      WHERE   NOT EXISTS
            ( SELECT DISTINCT PX.*
              FROM    P PX
              WHERE   EXISTS
                    ( SELECT DISTINCT SPX.*
                      FROM    SP SPX
                      WHERE   SPX.S# = 'S2'
                      AND     SPX.P# = PX.P# )
              AND     NOT EXISTS
                    ( SELECT DISTINCT SPY.*
                      FROM    SP SPY
                      WHERE   SPY.S# = SX.S#
                      AND     SPY.P# = PX.P# ) ) ;
```

("names of suppliers SX such that there does not exist a part PX such that (a) there exists a shipment SPX saying that supplier S2 supplies part PX but (b) there does *not* exist a shipment SPY saying that supplier SX supplies part PX also").

In this final transformation, I have made use of De Morgan's Law: The truth-valued expression

```
NOT ( p OR q )
```

can always be replaced by the logically equivalent expression

```
NOT ( p ) AND NOT ( q )
```

Two NOTs cancel out in the simplified form—i.e., the expression "NOT (NOT (EXISTS (. . .)))" becomes simply "EXISTS (. . .)". Some obviously redundant parentheses have also been eliminated. Eliminating the explicit tuple variables is left as an exercise for the reader.

4. QUERIES INVOLVING AGGREGATION

In this section I will be making use of an extended form of the original relational calculus, one that supports the aggregate functions COUNT, SUM, AVG, MAX, and MIN (and potentially others also, of course). Let me therefore begin with a brief explanation of those functions (taken from reference [5]). In general, an aggregate function reference takes the form

```
aggregate ( expression [, attribute ] )
```

where "aggregate" is COUNT, SUM, AVG, MAX, or MIN, "expression" is a relational calculus expression (which thus evaluates to a relation), and "attribute" is the attribute of that relation over which the aggregation is to be performed. The "attribute" argument is irrelevant (and must therefore be omitted) for COUNT; for the other aggregates, it may optionally be omitted if and only if the "expression" argument evaluates to a relation of degree one. If it is omitted, the sole attribute of the result of "expression" is assumed by default.

For interest, I list below some of the major differences between aggregate functions as I have just (briefly) defined them and the corresponding functions of SQL:

- The functions are orthogonally defined. In particular, they can be nested.

- By allowing two arguments ("expression" and "attribute"), I avoid the need for an optional DISTINCT specification. The "expression" argument evaluates to a relation, from which duplicate tuples are always eliminated by definition. The "attribute" argument then specifies the attribute of that relation over which the aggregation is to be performed, and duplicate values are *not* eliminated from that attribute before the aggregation is done. (Of course, the attribute might not contain any duplicates anyway. In particular, this will be the case if the attribute in question is the primary key of the relation.)

- There is no need for a GROUP BY clause.

- There is no need for a HAVING clause.

- The functions are defined to operate correctly if their "expression" argument evaluates to an empty set. Specifically, COUNT and SUM both return zero, MAX returns "minus infinity," MIN returns "plus infinity," and AVG returns an error [4]. By contrast, the SQL aggregates all incorrectly return *null* in such a case (except for COUNT, which does correctly return zero). I will return to this point later.

My first few examples all make use of the suppliers-and-parts database. As usual, I assume that SX, SY, . . . , PX, PY, . . . , SPX, SPY, . . . , are tuple variables ranging over relations S, P, and SP, respectively. *Note:* In some cases (particularly where the examples are rather simple), the reader might be forgiven for thinking that the relational calculus queries are more difficult to understand than their SQL equivalents. But the superior orthogonality (etc.) of relational calculus quickly begins to pay off as the queries become more complex.

Example 1 (aggregate function in the target list): Find the average shipment quantity, taken over all parts supplied.

In relational calculus:

(4.1)   A = AVG (SPX, QTY)

Note that my dialect of the calculus requires the introduction of a name ("A" in the example) for the sole attribute of the result relation [5]. Note too that a simple tuple variable name such as SPX is a legal relational calculus expression in that dialect. It evaluates, of course, to the entire relation over which the specified tuple variable ranges.

The SQL equivalent is

(4.2) `SELECT A = AVG ( QTY )`
`      FROM    SP SPX ;`

The mapping to SQL is obvious in this case, except that at the time of writing the "A =" phrase would have to be omitted in most SQL dialects.

Example 2 (aggregate function in the target list, with "duplicate elimination"): Find the average of *distinct* shipment quantities, taken over all parts supplied.

In relational calculus:

(4.3) `A = AVG ( SPX.QTY, QTY )`

(the second argument to AVG here could optionally be omitted).

The SQL equivalent is

(4.4) `SELECT A = AVG ( DISTINCT QTY )`
`      FROM    SP SPX ;`

The argument to the SQL aggregate includes the specification DISTINCT because the calculus "attribute" argument specifies the sole attribute of the "expression" argument.

Example 3 (aggregate function in the target list, with a more complex "expression" argument): For each part supplied, find the average shipment quantity.

In relational calculus:

(4.5) `SPX.P#, A = AVG ( SPY WHERE SPY.P# = SPX.P#, QTY )`

SQL equivalent:

(4.6) `SELECT SPX.P#, A = AVG ( QTY )`
`      FROM    SP SPX`
`      GROUP  BY SPX.P# ;`

The calculus "expression" argument "SPY WHERE SPY.P# = SPX.P#" maps to the SQL clause "GROUP BY SPX.P#".

Example 4 (aggregate function in the target list, with a more complex "expression" argument and with "duplicate elimination"): For each part supplied, find the average of *distinct* shipment quantities.

In relational calculus:

(4.7) `SPX.P#, A = AVG ( SPY.QTY WHERE SPY.P# = SPX.P# )`

SQL equivalent:

```
(4.8) SELECT SPX.P#, A = AVG ( DISTINCT QTY )
      FROM    SP SPX
      GROUP   BY SPX.P# ;
```

Example 5 (aggregate function in the qualification): Find part numbers for parts supplied in a total quantity greater than 500.
    In relational calculus:

```
(4.9) SPX.P# WHERE SUM ( SPY WHERE SPY.P# = SPX.P#, QTY ) > 500
```

SQL equivalent:

```
(4.10) SELECT SPX.P#
       FROM    SP SPX
       WHERE   500 < ( SELECT SUM ( QTY )
                       FROM    SP SPY
                       WHERE   SPY.P# = SPX.P# ) ;
```

Observe in this case that the calculus "expression" argument "SPY WHERE SPY.P# = SPX.P#" does *not* map to a SQL GROUP BY clause (contrast Example 3 above); instead, it maps to a FROM clause and a WHERE clause in a fairly straightforward fashion. *Note:* Most current dialects of SQL have a stupid rule by which a comparison expression of the form "scalar comparison subquery" is legal, whereas one of the form "subquery comparison scalar" is not. This fact accounts for the inversion involved in the mapping of the outer WHERE clause in this example.

Example 6 (multiple aggregate functions in the target list): For each part supplied, find the maximum and minimum shipment quantity.
    In relational calculus:

```
(4.11) SPX.P#, X = MAX ( SPY.QTY WHERE SPY.P# = SPX.P# ),
              Y = MIN ( SPY.QTY WHERE SPY.P# = SPX.P# )
```

SQL equivalent:

```
(4.12) SELECT SPX.P#, X = MAX ( QTY ), Y = MIN ( QTY )
       FROM    SP SPX
       GROUP   BY SPX.P# ;
```

The mapping is possible in this case because the "expression" arguments of the two calculus aggregates are identical.

Example 7 (nested aggregates): Find the average total shipment quantity per part, taken over all parts supplied.
    In relational calculus:

```
(4.13) A = AVG ( ( SPX.P#,
                   T = SUM ( SPY WHERE SPY.P# = SPX.P#, QTY ) ), T )
```

This example cannot be expressed as a single statement in conventional SQL, because SQL aggregates cannot be nested.* Instead, we have to "unnest" the aggregates first:

(4.14) X = (SPX.P#, T = SUM (SPY WHERE SPY.P# = SPX.P#, QTY))

(4.15) A = AVG (XX, T)

Line (4.14) here might be thought of as a "temporary view definition" [6]: It has the effect of assigning the name *x* to the relational calculus expression on the right hand side of the equals sign. Line (4.15) then computes the desired average; XX is a tuple variable, ranging over the (virtual) relation X.

SQL, however, does not support "temporary views"; instead, therefore, we have to make use of (SQL's version of) *relational assignment,* in which the intermediate result has to be physically materialized:

```
(4.16) INSERT INTO X ( P#, T )
              SELECT SPX.P#, T = SUM ( QTY )
              FROM   SP SPX
              GROUP  BY SPX.P# ;
```

```
(4.17) SELECT AVG ( T )
           FROM   X XX ;
```

Now let us turn to some more complex examples. In the first one, we are given a simple EMP relation:

```
EMP ( EMP#, JOB, SALARY, DEPT# )
```

The query is: "Find departments employing more than five programmers." Here is a "natural"—and correct—SQL formulation of this query (I deliberately show this SQL formulation first in order to make a specific point):

```
(4.18) SELECT DEPT#
           FROM    EMP
           WHERE   JOB = 'Programmer'
           GROUP   BY DEPT#
           HAVING COUNT (*) > 5 ;
```

Now consider the obvious inverse query: "Find departments employing less than five programmers." Here is the obvious inverse SQL formulation:

---

*The reason aggregates cannot be nested in conventional SQL is because of SQL's unorthodox syntax for function references [1]. Actually, certain "unconventional" SQL products *are* able to nest aggregates, but only in an ad hoc manner—supporting, for example, nesting to two levels but not to three.

```
(4.19) SELECT DEPT#
       FROM    EMP
       WHERE   JOB = 'Programmer'
       GROUP   BY DEPT#
       HAVING COUNT (*) < 5 ;
```

The first point to make is that this latter formulation is incorrect!—it misses those departments that employ no programmers at all. The problem is, of course, that the WHERE clause has the effect of eliminating such departments before the grouping is done, and thus before the HAVING-condition is applied.

Now let us see how these two queries would be formulated in relational calculus. The first is:

```
(4.20) EX.DEPT#
       WHERE COUNT ( EY.EMP# WHERE EY.DEPT# = EX.DEPT#
                             AND    EY.JOB = 'Programmer' ) > 5
```

(EX and EY are tuple variables ranging over EMP.) The second query (4.21) is identical to (4.20), except that the ">" is replaced by a "<". And the SQL equivalents of these two queries are:

```
(4.22) SELECT EX.DEPT#
       FROM    EMP EX
       WHERE   5 < ( SELECT COUNT ( DISTINCT EMP# )
                     FROM    EMP EY
                     WHERE   EY.DEPT# = EX.DEPT#
                     AND     EY.JOB = 'Programmer' ) ;
```

```
(4.23) SELECT EX.DEPT#
       FROM    EMP EX
       WHERE   5 > ( SELECT COUNT ( DISTINCT EMP# )
                     FROM    EMP EY
                     WHERE   EY.DEPT# = EX.DEPT#
                     AND     EY.JOB = 'Programmer' ) ;
```

Note: The argument to COUNT in SQL is always required to include the specification DISTINCT, except for the special case of COUNT (*); this fact accounts for the appearance of DISTINCT in the two SQL COUNT references above.

Much more to the point: These two SQL formulations are now both correct! We have avoided the GROUP BY operation entirely, and the condition that was previously specified as part of the HAVING clause has now been folded into the WHERE clause instead (and therefore applied at the logically correct point during the evaluation of the query).

For our next example, let us again consider two inverse queries: "Find departments for which the total salary of programmers is (a) greater than, (b) less than, $1,000,000." These two queries are clearly similar to the ones just discussed, and arguments analogous to those presented above would naturally lead us to the following SQL formulations:

```
(4.24) SELECT  EX.DEPT#
       FROM    EMP EX
       WHERE   1000000 < ( SELECT  SUM ( SALARY )
                           FROM    EMP EY
                           WHERE   EY.DEPT# = EX.DEPT#
                           AND     EY.JOB = 'Programmer' ) ;

(4.25) SELECT  EX.DEPT#
       FROM    EMP EX
       WHERE   1000000 > ( SELECT  SUM ( SALARY )
                           FROM    EMP EY
                           WHERE   EY.DEPT# = EX.DEPT#
                           AND     EY.JOB = 'Programmer' ) ;
```

Expression (4.24) here is indeed correct. Expression (4.25), however, is not!—it misses those departments that employ no programmers at all. The flaw this time is nothing to do with GROUP BY, however (obviously, since there is no GROUP BY clause). Instead, it has to do with SQL's incorrect definition of the SUM aggregate; as already noted, SQL defines the sum of an empty set to be *null* instead of zero. In order to fix the problem, we need to convert that *null* into a zero as quickly as possible "before it has a chance to do any more damage" [2]. In DB2, for example, we can use the VALUE function for this purpose [7]. Here is a correct version of (4.25) that makes use of that function:

```
(4.26) SELECT  EX.DEPT#
       FROM    EMP EX
       WHERE   1000000 > ( SELECT  VALUE ( SUM ( SALARY ), 0 )
                           FROM    EMP EY
                           WHERE   EY.DEPT# = EX.DEPT#
                           AND     EY.JOB = 'Programmer' ) ;
```

The next example also illustrates a shortcoming with the SQL GROUP BY and HAVING clauses. The query is: "For each department, find the number of programmers employed and the number of analysts employed." In relational calculus:

```
(4.27) EX.DEPT#, P = COUNT ( EY.EMP#
                             WHERE EY.DEPT# = EX.DEPT#
                             AND   EY.JOB = 'Programmer' ),
              A = COUNT ( EY.EMP#
                             WHERE EY.DEPT# = EX.DEPT#
                             AND   EY.JOB = 'Analyst' )
```

There is no direct SQL formulation of this query using GROUP BY and HAVING (at least not in any SQL dialect that I am familiar with). The best we can do is produce two intermediate results

```
DP ( DEPT#, P )
DA ( DEPT#, A )
```

and then join DP and DA together over DEPT#. The details are left as an exercise for the reader.

My final example is based on a problem first posed to me by an attendee at one of my seminars. We are given a relation

```
EDT ( E, D, T, ... )
     PRIMARY KEY ( D, T )
```

where E is an event, D is a date, and T is a time. Note that the "same" E can appear any number of times in the relation. A given E is said to be a *winner* if it occurs on some given D more times than any other E does (or, rather, if no other E occurs on that D more times than the given E does). The required result is a relation

```
RESULT ( W, N )
       PRIMARY KEY ( W )
```

containing one row for each winner W. For a given W, N is the number of days on which W was a winner.

This example illustrates the point very clearly that some queries are best attacked by some kind of "divide and conquer" strategy. The problem here is simply too difficult (for most users, at any rate) even to contemplate trying to formulate it immediately as a single statement—even given a clean, orthogonal formalism like the relational calculus. Instead, it seems clearly better to break the problem down into a sequence of steps, as follows.

(4.28) C = (EX.E, EX.D,
            M = COUNT (EY WHERE EY.E = EX.E AND EY.D = EX.D))

EX and EY are tuple variables that range over relation EDT. Relation C contains a tuple for each unique event/date (E/D) combination, giving the number of times (M) that event E occurred on date D.

(4.29) B = (W = CX.E, CX.D
            WHERE CX.M = MAX (CY.M WHERE CY.D = CX.D))

CX and CY are tuple variables that range over relation C. Relation B contains a tuple for each unique winner/date (W/D) combination.

(4.30) A = (BX.W, N = COUNT (BY WHERE BY.W = BX.W))

BX and BY are tuple variables that range over relation B. Relation A is the desired answer.*

Now we can map these relational calculus queries into SQL:

(4.31) INSERT INTO C (E, D, M)
               SELECT EX.E, EX.D, M = COUNT (*)
               FROM   EDT EX
               GROUP BY EX.E, EX.D ;

---

*Note that this approach of breaking the query down into several smaller queries need not even have any undesirable performance implications, if the system includes a lazy evaluation feature [6].

```
(4.32) INSERT INTO B ( W, D )
       SELECT CX.E, CX.D
       FROM   C CX
       WHERE  CX.M = ( SELECT MAX ( M )
                       FROM   C CY
                       WHERE  CY.D = CX.D ) ;
```

```
(4.33) INSERT INTO A ( W, N )
       SELECT BX.W, N = COUNT (*)
       FROM   B BX
       GROUP  BY BX.W ;
```

Of course, the query can be expressed as a single statement in the relational calculus if desired:

```
(4.34) W = EV.E,
       N = COUNT
           ( EW WHERE EW.E = EV.E AND
           COUNT
           ( EX WHERE EX.E = EW.E AND EX.D = EW.D ) =
           MAX ( ( EY.E, EY.D, M = COUNT
                               ( EZ WHERE EZ.E = EY.E
                                 AND    EZ.D = EY.D )
                    WHERE EY.D = EW.D ),   M ) )
```

I *think* this formulation is correct, though I wouldn't swear to it! (EV, EW, EX, EY, and EZ are tuple variables, all ranging over relation EDT.)

5.   CONCLUSION

This brings me to the end of my set of examples. I have discussed a variety of techniques for dealing with "complex" queries—specifically, queries involving universal quantification, logical implication, and (especially) aggregation, both in the target list and in the qualification. One further point with which to close: Obviously, the calculus-to-SQL mappings discussed in this paper have not been formally defined; such was not my intent. Nevertheless, it is tempting to suggest that those mappings might form the basis for implementing a "new, improved" relational language (essentially an extended relational calculus) on top of SQL. Such a language could serve as a common interface to all (or at least a large number) of the myriad SQL products found in the marketplace today. The advantages of such an interface would include all of the following:

- It would be a more genuinely useful and usable ad hoc query interface than the current SQL implementations.

- It could mask differences among different SQL dialects.

- It could serve as a basis for intersystem connectivity and application portability.

▪ It could serve as a vehicle for teaching relational concepts (one that would be much more satisfactory for the purpose than the current SQL interface).

REFERENCES AND BIBLIOGRAPHY

1. C. J. Date, "A Critique of the SQL Database Language," *ACM SIGMOD Record* 14, No. 3 (November 1984). Republished in C. J. Date, *Relational Database: Selected Writings* (Reading, MA: Addison-Wesley, 1986). Republished again in revised form in C. J. Date, *A Guide to the SQL Standard,* 2nd edition (Reading, MA: Addison-Wesley, 1989).

2. C. J. Date, "SQL Dos and Don'ts," in C. J. Date, *Relational Database Writings 1985-1989* (Reading, MA: Addison-Wesley, 1990).

3. C. J. Date, "EXISTS Is Not "Exists"! (Some Logical Flaws in SQL)," in C. J. Date, *Relational Database Writings 1985-1989* (Reading, MA: Addison-Wesley, 1990).

4. C. J. Date, "Oh No Not Nulls Again" (in this volume).

5. C. J. Date, "Relational Calculus," Chapter 14 of C. J. Date, *An Introduction to Database Systems: Volume I,* 5th edition (Reading, MA: Addison-Wesley, 1990).

6. C. J. Date, "Views," Section 15.5 of C. J. Date, *An Introduction to Database Systems: Volume I,* 5th edition (Reading, MA: Addison-Wesley, 1990).

7. C. J. Date and Colin J. White, *A Guide to DB2,* 3rd edition (Reading, MA: Addison-Wesley, 1989).

10

The Role of
Functional Dependence
in Query Decomposition

ABSTRACT

Current relational DBMSs permit certain **functional dependencies** (FDs) to be declared for base relations, either explicitly or (more commonly) implicitly. We show how the DBMS can use these declared FDs during the process of *query decomposition* to determine FDs that hold in derived relations (i.e., intermediate and final results of relational expressions). We also show how that knowledge can significantly improve the performance, functionality, and usability of those DBMSs.

COMMENTS ON PUBLICATION

In one of his contributions to this book's predecessor—"The Keys of the Kingdom" [12], to be precise—Hugh Darwen sketched some rules for determining the primary key of the result of any given expression of the rela-

---

Previously unpublished.

tional algebra. He also stated that he was "currently working on several refinements to these rules," which he hoped to publish at some future time. The paper that follows is the result of that work.

1. INTRODUCTION

As noted in the Abstract, current relational systems usually permit certain **functional dependencies** (FDs) to be declared, at least for base relations (although such declarations are usually implicit, being implied by the declaration of, e.g., a candidate key or a unique index). By using these declarations to infer FDs that hold in derived relations (i.e., relations that result from the evaluation of relational expressions), system performance, functionality, and usability can all be significantly enhanced. This paper gives a means by which the system can perform such inferences, and illustrates by example some of the benefits that can accrue.

Note: Ideally, of course, the system should be aware of *all* of the FDs that hold in base relations. We remark that in the case of a base relation in Boyce-Codd normal form (BCNF), the only nontrivial FDs are those that are implied by candidate keys [9]; for such a relation, therefore, it is sufficient that every candidate key be explicitly declared for the DBMS to know all of the FDs that hold in that relation.

The structure of the paper is as follows. Following this brief introduction, Section 2 presents a set of examples of situations in which current systems fall short. Section 3 gives formal definitions. Section 4 states and proves an important **General Unification Theorem**. Section 5 defines a subclass of FDs called **interesting** FDs and applies the General Unification Theorem to the task of deducing all of the interesting FDs that are implied by a given set of FDs. Section 6 then shows how interesting FDs can be noted during "query decomposition," i.e., the process of decomposing an arbitrary expression of the relational algebra. Finally, Section 7 shows how the foregoing ideas can be used to address each of the problem situations identified in Section 2.

2. OPPORTUNITIES FOR IMPROVEMENT

In this section, we discuss six specific opportunities for improvement, presenting each one in terms of a particular imaginary scenario. The example database contains two tables:

- DEPT, containing data about departments in some corporation, with columns DEPT# (primary key), DNAME, and LOCATION;

- EMP, containing data about employees in that same corporation, with columns EMP# (primary key), ENAME, JOB, SALARY, and DEPT#. (*Note:* Whether or not DEPT# is a foreign key is not pertinent to the matters discussed in this paper.)

Other columns will be added to these tables for illustrative purposes as the need arises. Coding examples are given in SQL.

Example 1: View updatability

Using some general-purpose table displayer/modifier, the user obtains a display of the result of the query

```
SELECT E.EMP#, E.ENAME, E.SALARY, D.LOCATION
FROM    EMP E, DEPT D
WHERE   E.DEPT# = D.DEPT#
AND     E.JOB = 'Programmer' ;
```

The result shows, for each person employed as a programmer, that person's employee number, name, salary, and department location.

For some of the employees thus displayed, the user would like to change the salary by overtyping the current value on the screen. However, such a change is disallowed: Current SQL says that *no* column of this result is updatable, because its definition involves a join.

The user thinks that salary values ought to be updatable, because each row in the result corresponds to exactly one row in the base table EMP, no two rows in the displayed table correspond to the same row in EMP, and the displayed SALARY column corresponds directly to a column of the same name in EMP. And the user's intuitive reasoning is correct: It could be formalized in terms of functional dependencies and candidate keys, and that formalization would lead to the same conclusion.

Of course, the general issue of which the foregoing example is a particular case, namely *view updatability,* has been discussed by many writers—see, e.g., references [5], [7], and [10].

Example 2: Primary keys of results not reported

Using the same tool as in the previous scenario, the user displays the result of

```
SELECT *
FROM    EMP ;
```

Now, EMP has a large number of columns, too many to be shown simultaneously in the display window. The window initially shows the columns for EMP#, ENAME, SALARY, and DEPT#. By scrolling right, the user is able to see other columns such as JOB, SEX, MARITAL_STATUS, and so on, but the all-important EMP# column is thereby lost from view.

In fact, the user can "click" on columns to be kept in view during horizontal scrolling, and may well choose ENAME as well as, or instead of, EMP#, but it is tedious to have to do that every time, and system preselection of the **primary key** of the table being displayed would be a great advantage in many cases.* Indeed, the columns of the primary key might even be displayed in some distinguishing color or typeface, thus conveying very useful information to the casual user (perhaps some consultant) who is not too familiar with the database.

Although the DBMS's data definition language supports the declaration of primary keys (and alternate keys) for base tables, such keys are not recognized (in SQL) as properties of tables in general, and that is why even the trivial query above produces a table that (so far as SQL is concerned) has no key.

Example 3: The GROUP BY problem

The user wishes to see, for each department that has at least one employee, the department number, location, and average salary of employees in that department. First attempt:

```
SELECT  D.DEPT#, D.LOCATION, AVG ( E.SALARY )
FROM    DEPT D, EMP E
WHERE   D.DEPT# = E.DEPT#
GROUP   BY D.DEPT# ;
```

However, standard SQL will reject this query on the grounds that D.LOCATION is disallowed in the SELECT-list, because it is neither an aggregate function reference nor a column specified in the GROUP BY clause.

The user who has been shown the trick can bypass this problem by adding D.LOCATION to the GROUP BY clause. This trick works because, as can easily be seen by intuition, D.LOCATION is functionally dependent on D.DEPT#. If the system were able to recognize this functional dependency, it could allow D.LOCATION to be omitted from the GROUP BY clause even if it is specified in the SELECT-list. And the query would probably then run a little faster, thanks to the reduction in the number of grouping columns.

Example 4: Scalar subqueries

A senior employee, Pentstemon Smith, likes to find out, every month, about any colleagues who are earning more than he. He uses the query:

---

*This paper subsequently discusses techniques for identifying *candidate* keys. Selecting one *candidate* key to be the primary key (when there is a choice) is not discussed, but a fairly simple scheme could no doubt be implemented to make the psychologically most suitable choice in most cases. Reference [12] describes a scheme that has been tried out, not unsuccessfully, in practice.

```
SELECT  ENAME, SALARY
FROM    EMP
WHERE   SALARY >
      ( SELECT  SALARY
        FROM    EMP
        WHERE   ENAME = 'Pentstemon Smith' ) ;
```

The subquery in the WHERE clause here is a "scalar subquery"—i.e., it is a subquery that (because it is used within a scalar comparison) is supposed to return a table containing exactly one column and at most one row. If it does return just one row, the comparand is taken to be the single scalar value within that row. If it returns no rows at all, the comparand is taken to be null.* And if it returns more than one row, an exception is raised.

Pentstemon's query works fine for several years, until his son, Pentstemon junior, joins the company. That month, when he submits his usual query, he is told: "Exception raised, *cardinality violation.*" This was because his subquery suddenly, for the first time ever, yielded two rows instead of the usual one.

As a result of this experience, he learns all about employee numbers and primary keys, and thinks: "Why couldn't the system have told me that in the first place?"

Example 5: The DISTINCT problem

Some advanced **query generator** (perhaps a natural language interpreter) is being used to submit queries. Because this query generator is founded firmly (under the covers) on **predicate logic**, it cannot countenance SQL's "duplicate row" phenomenon. It therefore makes the "safety play" of including the specification DISTINCT after every SELECT.†

The user is irritated by the slow response to simple queries like "Show me the employee number, name, and location of every employee," and tries the same query in native SQL:

```
SELECT  E.EMP#, E.ENAME, D.LOCATION
FROM    EMP E, DEPT D
WHERE   E.DEPT# = D.DEPT# ;
```

The user didn't think of specifying DISTINCT in this query, because it was obvious from the semantics of the situation that every row of the result was distinct from every other row. This query went very much faster, and the user wondered why the version with DISTINCT shouldn't be equally fast— and so it should be, if the system could determine that the DISTINCT is effectively a "no-op."

---

*This is the way the SQL standard is defined, even though such behavior is clearly incorrect [6].

†At least two query generators known to this writer behave in this fashion.

This example also illustrates another opportunity for optimization (if functional dependencies are noted): The query decomposition process could determine that the join is **many-to-one**, and the optimizer could take advantage of that knowledge.

Furthermore, a view defined by means of the above query (first version, with DISTINCT) should be just as updatable as that in the first scenario, even though SQL says it is not, because of the DISTINCT.

Example 6: CREATE TABLE AS expression

The user in Example 5, *user1*, would like to make a snapshot of that query and export it to a colleague, *user2*, who would like to import it into another database for some further analysis.

User1's DBMS allows an arbitrary relational expression to be used in the definition of a new table. That new table acquires its definition and initial data values from the result of that expression. For example:

```
CREATE TABLE EMP_LOC AS
        SELECT DISTINCT E.EMP#, E.ENAME, D.LOCATION
        FROM    EMP E, DEPT D
        WHERE   E.DEPT# = D.DEPT# ;
```

This operation very conveniently creates the desired snapshot. However, that snapshot has, as yet, no primary key (so far as the system is concerned). If it did have a primary key that was known to the system, of course, then that knowledge could be preserved across the export and import operations that are needed to deliver EMP_LOC to *user2*. Because the knowledge will help *user2* both to understand and use EMP_LOC, *user1* goes to the trouble of working out that the primary key is in fact EMP#, and executes an appropriate ALTER TABLE before exporting the snapshot:

```
ALTER TABLE EMP_LOC ADD PRIMARY KEY ( EMP# ) ;
```

User1 thinks: "Hmm. Couldn't the system have figured this out and done the work for me?" And, of course, it could.

3. DEFINITIONS

Let *R* be a relation. The *heading* HR of *R* is the set of attributes of *R;* the *body* BR of *R* is the set of tuples of *R*. In what follows, A, B, C, and D denote arbitrary subsets of HR, not necessarily nonempty, and not necessarily disjoint.

A *functional dependency* (FD) is a truth-valued expression, written as

$$A \rightarrow B$$

and pronounced "A determines B," "B depends on A," or just "A arrow B." Such an FD is a proposition that is either *true* or *false* in *R:* It is *true* if every pair of tuples in BR that agree in value for each of the attributes in A also agree in value for each of the attributes in B, and *false* otherwise.

The left operand of A → B is the *determinant;* each member of the right operand is a *dependant* of that determinant, and the right operand considered in toto is the *dependent set.*

We now state a number of simple but important theorems regarding FDs that we will be needing in our development. Each one is identical to one of Armstrong's axioms [1] or is an immediate consequence of those axioms.

1. **Self-determination**

   A → A

2. **R-augmentation**

   A → B & A → C ⟹ A → B ∪ C

   In fact, the inverse also holds:

   A → B ∪ C ⟹ A → B & A → C

   We use the term **joint dependence** for both implications together:

   A → B & A → C ≡ A → B ∪ C

3. **Determinant subset**

   B ≤ A ⟹ A → B

   This theorem follows from the previous two.

4. **L-augmentation**

   A → B ⟹ A ∪ C → B

5. **Transitivity**

   A → B & B → C ⟹ A → C

6. **Composition**

   A → B & C → D ⟹ A ∪ C → B ∪ D

Either the determinant or the dependent set can be ϕ (the empty set), of course. We note that A → ϕ for any A, and therefore (a) ϕ → ϕ, and (b) if ϕ → B, then all tuples in BR agree in value for all attributes in B.

We can now state and prove the **General Unification Theorem.**

4.   THE GENERAL UNIFICATION THEOREM

Theorem: A → B & C → D ⟹ A ∪ (C − B) → B ∪ D

Proof:

<1>	A → B	(given)
<2>	C → D	(given)
<3>	A → B ∩ C	(joint dependence, <1>)
<4>	C − B → C − B	(self-determination)
<5>	A ∪ (C − B) → (B ∩ C) ∪ (C − B)	(composition, <3> and <4>)
<6>	A ∪ (C − B) → C	(simplifying <5>)
<7>	A ∪ (C − B) → D	(transitivity, <6> and <2>)
<8>	A ∪ (C − B) → B ∪ D	(composition, <1> and <7>)

This completes the proof. ∎

We remark that the General Unification Theorem can be seen as a slight generalization of what Beeri and Bernstein [2] and others have called "pseudotransitivity."

Corollary: Substituting C, D, A, B for A, B, C, D, respectively, we have C → D & A → B (which is of course the same proposition as A → B & C → D) ⟹ C ∪ (A − D) → B ∪ D.

The foregoing theorem can be used to infer an FD from two given ones. The name "General Unification Theorem" is justified by the fact that all of the following are special cases:

- A → B & A → C ⟹ A → B ∪ C   (R-augmentation)

- A → B & B → C ⟹ A → C   (transitivity)

- If A, B, C, and D are pairwise disjoint, the theorem degenerates to composition.

Furthermore:

- A → B & C → φ ⟹ A ∪ C → B   (L-augmentation)

- A → B & φ → φ ⟹ A → B

  (so "φ → φ" is the identity under "and").

5. MAXIMAL AND INTERESTING DEPENDENCIES

Reference [1] defines the *dependency structure* Fr of a relation R as the family

```
{ (A,B) : A → B }
```

where A and B are subsets of HR. Reference [1] further defines a useful partial ordering of the set Fr, as follows. Let (A,B) and (A′,B′) be members of Fr. Then (A′,B′) ≥ (A,B) if and only if A′ is a subset of A and B′ is a superset of B.

This ordering allows us to define *maximal* functional dependencies. The FD (A,B) ϵ Fr is *maximal* if and only if, for each (A′,B′) ϵ Fr, (A′,B′) ≥ (A,B) only if A′ = A and B′ = B. (In other words, (A,B) is maximal if A is as small as possible and B is as large as possible, loosely speaking. Note in particular that B must be a superset of A, by self-determination and R-augmentation.)

Example: Given the familiar shipments relation SP(S#,P#,QTY), in which the only nontrivial FDs are those that are implied by the primary key {S#,P#}, the following are true statements:

```
({S#},{S#}) ≥ ({S#,P#},{S#}) ;
```

```
({S#},{S#}) ≥ ({S#},{S#}) ;
```

```
({S#,P#},{S#,P#,QTY}) ≥ ({S#,P#,QTY},{QTY}) ;
```

({S#},{S#}) is maximal ;

({S#,P#},{S#,P#,QTY}) is maximal ;

({S#,P#},{QTY}) is not maximal. ∎

Reference [1] goes on to prove that the family Mr of maximal dependencies of R is "just as informative" as the family Fr, because:

Assume A′ → B′ holds in R, and assume (A′,B′) ≥ (A,B).

Then (a) A′ is a subset of A and (b) B′ is a superset of B.

Therefore (c) A → B′ (using (a) and L-augmentation).

Therefore A → B (using (b), (c), and determinant subset).

Thus every FD in Fr is implied by an FD in Mr. Therefore, to obtain the dependency structure of R, it is sufficient to obtain the family Mr, a subset of Fr from which Mr can be inferred.

Now, the cardinality of the set of all possible FDs (true or false) in an n-ary relation R is 4^n, of which at least 2^n (all the instances of self-determination) hold true and are maximal. The set Mr is thus still quite large, in general. There is therefore an incentive to find a much smaller set—a subset of M*r*—that will still characterize the complete dependency structure of *R*.

To this end, we introduce the subclass of *interesting FDs*. We define an FD A → B to be *interesting* if and only if it is maximal and B is not equal to A (i.e., the instances of self-determination are excluded). The cardinality of the set of interesting FDs is less than or equal to 2^n (very much less if *n* is large and only a small number of FDs are observed to hold true).

Example: Consider the shipments relation SP(S#,P#,QTY) once again. The only interesting FD in this relation is the FD {S#,P#} → {S#,P#,QTY}.

As another example, consider the relation that is obtained from relation SP by discarding the QTY attribute (via projection). This relation has no interesting FDs at all (the only FDs are instances of self-determination). ∎

Inferring FDs

Given any two FDs, FD1 and FD2, in *R,* the General Unification Theorem, and its corollary, can be used to derive two further FDs, FD3 and FD4, in *R* (not necessarily distinct), either or both of which might be distinct from both FD1 and FD2.

Let *R* be a relation, and let F = {FD1,FD2, . . . } be a set of FDs that hold true in *R*. The function *SimplifyFamily,* defined in detail in Appendix A, develops a set M from set F, such that MDi = (DETi,DEPi) ∈ M if and only if:

1. MDi is implied by the General Unification Theorem in consideration of some pair of FDs, each of which is a member of either F or M;
2. If MDj = (DETj,DEPj) ∈ M and DETj = DETi, then DEPj = DEPi (i.e., MDj = MDi);
3. If MDj = (DETj,DEPj) ∈ M and DETj is a superset of DETi and DEPj is a subset of DEPi, then DETj = DETi and DEPj = DEPi (i.e., MDj = MDi).

Condition 2 here says that M contains at most one FD with a given determinant. Condition 3 says that if M contains a given FD, then it does not contain any distinct FD′ such that FD′ ≥ FD. In other words, M is a family of FDs in *R,* including all of the interesting FDs that can be inferred from F, and certainly excluding all nonmaximal FDs. M might include some uninteresting maximal FDs (i.e., instances of self-determination), but only if F includes any.

Candidate keys of *R** can easily be discovered by inspection of M for

---

*CK is a *candidate key* of *R* if (a) it is a subset of HR, (b) CK → HR holds *true* in *R*, and (c) there is no proper subset CK′ of CK such that CK′ → HR holds *true* in *R*.

"key dependencies" (i.e., FDs in which the dependent set is HR; the determinant in such an FD will be a candidate key). However, it is important to note that M might show no candidate keys at all if F is in a certain sense "incomplete." To be specific (as shown by example above), the set of interesting dependencies might be empty, in which case we must resort to including the uninteresting dependency HR → HR in F in order to generate a key dependency in M.

6. DEPENDENCIES IN DERIVED RELATIONS

Let Q be a query—i.e., an expression of the relational algebra. A DBMS typically applies a process of **query decomposition** on Q in order to develop an optimized execution model of the query. If this process includes the noting of FDs and makes use of the unification algorithm described in Appendix A, then it can determine all of the interesting FDs* in each result delivered by Q's use of some operator in the relational algebra, including the overall result of Q itself. Furthermore, the set of such FDs for any such result can easily be examined to see which of them have as dependents all of the attributes of that result; the determinants in those FDs are then either genuine candidate keys for that result or proper supersets thereof, and can be treated by the system as genuine candidate keys for the purposes of this paper.

Let R be the result of some operation used in Q. We now present some suggestions and guidelines for developing a suitable set F such that the unification algorithm applied to F delivers M, a set including all of the interesting FDs in R.

F can be built by initializing it to "Fifi" (the singleton set containing the tautology $\phi \to \phi$) and, whenever some functional dependency FD is noted, assigning *AddToFamily*(F,FD) to F (see Appendix A). If it is required to develop M, the tautology HR → HR should be added to F before invoking *SimplifyFamily* (again, see Appendix A).

Several very simple theorems are stated without proof in what follows. For example, if two attributes A and B of some relation R are constrained to be equal in every tuple of R, then A → B and B → A both hold true in R.[†]

Notation: R denotes the result of some relational operation. S, T, . . . , denote the operands of that operation. If X is a relation, then:

- HX denotes the heading of X.

---

*All that are implied by the noted FDs, that is.

[†]We feel free to omit the enclosing braces when it is clear that singleton attribute sets are involved. Thus we write, e.g., A → B instead of the more strictly correct {A} → {B}.

- Fx denotes the family of FDs that should be developed.
- Mx denotes the family of interesting FDs in X given by *SimplifyFamily*(Fx).
- FDx denotes an arbitrary member of Fx.
- DETx and DEPx denote the determinant and the dependent set, respectively, of FDx.

When to use *SimplifyFamily* to develop Mx from Fx is by and large an implementation decision, but in what follows we note some places where such development would be recommended.

FromSchema

We add this operator to the conventional relational algebra merely to designate the use within Q of some base relation. Let R be FromSchema(S), where S is a base relation.

Fr = Fs (the set of declared FDs for S). Mr should be developed, if the DBMS permits Fs to be empty (in which case HS is the only candidate key) or permits redundant FDs to be declared (e.g., if it allowed one declared "candidate key" to be a proper superset of another).

Projection

Let R be the projection of S over some set of attributes P. Fr is given by the rule:

DETs → P ∩ DEPs ∈ Fr if and only if DETs is a subset of P

(by joint dependence).

Mr should be developed, and the precaution of adding P → P to Fr should be taken (because otherwise it may be the case that Fr neither contains nor implies any FD with determinant equal to P).

Extended Cartesian Product

Let R be the extended Cartesian product of S and T. Fr is *CombineFamilies*(Fs,Ft), and Mr is *Unite*(Ms,Mt) (again, see Appendix A).

Rename

As this operator merely "copies" its relational operand, renaming one or more attributes in the result, the set of FDs in the result is the same as that in the operand, except that some attributes in determinants and dependent sets have new names.

Extension

It is obviously sufficient to consider just the simple case where extension of some relation S delivers a relation R with one more attribute, A say, than S, A being the result of some function f over attributes of S.

Let FA be the set of attributes of S that are arguments to f. Then, by definition, FA $\rightarrow$ A. In the special case where f involves no attributes of S at all (e.g., f is a literal), FA is the empty set. In some cases further FDs might be noted, arising from our knowledge of inverse functions. For example, if f is the Boolean function NOT(B), then $A \rightarrow B$. And if f is $B + C$, then $\{A,B\} \rightarrow C$ and $\{A,C\} \rightarrow B$ also hold true.

Let Fa be the set of FDs noted from the assignment of f(FA) to A. Since every FD in S is an FD in R, Fr is *CombineFamilies*(Fs,Fa).

Restriction

Let R be the restriction of S by some restriction condition *cond*. It is obviously sufficient to consider restriction conditions of the form "A θ B," where θ is some scalar comparison operator (because when *cond* is more complicated than this, the restriction can be reformulated using extension, union, intersection, and difference as appropriate).

Every member of Fs is a member of Fr.

The query decomposition process must examine *cond* and note any further FDs that are thereby constrained to hold true in R. In practice, those arising when θ is "$=$" are the most important and possibly the only ones that can feasibly be inferred.

If *cond* is "$A = B$," the FDs $A \rightarrow B$ and $B \rightarrow A$ should both be added to Fr. Mr can be developed using the same method as for extension.

Union

Let R be the union of union-compatible relations S and T.

In general, FDs in S and T do not hold true in R, and we have to note HR $\rightarrow$ HR as the only member of Fr.

In the special case where S and T are known to be both subsets of some relation U, then the family Fu can be carried forward to Fr. This case applies, for instance, when the logical operator OR is used in a complex restriction condition.

Intersection

Let R be the intersection of union-compatible relations S and T.

In general, all FDs in S and T hold true in R, so Fr is *CombineFamilies*(Fs,Ft).

Difference

Let *R* be the difference of union-compatible relations *S* and *T* (in that order).

In general, all FDs in *S* hold true in *R,* and F*s* can be carried forward to F*r*.

A difficulty (probably not important) arises in the special case where *S* and *T* are known to be both subsets of some relation *U.* Suppose *T* is the restriction of *U* by some condition *cond.* The negation of *cond* might imply some new FD in *R.* For instance, if *cond* is NOT ($A = B$), then $A = B$ holds true in *R,* and therefore $A \rightarrow B$ and $B \rightarrow A$ should, for completeness, both be included in F*r*.

Summarize

This operator involves two steps, a "grouping" step and an "aggregation" step. Matters are greatly simplified if we consider just the grouping step; the aggregation step can then be regarded as a projection of an extension of the result of the grouping step.

To isolate the grouping step, we define the operator

Group *S* Over *A* Into *B*

where *A* is a subset of HS. Let *R* be the result of this operation. Then HR is just *A* plus the new attribute *B.* *B* is a relation-valued attribute [4] whose value, in any row of *R,* is some subset (strictly, restriction) of *S.*

In any tuple *t* of *R,* the value of *B* is that subset of the tuples of *S* that agree, for all attributes in *A,* with corresponding values for all of the attributes of *A* in *t.*

The FDs $A \rightarrow B$ and $B \rightarrow A$ both hold true in *R,* as do all of the FDs in the projection of *S* over *A.* F*r* and M*r* can be developed accordingly.

In treating the aggregation step as an extension of the result of the grouping step (followed by a projection to remove *B*), we note that if *C* is the result of some aggregating function, then $B \rightarrow C$ holds true, and leave the rest to *SimplifyFamily.*

Unless *A* is a proper superset of some candidate key of *S,* in which case grouping over *A* is a rather strange thing to do, *A* will turn out to be a candidate key of the result of a summarize.

Natural Join

Let *R* be the natural join of *S* and *T.* Let *Cs* be the attributes of *S* that are also attributes of *T,* and let *Ct* be the attributes of *T* that are also attributes of *S.* *R* can be expressed as the extended Cartesian product of *S* and *T,* restricted where the combined value of the attributes in *Cs* is equal to the combined value of the corresponding attributes in *Ct,* projected over all attributes except those of *Ct* (or *Cs*). Therefore, the FDs holding in *R* can be determined by suitable application of the rules already given for extended Cartesian product, restriction, and projection. It is of great interest, nonetheless, to note what candidate keys those rules will deliver, and thereby to determine whether the join is many-to-many, many-to-one, or one-to-one.

As *Cs* and *Ct* are the same set, call it just *C.* Let *Ks* be some candidate key of *S,* and let *Kt* be some candidate key of *T.* Then the General Unification Theorem gives:

```
Ks ∪ ( Kt - HS ) → HS ∪ HT
```

and

```
Kt ∪ ( Ks - HT ) → HS ∪ HT
```

As the only members of HS that are also members of HT are precisely the members of *C,* and as the union of HS and HT is HR, we can easily see that

```
Ks ∪ ( Kt - C ) → HR
```

and

```
Kt ∪ ( Ks - C ) → HR
```

If neither of these two determinants is a superset of the other, then they are distinct candidate keys of *R.* In the case where *C* is a superset of some candidate key of either operand, every candidate key of the other operand is clearly a candidate key of *R;* for instance, if *C* is a superset of *Kt,* then the determinant in the first of the two FDs above reduces to just *Ks.* When some candidate key of either operand is a candidate key of *R,* then the join is many-to-one from that operand to the other. If both operands have a candidate key that is also a candidate key of *R,* then the join is one-to-one.

7. GRASPING THE OPPORTUNITIES

We now revisit the "opportunities for improvement" discussed in Section 2.

Example 1: View updatability

Using some general-purpose table displayer/modifier, the user obtains a display of the result of the following query:

```
SELECT  E.EMP#, E.ENAME, E.SALARY, D.LOCATION
FROM    EMP E, DEPT D
WHERE   E.DEPT# = D.DEPT#
AND     E.JOB = 'Programmer' ;
```

The reader is invited to write down all of the FDs implied by the primary keys of DEPT and EMP and by the condition in the WHERE clause. Given that set, *SimplifyFamily* will show that EMP# is a candidate key of the result. Because the result includes a candidate key of EMP, and some candidate key of the result is a subset of some candidate key of EMP, the DBMS can conclude that the result is updatable with respect to the columns of EMP. (Discussion of its updatability with respect to the columns of DEPT is beyond the scope of this paper.)

Example 2: Primary keys of results not reported

To report a candidate key that the system has chosen to be the primary key needs only a truth-valued flag, "PK-member," to be included in the information carried for each column of the result.

Example 3: The GROUP BY problem

The user wishes to see, for each department that has at least one employee, the department number, location, and average salary of employees in that department, and issues the query:

```
SELECT  D.DEPT#, D.LOCATION, AVG ( E.SALARY )
FROM    DEPT D, EMP E
WHERE   D.DEPT# = E.DEPT#
GROUP   BY D.DEPT# ;
```

This query can now be accepted. If we treat the GROUP BY operation as the grouping step of a summarize, then the SELECT-list specification D.LOCATION can be treated as invoking a (hypothetical) aggregate function that returns the only distinct value of D.LOCATION in each group (i.e., it would be an error if any group contained multiple distinct D.LOCATION values). The set of FDs developed for the result of the FROM–WHERE part of the query shows D.LOCATION to be functionally dependent on D.DEPT#; it follows that in the result of the GROUP BY clause (which is a relation that includes both a LOCATION attribute and a relation-valued attribute B, say, whose relation values each also contain a LOCATION attribute in turn), each tuple t must have the same value for LOCATION as does every tuple within t's B value (i.e., within the relevant "group"). Hence D.LOCATION is indeed "single-valued per group."

Example 4: Scalar subqueries

A senior employee, Pentstemon Smith, likes to find out, every month, about any colleagues who are earning more than he. He uses the query:

```
SELECT  ENAME, SALARY
FROM    EMP
WHERE   SALARY >
    ( SELECT  SALARY
      FROM    EMP
      WHERE   ENAME = 'Pentstemon Smith' ) ;
```

Even though there happens to be only one Pentstemon Smith, the query is now rejected, because the DBMS enforces the rule that a query can be used as a "scalar subquery" only if the result of that query necessarily has the empty set is a candidate key, which is not the case here. Note, however, that it *would* be the case if the condition ENAME = 'Pentstemon Smith' were replaced by the condition EMP# = '54321' (54321 being Pentstemon's employee number).

Example 5: The DISTINCT problem

The query

```
SELECT DISTINCT E.EMP#, E.ENAME, D.LOCATION
FROM    EMP E, DEPT D
WHERE   E.DEPT# = D.DEPT# ;
```

can now be just as fast as the same query with DISTINCT omitted. There are no duplicate rows in DEPT or EMP, because of the way the system enforces the constraints implied by their primary keys, and therefore the FROM–WHERE part cannot deliver any duplicate rows. EMP# is seen to be a candidate key of the result of the FROM -WHERE part, and is retained in the projection implied by the SELECT part. Therefore the projection can be done by just throwing away the unwanted columns. Furthermore, the result table is just as updatable as the result of the same query without DISTINCT.

The query can be made to run even faster if query decomposition can note that the join is many-to-one. This latter fact is implied by the fact that some candidate key of the result of the FROM–WHERE part is also a candidate key of the first operand of the join. If a nested loop or index lookup is used to match EMP rows with DEPT rows, the system need not look more than once in DEPT, for any row of EMP, and thus an expensive search-not-found is avoided.

Example 6: CREATE TABLE AS expression

The problem discussed in this scenario is deemed solved without further discussion.

ACKNOWLEDGMENTS

Above all, my thanks go to **Adrian Larner,** who has saved me from many embarrassing mistakes, and has shared my exhilaration at some of the results. My original proof of the General Unification Theorem was about three times as long as the one in the paper, which was supplied by Adrian.

Chris Date has been the main source of encouragement to get this work completed and published.

In addition to the above two, **Ron Fagin** and **Alan Best** reviewed an earlier attempt. While it was my own decision to discard that attempt, all of these people's comments have been of great help to me.

REFERENCES AND BIBLIOGRAPHY

1. W. W. Armstrong, "Dependency Structures of Data Base Relationships," *Proc. IFIP Congress,* Stockholm, Sweden (1974) (Amsterdam, North-Holland Publishing Company, 1974).

2. Catriel Beeri and Philip A. Bernstein, "Computational Problems Related to the Design of Normal Form Relational Schemas," *ACM Transactions on Database Systems* 4, No. 1 (March 1979).

> This paper shows that some problems in the theory of functional dependencies are "NP-complete," meaning that they cannot be solved in polynomial time. Indeed, the simple algorithm given in Appendix A clearly suffers from this defect—the time taken to find all the interesting FDs implied by a given set of *n* FDs is proportional to 2^n.

3. C. Beeri, R. Fagin, and J. H. Howard Jr., "A Complete Axiomatization for Functional and Multivalued Dependencies in Database Relations," *Proc. 1977 ACM SIGMOD International Conference on Management of Data,* Toronto, Canada (August 1977).

4. Hugh Darwen and C. J. Date, "Relation-Valued Attributes" (in this volume).

5. C. J. Date, "Updating Views," in C. J. Date, *Relational Database: Selected Writings* (Reading, MA: Addison-Wesley, 1986).

6. C. J. Date, "EXISTS Is Not "Exists"! (Some Logical Flaws in SQL)," in C. J. Date, *Relational Database Writings 1985–1989* (Reading, MA: Addison-Wesley, 1990).

7. Umeshwar Dayal and Philip A. Bernstein, "On the Correct Translation of Update Operations on Relational Views," *ACM Transactions on Database Systems* 7, No. 3 (September 1982).

8. R. Fadous and J. Forsyth, "Finding Candidate Keys for Relational Data Bases," *Proc. 1975 ACM SIGMOD International Conference on Management of Data,* San Jose, CA (May 1975).

9. Ronald Fagin, "Normal Forms and Relational Database Operators," *Proc. 1979 ACM SIGMOD International Conference on Management of Data,* Boston, MA (May/June 1979).

10. Nathan Goodman, "View Update Is Practical," *InfoDB* 5, No. 2 (Summer 1990).

11. C. L. Lucchesi and S. L. Osborn, "Candidate Keys for Relations," *Journal of Computer and Systems Sciences* 17, No. 2 (October 1978).

> This paper shows that the problem of determining whether a particular set of attributes is a candidate key can be solved in polynomial time, using a method very different from that given in Appendix A. This method is probably very suitable for determining the updatability of joins.

12. Andrew Warden, "The Keys of the Kingdom," in C. J. Date, *Relational Database Writings 1985–1989* (Reading, MA: Addison-Wesley, 1990).

APPENDIX A:
FUNCTIONAL DEPENDENCY ALGORITHMS

A design for the function *SimplifyFamily* is given in this appendix, along with two further functions, *CombineFamilies* and *Unite,* both trivial, that might be useful in query decomposition. The functions are expressed in an informal design language. The complete set of functions is referred to as *FDpackage.*

```
UNDEFINED ( ←, SET, subset of, ε, Attribute, TUPLE,
            project ... over ..., U, difference, {...} ) ;

TYPE Relation is SET of Attribute ;
TYPE FD       is TUPLE of ( det Relation, dep Relation ) ;
TYPE FDset    is SET of FD ;


/****************************************************************/
/*                                                            */
/*  DET and DEP return the determinant and the dependent set, */
/*  respectively, of a given FD.                              */
/*                                                            */
/****************************************************************/

FUNCTION DET ( fd1 FD ) returns Relation is project fd1 over det ;
FUNCTION DEP ( fd1 FD ) returns Relation is project fd1 over dep ;

INFIX OPERATOR set1 SET - set2 SET returns SET is
              set1 difference set2 ;


/****************************************************************/
/*                                                            */
/*  ImpliedBy operates on two FDs and returns "true" if and   */
/*  only if the first is implied by the second (by            */
/*  L-augmentation or joint dependence).                      */
/*                                                            */
/****************************************************************/

INFIX OPERATOR fd1 FD ImpliedBy fd2 FD returns Boolean is
        DET( fd1 ) subset of DET( fd2 ) &
        DEP( fd2 ) subset of DEP( fd1 ) ;


/****************************************************************/
/*                                                            */
/*  Unify applies the General Unification Theorem to deliver  */
/*  an FD implied by the given two FDs.                       */
/*                                                            */
/****************************************************************/

FUNCTION Unify( fd1 FD, fd2 FD ) returns FD is
        ( DET( fd1 ) U ( DET( fd2 ) - DEP ( fd1 ) ),
          DEP( fd1 ) U DEP ( fd2 ) ) ;
```

```
CONSTANT phi SET is {} ;
CONSTANT Fifi FDset is {(phi,phi)} ;


/****************************************************************/
/*                                                              */
/*  SimplifyFamily removes redundancies from a family of FDs,   */
/*  and makes sure all of the FDs implied by the General        */
/*  Unification Theorem are included.                           */
/*                                                              */
/*  The result can be inspected to determine candidate keys     */
/*  of the relation, R, provided that the tautological FD       */
/*  R → R has been included in the input family.                */
/*                                                              */
/****************************************************************/

FUNCTION SimplifyFamily( notsimple FDset ) returns FDset is

        SimplifyFamily:

            DECLARE newfam FDset ;

            newfam ← Fifi ;             /* prime the pump         */

            For each fd ε notsimple ;
               newfam ← TakeNewFD( newfam, fd ) ;
            End of For ;

            If newfam ¬= notsimple   /* keep on doing it until */
            Then                     /* until it's all done    */
               newfam ← SimplifyFamily( newfam ) ;

            Return newfam ;

End of SimplifyFamily ;


/****************************************************************/
/*                                                              */
/*  TakeNewFD updates a set of FDs with a new FD,               */
/*  incorporating what is implied by the General Unification    */
/*  Theorem, applied in turn to each member of the family       */
/*  being updated.                                              */
/*                                                              */
/****************************************************************/

FUNCTION TakeNewFD( family FDset, nfd FD ) returns FDset is

        TakeNewFD:

            DECLARE newfam FDset ;

            newfam ← Fifi ;             /* prime the pump         */

            For each ofd ε family ;
               nfd1 ← Unify( ofd, nfd ) ;
               nfd2 ← Unify( nfd, ofd ) ;
               newfam ← AddToFamily( newfam, nfd1 ) ;
               newfam ← AddToFamily( newfam, nfd2 ) ;
            End of For ;

            Return newfam ;

End of TakeNewFD ;
```

```
/****************************************************************/
/*                                                              */
/*  AddToFamily updates a family of FDs, given a new FD to be   */
/*  incorporated.  We avoid adding redundant members that are   */
/*  implied by L-augmentation or joint dependence, and we       */
/*  enforce that criterion for "interesting" that requires the  */
/*  determinant to be a subset of the dependent set.            */
/*                                                              */
/****************************************************************/

FUNCTION AddToFamily( family FDset, nfd FD ) returns FDset is

        AddToFamily:

            DECLARE newfam FDset, newfd FD, wanted Boolean ;

            newfd ← ( DET( nfd ), DET( nfd ) U DEP( nfd ) ) ;

            newfam ← Fifi ;              /* prime the pump         */
            wanted ← true ;

            For each oldfd ε family ;
               Case
                  When newfd ImpliedBy oldfd
                  Then                   /* don't need newfd       */
                     wanted ← false ;
                                         /* do need oldfd          */
                     newfam ← newfam U { oldfd } ;
                  When oldfd ImpliedBy newfd
                  Then                   /* don't need oldfd       */
                     do nothing ;
                  Otherwise              /* do need oldfd          */
                     newfam ← newfam U { oldfd } ;
               End of Case ;
            End of For ;

            If wanted
            Then
               newfam ← newfam U { newfd } ;

            Return newfam ;

End of AddToFamily ;


/****************************************************************/
/*                                                              */
/*  CombineFamilies makes two families into one family.         */
/*                                                              */
/*  It might be needed if two distinct components of a query    */
/*  decomposer have each noted a set of FDs, and it is          */
/*  required to combine those into a single set.                */
/*                                                              */
/****************************************************************/

FUNCTION CombineFamilies( family1 FDset, family2 FDset ) is

        CombineFamilies:

            DECLARE newfam FDset ;

            newfam ← family1 ;          /* prime the pump         */
```

```
                     For each fd ε family2 ;
                         newfam ← TakeNewFD( newfam, fd ) ;
                     End of For ;

                     Return newfam ;

        End of CombineFamilies ;


        /***************************************************************/
        /*                                                             */
        /*  Unite makes a simplified family out of two arbitrary sets  */
        /*  of FDs.                                                     */
        /*                                                             */
        /*  It might be useful in analysis of joins.  If family1 and   */
        /*  family2 have both been simplified, then their candidate    */
        /*  keys, and the candidate keys of Unite(family1,family2),    */
        /*  can be examined to determine if the join is many-to-one,   */
        /*  many-to-many, one-to-many, or one-to-one, and whether or   */
        /*  not the join should be considered updatable.               */
        /*                                                             */
        /***************************************************************/

        FUNCTION Unite(family1 FDset, family2 FDset ) returns FDset is

                SimplifyFamily( CombineFamilies( family1, family2 ) ) ;

        End of FDpackage ;
```

11

Into the Great Divide

ABSTRACT

We investigate the relational divide operation, paying special attention to the problems that can arise in the presence of empty relations.

COMMENTS ON PUBLICATION

References [2] and [7] both discuss a "generalized" version of the relational divide operation; in particular, both make the claim that the operation is an upward-compatible extension of the original divide operation as defined by Codd in reference [1]. It turns out (regrettably) that this claim is not quite accurate. Furthermore, it turns out that *neither* version of the operation is quite what is needed to handle the kind of problem that is usually stated, informally, to be "what divide is good for"—problems, that is, of the form typified by the query "Find suppliers who supply all parts." The paper that follows, a joint production by Hugh Darwen and myself, explores such matters in detail.

Note: I wanted to call the paper "*Across* The Great Divide," partly because that's the conventional cliché, partly because of the tiny pun on

Previously unpublished.

"cross" (= Cartesian product), and partly as a tribute to Kate Wolf and her song of that name. But Hugh argued that "Into" really made more sense, and I agreed, albeit a little reluctantly.

1. INTRODUCTION

Relational division tends to be one of the least well understood operators of the relational algebra. It is usually characterized, informally, as an algebraic counterpart to the universal quantifier ("for all")—indeed, Codd characterized it in exactly these terms when he first introduced the operator in reference [1]. As we shall see, however, this characterization can be somewhat misleading; specifically, it can cause confusion in the case where the divisor is empty. (Note, however, that the confusion arises not from the well-known—though arguably counterintuitive—fact that "for all" applied to the empty set always returns *true,* but rather from the intuitive interpretation of the word "all" in ordinary English.)

Now, Codd's divide (referred to hereinafter as the Small Divide) was somewhat limited in its application, inasmuch as it required the divisor relation to have a heading that was a subset of the heading of the dividend. Subsequently, Todd [12] introduced a "generalized" divide operation (referred to hereinafter as the Great Divide) that applied to *any pair of relations whatsoever.* Unfortunately, the Great Divide also suffers from certain difficulties over empty relations, as we shall see. Furthermore, it turns out that the Small Divide is not (quite) a special case of the Great Divide,* and hence that the name "generalized divide" for the latter operation is not (quite) apt. The purpose of this paper is to discuss such matters in depth.

The structure of the paper is as follows. Following this introductory section, Section 2 discusses the Small Divide in detail, and proposes a new operator that fixes the empty divisor problem. Section 3 then performs analogous functions for the Great Divide. Section 4 provides a precise characterization of the circumstances in which the Small Divide is a special case of the Great Divide. Finally, Section 5 briefly discusses a different solution to some of the empty set problems, using *relation-valued attributes.*

2. CODD'S DIVIDE

We introduce the Small Divide by means of an example. Given the usual suppliers-and-parts database—

---

*As noted in the "Comments on Publication," references [2] and [7] both incorrectly state the opposite.

```
S    ( S#, ... )
SP   ( S#, P#, ... )
P    ( P#, ..., COLOR, ... )
```

—the expression

```
SP [ S#, P# ] DIVIDEBY P [ P# ]
```

gives supplier numbers S# such that the pair of values (S#,P#) appears in relation SP for all part numbers P# appearing in relation P. This result is usually characterized, informally, as "supplier numbers for suppliers who supply all parts." And indeed, this characterization is accurate so long as there does exist at least one part. The case where there are no parts at all requires special consideration, however, and we will return to that case below.

Here then is a definition of the Small Divide. Let relations A and B have headings (X, Y) and (Y), respectively. (X and Y here represent *combinations* of zero or more attributes;* Y is all of the attributes of B, and X is the attributes of A not included in B. Note that, as already mentioned, the heading of B must be a subset of the heading of A.) Then the division of A by B, A DIVIDEBY B, is a relation with heading (X) and with body consisting of all tuples $(X{:}x)$ such that a tuple $(X{:}x, Y{:}y)$ appears in A for all tuples $(Y{:}y)$ appearing in B:

```
{ (X:x) : FORALL b EXISTS a ( x = a.X AND a.Y = b.Y ) }
```

(where a and b are tuple variables that range over A and B respectively).

Here is a relational algebra equivalent of this definition:

```
A [ X ] MINUS ( ( A [ X ] TIMES B ) MINUS A ) [ X ]
```

(The Small Divide is thus not a primitive operation of the relational algebra, as is well known.) Or to spell it out one step at a time:

```
T1   :=   A [ X ] ;
T2   :=   T1 TIMES B ;
T3   :=   T2 MINUS A ;
T4   :=   T3 [ X ] ;
ANS  :=   T1 MINUS T4 ;
```

Readers who are not familiar with this expansion of the Small Divide should take the time to convince themselves that it is correct before continuing.

Now let us revisit the "supplier numbers for suppliers who supply all parts" example. We have already suggested that a problem arises with this query if there are no parts at all. To suppose that there are no parts at all

---

*And we will adopt this notational convention throughout the remainder of this paper.

is intuitively unattractive, however; in particular, it implies not only that relation P will be empty, but that relation SP will be empty as well, because attribute SP.P# is a foreign key that references P. Let us therefore modify the example slightly, as follows. Let relation PP consist of relation P restricted to just tuples for parts that are purple—

```
P WHERE COLOR = 'Purple'
```

—and consider the expression ("Expression 1"):

```
SP [ S#, P# ] DIVIDEBY PP [ P# ]
```

(informally, "supplier numbers for suppliers who supply all purple parts").

Now, it might quite reasonably be the case that relation PP is empty (meaning that there are no purple parts), while relation SP is nonempty. And if there are no purple parts, then it is true of *every supplier* that that supplier supplies every purple part. However, Expression 1 does *not* give supplier numbers for "every supplier" if relation PP is empty. Instead, it gives supplier numbers *only for suppliers who supply at least one part—* suppliers, that is, who are represented in relation SP; it does not include any suppliers who happen to supply no parts at all (such suppliers will be represented in relation S but not in relation SP). More generally, the expression A DIVIDEBY B reduces to just $A[X]$ if B is empty (this fact is immediate from the algebraic definition).

So we see that Expression 1 is not quite sufficient, in general, to represent the query "supplier numbers for suppliers who supply all purple parts." Or, looking at it another way, a more accurate English translation of that expression is "supplier numbers for suppliers *who supply at least one part and* supply all purple parts."

How can we fix this problem? Well, here is the step-at-a-time expansion of Expression 1:

```
T1   :=  SP [ S# ] ;
T2   :=  T1 TIMES PP [ P# ] ;
T3   :=  T2 MINUS SP [ S#, P# ] ;
T4   :=  T3 [ S# ] ;
ANS  :=  T1 MINUS T4 ;
```

If we replace the reference to table SP in the first step by a reference to table S, as follows:

```
T1   :=  S [ S# ] ;
```

(while leaving the other steps unchanged), then we obtain a representation of the query "supplier numbers for suppliers who *exist* (i.e., are represented in relation S) and supply all purple parts"—in other words, the query that we really want. And this modified step-at-a-time sequence now correctly represents the query *regardless* of whether or not there are actually any purple parts.* But note clearly that, whatever else it may be, this modified sequence is not equivalent to an expression of the form *A* DIVIDEBY *B for any A or B whatsoever.* That is, the Small Divide is not quite the operation we need to express queries of the kind under consideration (and it should therefore be used with a certain degree of caution).

The foregoing discussion strongly suggests that it would be desirable to define a revised version of the Small Divide, a version that does correspond to the modified step-at-a-time expansion discussed in the example. We might refer to this operation as "divide per".[†] Here is the definition. Let relations *A, AB,* and *B* have headings (X), (X, Y), and (Y), respectively. Then the division of *A* by *B* per *AB, A* DIVIDEBY *B* PER *AB*, is a relation with heading (X) and body consisting of all tuples $(X:x)$ such that a tuple $(X:x, Y:y)$ appears in *AB* for all tuples $(Y:y)$ appearing in *B*:

```
{ (X:x) : EXISTS a FORALL b EXISTS ab
          ( x = a.X AND a.X = ab.X AND ab.Y = b.Y ) }
```

(where *a, b,* and *ab* are tuple variables that range over A, B, and AB respectively). *Note:* We might express this definition more intuitively—less formally—as

```
{ A.X : FORALL B EXISTS AB ( A.X = AB.X AND AB.Y = B.Y ) }
```

Here is a relational algebra equivalent:

```
A MINUS ( ( A TIMES B ) MINUS AB [ X, Y ] ) [ X ]
```

Step-at-a-time version:

```
T1   :=  A TIMES B ;
T2   :=  AB [ X, Y ] ;
T3   :=  T1 MINUS T2 ;
T4   :=  T3 [ X ] ;
ANS  :=  A MINUS T4 ;
```

The query "supplier numbers for suppliers who supply all purple parts" can now be simply (and correctly) expressed as

```
S [ S# ] DIVIDEBY PP [ P# ] PER SP [ S#, P# ]
```

---

*Observe, however, that we are relying on the fact that every supplier number appearing in relation SP must also appear in relation S. We could avoid this reliance by replacing SP[S#] by SP[S#] UNION S[S#] in the assignment to T1.

†The term "divide" is perhaps no longer very apt. Codd's original divide had the property that it was (approximately) the inverse of the product operation; at least, given relations *Q* and *R*, it was certainly the case with Codd's divide that forming the product of *Q* and *R* and then dividing the result by *R* yielded the original relation *Q* again. No obvious analog of this property applies to "divide per."

Note: It would obviously be possible to extend the definition of "divide per" to allow the headings of relations *A, B,* and *AB* to be supersets of (*X*), (*Y*), and (*X, Y*), respectively. We omit the details here.

3. TODD'S DIVIDE

We turn now to the Great Divide, which allows any relation to be divided by any relation. As in Section 2, we start with an example, or rather two examples. Given the following extended version of suppliers-and-parts—

```
S    ( S#, ... )
SP   ( S#, P#, ... )
P    ( P#, ..., COLOR, ... )
PJ   ( P#, J#, ... )
J    ( J#, ... )
```

(where "J" stands for "projects")—the expression

```
SP [ S#, P# ] DIVIDEBY PJ [ P#, J# ]
```

gives (S#,J#) pairs such that supplier S# supplies all the parts used in project J#, and the expression

```
PJ [ J#, P# ] DIVIDEBY SP [ P#, S# ]
```

gives (J#,S#) pairs such that project J# uses all parts supplied by supplier S#. (At least, these are the intuitive interpretations of the two expressions, but matters are not quite as clearcut as we might like, as we shall see.)

Here is the Great Divide definition. Let relations *A* and *B* have headings (*X, Y*) and (*Y, Z*), respectively. Then the division of *A* by *B*, *A* DIVIDEBY *B*,* is a relation with heading (*X, Z*) and with body consisting of all tuples (*X:x, Z:z*) such that a tuple (*X:x, Y:y*) appears in *A* for all tuples (*Y:y, Z:z*) appearing in *B*:

```
{ (X:x,Z:z) : FORALL b EXISTS a
              ( x = a.X AND a.Y = b.Y AND b.Z = z ) }
```

(where, once again, *a* and *b* are tuple variables that range over *A* and *B*, respectively).

Relational algebra equivalent:

```
( A [ X ] TIMES B [ Z ] ) MINUS
    ( ( A [ X ] TIMES B ) MINUS ( A JOIN B ) ) [ X, Z ]
```

Step-at-a-time version:

---

*Strictly speaking we should use a different syntax here, because (as we shall see) the Great Divide is *not* a true generalization of the Small Divide. Indeed (as mentioned earlier in this paper), we should not really refer to the Great Divide as a "generalized" divide at all.

```
T1   :=   A [ X ] ;
T2   :=   B [ Z ] ;
T3   :=   T1 TIMES T2 ;
T4   :=   T1 TIMES B ;
T5   :=   A  JOIN  B ;
T6   :=   T4 MINUS T5 ;
T7   :=   T6 [ X, Z ] ;
ANS  :=   T3 MINUS T7 ;
```

We do *not* at this juncture consider the question of an empty divisor (though readers might like to take a moment to consider that question for themselves). Instead, we examine a different problem, namely as follows. Let relation RPJ consist of relation PJ restricted to just tuples for parts that are red—

```
PJ JOIN ( P WHERE COLOR = 'Red' )
```

—and consider the expression ("Expression 2"):

```
SP [ S#, P# ] DIVIDEBY RPJ [ P#, J# ]
```

Informally, this expression represents the query "(S#,J#) pairs such that supplier S# supplies all red parts used in project J#." Now we make a couple of assumptions:

- First, we assume that there does exist at least one supplier, say S3, who supplies at least one part (which may or may not be red); thus, relation SP is not empty.

- Second, we assume that there does exist at least one project, say J3, that uses at least one part but does not use any red parts; thus, project J3 is represented in relation PJ but not in relation RPJ.

By contrast, we do *not* assume that there are no red parts; thus, relation RPJ is not necessarily empty (and so the problem under consideration is not simply the empty divisor problem).

Given the foregoing assumptions, the statement "Supplier S3 supplies all red parts that are used in project J3" certainly evaluates to *true* (because the set of such parts is empty, and it is true that every supplier supplies all the parts in an empty set). So the pair (S3,J3) ought really to appear in the result of evaluating Expression 2. But will it? Sadly, the answer is "No." The value J3 does not appear in RPJ, as explained above, and it certainly does not appear in SP, because SP does not have a J# attribute; there is thus no possibility of J3 appearing anywhere in the result of the overall expression.

As with the Small Divide, therefore, the informal English interpretation of the expression is insufficient. Of course, we must add the qualification "suppliers who supply at least one part," as with the Small Divide, but we must add a similar qualification for the divisor too, so that the overall query is actually "(S#,J#) pairs such that supplier S# supplies at least one part, *project J# uses at least one red part,* and supplier S# supplies all red parts used in project J#."

How can we fix this problem? Well, here is the step-at-a-time expansion of Expression 2:

```
T1    :=  SP [ S# ] ;
T2    :=  RPJ [ J# ] ;
T3    :=  T1 TIMES T2 ;
T4    :=  T1 TIMES RPJ [ P#, J# ] ;
T5    :=  SP [ S#, P# ] JOIN RPJ [ P#, J# ] ;
T6    :=  T4 MINUS T5 ;
T7    :=  T6 [ S#, J# ] ;
ANS   :=  T3 MINUS T7 ;
```

If we want the result to include (S#,J#) pairs such as (S3,J3)—i.e., (S#,J#) pairs such that (a) supplier S# supplies at least one part, and (b) project J# uses at least one part *but no red parts*—then we must redefine T2 to include J#'s for all projects that use at least one part (not just J#'s for projects that use at least one *red* part):

```
T2   :=  PJ [ J# ] ;
```

If we wish to extend the result further to include (S#,J#) pairs such that supplier S# supplies no parts at all (and project J# uses at least one part but no red parts)—for, again, it is true for such a pair that the supplier does supply all red parts used by the project—then we must redefine T1 also:

```
T1   :=  S [ S# ] ;
```

And if we wish to extend the result still further to include (S#,J#) pairs such that project J# uses no parts at all—for, yet again, it is true for such a pair that the supplier does supply all red parts used by the project—then we must redefine T2 once more:

```
T2   :=  J [ J# ] ;
```

At this point, it is probably worth taking a moment to convince ourselves that the overall (modified) sequence of operations is indeed correct. To summarize, that sequence is as follows:

```
T1    :=  S [ S# ] ;
T2    :=  J [ J# ] ;
T3    :=  T1 TIMES T2 ;
T4    :=  T1 TIMES RPJ [ P#, J# ] ;
T5    :=  SP [ S#, P# ] JOIN RPJ [ P#, J# ] ;
T6    :=  T4 MINUS T5 ;
T7    :=  T6 [ S#, J# ] ;
ANS   :=  T3 MINUS T7 ;
```

Explanation:

- T1 is S#'s for suppliers that exist.
- T2 is J#'s for projects that exist.
- T3 is (S#,J#) pairs such that supplier S# exists and project J# exists.
- T4 is (S#,P#,J#) triples such that supplier S# exists and part P# is a red part used in project J#.
- T5 is (S#,P#,J#) triples such that supplier S# supplies part P# and part P# is a red part used in project J#.
- T6 is (S#,P#,J#) triples such that part P# is a red part used in project J# but supplier S# does not supply part P#.
- T7 is (S#,J#) pairs such that project J# uses some red part but supplier S# does not supply that part.
- Finally, ANS is (S#,J#) pairs such that supplier S# exists, project J# exists, and it is not the case that project J# uses some red part that is not supplied by supplier S#—i.e., supplier S# supplies all red parts that are used in project J#.

As in the case of the Small Divide, however, this modified sequence of operations no longer represents an expression of the form *A* DIVIDEBY *B* for any *A* or *B* whatsoever. Like the Small Divide, therefore, the Great Divide is not quite the operation that we need to express queries of the kind under consideration; again, therefore, it should be used with a certain degree of caution.*

As with the Small Divide, it is possible to define a "divide per" version of the Great Divide, as follows. Let relations *A, AB, BC,* and *C* have headings (X), (X,Y), (Y,Z), and (Z), respectively.† Then the division of *A* by *C* per *AB* and *BC, A* DIVIDEBY *B* PER (AB,BC), is a relation with heading (X,Z) and body consisting of all tuples $(X:x,Z:z)$ such that a tuple $(X:x)$ appears in *A,* a tuple $(Z:z)$ appears in *C,* and a tuple $(X:x,Y:y)$ appears in *AB* for all tuples $(Y:y,Z:z)$ appearing in *BC*:

---

*An argument might be made that the two divides nevertheless behave in a manner that accords better with intuition (better, that is, than the universal quantifier does). For instance, how does an only child respond to the question "Are all your brothers and sisters married?" And what would we think of such a child who correctly replied with an unqualified "Yes"? On the other hand, if Expression 2, which we intuitively take to mean "(S#,J#) pairs such that supplier S# supplies all red parts used in project J#," fails to give the pair (S3,J3), might we not wrongly conclude that there is some red part that is used by J3 and not supplied by S3?

†Again it would be possible to extend the definition to allow the headings of the relations to be supersets of what is specified here. Again, we omit the details.

```
{ (X:x,Z:z) : EXISTS a EXISTS c FORALL bc EXISTS ab
              ( x = a.X AND a.X = ab.X AND ab.Y = bc.Y
                    AND bc.Z = c.Z AND c.Z = z ) }
```

(where *a, ab, bc,* and *c* are tuple variables that range over *A, AB, BC,* and *C,* respectively). *Note:* We might express this definition more intuitively— less formally—as

```
{ A.X,C.Z : FORALL BC EXISTS AB
            ( A.X = AB.X AND AB.Y = BC.Y AND BC.Z = C.Z ) }
```

Relational algebra equivalent:

```
( A TIMES C ) MINUS
              ( ( A TIMES BC ) MINUS ( AB JOIN BC ) ) [ X, Z ]
```

Step-at-a-time version:

```
    T1  :=  A TIMES C ;
    T2  :=  A TIMES BC ;
    T3  :=  AB JOIN  BC ;
    T4  :=  T2 MINUS T3 ;
    T5  :=  T4 [ X, Z ] ;
   ANS  :=  T1 MINUS T5 ;
```

The query ''(S#,J#) pairs such that supplier S# supplies all red parts used in project J#'' can now be simply (and correctly) expressed as

```
S [ S# ] DIVIDEBY J [ J# ]
                  PER ( SP [ S#, P# ], RPJ [ P#, J# ] )
```

4. DOES THE GREAT DIVIDE DEGENERATE TO THE SMALL DIVIDE?

In order to study this question, it is convenient to begin by repeating the step-at-a-time definition of the Great Divide:

```
    T1  :=  A [ X ] ;
    T2  :=  B [ Z ] ;
    T3  :=  T1 TIMES T2 ;
    T4  :=  T1 TIMES B ;
    T5  :=  A  JOIN  B ;
    T6  :=  T4 MINUS T5 ;
    T7  :=  T6 [ X, Z ] ;
   ANS  :=  T3 MINUS T7 ;
```

It is clear that the only situation in which the Great Divide can possibly degenerate to the Small Divide is that in which *Z* (the set of attributes appearing in *B* and not in *A*) is empty, so that the heading of *B* is a subset of the heading of *A*.* In this case, T2 is a relation of degree zero, either

---

*The situation in which *X* is empty is totally different and does not degenerate to the Small Divide of *B* by *A* (contrary to what is stated in references [2] and [7]).

TABLE_DEE if *B* is nonempty, or TABLE_DUM otherwise. (TABLE_DEE and TABLE_DUM are the only possible degree-zero relations; TABLE_DEE contains exactly one tuple and TABLE_DUM is empty. See reference [3] for further discussion.) If T2 is TABLE_DEE, then T3 is equal to T1, and it is easy to verify that ANS is the same as that given by the expansion shown earlier for the Small Divide.

However, if T2 is TABLE_DUM (which it is only if *B*, the divisor, is empty), then T3 is also empty, and ANS (= T3 MINUS T7) is therefore empty also. By contrast, the Small Divide returns *A*[*X*] when the divisor is empty, as already noted in Section 2.

We are therefore forced to conclude that the Small Divide is *not* a special case of the Great Divide in the (presumably unusual) situation in which the divisor is empty. In all other situations, however, it is.

Note: For much the same reasons, it turns out that the "Small Divide per" is not quite a special case of the "Great Divide per" either. The details are left as an exercise for the reader.

5. IS FIRST NORMAL FORM THE CULPRIT?

Note: The material of this section duplicates some of that of reference [6]. It is included here in order to make the present paper more self-contained.

The answer to the question in the title of this section depends (a) on what we really mean by first normal form and (b) on what the reader may think about the alternative way of thinking about division and universal quantification to be discussed below.

Those who have written about "nested relations"—i.e., relations that contain attributes that are themselves relation-valued—have tended to use the term "non first normal form," or NFNF, often further abbreviated to NF^2 ("NF squared"). But such attributes, and the relations that contain them, do not necessarily have to be seen as violating the first normal form requirement that each tuple must contain exactly one value for each attribute; it is only necessary to consider the nested relations as "atomic values." After all, the "atomic values" requirement is one that is very much open to interpretation.

Consider once again the Great Divide example SP DIVIDEBY RPJ, which we saw could be interpreted (loosely!) as "(S#,J#) pairs such that supplier S# supplies all red parts used in project J#." Let us now rephrase that interpretation in terms of a comparison between two sets (or rather relations):

"(S#,J#) pairs such that the set of all parts supplied by supplier S# is a superset (not necessarily a proper superset) of the set of red parts used in project J#."

Note that if (say) project J3 uses no red parts, then all possible (S#,J3) pairs satisfy this interpretation, even if supplier S# supplies no parts at all.

Now, suppose we can somehow* construct the binary relations

```
SP   ( S#, S_P#_SET )
```

and

```
RPJ ( J#, J_P#_SET )
```

where the attributes S_P#_SET and J_P#_SET are relation-valued, each containing, within each tuple of the relevant containing relation, a set (actually a unary relation) of part numbers. Furthermore, S_P#_SET (set of P#'s for supplied parts) is functionally dependent on S# in SP, and J_P#_SET (set of P#'s for red used parts) is functionally dependent on J# in RPJ—each supplier number is mapped to exactly one set of part numbers, and so is each project number. Since each set of part numbers is in fact represented by a unary relation, with sole attribute P#, defined on the domain "part numbers," we could describe SP and RPJ in terms of "nested relations" if we liked.

An example of a tuple in SP might be

```
( S2, { P2, P5, P6 } )
```

meaning that supplier S2 supplies parts P2, P5, P6, and no others (no other tuple in SP can have supplier number S2, because S# is a candidate key). Another example might be

```
( S9, { } )
```

meaning that supplier S9 supplies no parts at all.[†]

Analogously, examples of tuples in relation RPJ might be

```
( J2, { P2, P6 } )
```

and

```
( J3, { } )
```

meaning, respectively, that project J2 uses red parts P2 and P6 (only), and project J3 uses no red parts at all.[‡]

---

[*]Reference [6] shows how this might be done.

[†]Note that suppliers who supply no parts at all must be represented by tuples such as this one, not excluded from relation SP altogether, for the technique we are about to describe to work. Note too that the method described in reference [6] for constructing relations like relation SP will in fact satisfy this requirement.

[‡]Again, projects that use no red parts at all must be included in relation RPJ for our technique to work.

Now, when we have numeric attributes in relations, we are allowed to use numeric operators (such as "+", "−", "<", "ABS", and so on) in queries involving such attributes. Similarly, if we were to take the bold step (actually not so bold) of allowing relationss as values—and note, **most importantly**, that we do so without requiring any extension to the relational algebra*—then we would define operators on relations for use in queries. And one such operator would most certainly be the truth-valued (comparison) operator "is a superset of." Given that operator, we could then express the query "(S#,J#) pairs such that supplier S# supplies all red parts used in project J#" as follows:

```
( ( SP TIMES RPJ ) WHERE S_P#_SET ≥ J_P#_SET ) [ S#, J# ]
```

(using "≥" for "is a superset of").

Not for the first time, we note how the use of relation-valued attributes neatly solves a problem that "classical" relational theory has great difficulty with—to be specific, a problem arising from the possibility that some set might be empty. *Note:* Those who would stick rigidly to the atomicity requirement of first normal form (in the sense that we do not) typically address such problems by the highly dubious device of introducing an outer join operation that generates a "null" to represent the empty set. We have argued elsewhere that such an approach suffers from major problems of its own [4,5,8,9,10].

REFERENCES AND BIBLIOGRAPHY

1. E. F. Codd, "Relational Completeness of Data Base Sublanguages," in R. Rustin (ed.), *Data Base Systems,* Courant Computer Science Symposia Series 6 (Englewood Cliffs, NJ: Prentice-Hall, 1972).

2. Hugh Darwen (writing as Andrew Warden), Preface to "Adventures in Relationland," in C. J. Date, *Relational Database Writings 1985–1989* (Reading, MA: Addison-Wesley, 1990).

3. Hugh Darwen (writing as Andrew Warden), "Table_Dee and Table_Dum," in C. J. Date, *Relational Database Writings 1985–1989* (Reading, MA: Addison-Wesley, 1990).

4. Hugh Darwen (writing as Andrew Warden), "Into the Unknown," in C. J. Date, *Relational Database Writings 1985–1989* (Reading, MA: Addison-Wesley, 1990).

5. Hugh Darwen, "Outer Join with No Nulls and Fewer Tears" (in this volume).

6. Hugh Darwen and C. J. Date, "Relation-Valued Attributes" (in this volume).

---

*Contrast the approach adopted in reference [11], which introduces additional algebraic operators "nest" and "unnest" and extends the definitions of projection and natural join.

7. C. J. Date, "Relational Algebra," Chapter 13 of C. J. Date, *An Introduction To Database Systems: Volume I,* 5th edition (Reading, MA: Addison-Wesley, 1990).

8. C. J. Date, "NOT Is Not "Not"! (Notes on Three-Valued Logic and Related Matters)," in C. J. Date, *Relational Database Writings 1985–1989* (Reading, MA: Addison-Wesley, 1990).

9. C. J. Date, "Three-Valued Logic and The Real World" (in this volume).

10. C. J. Date, "Watch Out for Outer Join" (in this volume).

11. Mark A. Roth, Henry F. Korth, and Abraham Silberschatz, "Extended Relational Algebra and Relational Calculus for Nested Relational Databases," *ACM Transactions on Database Systems* 13, No. 4 (December 1988).

12. Stephen Todd, private communication (1988).

3. LEMMAS

Note: In what follows, the symbols *X, Y, Z,* etc. stand for logical (truth-valued) expressions.

The first few lemmas are well-known results from logic. We state them without proof.

```
X AND ( X OR  Y )  ≡  X
X OR  ( X AND Y )  ≡  X
X AND ( Y OR  Z )  ≡  ( X AND Y ) OR  ( X AND Z )
X OR  ( Y AND Z )  ≡  ( X OR  Y ) AND ( X OR  Z )

( X OR  Y ) AND ( Z OR  W )  ≡  ( X AND Z ) OR  ( X AND W ) OR
                                ( Y AND Z ) OR  ( Y AND W )

( X AND Y ) OR  ( Z AND W )  ≡  ( X OR  Z ) AND ( X OR  W ) AND
                                ( Y OR  Z ) AND ( Y OR  W )
```

And similarly for more complex expressions such as

```
( X AND Y ) OR ( Z AND W ) OR ( U AND V )
```

(of course).

The proof of the next four identities is trivial from the arithmetic meanings of the expressions A, I, etc.:

```
A OR I  ≡  true
C OR K  ≡  true
F OR J  ≡  true
H OR L  ≡  true
```

The proof of the next four pairs of identities is again trivial from the arithmetic meanings of the expressions B, I, etc. (note that combinations such as B *false*, I *true* are impossible):

```
B AND I  ≡  I        B OR I  ≡  B
D AND K  ≡  K        D OR K  ≡  D
E AND J  ≡  J        E OR J  ≡  E
G AND L  ≡  L        G OR L  ≡  G
```

The proof of the next four pairs of identities is again trivial from the arithmetic meanings of the expressions A, E, etc. (note that $X2 >= X1$ and $Y2 >= Y1$, and hence that combinations such as E *false*, A *true* are impossible):

```
A AND E  ≡  A        A OR E  ≡  E
C AND G  ≡  C        C OR G  ≡  G
F AND B  ≡  F        F OR B  ≡  B
H AND D  ≡  H        H OR D  ≡  D
```

4. PROBLEM SOLUTION

The following solution depends on a systematic grouping together of terms of the original expression according to shared subexpressions. For example, *t1, t3,* and *t7* share the subexpression A AND B. Hence:

```
t1 OR T3 OR t7

≡   [ A AND B ] AND [ ( C AND D ) OR ( G AND H ) OR ( K OR L ) ]

≡   [ A AND B ] AND [ ( C OR G OR K ) AND ( C OR G OR L ) AND
                      ( C OR H OR K ) AND ( C OR H OR L ) AND
                      ( D OR G OR K ) AND ( D OR G OR L ) AND
                      ( D OR H OR K ) AND ( D OR H OR L ) ]
```

Examining the eight triplet terms (C OR G OR K), etc., we have:

```
C OR K  ≡   true,  so terms 1 and 3 vanish;
H OR L  ≡   true,  so terms 4 and 8 vanish;
G OR L  ≡   G,     so L vanishes from terms 2 and 6;
C OR G  ≡   G,     so C vanishes from term 2;
D OR K  ≡   D,     so K vanishes from terms 5 and 7;
D OR H  ≡   D,     so H vanishes from term 7;
terms 5 and 6 are now identical, so we can drop one of them.
```

What is left is

```
G AND ( D OR G ) AND D
```

which reduces to just

```
D AND G
```

Hence we see that

```
t1 OR t3 OR t7  ≡   A AND B AND D AND G
                ≡   ( B AND D AND E AND G ) AND A
```

because A ≡ (A AND E).

Analogous arguments can be used to show that

```
t1 OR t4 OR t6  ≡   ( B AND D AND E AND G ) AND C
```

(common subexpression C AND D); also that

```
t2 OR t4 OR t8  ≡   ( B AND D AND E AND G ) AND F
```

(common subexpression E AND F); also that

```
t2 OR t3 OR t9  ≡   ( B AND D AND E AND G ) AND H
```

(common subexpression G AND H); also that

```
t5 OR t6 OR t9  ≡   ( B AND D AND E AND G ) AND ( I AND J )
```

(common subexpression I AND J); and finally that

```
t5 OR t7 OR t8  ≡  ( B AND D AND E AND G ) AND ( K AND L )
```

(common subexpression K AND L). *Note:* Of course, it is legitimate to use terms of the original expression over and over again in the foregoing reductions as we have done, because $X \equiv (X \text{ OR } X)$ for all X.

It follows that the complete original expression

```
t1 OR t2 OR t3 OR t4 OR t5 OR t6 OR t7 OR t8 OR t9
```

reduces to

```
( B AND D AND E AND G ) AND term
```

where "term" is

```
( A OR C OR F OR H OR ( I AND J ) OR ( K AND L ) )
```

Regrouping:

```
( A OR F ) OR ( I AND J ) OR ( C OR H ) OR ( K AND L )
```

Taking the 1st and 2nd parenthesized terms together and the 3rd and 4th likewise:

```
[ ( A OR F OR I ) AND ( A OR F OR J ) ]   OR
[ ( C OR H OR K ) AND ( C OR H OR L ) ]
```

But (A OR I) ≡ (F OR J) ≡ (C OR K) ≡ (H OR L) ≡ *true,* so each of the four triplet terms here reduces to *true,* and hence the overall expression is identically *true.* So the entire original expression reduces to just

```
B AND D AND E AND G
```

—i.e., to the desired target expression. ∎

5. DISCUSSION

We have now formally proved that the two versions of the query are indeed equivalent as claimed. As indicated earlier, however, the real question is whether the system optimizer would be able to transform the original long version into the equivalent short one. In this regard, let me first of all remark that the proof presented in Section 4 is at least *constructive* in nature, in the sense that it actually does what an optimizer would have to do (i.e., it actually reduces the long expression to the short one). By contrast, most of the other proofs I have seen have been *existential* in nature—by which I mean that they showed that each expression implies the other (and hence that the two expressions were logically equivalent and that a transformation procedure must therefore exist), but they did not actually perform the transformation. Such an approach would not be of much use if the short expression were not known ahead of time.

However, if we examine the transformations of Section 4 a little more closely, a number of facts, some of them perhaps a trifle unfortunate, will become apparent:

1. The transformations rely on a knowledge of elementary properties of logic—for example, knowledge of the "absorption law" that X AND $(X \text{ OR } Y) \equiv X$. Some relational optimizers (the better ones) probably do possess such knowledge; almost certainly, however, others do not.

2. The transformations also rely on a knowledge of elementary properties of arithmetic—specifically, knowledge of the fact that zero is less than one (and one is greater than zero). Most current relational optimizers probably do not possess such knowledge; some probably do not even know that ">" is the inverse of "<", i.e., that "$a > b$" is *true* if and only if $b < a$ is *true*.

3. The transformations also rely on knowledge of certain *integrity constraints*—specifically, the constraints that X1 $< =$ X2 and Y1 $< =$ Y2. Transformations that rely on certain integrity constraints being satisfied are referred to as *semantic* transformations, and an optimizer that performs such transformations is said to be doing *semantic optimization* [5]. So far as I know, no DBMS on the market today does anything significant by way of semantic optimization. In fact, most current DBMSs do not even allow integrity constraints to be declared, nor—a fortiori—do they enforce them. (See also the further remarks on this topic in Appendix A to this paper.)

4. The transformations also rely on an arguably tricky set of choices regarding exactly which transformation laws to use, and in which order. For example, we noted in the presentation of the proof in the previous section that certain terms of the original expression had to be used over and over again in the overall transformation process. This fact effectively implies that a certain term, X say, had to be transformed into the expression $X \text{ OR } X \text{ OR } X \text{ OR } \ldots \text{ OR } X$ (as many X's as needed for the said repeated use). Such a transformation does not seem particularly obvious, to say the least. Considerations such as this one tend to suggest that the optimizer might run into combinatorial explosion problems.

From all of the foregoing, I conclude that it is unlikely, given the present state of the art, that a conventional relational optimizer—even a "good" one—would in fact be able to perform the desired transformation (though I would be delighted to be proved wrong in this regard).

6. CONCLUSION

There seem to be a number of conclusions that can be drawn from the discussions of this paper.

1. We should of course continue to strive to make optimizers more and more "intelligent." However, there will always be optimizations that are beyond the capability of the system optimizer at any given stage of its development. Thus, there needs to be a mechanism by which an appropriately skilled user can add specialized, user-written optimization code to the vendor-provided optimizer. This mechanism will probably be part of the "user-defined data type" facility (see point 2 below).

2. I have argued elsewhere [2] that a "full-function" relational system (specifically, one that supported domains properly) would allow appropriately skilled users to define their own data types.* Such data types could be of arbitrary internal complexity (but they would be "encapsulated," meaning that details of their internal structure would not show through to the data type user). The user-defined data type mechanism would also support the specification of user-defined operators for those data types. For example, we might define a RECTANGLE data type, together with an OVERLAPS operator that returns *true* if its two RECTANGLE operands overlap. The code that supports the OVERLAPS operator would be, precisely, an "efficient" (optimized) implementation of the query discussed in the body of this paper (or, rather, a generalized version thereof).

3. The discussions of Section 5 show clearly that it is not enough for the optimizer to be familiar with *relational* transformations. A good optimizer should understand *logical* transformations, *arithmetic* transformations, and so on. A good optimizer should also be aware of *integrity constraints* and be able to take advantage of them.

4. Finally, "doing logic is hard and error-prone for humans, and should be left to computers" (I am indebted to Adrian Larner [6] for this observation; readers who tried to prove the equivalence of the two versions of the query discussed earlier in the paper should readily be convinced of its truth).

---

*This is exactly the point that Stonebraker was making when he argued that relational systems should be extended to incorporate certain object-oriented features [7].

ACKNOWLEDGMENTS

I am grateful to Mike Stonebraker for attracting my attention to the rectangles query in the first place. I am also grateful to Hugh Darwen and Adrian Larner for alternative proofs of the equivalence of the long and short forms of the query and for much enlightening correspondence on the larger matters discussed in this paper.

REFERENCES AND BIBLIOGRAPHY

1. ANSI X3H2 / ISO/IEC JTC1 SC21 WG3 Data Base Languages, (*ISO working draft) Database Language SQL2,* Document X3H2-90-264 (July 1990).

2. C. J. Date, "What Is a Domain?" in C. J. Date, *Relational Database Writings 1985–1989* (Reading, MA: Addison-Wesley, 1990).

3. C. J. Date, "A Contribution to the Study of Database Integrity," in C. J. Date, *Relational Database Writings 1985–1989* (Reading, MA: Addison-Wesley, 1990).

4. C. J. Date and Colin J. White, *A Guide to SQL/DS* (Reading, MA: Addison-Wesley, 1989).

5. Jonathan J. King, "QUIST: A System for Semantic Query Optimization in Relational Databases," *Proc. 7th International Conference on Very Large Data Bases,* Cannes, France (September 1981).

6. Adrian Larner, private communication (July 12th, 1990).

7. Michael Stonebraker, "Three-Dimensional DBMSs," presentation given at DB Expo 90: The National Database Exposition and Conference, San Francisco, CA (May 27–29, 1990).

APPENDIX A:
A NOTE REGARDING CONSTRAINT DEACTIVATION

It is well known that certain integrity constraints cannot be checked "immediately" (i.e., during the processing of individual update operations), but rather have to be deferred to some later time, typically COMMIT time [3]. The preferred approach to this problem (as to so many problems) is *declarative,* meaning that the integrity constraint in question should be explicitly flagged in the database definition by some clause such as "CHECK AT COMMIT."

However, the SQL2 committee [1] is currently proposing an extension to the existing SQL standard by which constraints can be deactivated (and subsequently reactivated) *dynamically:*

```
SET CONSTRAINTS constraints { DEFERRED | IMMEDIATE } ;
```

Furthermore, there is at least one product, namely SQL/DS [4], that already supports such a facility for certain constraints (basically primary and foreign key constraints).

Now, such a facility can clearly be used to defer integrity checks to some later time; indeed, of course, this is the rationale for providing such a feature in the first place. The problem* is that it seriously undermines the potential for semantic optimization. Semantic optimization, to repeat from the body of this paper, is optimization based on semantic knowledge—i.e., on knowledge of the fact that the database satisfies certain integrity constraints. Clearly, if some given constraint can be dynamically deactivated, then the optimizer cannot rely on that constraint being satisfied, and so *cannot use it for semantic optimization purposes.*

Of course, it is true, as already stated in the body of this paper, that products typically do not perform semantic optimization anyway at the time of writing. But they *could,* and in the future I trust they will; the potential payoff could be very significant indeed [5]. It seems a shame to "shoot ourselves in the foot" on this issue before we have even started. (Of course, SQL/DS has already done as much. But that is SQL/DS's problem.)

It is also true, of course, that the preferred approach of stating declar-

---

*The problem we are concerned with here, that is. There are other problems with this feature too, beyond the scope of this appendix. See reference [3].

179

atively that certain constraints are to be checked AT COMMIT also means that those constraints cannot be guaranteed to be satisfied except at transaction boundaries, and hence that the potential for using those constraints for semantic optimization purposes is also somewhat limited. But at least with the declarative approach:

1. The system knows which constraints are deferred and which immediate, and can make use of the immediate ones freely for optimization purposes.

2. Even the deferred ones can be used freely for optimizing read-only transactions.

Note: In the case of the SQL2 proposal, I believe the intent is that COMMIT should force all constraints back into IMMEDIATE mode, meaning that constraints will at least always be satisfied at transaction boundaries—though in fact it is hard to tell from reference [1] exactly *what* the intent is, and in any case the proposals are still subject to change at the time of writing. In the case of SQL/DS, however, a dynamically deactivated constraint remains deactivated—for *everybody*—until such time as the constraint is successfully reactivated, which might be an arbitrarily long time (e.g., days or weeks) later.

13

The Nullologist in Relationland
or
Nothing Really Matters

ABSTRACT

An introduction to the science of *nullology* and its fundamental significance.

COMMENTS ON PUBLICATION

As I explained in my "Comments on Publication" for Chapter 3 of this book, readers were first introduced to Relationland by Hugh Darwen (writing as Andrew Warden) in this book's predecessor *Relational Database Writings 1985–1989*. Chapter 22 of that earlier book in particular discussed the concept—at first sight mind-boggling, but crucially important—of *tables with no columns at all*. Such tables represent just one of the many

Previously unpublished.

places in Relationland where "nullology" rears its head (not at all an ugly head, be it noted). In the paper that follows, Hugh discusses such matters in depth.

Note: I will leave it to Hugh to explain exactly what he means by "nullology," but perhaps I should point out immediately that it has nothing to do with *nulls!*

1. INTRODUCTION

Apropos of nothing in particular, let me tell you a couple of horror stories. They both relate to incidents that occurred to me during my computer programming days. In neither case was I in Relationland at the time. Of course not. Nothing horrid *ever* happens in Relationland.

In the first story, I was in a little-known corner of Pliland. I had decided to write this procedure, you see, to provide myself with a certain user-defined function for use by the other procedures in my program. Unfortunately, the experience I am about to relate was so horrid that I can remember nothing at all about the actual problem at hand. All I can remember is that I decided to implement the function by declaring a one-dimensional array of integers, whose cardinality was given by one of the parameters to the function. If that parameter was called N, then the declaration of the array looked something like this—

```
DECLARE A ( N ) INTEGER ;
```

—and the important part of the code of the procedure was inside loops such as the following:

```
DO I = 1 TO N ;
    things done inside the loop
END ;
```

Using well-known techniques I had just learned at the Software Engineering school, I was able to prove the correctness of this procedure without even testing it. It was a doddle—I quickly discovered the required things called loop invariants, and then I did something called induction, and the mathematics said "Nice one, Hugh, that'll work fine!"

It didn't.

It worked fine most of the time. If I were dishonest, I'd embellish the tale and say that it worked fine in production for several years, until long after I had left that job. But no. I don't distrust mathematics, much, but I *have* learned to distrust computer software, mine and other people's. So, although my Software Engineering teachers had told me this would never be necessary, I decided to *test* my program before shipping it to production. I compiled a list of test cases, insidiously including the one that would pass zero as the value of N to my function (as it happened, this was not at all an unreasonable case to expect).

It was the test case with N = zero that fell over. A run-time error message muttered something to the effect of "Don't be so silly, how can you have an array with zero elements?", followed by "Abort, abort!" and several hundred sheets of memory dump in hexadecimal (this was quite a long time ago, you see).

After a few days and nights agonizing over this—for I was faced with the unbearable prospect of having to rewrite the whole of my *beautiful* 25-line procedure using some mundane and obvious technique that any old hack might have churned out—I hit upon a fix to beat this damn compiler at its own game:

```
DECLARE A ( 0:N ) INTEGER ;
```

For those of you who don't speak this language, what I was now doing was declaring an array of N + 1 elements, of which the first was numbered 0 and the last N. When N was zero, my array had just one element, numbered zero, and all my loops controlled by DO I = 1 TO N worked fine, just as the mathematics had proved they would, being iterated zero times.

My documentation of the final working version included:

"Memory requirement: 125,948 bytes (should have been 125,944)."

At the very instant in which I saw my "N = zero" test case fail, I became, although I did not know this word at the time, a **nullologist**.*

Nullology, the study of nothing at all, was founded by Bob Engles of IBM's Santa Teresa Laboratory. Actually, he subfounded it, as a substudy of what he calls **representology**, the study of the representation of things. According to Engles, the study of the representation of numbers is **number-ology**, and the study of the representation of characters is **characterology**.

Now, nothing at all is, well, just nothing at all. Or, as a mathematician would have it, there's only one *empty set*. Nullologists agree, but note that nothing at all does come in lots of different guises. Hence the worthwhile study of the representation[†] of nothing at all, nullology.

---

*As the example illustrates, it is very often the nullological cases that cause programs (or algorithms, or procedures, or plans, or whatever) to fail. Indeed, an interesting case in point is discussed elsewhere in the present volume [6]. Thus, one great virtue of nullology is that it provides us with a "final" check of correctness, a check that we should take care never to overlook.

[†]Representologists sometimes study how to represent things (particularly interesting to characterologists), sometimes what things represent. Nullologists do a bit of both, but this chapter is mostly to do with what nothing at all can represent.

The nullologist cares about nothing. Really cares about it. The nullologist thinks nothing *really* matters.

Oh, I promised *two* horror stories, didn't I. On the second occasion I was in Rexxland (a rather pleasant, unaggressive country, on the whole—I quite like being there). I devised a form to be presented on the screen for the end-user of my program. The user would type a few things into the indicated places on the form, and my program would use the typed information to conduct a search of a database of documents.

One of the places in the form was for the user to type, optionally, an arbitrary sequence of characters. My program would then list only those documents whose titles included that sequence of characters. For instance, the user might type "elation" to obtain all documents whose title contained the word "relation" (or any derivative thereof), whether spelled with a capital R or a small one. (Of course, titles including words like "correlation" and "elation" would also satisfy this search criterion, but that was a small risk the user was presumably happy to take.)

Inside a "for each document title" loop, therefore, I wrote the following Rexx code:

```
IF POS ( SEARCH_ARG, TITLE ) > 0
THEN
    /* this document required */
ELSE
    /* this document not required */
```

The builtin function POS(*s1,s2*) is defined to return a positive integer *p* if the string *s1* occurs as a substring of the string *s2* starting at position *p* (and does not occur at any position prior to *p*); otherwise it returns zero. At least, that is how I intuitively thought it was defined, until I discovered that my program listed no document titles at all, instead of all of them, when the user typed nothing at all into the form field for the search argument. I therefore had to replace my code by something like the following:

```
IF LENGTH ( SEARCH_ARG ) > 0
THEN
    IF POS ( SEARCH_ARG, TITLE ) > 0
    THEN
        /* this document required */
    ELSE
        /* this document not required */
ELSE
    /* this document required */
```

When you look up POS in the Rexx manual, you find something similar to my definition, but with the proviso ". . . except that zero is returned if *s1* is the empty string" (or words to that effect). So nobody can say the Rexx interpreter wasn't working as specified. That doesn't stop the nullologist from screaming: "But it's *plain wrong!*"

In case you need convincing that it's plain wrong, I could show you the argument that the empty string "occurs" at every position in every string, because if the concatenation of $s3$, $s1$, and $s4$ in that order is equal to $s2$, then $s1$ occurs in $s2$ at position LENGTH($s3$) + 1, and we always feel, don't we, that things are somehow *right* if we find that we have a set of interrelated operators that can neatly be defined in terms of one another (in this case, substring, concatenate, and position). And if you don't care for that argument, I bet you would at least be persuaded that, surely, it is always the case that POS(s,s) = 1. For any s. Even for $s = $ ''.

What's even more convincing is that it's quite difficult to think of a case where you'd be really grateful for POS('',s) returning 0 instead of 1.

So much for my two horror stories. Now let's leave Pliland and Rexxland and go to Relationland, where such nasty things as I have been describing of course never occur. Now, there are sets all over the place in Relationland, and that means the empty set is ubiquitous. Relationland is just the place for a nullologist's field day. And that, I am afraid, inevitably means that the tunnels inside the Askew Wall [1] are littered with nullological blunders—and on this occasion I am, perhaps to your surprise, not even mentioning those nasty, biting things called *nulls!* There aren't any of those in *my* Relationland, but the empty set does present itself—in many utterly respectable guises.*

2. TABLES WITH NO ROWS

The first and perhaps most obvious—certainly the most familiar—of the many manifestations of the empty set in Relationland is in *empty tables.* When we say a table is empty, we mean that its body has no rows.

Now, "table" is a friendly word for the mathematical "relation," as you know, and "relation" is in a sense just another word for "predicate." Seen that way, every row in a table represents a *proposition,* an instantiation of the predicate. If the row is (Renoir,Sisley) and the relation is PAINTED (ARTIST,MODEL), then the predicate is "*artist* painted *model,*" and the row (Renoir,Sisley) provides instances to replace the placeholders *artist* and *model,* yielding the proposition "Renoir painted Sisley." The instances have to be genuine instances of what those placeholders represent (people who were artists or models)—in other words, they have to be members of the *domains* on which the corresponding columns in PAINTED are defined.

---

*I may as well mention right away that there is one such "respectable" guise, namely *empty domains,* for which I was (regretfully) unable to find a truly useful application. I would be delighted to hear from any reader who is able to find such an application.

More generally, the presence of a row *r* in the body of a table T is interpreted as "P*r* is *true*" (where P is the predicate for T). When the body of T is empty, therefore, the interpretation is "There is no row *r* such that P*r* is *true*."

Mathematicians are often very fussy about the uniqueness of the empty set, ϕ. They won't even let you say "Hmm, one empty set is very much the same as any other empty set, really," because such talk is admitting the absurd (to them) possibility that there is more than one empty set. Unfortunately, the same is not true of empty tables. If PAINTED is empty, then nobody painted anybody. If the one-column table USED_OILS (ARTIST) is empty, then nobody used oils. So, those two empty tables aren't the same thing, even though their bodies are both the empty set. Why did I write "unfortunately"? Only because that pleasing nullological observation in set theory, that the empty set is the identity of sets under union—

```
FORALL A ( A UNION φ = A )
```

—doesn't have a direct equivalent in relational algebra. It is, however, the case that T UNION MT, where T is any table and MT is an empty table with the same heading as T, is equal to T. Similarly, T INTERSECT MT is equal to MT, T MINUS MT is equal to T, and MT MINUS T is equal to MT. *Note:* Here and throughout this chapter, I use the dialect of the relational algebra defined in reference [5]. In that dialect, the expressions A UNION B, A INTERSECT B, and A MINUS B are defined only if tables A and B have the same heading. "Having the same heading" is thus the analog in that dialect of what is usually called *union-compatibility*.*

With regard to the other operators of the relational algebra, we can make the following nullological observations. Let MT be an empty table. Then:

- *Restriction:* MT WHERE *cond* is equal to MT, for any restriction condition *cond*.

- *Projection:* MT [*cols*] is an empty table, for any set of column names *cols*. It is not equal to MT, however, unless *cols* names all columns in the heading of MT.

- *Extension:* EXTEND MT *ext-spec* is an empty table, for any extension specification *ext-spec*.

---

*The terms "union-compatible" and "union-compatibility" are not really very good, because union is not the only context in which the concept is relevant. If one-word terms are really necessary, I would vote for *isomorphic* and *isomorphism* (even though these latter terms do tend to be over-used).

- *Cartesian product:* MT TIMES T (or T TIMES MT) is an empty table, for any table T, so long as the headings of T and MT are disjoint (otherwise the operation is not defined). It follows that any variety of (inner) join, natural or otherwise, of MT with T is also an empty table.

- *Division:* MT DIVIDEBY T is an empty table; so too is T DIVIDEBY MT, except in the interesting case where the heading of MT is a subset of the heading of T.* An example of this latter situation is the query

```
SP[S#,P#] DIVIDEBY (P WHERE COLOR = 'Purple')[P#]
```

which gives supplier numbers for suppliers who supply all the purple parts (more precisely, suppliers who *supply at least one part* and supply all the purple parts). If there are no purple parts, then all suppliers mentioned in table SP qualify (i.e., the result is the projection of SP over S#).

- *Summarize:* SUMMARIZE MT *sum-spec* is an empty table, for any summary specification *sum-spec.* This is the cause of a certain amount of grief, because the empty set result is a little counterintuitive in some cases. If nobody painted anybody, then the empty result given by

```
SUMMARIZE PAINTED GROUPBY ( ARTIST )
             ADD COUNT AS NUMBER_OF_MODELS
```

is fine—since there are no artists, there can be no instantiation of the predicate "*artist* painted *number_of_models* people." However,

```
SUMMARIZE PAINTED GROUPBY ( )
             ADD COUNT AS NUMBER_OF_PORTRAITS
```

looks as if it should return the answer to the question "How many portraits were there in total?", which is clearly zero, not nothing at all. Well, I didn't invent SUMMARIZE, but I do take some credit and blame for its tentative appearance in the definition of the relational algebra in reference [5]. If, like many, you are particularly irritated by this little glitch, I offer a remedy, by way of atonement, elsewhere in this book [3].

Strange, that they tried to avoid this glitch inside the Askew Wall, but still managed to go astray:

```
SELECT COUNT(*) AS NUMBER_OF_PORTRAITS
FROM    PAINTED
WHERE   MODEL = 'Manet' ;   /* assume nobody painted Manet */
```

---

*DIVIDEBY here refers to the *generalized* division operator [4].

does indeed deliver a one-row table, with zero for NUMBER_OF_ PORTRAITS. But, as so many authorities and disappointed users have noted:

```
SELECT SUM (SALARY) AS TOT_SAL
FROM    EMP
WHERE   AGE > 109 ;   /* there aren't any employees that old */
```

delivers, not zero, but one of those nasty biting things. The nullological observation here is that when some operation (usually, but not necessarily, commutative and associative) is applied iteratively over an empty list of operands, then the result is the value that is the *identity* under that operation [7]. SUM is the iterative application of "plus," whose identity is 0. If PRODUCT were supported, we would hope to see 1, the identity under "times," when the input table is empty. If the iterative operators ALL and ANY were supported, over a truth-valued data type, then ALL of nothing is *true,* the identity under AND, and ANY of nothing is *false,* the identity under OR.* Where there is no identity (as is the case with AVG, for example), the result is undefined.

3. TABLES WITH NO COLUMNS

This nullological delight is not so well known as the one discussed in the previous section. A good way to approach it is to study the relational *projection* operator. Normally, we talk about projecting a given table, T say, over some subset S of its columns, thereby specifying the columns that we want to keep in the result. But users often say they would like to be able to specify the columns they *don't* want, rather than the ones they do. And Relationlanders often, in lively discussions over a drink or something, talk about "projecting out," to "get rid of" a column, rather than "projecting over" the columns to be retained.

What's really going on? What's really going on is actually *existential quantification,* and we shall soon see that "projecting out" is really the more appropriate way to think about projection. That being the case, anybody with the teeniest little nullological inclination would inquire, "Oh, what on earth does it mean, then, to project out the only (remaining) column?"

The answer, of course, is that you get a table with no columns at all. Can that table have any rows? Yes, it can have one row, but no more than one. If it has one row, that row is necessarily a zero-tuple. Sorry, *the* zero-

---

*As a consequence, if (a) *r* is a variable ranging over table T, (b) C*r* is a truth-valued expression, and (c) T happens to be empty, then EXISTS *r* (C*r*) is *false,* and FORALL *r* (C*r*) is *true.*

tuple. The zero-tuple is the row with no values. If you like to order the attributes of a relation, then the zero-tuple is an empty list. If you prefer to regard tuples as sets of (attribute:value) pairs, then the zero-tuple is an empty set (sorry, *the* empty set). But let's get back to what's *really* going on.

PAINTED [ARTIST]—the projection of PAINTED over ARTIST—is equivalent to the predicate "There exists some *model* such that *artist* painted *model,*" and you are welcome to write that using a backward E if you like. This predicate takes our "base" predicate "*artist* painted *model*" and disposes of one of the placeholders, *model,* not by instantiating it (such as replacing it by the proper name Sisley), but by *quantifying* over it ("*there exists* some *model* such that . . .").

If we repeat this process for the only remaining column, ARTIST— that is, we project the previous result over no columns at all, or we project ARTIST out—we are expressing the predicate "There exists some *artist* such that there exists some *model* such that *artist* painted *model.*" Now both placeholders are wrapped up in quantifiers, so there is nothing left to be instantiated—we already have something that is either *true* or *false.* Such a predicate is the degenerate case, a proposition (and that is a nullological observation in logic).

By the way, if PAINTED is empty, then the result of projecting out both of its columns is also empty; otherwise it is not (it contains the zero-tuple). And those two results are the only possible instances of a table with no columns. Such distinguished beings clearly demand special names of their own, and in reference [9] I introduced them as TABLE_DUM and TABLE_DEE. DUM is the empty one. DEE has a tiny voice, just about able to whisper *yes,* meaning "Yes, the only possible instantiation of my predicate happens to yield a proposition that is *true,*" while poor DUM can manage no more than an apologetic shake of the head.

So, we can immediately note two of the many nullological mistakes that have been made in the Askew Wall. The first is that you are not permitted to specify an empty SELECT-list, as in, e.g.:

```
SELECT
FROM    PAINTED P, USED_OILS U
WHERE   P.ARTIST = U.ARTIST ;
```

As a matter of fact, the foregoing is exactly what a Natural Language Query processor would like to generate in response to the query: "Was anybody painted by an artist who used oils?" Such a processor typically generates an intermediate logical form of the query, looking very much like a predicate. The placeholders in the predicate determine the column names that will be written in the Askew Wall's SELECT-list. When there are no placeholders left in the predicate, the poor old NLQ has to think of something to write. My own suggestion is:

```
SELECT DISTINCT 'Yes' AS ANSWER
FROM    PAINTED P, USED_OILS U
WHERE   P.ARTIST = U.ARTIST ;
```

This query gives a table with one column, called ANSWER, containing the value "Yes" if the answer to the original question is "Yes," but empty otherwise.

Is it possible to write a relational query that will give a real yes-or-no answer to a yes-or-no question? Yes! I will show one way to do it, using relational algebra. Let *R* be an arbitrary relation (specified, in general, by any arbitrary expression of the relational algebra), and let the user's query be (in effect) "Are there any rows in *R*?"

```
T1  :=  R [ ] ;
T2  :=  EXTEND T1 ADD 'Yes' AS ANSWER ;
T3  :=  EXTEND TABLE_DEE ADD 'No' AS ANSWER ;
T4  :=  T2 UNION T3 ;
ANS :=  SUMMARIZE T4 GROUPBY ( ) ADD MAX ( ANSWER ) AS ANSWER ;
```

Yes, it's a little messy, to rely on the alphabetical ordering of the words "Yes" and "No," but the search for neater, more elegant solutions can be left as an exercise for the reader. Note that I expect the constants TABLE_DEE and TABLE_DUM to be available as such in the language, though a one-word shorthand for "EXTEND TABLE_DEE ADD" (such as GENERATE) might be a little less esoteric.

The second of the two nullological mistakes referred to above (concerning columnless tables) in the Askew Wall is that

```
ALTER TABLE T DROP COLUMN C ;
```

is not guaranteed to be acceptable, even if there really is a table called T having a column called C. Specifically, it is not acceptable when C is the *only* column of T. Of course, dropping the only (or last) column may be a problem, if T is already populated and has more than one row. But in that case either C is the primary key of T (and dropping a primary key column from a populated table is dangerous in any case), or T is one of those strange nonrelational tables—the ones that permit duplicate rows—that you are allowed to have inside the Askew Wall.

By the same token, you are not permitted to create a base table with no columns at all. Such a facility could be handy, if you are using a modern tool for designing your database. Perhaps you like to identify your entities, and draw relationship lines connecting them, before you have decided on any attributes.

In reference [9] I list various interesting properties of TABLE_DUM and TABLE_DEE when they are operands of relational operations. For instance, the following tables for UNION, INTERSECT, and MINUS are remarkably reminiscent of the truth tables, in logic, for OR, AND, and AND NOT:

UNION	DEE	DUM
DEE	DEE	DEE
DUM	DEE	DUM

INTERSECT	DEE	DUM
DEE	DEE	DUM
DUM	DUM	DUM

MINUS	DEE	DUM
DEE	DUM	DEE
DUM	DUM	DUM

4. EMPTY LISTS OF OPERANDS

One particularly important observation concerning the use of columnless tables is that T TIMES TABLE_DEE = T, for any T. That is to say, TABLE_DEE is the identity of tables under Cartesian product. Furthermore, T TIMES TABLE_DEE must be the same as T JOIN TABLE_DEE (where JOIN means *natural* join), since no table can have any columns in common with a columnless table. So TABLE_DEE is also the identity under natural join.

I have previously observed that the sum of an empty list of numbers is zero, the identity under addition, that the product of an empty list of numbers is 1, the identity under multiplication, and so on. As Cartesian product and natural join are commutative and associative, we can talk about forming the product or join of a list of tables, without worrying about the order of tables in the list. We can observe that the product or join of exactly one table T is T, so that makes sense of a FROM clause that specifies exactly one table. But we can also observe that the product or join of no tables at all is TABLE_DEE, so the FROM list really ought to be allowed to be empty. Have you ever tried giving the relational query that delivers the time of day, using a builtin function, say TIMENOW? Inside the Askew Wall you probably tried something like this:

```
SELECT TIMENOW AS TIME
FROM    SYSTEM.TABLES ;
```

where SYSTEM.TABLES is the name of the catalog table that tells you what base tables you have in your database. As you happened to have 19 base tables, you saw the time repeated 19 times on your screen, and fixed that by writing the word DISTINCT after SELECT (did you think to yourself "Hmm . . . I thought this stuff was supposed to be based on predicate calculus"?).

Of course, you really should have been able to write

```
SELECT TIMENOW AS TIME
FROM    ;
```

or perhaps just

```
SELECT TIMENOW AS TIME ;
```

where DISTINCT would be what it ought really always to be: superfluous.
Translated into relational algebra, this is

```
EXTEND TABLE_DEE ADD TIMENOW AS TIME
```

for which I have already suggested the shorthand

```
GENERATE TIMENOW AS TIME
```

Having discovered what would be represented by an empty SELECT-
list and an empty FROM-list, if only we were allowed to write such things,
we can now note, in nullological wonder, that the following should be a
legitimate query:

```
SELECT
FROM    ;
```

And if we agree to allow keywords to be omitted when their associated
list is empty, so should this:

```
;
```

In either case, TABLE_DEE is the result (and we could make
TABLE_DUM by adding a WHERE clause such as WHERE 1 = 0—
or, much more elegantly, WHERE *false*).

Relational union is commutative and associative, too, but unfortunately there is no general identity under relational union, because of the
constraint of union-compatibility. We can support unions of unordered lists
of tables, down to a list of one (the union of a single table T is equal to T),
but we cannot define the union of no tables at all. Analogous remarks apply
to relational intersection, of course.

5. EMPTY PARTITIONS OF HEADINGS

Consider the expressions A JOIN B and A DIVIDEBY B (where JOIN
means natural join). In both cases, we have to define *partitions* of the headings of the two relations; in fact, we have to distinguish the "common columns," the columns unique to A, and the columns unique to B. Let us
agree to refer to these three sets of columns as Y, X, and Z, respectively.
Since (a) X and Y are disjoint, Y and Z are disjoint, and X and Z are
disjoint, and (b) JOIN and DIVIDEBY involve only equality comparisons
between column values, we can treat each of X, Y, and Z as though it were
a single column (and note that this simplification is sound even if X or Y

or Z is the empty set). Then the result of A JOIN B has columns X, Y, and Z, and the result of A DIVIDEBY B has columns X and Z (the common column Y is removed).

As I explained earlier in this paper, any relation has a corresponding *predicate*. Loosely speaking, the predicate is what the relation *means*. What then are the predicates for (the results of) A JOIN B and A DIVIDEBY B? In order to discuss this question, we first need to know the predicates for A and B. Let's say those predicates are "*x* is A-related to *y*" and "*z* is B-related to *y*" (*x, y,* and *z* being placeholders corresponding to columns X, Y, and Z, respectively). Then the predicate for A JOIN B is "*x* is A-related to *y* and *z* is B-related to *y*," and the predicate for A DIVIDEBY B is "For every *y* such that *z* is B-related to *y, x* is A-related to *y*."

If any of the placeholders *x, y,* or *z* corresponds to an empty set of columns, then the predicate can be abbreviated by removing that place-holder and the words that connect it with other placeholders, and writing "is an A" or "is a B" (as appropriate) after the placeholder it was connected to. For instance, if X is empty, the predicate for A becomes simply "*y* is an A," and the predicate for A JOIN B becomes "*y* is an A and *z* is B-related to *y*."

Now we can make the following nullological observations. *Note:* For brevity I will not bother to keep repeating "the predicate for" in what follows, but will simply say, e.g., "A JOIN B becomes . . ."—meaning "*the predicate for* A JOIN B becomes [etc.]."

- If Y is empty, A JOIN B and A DIVIDEBY B are both the same as A TIMES B. A JOIN B becomes "*x* is an A and *z* is a B," and A DIVIDEBY B becomes "*z* is a B, *x* is an A," both of which are clearly Cartesian product.

- If X is empty, A JOIN B becomes "*y* is an A and *z* is B-related to *y*" (in fact, it reduces to the semijoin [8] of B with A). An optimizer could usefully note that the join is one-to-many. Conversely, if Z is empty, we have a many-to-one join, "*x* is A-related to *z* and *z* is a B" (the semijoin of A with B).

- If X is empty, A DIVIDEBY B becomes "For every *y* such that *z* is B-related to *y, y* is an A".* On the other hand, if Z is empty, then A DIVIDEBY B becomes "For every *y* such that *y* is a B, *x* is A-related to *y*" (and this is—almost [4]—the special case of division originally proposed by Codd).

---

*Reference [5], page 317, is incorrect in stating that A DIVIDEBY B becomes the same as B DIVIDEBY A when X is empty. Mea culpa, for I say the same in the preface to "Adventures in Relationland," my contribution to this volume's predecessor [8].

- If both X and Z are empty, A JOIN B becomes "*y* is an A and *y* is a B," otherwise known as *intersection*. An intersection is necessarily one-to-one, and an optimizer might do very well to note that fact.

- If both X and Z are empty, A DIVIDEBY B becomes "For every *y* such that *y* is a B, *y* is an A," usually abbreviated to "Every B is an A." On the other hand, B DIVIDEBY A becomes the very different "Every A is a B."

   Notice that the abbreviated forms of these two predicates have no placeholders. That is because the *y* is (universally) quantified, and we already know from our study of projection that quantifying over a placeholder has the effect of "removing" the corresponding column. Therefore A DIVIDEBY B, when A and B are union-compatible, yields a table with no columns, either TABLE_DEE (if it is true that all A's are B's) or TABLE_DUM (otherwise). A DIVIDEBY B thus becomes a way of determining the truth of "B is a subset of A" (do not conclude that these two expressions are equivalent, however—the first is relation-valued, the second truth-valued).

6. EMPTY DETERMINANTS IN FUNCTIONAL DEPENDENCIES

A functional dependency in Relationland is a truth-valued statement about two sets of columns of a table [2]. The notation is

   A → B

pronounced "A determines B" or "B is dependent on A," or simply "A arrow B." The left-hand operand is called the **determinant**, and each member of the right-hand operand is called a **dependant**.

   When A → B is *true,* and B is the empty set, we might be tempted to conclude that A has no dependants, but such a conclusion would be incorrect: We are merely failing to note any such dependants (not even the members of A itself, which are all trivially dependent on A). In fact, A → B, when B is empty, is trivially *true* for all A. If it were not, the axioms of functional dependency theory would be inconsistent, for we have:

   A ≥ B   implies   A → B

(using "≥" to mean "is a superset of") for all A and all B. As every set A is a superset of the empty set, we must conclude that "B is empty" implies "A → B."

   Much more interesting is the case when A, the determinant, is empty. When ϕ → B in a table T, then any two rows in T must agree in value in all columns of B. (This follows from the fact that all rows agree in that mysterious value that is the combination of the values in the empty set of columns, and, by the definition of functional dependence, any two rows that thus agree must also agree in all columns of B.) In the special case where A is empty and B is all of the columns of T, we can note that the empty set satisfies both the uniqueness and minimality requirements for candidate keys, and is therefore a candidate key of T. Furthermore, it must be the *only* candidate key (any other subset of the columns of T would be a superset of A, thus violating the minimality rule), and it is therefore the primary key.

> *Aside:* Incidentally, the foregoing gives the lie to the commonly held belief that a binary relation is necessarily in third normal form! Consider the table USA (COUNTRY,STATE), interpreted as "*state* is a member of *country* (the United States of America)." The FD $\phi \rightarrow$ COUNTRY holds in this table (COUNTRY is, of course, "USA" in every row), and yet the empty set is not a candidate key. *End of aside.*

A table that has the empty set as primary key is constrained to contain at most one row. This property is occasionally useful in database design; as noted in reference [2], it is even more useful when it can be deduced during query decomposition.

Of course, if a primary key can be empty, then so can a foreign key. Let T2 be a table with an empty foreign key, and let T1 be the corresponding target table. Then the referential constraint will be satisfied whenever T1 is nonempty (i.e., contains a single row), and will be violated whenever T1 is empty but T2 is nonempty. Note that *any table whatsoever* can reference T1, since the empty set is a subset of the heading of every table. In particular, any table can reference TABLE_DEE or TABLE_DUM. Referencing TABLE_DEE achieves nothing—the constraint can be violated only if TABLE_DEE were empty, which by definition it is not. On the other hand, a table that references TABLE_DUM is, perhaps usefully, constrained to be empty.

Here's a useful trick, to save you a lot of typing when there's a whole bunch of tables in your database that all need to be emptied at the start of some processing cycle. You set up a table with as few columns as your DBMS permits, and declare the empty set as the primary key of that table. You declare foreign keys referencing this table in all of the tables in the aforementioned bunch. You call the current state "square one," and then you insert a row into the referenced table. Then you populate all of the referencing tables, thereby starting the cyclic process. When the process is to be restarted, you delete the single row from the referenced table. As you had been careful to write ON DELETE CASCADE in all of the foreign key declarations, you are now back to square one. Furthermore, when an extension to the process involves adding a new table to the bunch, you won't have to make any changes to the "getting back to square one" routine. But of course you will need a DBMS that supports empty keys . . .

That keys can be empty lets us breathe a little sigh of relief. It would be awful, indeed, if TABLE_DEE and TABLE_DUM proved to be nasty exceptions to the well-known properties of tables, that every table has at least one candidate key. Indeed, the statement

"none of the columns" determines "all of the columns"

(in connexion with my two very diminutive friends) is not only *true* but degenerates to

$$\phi \to \phi$$

which is, of course, *always* true—a tautology—in any table. Yet, as you can see in the algorithm given in reference [2] for noting interesting functional dependencies during query decomposition, it is not without its uses! There, it is used to "seed" a set of functional dependencies, where starting with the empty set would be very awkward as, the way this algorithm works, no nonempty set can be generated from the empty set.

Such a nullological delight as $\phi \; \phi$ deserves an affectionate name. "Fifi," a tiny and obvious pun, is my pet name for what, I suggest, is the least momentous observation that can be made in Relationland.

ACKNOWLEDGMENTS

I am grateful to Stephen Todd, who first drew my attention to the idea of tables with no columns at all, and thereby set me wondering about all of the other nullological possibilities in Relationland.

REFERENCES AND BIBLIOGRAPHY

1. Hugh Darwen, "The Askew Wall: A Personal Perspective" (in this volume).

2. Hugh Darwen, "The Role of Functional Dependence in Query Decomposition" (in this volume).

3. Hugh Darwen and C. J. Date, "Relation-Valued Attributes" (in this volume).

4. Hugh Darwen and C. J. Date, "Into the Great Divide" (in this volume).

5. C. J. Date, "Relational Algebra," Chapter 13 of *An Introduction to Database Systems: Volume I,* 5th edition (Reading, MA: Addison-Wesley, 1990).

6. C. J. Date, "An Anomaly in Codd's Reduction Algorithm" (in this volume).

7. C. J. Date, "Oh No Not Nulls Again" (in this volume).

8. Andrew Warden, "Adventures In Relationland," in C. J. Date, *Relational Database Writings 1985–1989* (Reading, MA: Addison-Wesley, 1990).

9. Andrew Warden, "Table_Dee and Table_Dum," in C. J. Date, *Relational Database Writings 1985–1989* (Reading, MA: Addison-Wesley, 1990).

14

Relational Database:
Further Misconceptions
Number Three

ABSTRACT

A further selection of strange pronouncements on the topic of relational technology.

COMMENTS ON PUBLICATION

This paper is the latest in an occasional series. The first, entitled "Some Relational Myths Exploded" (subtitle "An Examination of Some Popular Misconceptions Concerning Relational Database Management Systems"), was originally published in two parts in *InfoIMS* (2nd and 3rd Quarter, 1984), and was then republished in my book *Relational Database: Selected*

Previously unpublished.

Writings [1]. That paper was followed by two more, entitled "Relational Database: Further Misconceptions Number One" and "Relational Database: Further Misconceptions Number Two," which were published in the first two issues of *InfoDB* (Spring and Summer, 1986), and then republished (in considerably revised form) in this book's predecessor under the title "Further Relational Myths" [2].

In each of those earlier papers, I documented a few (*very* few!) of the numerous misconceptions regarding relational technology that had recently found their way into print, and attempted to respond to them by pointing out just what the errors were. In the case of references [1] and [2], I also attempted to classify the various misconceptions into categories, picking out themes that seemed to be common to several of the individual misunderstandings and thus identifying a number of what I referred to as "relational myths."

The present paper continues the pattern established by its predecessors, inasmuch as it again quotes a number of recent erroneous statements on the same general subject, from the trade press and elsewhere. This time around, however, I have decided that it is not worth the effort of trying to classify the misconceptions into groups or to identify any more generic "myths." Instead, I have simply allowed the quotes to speak for themselves. Indeed, I have also decided in most cases that it is not even worth bothering to respond, in the belief that the errors are mostly so obvious that additional commentary would be superfluous. In fact, the entire paper could be taken just as a little light relief, were it not for the sad fact that some people who really ought to know better clearly *still* do not understand what relational technology is all about.

1.   INTRODUCTION

By way of introduction, I cannot do better than give a slightly updated version of the abstract from the first paper in this series [1]:

> "Relational database management is one of the key technologies for the 1980s (and beyond), yet the field of relational technology still suffers from a great deal of misunderstanding and misrepresentation. Misconceptions abound. The purpose of this paper is to identify some of those misconceptions."

Without further ado, let us proceed to examine some of the more recent pronouncements. Section titles are taken from the articles or papers from which the quotes themselves have been extracted.

2. WHY LARGE ON-LINE RELATIONAL SYSTEMS DON'T (AND MAY NOT EVER) YIELD GOOD PERFORMANCE

This article was published by W. H. Inmon in 1986 [3]. The best way to sum up the article's general message is in Inmon's own words: "This article will clearly spell out why—**if the relational model consists of only/both a nonprocedural DML and an underlying data base structure for its definition and implementation, then in the face of large amounts of on-line processing and/or large amounts of data, consistent, satisfactory on-line performance is not attainable**" (boldface as in the original article).

1. "There is evidence that relational systems, as they come of age, are fulfilling some of the predictions of poor performance."

2. ". . . there is a major problem with set-at-a-time processing in regard to resource utilization [—namely, that the] number of records to be processed is indeterminate."

    Not always. The number of records to be processed in response to the SQL request

```
SELECT *
FROM    ACCOUNTS
WHERE   ACCOUNT# = '123456' ;          /* access by primary key */
```

    (a typical OLTP-style request, of course) is *very* "determinate." It is important in these matters to compare apples and apples, not apples and oranges.

3. "Another factor contributing to the indeterminate nature of nonprocedural languages is the capability to join data on a common data field. If accessing records using an indeterminate number of resources were not bad enough, joining sets of records exaggerates the extremes that a nonprocedural language can be extended to."

4. "Consistent, satisfactory on-line performance *demands* that there be discipline in the usage of resources, and the very essence of nonprocedural processing is unstructured, undisciplined processing."

    Apples and oranges again. See Quote No. 6 below.

5. "In the general case it is not possible to identify a resource-intensive process *until* the process has already reached the server."

    Not so. Resource-intensive processes can (and must) be identified in a relational system by the system optimizer, prior to execution.

6. "A good example of a large relational data base system that achieves good on-line performance is an airlines reservation system that runs on a Tandem processor. During the peak processing periods, data is ac-

cessed in a structured, disciplined fashion with requests that predictably access limited amounts of data. Nonprocedural requests that do indeterminate set-at-a-time processing are not allowed to run when on-line performance is an issue. But when on-line performance is not an issue, nonprocedural indeterminate processing is done. Performance is achieved by separating the DML from the data base, and restricting DML processing at critical times of the day.''

So controls *are* possible? So good performance *can* be achieved with a large, online relational system? Doesn't this paragraph undermine the entire argument of Inmon's paper?

7. "For IBM to ever achieve high performance levels with DB2, either SQL must be altered to do record-at-a-time processing, or some artificial method (such as limiting the records accessed underneath the covers and, in essence, doing incomplete operations) must be employed. In any case the holy grail of relational theory must be compromised."

8. "One of the great mystiques proclaimed by the relational theorists is that relational theory has a firm mathematical foundation and that is supposed to give relational systems a long term basis for stability. If we are to accept the fact that a nonprocedural DML is the only means to manipulate relational data, then relational theory is at odds with queueing theory, which also has a firm mathematical foundation. An interesting question then becomes, which is more relevant in the real world— queueing theory or relational theory? Queueing theory is a daily fact of life—on the crowded freeways, in the supermarket, at the lunch counter, in the bank, in the bathroom in the morning, and so forth. Applied queueing theory is observable 100 times a day in the life of modern man. Where then is relational theory observable and relevant?"

This one does demand a response (or rather, several responses). First, it is absurd to label the fact that "relational theory has a firm mathematical foundation" a "mystique"; it is only detractors who do not understand the technology that like to decry theory and claim that relational databases are somehow mysterious. Second: Yes, that firm mathematical foundation does provide "a long term basis for stability," for numerous sound and well-known reasons. Third, the point about relational theory being "at odds with queuing theory" (a) is not demonstrated in Inmon's paper, and (much more important) (b) is a complete red herring! (Which do you prefer, Thursdays or porridge? The comparison is about as meaningful.) Fourth, *queues* are a "daily fact of life," but queuing theory (regrettably) is not; indeed, if it were, we might see fewer queues. Fifth, relational theory is certainly "observable and relevant,'' because it consists (in large part) of elements from set theory and predicate logic, which form the basis of much of mathematics (or is Inmon arguing that mathematics is not observable and relevant?). Furthermore, a knowledge of predicate logic enables people to pinpoint the logical errors in arguments such as Inmon's, which I think makes it very relevant indeed.

Finally, this entire quote is an illustration of what is sometimes known as *ignoratio elenchi*—the fallacy of arguing to the wrong point.

9. "If the issue does boil down to a conflict of theories, and the resolution of the conflict is relevancy, then it is a good bet that relational theory must be compromised if it is ever to be useful for large on-line systems. Perhaps a relational foundation is best suited to theoretical mathematicians."

10. "In the final analysis, the marketplace and the end-users in that marketplace will be the best gauge of conflicting theories, set-at-a-time and record-at-a-time, nonprocedural DMLs, and the like. The rhetoric, debate, and hype will all fall away, and the final truth will be molded in the reality of the marketplace."

Now this quote I agree with . . . but prejudiced, uninformed, and misleading articles like this one by Inmon do not help.

3.   A CRITICAL REVIEW OF THE RELATIONAL MODEL – ITS DEFICIENCIES AND INADEQUACIES

This was the title of a presentation by Herbert J. Spencer to the Spring 1986 FOCUS User Group meeting [4]. As in the case of Inmon's article above, the best way to sum up the general message of the presentation is in the speaker's own words: "This session will review several major problems with the Relational Data Model. . . . Special attention will be focused on the functional, semantic and mathematical weaknesses and the inadequacy of this approach when developing full-scale information systems. . . . The theoretical Relational Model [will be] contrasted with the pragmatic data structures available in FOCUS."

1. "*Functionality:* The central JOIN concept forces users to think at a needlessly low level of structural detail, combining three orthogonal concepts:

   (a) one-to-many relationships;
   (b) user-visible navigation;
   (c) existence dependency."

Spencer gives the following by way of "evidence" to support this ludicrous claim:

"(a) Arbitrary assignment of data to relations based on evolving user perspectives of one-to-one or one-to-many relationships between attributes.

"(b) This attribute migration means that programs must be significantly altered and extended in order to meet the evolving requirements thereby generating excessive program maintenance and user re-education.

"(c) The primary/foreign key concept is an add-on by E. F. Codd and does not form any part of the mathematical theory of relations, resulting [sic] in "foreign-key" referential integrity problems."

2. "*Semantics:* The Relational Model captures minimal knowledge of the application environment creating a semantic overload on the TABLE and ATTRIBUTE names. The designer can assign meaning to either a TABLE, KEY, ATTRIBUTE, or FOREIGN.KEY, which must be 'decoded' by each end-user."

3. "*Mathematical bias:* The Relational Model is based on the mathematics of relations and set theory using non-semantic operations (e.g., θ-joins, Cartesian product, etc.) confusing 'unknown-value' with generated-nulls. This forces users seeking information to translate semantic operations (e.g., WHO, WHEN, etc.) into abstract mathematics."

4. "*Artificiality:* [The Relational Model] introduces data structuring concepts which are not familiar to end-users who think in Natural Languages (e.g., 'no component of a *primary key* of a *base relation* can have a *null* value')."

5. "*Transitivity:* Certain column-orderings are semantically significant."

6. "*Key significance:* No agreement exists in the implementations of the Relational Model on the approach to the concept of Primary Keys (e.g., DB2, SQL). The standard theory fails to recognize the dual semantic role of EVENT representations as both a NOUN and a STATEMENT. . . . The concept of primary key is central to data processing but forms no part of the mathematical Theory of Relations (c. 1900) although it is claimed that the relational model relies on a solid theoretical foundation."

7. "*Weak mathematics:* Users are easily confused by creating relations with non-unique rows, by projecting attributes without their corresponding primary keys. This reflects the fundamental problem of the failure of the mathematical Theory of Relations to respect the 'group' property of mathematics, which is found in all useful applications of

mathematics, i.e., the PROJECT operation has no inverse. This corresponds to the semantic inability of the Relational Model to represent relative clauses (or sub-setting).''

8. *"Semantic insensitivity:* Only natural joins are semantically significant, all others are separate selections followed by combination (i.e., set union).''

9. *"Logical data dependency:* [The Relational Model] forces programmers of updates to know if data [is] stored [sic] in REAL or only VIEW representations, as updates cannot be performed on VIEWS formed from more than one real (base) table (e.g., DB2). This forces programs to explicitly 'navigate' through the data structures, thereby eliminating logical data independence, which 'will result in skyrocketing costs in both money and time'.''

10. *"Artificial query syntax:* Users need to introduce temporary programming variables to specify non-trivial queries.''

11. *"Conceptual hierarchies:* The Relational Model cannot represent conceptual hierarchies ('IS-A').''

12. *"Categorical subtypes:* The Relational Model cannot readily represent 'categorical sub-typing' (especially exclusive 'roles').''

13. *"Inferences:* The Relational Model cannot represent logical deductions or inferences, relying exclusively on explicit data occurrences. Accordingly, it cannot represent implicit recursion.''

14. *"Time durations:* The Relational Model cannot represent semantic time durations (inter-record inferences).''

15. *"Sorted data:* The Relational Model explicitly denies the significance of ordered occurrences of data, as it is based on set theory, not lists. As a result, the intrinsic linear ordering of events cannot be adequately represented.''

16. *"Existence:* The Relational Model has no mathematical operators to represent the existential functions, such as COUNT, MAXIMUM, etc., where the results do not form a new table.''

17. *"Names:* [There is a] major impact [in] changing NAME strings once [the] system [is] operational, reflecting unique naming conventions rather than 'names in context'.''

Spencer concludes that: ''The Relational Model forces *all* users to know where all attributes reside (i.e., access by NAMED ASSOCIATION rather than by NAME alone) and to understand the implied semantics for both data integrity and queries and can easily generate anomalous mathematical results from ill-considered use of the PROJECT operator. This results in a minimal level of usability in the real-world for non-programmers and limited productivity gains for programmers. The model reflects the "electro-mechanical" compromise of unit record devices and the discrepancies between access times of RAM and peripheral storage rather than the intrinsic relationships of knowledge."

My basic response to all of the above is:

Whew!!!

I would like to respond in more detail, but it is hard to know where to begin. It's harder still to know where to stop.

4. THE TROUBLE WITH SQL

This article was published by Frank Sweet in June 1988 [5]. It takes several column-inches to criticize SQL for not doing something that relational languages were deliberately never intended to do—namely, providing a means for defining databases at the physical or storage level. The paper also complains that SQL does not support CODASYL-style "sets," and further claims that CODASYL-style record-at-a-time programming is more suitable than SQL for performing database maintenance activity.

1. "The problem with SQL's physical DDL is that it does not exist . . . no one has invented a standard SQL physical DDL syntax yet, and SQL's logical DDL has no words to define inter-entity relationships."

2. ". . . physical choices are unavoidable. Making those choices is largely what we [i.e., physical database designers] get paid to do. It would be useful to employ a language that lets us express them. ANSI SQL does not."

3. ". . . one notorious SQL package offers only one way to access a record, given its parent's key: blindly stumbling about until bumping into it."

4. [Part of a discussion of the CODASYL committee's *modus operandi,* with an implied contrast to the way SQL was developed:] "Passions ran high . . . Every issue seemed to become a matter of principle, and rightly or wrongly, principle was seldom compromised. In CODASYL meetings careers were risked, hairs grayed, and ulcers earned in the struggle to make it right, not necessarily popular."

5. "We use the terms box, entity, base table, and record interchangeably. All three [sic] mean the same thing."

6. ". . . one prophet of the relational model claims that a database must avoid . . . physical access mechanisms to be relationally pure. The gen-

tleman becomes irate with those of us who make a living writing programs—rather than just talking about it—when we point out that the
inescapable consequence of such ideological purity is grinding inefficiency."

7. "All this . . . activity is inside the program's main loop . . .
   CODASYL's record-at-a-time syntax lends itself to this role because
   each OBTAIN retrieves one record. SQL's only way of handling such
   procedural processing is with an imaginary cursor or pointer. You retrieve the entire file with one command (in housekeeping) and then in-
   crement the pointer inside the loop. The process is clumsy, tedious,
   and error-prone. Twenty years ago we called it manual deblocking. We
   thought we had laid it to rest by inventing operating systems."

Now, I am certainly not a fan of cursors—I think there are more elegant
solutions to the problem that cursors are intended to solve—but the senti-
ments expressed in this particular quote are really nonsense. SQL's FETCH
(via a cursor) is directly comparable to CODASYL's OBTAIN, except that
no predefined "sets" are needed. "Entire files" are *not* retrieved. The process is no more "clumsy, tedious, and error-prone" than its CODASYL
analog (though I might agree that it is not much *less* clumsy [etc.] than
CODASYL). Anyway, it has absolutely nothing to do with "manual deblocking." And in what sense, exactly, are cursors "imaginary"?

5. TECHNIQUES FOR PHYSICAL DATA MODELING

This article was published by Frank Sweet in August 1988 [6]. As its title
indicates, its primary concern is with physical, not logical, aspects of the
system. However, the author contends that "Codd's relational model forbids application builders from letting . . . DBMS builders . . . know how
entities are inter-connected," and hence claims that it is not possible in a
relational system for the DBMS "to know what chains, arrays or B-trees it
must maintain."

1. ". . . [the second solution] is to devise a means for our DBMS to access
   statistics, infer relationships from retrieval frequencies, and dynamically put links into the database on its own as it runs . . . no one has
   figured out how to carry out the second solution yet."

   Really? No one? Have you looked inside a good relational DBMS
   recently?

2. ". . . we are compelled to choose between supporting Codd's rules
   with a toy or building a real DBMS that breaks the rules. Such theologi-
   cal purity is pointless, of course. All serious DBMSs employ links de-

fined by developers during design. . . . They must, if they are to work. In practice, they follow Charles Bachman's network model, not Codd's relational model.''

3. "The irony is that [certain DBMSs, including IBM's DB2] claim to be truly relational because they enable explicit links when, in fact, Codd's model forbids precisely that. In reality, they are conceptually networks. But let us stop nitpicking. Real DBMSs use explicit links, they call themselves relational anyway, and no one but Codd seems to mind. In fact, there are signs that even he may be mellowing on this point. After all, he continues to improve the relational model.''

6.   SQL COMPROMISES INTEGRITY

This article was published by Robin Bloor in June 1990 [7]. I have two broad problems with it: its overall message on the one hand, and the quite extraordinarily imprecise language in which that message is expressed on the other. Let me address the message per se first. Bloor claims that "vendor implementations of SQL can . . . [cause] updates to be lost" if transactions run under an isolation level of CS ("cursor stability") instead of RR ("repeatable read"). He further claims that transactions *will* run under CS because "for update intensive applications, RR is not a practical option," a claim that I do not propose to address here, although I do not fully agree with it.

The crux of Bloor's argument is that opening a cursor will sometimes cause the implementation to create a copy of the data (e.g., if the cursor definition involves an ORDER BY clause and no index exists that supports the requested ordering directly): "[Cursors] may be implemented as pointers or as direct copies of data . . . where the cursor is more complex it is likely that the cursor will be held as an actual copy of information *from the buffer*" [7; emphasis added].

I would like to make a couple of points immediately in response to this first quote:

- First, whether the transaction has (a) a pointer into the buffer or (b) a copy of the data from the buffer is, or should be, *entirely irrelevant* so far as updating is concerned; it is merely the difference between what we used to call (in the old days of access methods) "locate-mode" vs. "move-mode" I/O. The point rather is whether the buffer is being used as an I/O area for the real data or as an I/O area for a copy of that data *on the disk;* in other words, the issue is whether the cursor is running through the real data or a copy *on the disk.* I assume that Bloor understands this point, but it's not what he says in his article.

- Second, if the system is going to permit updates via the cursor, then the cursor *will* be running through the real data on the disk (for otherwise updates will simply not be permitted). Indeed, to refer back to my remark above regarding the ORDER BY clause, it is precisely because ORDER BY might cause the cursor to run through a copy of the data that the SQL standard (and every SQL implementation I know) says that the presence of ORDER BY in the cursor declaration means that updates via that cursor will not be allowed. In other words, the whole question of whether the cursor is accessing the real data or a copy— either on the disk or in the buffer—is a *complete red herring* so far as the thesis of the article (i.e., that "SQL compromises integrity") is concerned.

Here now is a simplified version of one of Bloor's examples. It is assumed in this example that Transactions 1 and 2 are both executing under CS isolation level.

1. Transaction 1 retrieves a copy of the record for part 507, showing the price of that part as $155

2. Transaction 2 retrieves a copy of that same record

3. Transaction 1 adds 30 to the price (the $155 becomes $185), writes the record back to the database, and commits

4. Transaction 2 subtracts 10 from the price (the $155 becomes $145), writes the record back to the database, and commits

At Step 4, Transaction 1's update is lost.

Now, we obviously have to assume for the sake of discussion that Bloor is right in saying that some DBMS behaves as suggested by this example; but if so, the DBMS in question is simply *INCORRECT* (it is certainly not implementing cursor stability, whatever else it may be doing). Furthermore, the problem is NOTHING WHATSOEVER TO DO WITH RELATIONAL SYSTEMS; nor is it to do with SQL systems specifically. It is simply the classic "lost update" problem, which CANNOT OCCUR if all transactions execute under (at least) CS isolation level and the DBMS is correctly implemented—but which *can* occur (obviously) in a system, relational or otherwise, that is not correctly implemented. In my opinion it is somewhat mischievous, to say the least, to suggest that the problem is somehow a problem of SQL products or relational products specifically.

This is not the place to explain the lost update problem or CS isolation level in detail; comprehensive explanations can be found in many places— see, e.g., the discussion (under the title of "Level 3 isolation") in reference [8]. Suffice it to say that (under a correct implementation of CS isolation level) the foregoing example will lead either to deadlock or to a serialized execution, depending on whether the implementation uses shared locks (type S) or update locks (type U). It will *not* lead to a lost update.*

To recap, therefore: If some DBMS really does behave as Bloor's example indicates, then that DBMS is simply incorrect. The implication, of course, is that the DBMS vendor does not understand locking. And that implication is a little hard to believe, given that the kind of locking we are discussing here has been thoroughly understood, both pragmatically *and theoretically,†* since at least 1976 [9].

I turn now to my second criticism, the sloppy language in which the message of the paper is expressed. Here are some quotes:

1. "A cursor is a subset of information extracted from one or more tables. . . . More complex cursors can also be created, for instance JOINs can be used to join together data from a number of tables and the cursor can be sorted . . . the cursor allows the user to create subsets of data. . . . The Cursor [sic] is a versatile and useful structure and it is central to the whole idea of SQL, allowing data to be processed in sets."

2. "The Level 1 ANSI standard for SQL says that cursors may be implemented as pointers or as direct copies of data. When implemented as pointers each row in the cursor is a pointer, pointing to the original record which is held in a buffer. . . . Most [DBMSs] will hold simple cursors as pointers. . . . However, where the cursor is more complex it is likely that the cursor will be held as an actual copy of information from the buffer. . . . *This copying of information is the prime reason for updates being lost*" [7; emphasis added].

3. "An RR lock places a lock on the whole of the cursor. . . . However RR locking has a disastrous effect on throughput, especially for large cursors. . . . The situation becomes worse if the cursor consists of a join."

4. "With CS locking it is possible to lose updates."

5. "We have looked at a number of [relational DBMSs], and all of them hold the cursor as record copies on some occasions at least. Thus if they implement CS locking and it is used, they may lose updates."

---

*It is not my intent to mislead the reader here: CS certainly does suffer from certain integrity problems (which is why RR is provided as a safer alternative), but losing updates is not one of them.

†Given the general thrust of Bloor's article, incidentally, it is worth pointing out that this theoretical understanding was *first obtained* in the context of the relational model [9].

6. "There are some products which do not suffer from the problem. Products which do not yet implement SQL such as IDMS, and products like ADABAS and Model 204 which have yet to implement cursors in their versions of SQL are immune. Both Rdb and DBM (IBM's OS/2 database [sic]) do not yet offer CS locking, but both products promise it for a later version, when presumably this problem will manifest itself."

This quote is (again) just mischievous, in my opinion: It clearly suggests that nonSQL products are not subject to the lost update problem, but that introducing SQL support (with cursors and "CS locking") will introduce that problem. It would be more useful, and more honest, to name the products that do allegedly suffer from the problem, in order to allow other people to attempt to reproduce the erroneous results and to allow the vendors to respond publicly to the criticism.

7. "It is worth noting, that this is not the only lost update problem in SQL."

A fascinating remark. Do you believe it—given all of the foregoing discussion?

For the record, here are a few specific examples of sloppy use of technical terms in these quotes:

- A cursor per se is not a "subset of information."
- A cursor per se cannot be "sorted."
- The cursor per se is not what allows "data to be processed in sets."
- ". . . each row in the cursor is a pointer . . . pointing to the . . . record . . . in a buffer"—? Rows are not "in" cursors. A row is not a pointer. The pointer does not point into a buffer.
- "The situation becomes worse if the cursor consists of a join"—but, of course, most SQL dialects do not permit updates via a cursor whose definition involves a join. And a cursor per se cannot "consist of a join."
- "An RR lock" does not "place a lock on the whole of the cursor" ("the whole of the cursor" meaning, presumably, all records accessible via the cursor). Also, the phrase "RR lock" is confused in itself (see the next point below).
- The phrase "CS locking" (or "RR locking") mixes two distinct concepts, the concept of locking per se and the concept of isolation level.
- "DBM (IBM's OS/2 database)"—the product is not a database, it is a database management system.

It is very distressing to find such sloppiness in publications dealing with relational technology of all things, given that (to repeat from reference [1]) one of the objectives of the relational model was precisely to introduce some sorely needed precision and clarity of thinking into the database field.

7. CONCLUSION

This concludes the quotations—for now. It would be nice if Number Four in this sequence of articles turned out never to be needed, but I am not optimistic.

ACKNOWLEDGMENTS

I would like to thank an attendee at one of my seminars, Lucas Kapteijns of KLM Royal Dutch Airlines, for bringing the presentation by Spencer to my attention. I would also like to thank Hugh Darwen and Elliott Mc-Clements for their comments on an earlier draft of this article.

REFERENCES AND BIBLIOGRAPHY

1. C. J. Date, "Some Relational Myths Exploded," in C. J. Date, *Relational Database: Selected Writings* (Reading, MA: Addison-Wesley, 1986).

2. C. J. Date, "Further Relational Myths," in C. J. Date, *Relational Database Writings 1985–1989* (Reading, MA: Addison-Wesley, 1990).

3. W. H. Inmon, "Why Large On-Line Relational Systems Don't (And May Not Ever) Yield Good Performance," *System Development* 6, No. 2 (April 1986). Published by Applied Computer Research Inc., PO Box 9280, Phoenix, AZ 85068.

4. Herbert J. Spencer, "A Critical Review of the Relational Model—Its Deficiencies and Inadequacies," presentation to the FOCUS User Group meeting, New Orleans, LA (Spring 1986).

5. Frank Sweet, "The Trouble with SQL," *Database Programming and Design* 1, No. 6 (June 1988).

6. Frank Sweet, "Techniques for Physical Data Modeling," *Database Programming and Design* 1, No. 8 (August 1988).

7. Robin Bloor, "SQL Compromises Integrity," *Daemon* 1, No. 1, ButlerBloor Ltd., Milton Keynes, England (June 1990).

8. C. J. Date, "Concurrency," in C. J. Date, *An Introduction to Database Systems: Volume II* (Reading, MA: Addison-Wesley, 1983).

9. K. P. Eswaran, J. N. Gray, R. A. Lorie, and I. L. Traiger, "The Notions of Consistency and Predicate Locks in a Data Base System," *Communications of the ACM* 19, No. 11 (November 1976).

THE RELATIONAL MODEL

An Introduction

by
Hugh Darwen

As the founding father of the Relational Model of Data and author of one of the best known research papers in the history of computing, E. F. Codd richly deserves the unique position he occupies in the relational arena and the general high regard in which his vision of 1970 is held. I do not know of any other field in computer science that can be said to stem so entirely from the original contribution of a single researcher as much as the relational field does.

I am sure, therefore, that it is not without a very great deal of careful deliberation that Chris Date, in the next two chapters, takes on the daunting task of criticizing and, indeed, challenging two important recent works by Codd, namely his 1985 and 1990 definitions of the Relational Model (RM/V1 and RM/V2). These works by Codd are important because they are bound to be very widely read, and the task is daunting for two reasons. First, there is undoubtedly very much criticizing and challenging to be done—that is to say, I find myself in very broad agreement with what Date has to say in these chapters, which is why I offered to write these brief introductory remarks. Second, it is more than usually difficult, in the circumstances, to maintain the complete objectivity that one would expect in criticism of the work of any other writer in the field.

First, regarding RM/V1: It seems to me that Version 1 is, or should be, concerned with *the fundamental core* of the whole relational approach—i.e., with the definition of the term "relation" and various associated terms, and of the primitive operators available for the formulation of relational expressions. It is crucially important to get the fundamental core right first; yet, as Date explains in the first of his two chapters, there are numerous aspects of Codd's 1985 definition that are somewhat questionable, to say the least.

Second, turning to RM/V2: RM/V2 seems to be an attempt at an abstract prescription for a database management system that aims at a great diversity of objectives. Certainly it casts its net very wide. Of the several unfortunate consequences of this wide-ranging nature, the one that distresses me the most is the failure to distinguish the fundamental core (as discussed above) from all the other aspects of databases and database management. While the way we address these other topics is likely to be greatly influenced by our choice of data model, they are all—and this is one of the Relational Model's many great strengths—completely orthogonal to the definition of the fundamental core. And I find the prescriptions of RM/V2 to contain a mixture of proposals, some truly independent of the core (hence possibly debatable, but in a sense irrelevant), and others that are clearly part of the core but wrong.

An example of an area where I find RM/V2 irrelevant in the foregoing sense is that of data types (for attributes in relations) and their associated operators—Codd's class F (functions). This topic is indisputably orthogonal to the Relational Model; I maintain, therefore, that it is unreasonable to *require* that certain data types be supported. For instance, RM/V2 prescribes the usual scalar functions, "plus," "minus," "times," and "divide," implying that support for a numeric data type is a *sine qua non*. I find it much easier to imagine a fully relational system that fails to support numbers, than one that fails to support a truth-valued data type!

An example of the inverse, where RM/V2 is relevant but patently wrong, is in its prescription for the naming of columns. The model as I was taught it in the early seventies merely required that every column have a name, different from the name of every other column in the same table. Exactly how column names were to be assigned was left, quite reasonably, as an implementation choice.* Any implementation that now takes the RM/V2 prescription for column naming seriously will inevitably suffer from harmful defects.

These two examples should be sufficient to warn the reader to treat RM/V1 and RM/V2 circumspectly. Date's treatment of these and so many other debatable matters should serve to reassure the reader that alternative recommendations can be found elsewhere in the literature, and that the Relational Model of Data remains worthy of attention.

---

*Doing it right turned out to be a nontrivial matter!—so much so, that the first (and, so far, only) somewhat-relational language to achieve widespread use got it wrong.

15

Notes Toward a Reconstituted Definition of the Relational Model Version 1 (RM/V1)

ABSTRACT

Codd's 1985 definition of the relational model is summarized and criticized, and an alternative definition suggested.

COMMENTS ON PUBLICATION

In 1985, Codd published the latest in a succession of definitions of the relational model [9]. As the Abstract above indicates, the purpose of the present paper is (in part) to criticize that definition. Now, it is well known that I have been a relational advocate for many years, and I certainly do not

---

Previously unpublished.

wish to be thought of as criticizing the basic idea of the relational model per se; on the contrary, I felt at the time when Codd first introduced it, and I still feel now, that his original paper [5] was a work of genius, and he fully deserves all of the recognition that has come his way as a result of that major contribution.

But the 1985 definition bothered me in several respects—it extended the original ideas in what seemed to me to be some rather questionable ways—and I felt it necessary to offer a dissenting opinion. And indeed I did exactly that, articulating a variety of concerns, both in print and in live discussion, both with Codd himself and with other database professionals, on numerous occasions over the period 1985–1990. Until I wrote the present paper, however, I had not tried to draw all of my objections together into a single published document (although some of them did find their way, in somewhat muted form, into the 5th edition of my book *An Introduction to Database Systems: Volume I* [16]).

The paper that follows, then, originated as an attempt to identify the various aspects of Codd's 1985 definition that bothered me. For each such aspect, the paper either explains just why I felt there was cause for concern, or it gives a reference to some other publication that contains such an explanation. But, of course, the very act of articulating my concerns led me, inevitably, to a proposal—or at least the beginnings of a proposal—for an alternative definition of my own. The emphasis of the paper thus changed in the writing: I now feel its significance (what significance it may have) lies not so much in the fact that it documents a dissenting opinion, but rather in the fact that it makes a set of specific proposals for revision—in other words, it suggests a "reconstituted definition" of the relational model, offered (in all humility) as a replacement for the version of reference [9].

Note: In a recent book [12], Codd has described what he calls Version 2 of the model, referring to the previous version as Version 1.* As indicated above, the present paper is concerned with Version 1 only, although, since Version 2 is intended to be an upward-compatible extension of Version 1, the criticisms it levels at Version 1 apply to Version 2 also. I do feel strongly that it is important to get the foundation (i.e., "Version 1") right first before attempting to extend that foundation to any kind of "Version 2."

---

*I am assuming here that Codd is using the term "Version 1" to refer to the 1985 version specifically, although in fact his book [12] is not clear on this point: On the one hand, it says (page vi) that Version 1 consists of "the total content of [a series of papers published prior to 1979]"; on the other hand, it also says (page 10) that Version 1 contains "approximately 50 features," whereas the 1985 version (which certainly has more features than the pre-1979 versions did) still contains only 30.

tive features, although the boundaries between these categories are not completely clearcut, as will be seen. The present section considers the structural features, and Sections 6 and 7 consider the integrity and manipulative features respectively.

Before getting into details, there is one point I would like to make absolutely clear: I specifically do not wish to address the question at this juncture of what it is that constitutes a "relational DBMS".* I am much more interested in trying to define the scope and potential of (my preferred version of) the model; how much of that definition a system has to support in order to qualify as a "genuine" relational DBMS is an interesting but separate issue, one that is beyond the scope of the present discussion. I am specifically not claiming that a "genuine" relational system has to support all of the features described herein.

For brevity, however (and despite the foregoing disclaimer), the various features of the model are mostly described in a *prescriptive manner*—i.e., the definitions typically take the form "The system must support [the feature in question]"—even though this style of definition is not my preferred style.

Domain

- *Overall requirements:* I have indicated elsewhere what I believe full support for domains should consist of (see the proposals of reference [24], also the minor clarification of those proposals in reference [29]). Essentially, it is my position that a domain is nothing more nor less than a *data type,* either builtin (i.e., system-defined) or, more generally, user-defined. *Note:* For the benefit of readers who do not have access to reference [24], I should emphasize the point that I am using the term "data type" here in the sense in which that term is usually understood in modern programming language circles. I am most certainly NOT using it to refer merely to such elementary data types as FLOAT, FIXED DECIMAL, etc. See further discussion below.

- *Scalar values:* It is convenient to refer to the values in a domain as *scalars,* even though (as a consequence of the fact that domains can be user-defined) those values are potentially of arbitrary internal complexity. The point is, however, that the internal structure of such values is not visible to or "understood by" the DBMS (at least in principle). On the contrary, domain values (and therefore attribute values—see later) are always "atomic," and relations are thus always normalized, from

---

*Reference [9], by contrast, does consider this question. See Appendix D.

the DBMS's point of view [29]. Access to the internals of any given value, where such access is necessary, should be by means of appropriate operators or functions that are provided as part of the domain definition.

- *Builtin domains:* The system must provide a set of builtin or system-defined domains, each with an appropriate set of operators (including conversion or coercion operators [24]). The precise set of required builtin domains is not important for present purposes, but will presumably include the usual primitive data types—boolean,* bit string, character string, integer, real, etc. Once again, however, note that the DBMS per se does not need to "understand" these data types and their associated operators—it only needs to know how to invoke the procedures that implement the operators, as and when appropriate.

- *User-defined domains:* As already indicated, the system must provide a mechanism for users to define their own domains or data types. That mechanism must include support for user-defined operators or functions and support for type inheritance (both "structural" and "behavioral" inheritance). Note yet again, however, that the DBMS per se does not need to understand these data types and operators, it just needs to know how to invoke the procedures that implement the operators as and when appropriate.

- *No composite domains:* As mentioned earlier in this paper, I now believe that "composite domains" (meaning combinations of other domains, where the specifics of that combination are *known to the DBMS*) should *not* be supported. The reason is that such a facility becomes unnecessary (and an unnecessary complication to boot) if full support for user-defined domains is available.

- *Closed set of domains:* The complete set of domains that applies to any given database must be a closed set, in the sense that the result of evaluating any legal scalar-valued expression (i.e., any legal expression whose operands are values from those domains) must itself be a value in some domain of the set. *Note:* "Scalar-valued expression" is abbreviated throughout the rest of this paper to just "scalar expression."

- *Literals:* For builtin domains, the system must provide a way of specifying literal values from those domains. For user-defined domains, it must provide a way of defining how such literal values can be specified.

---

*The system *must* support a boolean data type, given that (a) the complete set of domains is required to be a closed set (see later), and (b) the result of any comparison operation (or, more generally, any truth-valued expression) is obviously a boolean value. I note in passing that such a data type is conspicuous by its absence in most current dialects of SQL, including in particular the dialect of the SQL standard [2].

- *Scalar expressions:* The system must know exactly which scalar expressions are legal. For each such legal expression, it must know the domain of the result. In the case of expressions that involve a user-defined domain, it is the responsibility of the user defining the domain to specify the domain of the result of each such expression. Such specifications will be provided as part of the process of defining the domain in question.

- *Missing information:* The system does *not* support three- or four-valued logic or "nulls" based on such a logic. Instead, it supports a "default values" scheme for representing missing information along the lines sketched in reference [32].

Relations

- *Overall requirements:* The system must support relations* as described in reference [29]. All relations are *normalized* (i.e., in at least first normal form). Some relations (those that are explicitly declared) are *named,* others (those that are final or intermediate results of evaluating relation-valued expressions) are unnamed. All relations, named or unnamed, have a proper *heading* [18] and a system-known set of *candidate keys* [13]. *Base* relations have a declared (and hence system-known) *primary* key. Relations never contain duplicate tuples, by definition. *Note:* "Relation-valued expression" is abbreviated throughout the rest of this paper to just "relational expression."

- *Constructors:* The system must provide a way of constructing tuples from sets (possibly empty sets) of scalar expressions and a way of constructing relations from sets (possibly empty sets) of such constructed tuples. There must be a way of specifying the candidate keys for constructed relations.

- *Selectors:* The system must provide a way of selecting a tuple from a relation and a way of selecting an attribute value from a tuple. Selecting a tuple from a relation is done by first restricting the relation (see later) to that subrelation that contains just the tuple desired† and then extracting the desired tuple by means of an appropriate coercion (i.e., conversion) operation. Selecting an attribute value from a tuple is done by first specifying the relevant attribute name, which projects out a

---

*And nothing but relations! That is, the only kind of composite object in the model—the only kind of composite object that is "understood" by the DBMS—is the normalized relation. See reference [29] for further discussion of this point.

†In the common special case where the relation has a declared primary key—in particular, in the case of a base relation—the desired subrelation can be specified by means of the relevant primary key value.

subtuple of degree one from the given tuple, and then extracting the desired value by means of an appropriate coercion operation (again).

- *Relational expressions:* The system must know exactly which relational expressions are legal. Each such expression defines an *expressible relation*.

- *Base relations and derived relations:* The system must support both base relations and derived relations. A base relation is a named relation that is not expressible in terms of other named relations. A derived relation is an expressible relation that is not a base relation. (Note, however, that some writers use "derived relation" to refer to what I am here calling an expressible relation.)

- *Views:* The system must allow any legal relational expression to be given a name and saved as a view definition. All retrieval operations must be supported against views. Update operations must be supported where theoretically possible.

- *Snapshots:* The system must allow any legal relational expression to be given a name and saved as a snapshot definition. All retrieval operations are supported against snapshots. Update operations are not supported, except for the system-managed automatic refreshing that is performed at intervals in accordance with specifications in the snapshot definition.

- *Temporary relations:* The system should support temporary base relations and temporary views. (*Note:* A temporary view is basically just a mechanism for dynamically assigning a name to an arbitrary relational expression, for use in subsequent expressions [19].) Such relations are dropped automatically at some appropriate time—e.g., end-of-transaction or end-of-session—without the need for explicit "drop" actions on the part of the user.

- *Attributes:* All attributes of all relations, named and unnamed, have a proper attribute name, i.e., a simple (unqualified) name that is unique within the containing relation.* Composite attributes are not supported.

- *Relational assignment:* The system supports a relational assignment operator by means of which the value of a specified relational expression can be assigned to a named relation. The source and target of the assignment must be union-compatible. See reference [18] for further discussion.

---

*In this connexion, incidentally, I categorically reject the naming proposals of RM/V2 [12], for more reasons than we have room to discuss here. See reference [31].

■ *Relational comparisons:* The system supports a set of relational comparison operators ("equals," "subset of," etc.) by means of which the values of two relational expressions can be compared. The comparands must be union-compatible. *Note:* The comparison operator "ϵ" (for testing whether a specified tuple appears within a specified relation) might also be provided for reasons of usability. However, the operator is strictly unnecessary, given the combination of (a) the existence of the "subset of" operator and (b) the ability to construct a relation from a specified tuple (see the discussion of "Constructors" above).

6. THE INTEGRITY FEATURES REVISITED

It could be argued that the integrity features of the model are less fundamental than the structural and manipulative features. Certainly the basic objects (i.e., the relations themselves) and the basic operators (i.e., the relational algebra) are *more* fundamental, and it is crucially important to get those constructs right first; for if we get those parts of the model wrong in any way, then we will get everything else wrong a fortiori. But—in the perhaps pious hope that the objects and operators are *not* wrong—it clearly seems worthwhile to try to give a "definitive" set of requirements for the integrity features also (especially since those features are obviously of great practical significance). So here goes:

■ *Overall requirements:* The system should permit the declarative specification of integrity rules along the lines described in reference [27]. Domain vs. relation, single- vs. multi-variable, state vs. transition, and immediate vs. deferred rules should all be supported. All rules should be uniquely named and should include (a) an appropriate trigger condition (at least implicitly), (b) the constraint itself (an arbitrary truth-valued expression, in general), and (c) an appropriate violation response (again, at least implicitly). *Note:* See reference [27] for detailed explanations of the terms "trigger condition" and "violation response."

■ *Domain integrity:* For each domain, the system requires an explicit or implicit specification of the set of values that constitute that domain. For each attribute of each base relation, the system requires a specification of the underlying domain, and it enforces the constraint that every value of that attribute is indeed a legal value from that domain. For other named relations, the system will infer all relevant domains, though explicit specifications may still be desirable in some situations.

 Note: The foregoing requirements are in accordance with the basic domain integrity metarule of the relational model [17].

- *Candidate keys:* First, a definition. A *candidate key* for a given relation
  R is a subset (possibly an empty subset [37]) of the attributes of *R,* say
  K, such that, at any given time:

  1. (*Uniqueness property*) No two distinct tuples of *R* have the same
     value for *K.*

  2. (*Minimality property*) No proper subset of *K* has the uniqueness
     property.

  The system supports the declaration of zero or more candidate keys for
  each named relation. In the case of base relations (only), it *requires* at
  least one such declaration. In the case of other named relations, the
  system will infer a set of candidate keys anyway [13], but explicit declarations may still be desirable in some situations (see Appendix A). The
  system enforces the uniqueness property for all declared candidate
  keys.

- *Primary keys:* In the case of base relations, at least, the system requires
  that exactly one candidate key be designated as the primary key for that
  relation. *Note:* There is no direct counterpart of Codd's entity integrity
  rule (or rather metarule); see Appendix B for further discussion of this
  point. I could however easily be persuaded to reinterpret the term "entity integrity" and apply it to the requirement of the present paragraph—namely, that every base relation have exactly one primary key.
  (Especially as most people already think this is what the entity integrity
  rule says anyway [17].)

- *Foreign keys:* Again we start with some definitions. Let *R2* be a base
  relation and let *Y* be a subset (possibly an empty subset [37]) of the
  attributes of *R2*. If there exists a base relation *R1* (not necessarily distinct from *R2*) with primary key *X* such that at any given time, every
  value of *Y* in *R2* is equal to the value of *X* in some tuple of *R1*, then
  Y is called a *foreign key*. *R1* and *R2* are the *referenced* (or *target*) relation and the *referencing* relation, respectively. The constraint that each
  value of *Y* in *R2* must be equal to some value of *X* in *R1* is a *referential
  constraint.* The problem of ensuring that all referential constraints are
  satisfied is the *referential integrity* problem.*

  The system supports the declaration of zero or more foreign keys

---

*I have explained elsewhere (see, e.g., reference [17]) that the foreign key and referential integ-
rity concepts are inextricably interwoven. In fact, of course, they are defined in terms of one
another. Thus, "support for referential integrity" and "support for foreign keys" mean essentially the same thing.

for each base relation. Each such declaration specifies (at a minimum) the corresponding target relation. For each such declaration, the system enforces the corresponding referential constraint.

Note: The foregoing requirements are in accordance with the basic referential integrity metarule of the relational model [17], except that (a) for reasons discussed in Appendix B, I have excluded the possibility that a foreign key value might be null, and (b) for reasons discussed in reference [26], I have also excluded the possibility—tacitly allowed by Codd in reference [7]—that a foreign key might correspond to multiple distinct target relations. Also, the definition of what it means for a foreign key value and a primary key value to be equal is a trifle complex. For this reason, I defer that definition to Appendix C.

- *Database-specific integrity:* All of the integrity rules sketched above are database-specific in a sense, since they are clearly defined in terms of the domains, candidate keys, primary keys, and foreign keys that happen to apply to the database in question. However, those rules are all rules that are effectively demanded by the relational model per se (or rather by the domain and key constructs of the relational model); they can thus be thought of as *generic* rules, since every database will be subject to an analogous set of such rules. In contrast to those generic rules, every database will also be subject to an arbitrary number of arbitrarily complex *specific* rules. The system must support the declarative specification of such database-specific rules (and must enforce them, of course). See the "Overall requirements" above.

7. THE MANIPULATIVE FEATURES REVISITED

- *Overall requirements:* The system should support a version of the relational algebra* that:

(a) Is properly closed with respect to attribute naming [18,35];
(b) Is strongly typed [24], which implies (among other things) that it should *not* support any special "domain check override" operations;
(c) Is based firmly on traditional two-valued logic [28], which implies (among other things) that it should *not* support any special "maybe" operations, and that any "outer" operations it does support will require some redefinition; and

---

*Or a language that is functionally equivalent to such a version.

(d) Is able, given declarations of functional dependencies and candidate keys for base relations, to deduce functional dependencies and candidate keys for the result of any legal relational expression [13].

- *Name-based operations:* All operations* are defined in accordance with Warden's *marriage principle* [36], which guarantees the "proper closure" referred to in (c) above. An "attribute rename" operator is provided [18].

- *Restrict:* The system supports the restriction operator as defined in reference [18], except that, as suggested in Section 4 of this paper, the restriction condition is generalized to permit *any truth-valued expression*—provided only that the expression in question can be evaluated for a given tuple by examining just that tuple in isolation.

    Note: For reasons of familiarity and "user-friendliness," the particular case where the truth-valued expression is just a simple comparison, or combination of such comparisons, will probably enjoy special syntactic treatment. In other words, a restriction condition such as

    ```
    X = 3 OR Y > Z
    ```

    will probably be written exactly as shown, just as it is in (e.g.) SQL today. But this fact should not mislead the reader into thinking that the DBMS "understands" such expressions, any more than it "understands" the expression FOO(x) where FOO is an arbitrary, user-defined, truth-valued function.

- *Project:* The system supports the projection operator as defined in reference [18].

- *Cartesian product:* The system supports the Cartesian product operator as defined in reference [18]. Note that, in contrast to Codd [9], I do think it worthwhile to include the Cartesian product operator explicitly.[†] Here is a simple example of a query that needs it: "Find supplier-number / part-number pairs such that the indicated supplier does not supply the indicated part" (assuming the suppliers-and-parts database as usual [16]). Relational algebra formulation:

    ```
    ( S.S# TIMES P.P# ) MINUS SP [ S#, P# ]
    ```

    Or if you prefer SQL:

---

*All binary operations, that is. Marriage requires two players.

[†]Even though it can be regarded as a degenerate case of our version of natural join. The (perhaps rather minor) difference between TIMES and JOIN is that with TIMES it is an error if the operands have any column names in common.

```
SELECT  S.*,  P.*
FROM    S, P
WHERE   NOT EXISTS
      ( SELECT *
        FROM    SP
        WHERE   SP.S# = S.S#
        AND     SP.P# = P.P# ) ;
```

This SQL expression is an almost direct transliteration of the relational algebra version, of course.

- *Union:* The system supports the union operator as defined in reference [18].

- *Intersect:* The system supports the intersection operator as defined in reference [18]. Of course, intersection is not strictly necessary, since (as already explained) it is not primitive, but it is convenient to have a special name and special syntax for this comparatively common combination of primitive operators.

- *Difference:* The system supports the difference operator as defined in reference [18].

- *Natural join:* The system *directly* supports the natural join operator as defined in reference [18].

- *θ-join:* The system supports the θ-join operator as defined in reference [18]. Of course, the system *must* support θ-join, since I have already said that it must support restriction and Cartesian product, and I am not proposing any special syntax for the operation here (the syntax used in reference [18] is perfectly adequate). Nevertheless, it is convenient to have a single name ("θ-join") for the operation for use in informal discussion (formal discussion too, for that matter), in order to avoid tedious circumlocutions.

- *Divide:* The system supports a *generalized* version of the division operator, as discussed in reference [15].

- *Extend:* The system supports the "extend" operator as defined in reference [18]. For readers who may not be familiar with this operator, I give a single example here (taken from reference [18]). The expression

```
EXTEND P ADD ( WEIGHT * 454 ) AS GMWT
```

evaluates to a relation with the same heading as relation P, except that it additionally includes an attribute called GMWT, with values computed in accordance with the specified scalar expression (WEIGHT * 454). *Note:* The precise syntax is not important, of course.

■ *Summarize:* The system supports the "summarize" operator as defined in reference [18]. For readers who may not be familiar with this operator, I give a single example here (taken from reference [18]). The expression

```
SUMMARIZE SP GROUPBY ( P# ) ADD SUM ( QTY ) AS TOTQTY
```

evaluates to a relation with heading (P#,TOTQTY), in which there is one tuple for each distinct P# value in SP, giving that P# value and the corresponding total quantity. *Note:* Again, the precise syntax is not important. Also, of course, other aggregate operators (MAX, MIN, AVG, etc.) should be supported as well as SUM.

■ *Left outer natural join:* The system supports the left outer natural join operator as defined by Darwen in reference [14]. Actually this operator is not strictly necessary (once again it is not primitive); as with intersection and division, however, it is convenient to have a special name and special syntax for this comparatively common combination of primitive operators.

   Note: Darwen's version of outer join is deliberately *not* completely general. Instead, it is "constrained to a well-defined subset"—actually the sensible subset—"of the many varieties of outer join that can be distinguished" [14]. Furthermore, it does not generate nulls in its result.

   Note too that this is the only "outer" operation I choose to include. I reject other forms of outer join for essentially the reasons given by Darwen in reference [14]. I reject outer union for essentially the reasons given by Warden in reference [38]. I reject Codd's original outer intersection and difference operators [7] for reasons I have previously given in reference [18]. And I reject Codd's revised outer intersection and difference (and union) operators [12] for essentially the same reasons that I reject the original outer union—not to mention the fact that their definition seems extremely complex (and ad hoc).

■ *Single-tuple INSERT:* The system supports an INSERT operator that inserts a constructed tuple (see "Constructors" in Section 5) into a specified relation.*

■ *Multi-tuple INSERT:* The system supports an INSERT operator that inserts a specified set of tuples into a specified relation. The tuples to be inserted are specified by means of an appropriate relational expression.

---

*I include single- as well as multi-tuple versions of each of the operators INSERT, UPDATE, and DELETE. Strictly speaking, of course, the single-tuple versions are redundant (equivalent function can be provided in every case by means of [special cases of] the multi-tuple versions); however, experience in the use of relational systems strongly suggests that direct support of single-tuple operators is desirable in practice.

- *Single-tuple UPDATE:* The system supports an UPDATE operator that updates a specified tuple within a specified relation in accordance with a specified set of assignments to specified target attributes. The update values are specified by appropriate scalar expressions. The tuple to be updated is specified by means of its primary key value. It is an error if the specified relation has no declared primary key (as might be the case with a view, for example).

- *Multi-tuple UPDATE:* The system supports an UPDATE operator that updates a specified set of tuples within a specified relation in accordance with a specified set of assignments to specified target attributes. The update values are specified by appropriate scalar expressions. The tuples to be updated are specified by means of an appropriate relational expression.

- *Single-tuple DELETE:* The system supports a DELETE operator that deletes a specified tuple from a specified relation. The tuple to be deleted is specified by means of its primary key value. It is an error if the specified relation has no declared primary key.

- *Multi-tuple DELETE:* The system supports a DELETE operator that deletes a specified set of tuples from a specified relation. The tuples to be deleted are specified by means of an appropriate relational expression.

8. CONCLUSION

This concludes my—necessarily somewhat sketchy—presentation of my own "Version 1" of the relational model. As can be seen, it differs significantly from the version presented by Codd in reference [9], and I have given my reasons (or at least some of those reasons) for thinking it considerably preferable. So what should we conclude?

Well, there are clearly two broad options: We could just accept Codd's definition anyway; or we could try to agree on a set of changes to that definition, along the lines suggested in this paper. Naturally, I would vote for the second option. But note that, given the current state of affairs, it no longer really makes any sense to talk about "the" relational model; that is, I do not think we can even attach any unambiguous meaning to the phrase "the relational model" at this time. (In fact, it could be argued that this has been the situation for some time anyway [34].)

It seems to me, therefore, that, for better or worse, we simply have to accept that there are indeed several different versions of the model, and the industry—users, vendors, researchers, standards bodies, and anyone else who might be interested—will just have to decide which version it wants to run with. After all, Codd himself has described three distinct "official" versions, namely the original model (now referred to as RM/V1), the extended version RM/T [7], and "The Relational Model, Version 2" (RM/V2). He has also described at least four different versions of RM/V1 [5,7,8,9] (some of them mutually incompatible, incidentally—for instance, the definition of "foreign key" has changed several times [25]).

Whichever way the industry decides to go, however, one thing is certain: The model will continue to evolve. Indeed, Codd's book on RM/V2 [12] indicates that he is already thinking about a "Version 3" (RM/V3), and also hints that further versions (RM/V4, RM/V5, RM/V6, etc.) will continue to be defined at regular intervals.

ACKNOWLEDGMENTS

Among the numerous friends and colleagues who have helped me crystallize and organize my thinking on the topics discussed in this paper over the past several years, there are a few whose influence has been perhaps more significant than most. First of all, of course, there is Ted Codd, the prime mover in this field; I am grateful to him for his fundamental contribution, and trust that he will not take the criticisms in this paper as a personal attack! Second, I am enormously indebted to Hugh Darwen for his support, and especially for his help in clarifying my thinking on many specific points. Adrian Larner has also given me much food for thought on several occasions; Adrian is probably more responsible than anyone else for making me realize the importance of getting the foundations right first, for which I am most grateful to him. Discussions with David McGoveran and (especially) Charley Bontempo over the years have also proved very helpful. I am also grateful to Charley, David, Hugh Darwen, Chris Hultén, and Colin White for their careful and helpful reviews of earlier drafts of this paper. And, finally, I must pay tribute to the designers of the Peterlee Relational Test Vehicle (PRTV), a relational prototype built in the early seventies at the IBM Scientific Centre in England; they got so many things right that later systems got wrong [33]. It is a great pity—and no fault of theirs—that their ideas were not more widely disseminated, or accepted, at the time.

REFERENCES AND BIBLIOGRAPHY

1. Michel E. Adiba, "Derived Relations: A Unified Mechanism for Views, Snapshots, and Distributed Data," IBM Research Report RJ2881 (July 1980).

2. ANSI (American National Standards Institute), *Database Language SQL,* Document ANSI X3.135-1986. Also available as ISO (International Organization for Standardization) Document ISO/TC97/SC21/WG3/N117.

3. H. W. Buff, "Why Codd's Rule No. 6 Must Be Reformulated," *ACM SIG-MOD Record* 17, No. 4 (December 1988).

4. E. F. Codd, "Derivability, Redundancy, and Consistency of Relations Stored in Large Data Banks," IBM Research Report RJ599 (August 1969).

5. E. F. Codd, "A Relational Model of Data for Large Shared Data Banks," *Communications of the ACM* 13, No. 6 (June 1970). Republished in *Communications of the ACM* 26, No. 1 (January 1983).

6. E. F. Codd and C. J. Date, "Interactive Support for Nonprogrammers: The Relational and Network Approaches," *Proc. 1974 ACM SIGMOD Workshop on Data Description, Access, and Control,* Ann Arbor, MI (May 1974).

7. E. F. Codd, "Extending the Database Relational Model to Capture More Meaning," *ACM Transactions on Database Systems* 4, No. 4 (December 1979).

8. E. F. Codd, "Relational Database, A Practical Foundation for Productivity," *Communications of the ACM* 25, No. 2 (February 1982).

9. E. F. Codd, "Is Your DBMS Really Relational?" (*Computerworld,* October 14th, 1985); "Does Your DBMS Run by the Rules?" (*Computerworld,* October 21st, 1985).

10. E. F. Codd, "Missing Information (Applicable and Inapplicable) in Relational Databases," *ACM SIGMOD Record 15,* No. 4 (December 1986).

11. E. F. Codd, "More Commentary On Missing Information in Relational Databases (Applicable and Inapplicable Information)," *ACM SIGMOD Record* 16, No. 1 (March 1987).

12. E. F. Codd, *The Relational Model for Database Management Version 2* (Reading, MA: Addison-Wesley, 1990).

13. Hugh Darwen, "The Role of Functional Dependence in Query Decomposition" (in this volume).

14. Hugh Darwen, "Outer Join with No Nulls and Fewer Tears" (in this volume).

15. Hugh Darwen and C. J. Date, "Into the Great Divide" (in this volume).

16. C. J. Date, *An Introduction to Database Systems: Volume I,* 5th edition (Reading, MA: Addison-Wesley, 1990).

17. C. J. Date, "The Relational Model," Part III of C. J. Date, *An Introduction to Database Systems: Volume I,* 5th edition (Reading, MA: Addison-Wesley, 1990).

18. C. J. Date, "Relational Algebra," Chapter 13 of C. J. Date, *An Introduction to Database Systems: Volume I,* 5th edition (Reading, MA: Addison-Wesley, 1990).

19. C. J. Date, "Views," Section 15.5 of C. J. Date, *An Introduction to Database Systems: Volume I,* 5th edition (Reading, MA: Addison-Wesley, 1990).

20. C. J. Date, "Further Normalization," Chapter 21 of C. J. Date, *An Introduction to Database Systems: Volume I,* 5th edition (Reading, MA: Addison-Wesley, 1990).

21. C. J. Date, "An Introduction to the Unified Database Language (UDL)," in C. J. Date, *Relational Database: Selected Writings* (Reading, MA: Addison-Wesley, 1986).

22. C. J. Date, "Some Principles of Good Language Design," in C. J. Date, *Relational Database: Selected Writings* (Reading, MA: Addison-Wesley, 1986).

23. C. J. Date, "The Outer Join," in C. J. Date, *Relational Database: Selected Writings* (Reading, MA: Addison-Wesley, 1986).

24. C. J. Date, "What Is a Domain?" in C. J. Date, *Relational Database Writings 1985–1989* (Reading, MA: Addison-Wesley, 1990).

25. C. J. Date, "Referential Integrity and Foreign Keys Part I: Basic Concepts," in C. J. Date, *Relational Database Writings 1985–1989* (Reading, MA: Addison-Wesley, 1990).

26. C. J. Date, "Referential Integrity and Foreign Keys Part II: Further Considerations," in C. J. Date, *Relational Database Writings 1985–1989* (Reading, MA: Addison-Wesley, 1990).

27. C. J. Date, "A Contribution to the Study of Database Integrity," in C. J. Date, *Relational Database Writings 1985–1989* (Reading, MA: Addison-Wesley, 1990).

28. C. J. Date, "NOT Is Not "Not"! (Notes on Three-Valued Logic and Related Matters)," in C. J. Date, *Relational Database Writings 1985–1989* (Reading, MA: Addison-Wesley, 1990).

29. C. J. Date, "What Is a Relation?" (in this volume).

30. C. J. Date, "An Optimization Problem" (in this volume).

31. C. J. Date, "A Critical Review of the Relational Model Version 2 (RM/V2)" (in this volume).

32. C. J. Date, "The Default Values Approach to Missing Information" (in this volume).

33. P. A. V. Hall, P. Hitchcock, and S. J. P. Todd, "An Algebra of Relations for Machine Computation," *Conference Record of the 2nd ACM Symposium on Principles of Programming Languages,* Palo Alto, CA (January 1975).

34. Michael Stonebraker, *Introduction to* "The Roots," in M. Stonebraker, ed., *Readings in Database Systems* (San Mateo, CA: Morgan Kaufmann, 1988).

35. Andrew Warden, "The Naming of Columns," in C. J. Date, *Relational Database Writings 1985–1989* (Reading, MA: Addison-Wesley, 1990).

36. Andrew Warden, "In Praise of Marriage," in C. J. Date, *Relational Database Writings 1985–1989* (Reading, MA: Addison-Wesley, 1990).

37. Andrew Warden, "Table_Dee and Table_Dum," in C. J. Date, *Relational Database Writings 1985–1989* (Reading, MA: Addison-Wesley, 1990).

38. Andrew Warden, "Into the Unknown," in C. J. Date, *Relational Database Writings 1985–1989* (Reading, MA: Addison-Wesley, 1990).

APPENDIX A:
CANDIDATE KEYS AND NAMED RELATIONS

In the body of this paper, I suggested that it would be desirable to be able to declare candidate keys for all named relations (views and snapshots as well as base relations). The purpose of this appendix is to present some arguments in support of this position.

1. The first argument is simply *documentation*. If, for example, users are to interact with views instead of base relations, then it is clear that those views should look to the user as much like base relations as possible. Ideally, in fact, the user should not even have to know that they *are* views, but should be able to treat them as if they actually were base relations. And just as the user of a base relation needs to know what the primary key of that base relation is (in general), so the user of a view needs to know what the primary key of that view is (again, in general). Explicitly declaring that primary key is the obvious way to make that information available.

   Analogous arguments can be made for other kinds of named relation, and for alternate keys as well as primary keys—and, indeed, for all applicable integrity constraints for all named relations.

2. The DBMS might not be able to deduce the candidate keys for itself (this is certainly the case today in every DBMS I know). Explicit declarations are thus likely to be the only means available today (available to the DBA, that is) of informing the system—as well as the user—of the existence of those keys.

3. Even if the DBMS were able to deduce the candidate keys for itself, explicit declarations would at least enable the system to check that its deductions and the DBA's explicit specifications are not inconsistent.

4. The DBA might have some knowledge that the DBMS does not, and might thus be able to improve on the DBMS's deductions. For example, suppose we have the usual shipments relation (SP):

```
SP ( S#, P#, QTY )
   PRIMARY KEY ( S#, P# )
```

Now consider the following SQL view definition:

```
CREATE VIEW VSP ( S#, P#, QTY ) AS
       SELECT SP.S#, SP.P#, SP.QTY
       FROM   SP
       WHERE  SP.S# = 'S1' ;
```

This view is a restriction of relation SP. And the primary key of a restriction is usually the same as the primary key of the relation being restricted [18]; thus, the DBMS might very likely deduce that the primary key of VSP is (S#,P#). But in fact, of course, every tuple of VSP contains the same S# value; P# by itself thus possesses the necessary uniqueness property, and the primary key is therefore just P# (the combination (S#,P#) does not satisfy the minimality requirement). If the DBMS cannot deduce this fact for itself, then it would certainly be desirable for the DBA to be able to tell it.

APPENDIX B:
ENTITY INTEGRITY, REFERENTIAL INTEGRITY, AND NULLS

Dropping support for three-and four-valued logic has certain implications—on the whole, beneficial implications—for the entity and referential integrity rules. Those implications are summarized in this appendix.

First, it is convenient to continue to use the term "null" to refer to the representation of the fact that some piece of information is missing. For example, we might say, loosely, that "Joe's salary is null," meaning that (a) Joe's salary is unknown, and (b) that fact is represented in the database by some distinguished value, perhaps minus one. In other words, "nulls" as understood in this appendix—unlike the nulls of three-valued logic—are indeed *values.** As such, they possess the very desirable properties that:

(a) The expression "null = null" evaluates to *true;*

(b) The expression "null = x" evaluates to *false* for all nonnull values x from the relevant domain.

It follows that the arguments for the entity integrity rule [17] no longer have any meaning, and the rule can therefore be dropped. Thus—barring any explicit integrity constraint to the contrary—a given base relation will be allowed to contain *at most one* tuple at any given time with a "null" primary key value.

Now, there may well be good reasons to impose such an "explicit integrity constraint to the contrary" in many cases—perhaps even most cases—but it is certainly possible to think of examples where such a constraint does *not* make sense. In other words, the "entity integrity" rule might serve as a good guideline for database design, much as the ideas of further normalization serve as such a guideline; like those ideas, however, it should be seen as a guideline *only*—it cannot be taken as a hard requirement for all base relations.

By way of an example, here is a case in which a "null" primary key value does make sense. The relation below (SURVEY) represents the results

---

*In the three-valued approach, the term "null value" is deprecated, precisely because the three-valued logic null is not a value [28]. But in the approach advocated in this appendix, null *is* a value, and the expression "null value" (which is frequently heard anyway) is perfectly acceptable.

of a salary survey, showing the average, maximum, and minimum salary by birth year for a certain sample population:

SURVEY	BIRTHYEAR	AVGSAL	MAXSAL	MINSAL
	1940	85K	130K	33K
	1941	82K	125K	32K
	1942	77K	99K	32K
	1943	78K	97K	35K
	....	...	...	...
	1970	29K	35K	12K
	null	56K	117K	20K

BIRTHYEAR here is the primary key. And the tuple with a "null" BIRTH-YEAR value represents people who declined to answer the question "When were you born?"

I remark next that we might very well want to join this "null primary key" tuple to a tuple in another relation with a "null" in some attribute position—in particular, in a foreign key position. Which brings me to the referential integrity rule. Now, the referential integrity rule, unlike the entity integrity rule, cannot of course simply be dropped; however, it can be simplified slightly, as follows.

Since "null = null" now evaluates to *true*, not *unk* [28], there is no need to treat null foreign key values in any special manner. Thus, the referential integrity rule can be simplified to say just that every value of the foreign key must exist as a value of the target primary key. Note, however, that this simplification does imply that if a foreign key value *is* "null," a tuple with a "null" primary key value will have to exist in the target relation. This situation will undoubtedly be a trifle annoying in some cases, and the idea of continuing to give "null" foreign key values special treatment (i.e., not requiring a matching "null" primary key value) should probably be considered further.

APPENDIX C:
COMPARING COMPOSITE KEYS

One aspect of the relational model as defined in the body of this paper is that there is now no concept of a composite domain or composite attribute. I believe this simplification to be a significant improvement, but there is one tiny consequence that needs some attention, as follows.

First, keys—candidate, primary, alternate, and foreign keys—must now all be defined to be *sets* of attributes of the relation in question.* We thus run into a minor problem when we need to say what it means for a foreign key value and a primary key value to be equal. If the keys in question are "composite"—i.e., if the sets of attributes that constitute those keys have cardinality greater than one—we are faced with the need to define a way of comparing two sets. (*Note:* The two sets will have the same cardinality, of course.)

Now, it would clearly be undesirable to introduce some kind of left-to-right ordering and say that the "first" attribute of the composite foreign key must equal the "first" attribute of the composite primary key, the "second" must equal the "second," and so on. (It would be undesirable for the same reasons that it is undesirable within the heading of a relation [17].) Instead, therefore, we proceed as follows:

- Let $t1$ and $t2$ be tuples from relations $R1$ and $R2$, respectively, and let x and y be projections of $t1$ and $t2$, respectively, such that x and y have the same degree (i.e., the same number of attribute values).

- Then, if and only if there exists a one-to-one mapping between x and y such that all pairs of corresponding attributes under that mapping (a) have a common domain and (b) are equal in value,† then x and y are said to be equal (under the mapping in question).

In the case of interest (involving "composite" foreign and primary keys), it would be the responsibility of the user defining the foreign key to specify

---

*In previous writings—see, e.g., reference [17]—I have generally defined keys to be "[single] attributes, possibly composite." But I have at last seen the error of my ways; thinking of keys as sets of attributes (possibly singleton sets, of course) is much preferable, and indeed more correct.

†Observe the implication that if x and y each have degree zero, then they are equal—i.e., the truth-valued expression "$x = y$" evaluates to *true* [37].

the desired one-to-one mapping. A possible syntax for performing this function is illustrated by the following example (which is based on the education example of reference [21]). Note in particular the FOREIGN KEY clause for the STUDENT relation.

```
COURSE     ( COURSE#, TITLE )
           PRIMARY KEY ( COURSE# )

OFFERING   ( COURSE#, OFF#, DATE, LOCATION )
           PRIMARY KEY ( COURSE#, OFF# )
           FOREIGN KEY ( COURSE# ) REFERENCES COURSE

STUDENT    ( COURSE#, OFF#, EMP#, GRADE )
           PRIMARY KEY ( COURSE#, OFF#, EMP# )
           FOREIGN KEY ( COURSE# = OFFERING.COURSE#,
                         OFF#   = OFFERING.OFF# )
                         REFERENCES OFFERING
```

Points arising:

1. The example tends to suggest that the mapping could be specified by simple name matching (Warden's marriage principle again [36]), and indeed so it could in the vast majority of cases. But the marriage principle by itself would clearly not be adequate in all situations—it would sometimes have to be augmented by some kind of "attribute rename" operation. Nevertheless, this might be a fruitful direction to explore.

2. The mapping can obviously be left implicit in the (common) "singleton set" case (i.e., when the set of attributes constituting each key contains just one attribute).

3. If the mapping *is* spelled out explicitly, the REFERENCES phrase then effectively becomes redundant!

Taking points 1–3 together, it is clear that a small amount of language design work is needed. But we are beginning to stray rather a long way from the point of this appendix, and indeed from the point of the paper as a whole.

APPENDIX D:
AN ASSESSMENT OF CODD'S EVALUATION SCHEME

In the same paper in which he defined his 1985 version of the relational model (reference [9]), Codd also defined his—by now famous—"twelve rules" for relational DBMSs. He then used those rules, together with the "nine structural, three integrity, and 18 manipulative features" of the relational model, as a basis for an evaluation scheme to be used in assessing how relational a given DBMS might be, and applied that scheme to three specific products: DB2 (from IBM), IDMS/R (from Cullinet, as it then was), and DATACOM/DB (from Applied Data Research, as it then was).

Codd's evaluation scheme works as follows: For each of 42 items (the twelve rules, plus the nine structural, three integrity, and 18 manipulative features of the model), a system scores one point if and only if it supports that item *fully;* anything less than full support gets a zero. Then, if and only if the system achieves a score of 42 (the maximum), a bonus of eight is added; finally, the total is doubled to yield a percentage "fidelity rating." A system is then said to be "mid 80s fully relational" if and only if it gets a fidelity rating of 100 percent. (The qualifier "mid 80s" reflects the fact that "it is likely that there will be a few more requirements by the nineties" [9].)

According to this scheme, Codd awarded DB2, IDMS/R, and DATACOM/DB fidelity ratings of 46 percent, 8 percent, and 10 percent, respectively.

I do not endorse the foregoing scheme, and in this appendix I would like to explain why.

Preliminary Remarks

There are a couple of points that I would like to make quite clear at the outset:

1. I am not opposed to the idea of evaluating systems—far from it; on the contrary, the availability of an independent and objective evaluation scheme could be extremely beneficial to both users and vendors. But it is clearly desirable that any such scheme be very carefully thought out in order to be (as far as possible) above all reasonable criticism. In my opinion, Codd's scheme does not meet this requirement.

2. We should not lose sight of the fact that to measure how relational a system is only to measure that system along one of several possible axes. I would certainly agree that the relational axis is an extremely important and indeed fundamental one, but other axes are obviously possible, and relevant. For example, what about recovery support? What about concurrency control? How does the system perform? What frontend subsystems are available, and how well are they integrated with the DBMS? And so on. A fair assessment of a given system would consist of some weighted sum of its ratings along each of the various axes. Again, I would certainly agree that the weighting assigned to the relational axis should be very high, but different users will surely want to assign different weights to different axes.

General Comments

The overall intent behind Codd's twelve rules was that, first, satisfying those rules was by and large a technically feasible proposition,* and second, there were clear practical benefits to the user if the system did in fact satisfy them. The rules were all based on a single "foundation rule" (Rule Zero):

> *For any system that is advertised as, or claimed to be, a relational database management system, that system must be able to manage databases entirely through its relational capabilities* [9].

There can be no question that this Rule Zero is a good, though informal, guiding principle. However:

- It is not clear that all twelve of the rules are logical consequences of Rule Zero (see, e.g., Rule 11).

- It is not clear why Codd chose exactly the rules he did and not others that could be argued to be at least equally important (e.g., why not a proper closure rule?).

- Although I agree with most of the rules in spirit, some of them seem hard to justify other than in a purely intuitive manner (see, e.g., Rule 5).

- The rules are not all independent of one another (see, e.g., Rules 6 and 9).

- Some of the rules are effectively just a restatement of certain features of the underlying relational model (see, e.g., Rule 2); why those particular features and not others?

---

*Though it turned out subsequently (as we will see) that at least one of the rules, and arguably as many as three or four, could *not* in fact be fully satisfied—at least not within the current state of the art.

- Some of the rules are stated rather imprecisely and/or seem to be hard to apply (see, e.g., Rules 3, 6, and 11).

- Some of the rules do not seem to be particularly *relational* (see, e.g., Rule 11).

- Finally, the all-or-nothing scoring system seems unduly harsh. For example, it seems very unfair to give (say) IBM's DB2 the same score, zero, on Rule 6 as a system that does not support views at all—yet zero is the right score if we follow the evaluation scheme faithfully.

Detailed Comments

I now proceed to state the twelve rules and to offer some more specific comments on each of them. The names of the rules are taken from Codd's paper [9]; however, the explanations are not—I have deliberately chosen to rephrase them, in most cases. (In fact, the explanations are mostly taken from reference [17].)

1. *The information rule:* All information in the database must be represented explicitly in one and only one way, namely by scalar values in column positions within rows of tables.

   I have no objection to this rule, except to point out that it is really just a restatement of an essential aspect of the relational model. I might also mention that in an earlier paper [6], Codd did say that *inessential ordering* [17] could also be used as a means of representing information.

2. *Guaranteed access rule:* Every individual scalar value in the database must be logically addressable by specifying the name of the containing table, the name of the containing column, and the primary key value of the containing row.

   Again, my only comment here is that the rule is not new: It is merely a restatement of the underlying requirement that all (base) relations have named attributes and possess a known primary key.

3. *Systematic treatment of null values:* The DBMS is required to support a representation of "missing information and inapplicable information" that is systematic, distinct from all regular values (for example, "distinct from zero or any other number," in the case of numeric values), and independent of data type. It is also implied that such representations must be manipulated by the DBMS in a systematic way.

   Systematic treatment of missing information is clearly desirable. "Null values"—at least as that term is usually understood—are not, in my opinion [28].

4. *Dynamic online catalog based on the relational model:* The system is required to support an online, inline, relational catalog that is accessible to authorized users by means of their regular query language.

This is a good rule. No additional comment.

5. *Comprehensive data sublanguage rule:* The system must support at least one relational language* that (a) has a linear syntax, (b) can be used both interactively and within application programs, and (c) supports data definition operations (including view definitions), data manipulation operations (update as well as retrieval), security and integrity constraints, and transaction boundary operations (BEGIN TRANSACTION, COMMIT, and ROLLBACK).

I feel intuitively that this is a good rule, but find it hard to justify in any precise and objective way. Codd's argument that ". . . it should rarely be necessary to bring the database activity to a halt [and therefore] it does not make sense to separate the services listed above into distinct languages" is unconvincing. I certainly subscribe to the proposition that the same function should use the same syntax everywhere it appears in the system—but is that all there is to it?

Also, is the list of services meant to be exhaustive? If we are going to include operations such as BEGIN TRANSACTION (etc.), then what about concurrency control operations? What about load and unload operations? What about reorganization? Auditing? Other utility functions? (etc., etc.). All of these items surely have as much—or as little—right to be included as do BEGIN TRANSACTION, COMMIT, etc. in a list of "relational" requirements. (My point, in case it is not obvious, is that such matters are really nothing to do with the question of whether a given DBMS qualifies as relational or not.)

6. *View updating rule:* All views that are theoretically updatable must be updatable by the system.

Codd goes on to say that ". . . a view is theoretically updatable if there exists a time-independent algorithm for unambiguously determining a single series of changes to the base relations that will have as their effect precisely the requested changes in the view." Again, I agree with the general intent of this rule, but I have at least two problems with the detailed statement:

(a) First, the rule clearly implies that the system must support the *definition* of all updatable views. (Note that many systems will fail on

---

*Note that I say "language," not "sublanguage." I do not subscribe to the idea that there should be a strong separation between the database language and the host language, for reasons discussed in references [16] and [21].

this requirement alone; for example, as mentioned in the body of this paper, many systems do not support the use of UNION in a view definition, and yet it is clearly possible to support, e.g., DELETE operations on a union view.) But is there an implication that we know exactly what it is that characterizes the class of theoretically updatable views? Is the "time-independent algorithm" always known? I am not aware of any documented definition of that class or of such an algorithm. And if those definitions in fact do not exist (or at least are not yet known), then this rule is rather hard to apply, to say the least.*

(b) Compliance with this rule is a logical consequence of compliance with Rule 9; i.e., if a system satisfies Rule 9, it must satisfy this rule also. Surely independence among the rules is desirable, for exactly the same kinds of reasons that the rules themselves demand certain kinds of independence in relational systems. (Though I certainly accept the point that it might be difficult to come up with a set of fully independent rules.)

7. *High-level insert, update, and delete:* The system must support set-at-a-time INSERT, UPDATE, and DELETE operators.

This is another good rule. No additional comment.

8. *Physical data independence:* (I assume the reader is familiar with this concept and will not bother to define it here.)

Once again this is a good rule in principle. But the problem is that physical data independence is not an absolute; in fact, it is probably true to say that every system should get a "Partial" score on this one. In particular, the rule does not seem to have been fairly applied in the cases considered by Codd in his paper: DB2 is given a "Yes" (score one point) while IDMS/R and DATACOM/DB are both given a "No" (score no point), yet DB2 fails to provide full physical data independence in at least the following ways:

- Creating or dropping a UNIQUE index can affect the logic of existing queries or programs (this is partly a lack of *integrity* independence as well as a lack of physical data independence—see Rule 10)

- Fields of type LONG VARCHAR (equivalently, VARCHAR(n) with $n > 254$) are subject to numerous restrictions (e.g., they cannot be used in WHERE or GROUP BY or HAVING or ORDER BY or DISTINCT or PRIMARY KEY or FOREIGN KEY or . . .)

---

*After I first raised these questions, a paper appeared (reference [3]) that indicated that those definitions do *not* exist, at least not yet. As a consequence, Codd published a revised version of the rule in his RM/V2 book [12]. However, that revised version is much too long, in all of its details, to include here.

- Partitioning fields cannot be updated
- The meaning of "SELECT *" can change if the storage representation of the table is changed
- The meaning of "INSERT with an implicit field list" can change if the storage representation of the table is changed

Note too that the rule does not explicitly mention such matters as changes in field width or data type or units (etc.). Some systems (though not DB2) do provide a measure of independence in such areas also. The problem is, to repeat, there are really different *degrees* of physical data independence. Even a system like IMS does provide some such independence. I do not think such independence can be a simple "Yes" or "No" item.

9. *Logical data independence:* (I assume the reader is familiar with this concept and will not bother to define it here.)

Codd goes on to say that ". . . the DBMS must be capable of handling inserts, updates, and deletes on *all views* that are theoretically updatable" (emphasis as in the original)—in other words, Rule 9 implies Rule 6, as previously claimed.* Note too that, like the previous rule, this rule really is not a simple "Yes" or "No" item. (In fact, come to think of it, almost none of Codd's rules is a simple "Yes" or "No" item!)

10. *Integrity independence:* Integrity constraints must be specified separately from application programs and stored in the catalog. It must be possible to change such constraints as and when appropriate without unnecessarily affecting existing applications.

I have no real objection to this rule either, but note that:

(a) First, the requirement has already been specified as part of Rule 5 (the comprehensive data sublanguage rule).

(b) Second, it is stated (or at least implied) again later as one of "the three integrity features" of the relational model.

Again, therefore, we see that the requirements are not as independent of one another as they might be.

11. *Distribution independence:* Existing applications should continue to operate successfully (a) when a distributed version of the DBMS is first introduced; (b) when existing distributed data is redistributed around the system.

This seems to be another rule that is hard to apply in practice, since

---

*I might add here that the DBMS also needs to be capable of handling *retrievals* on all views—another area in which many DBMSs fail today [19].

it talks in terms of *future possibilities.* An argument could be made that any database language (e.g., IMS's DL/I) could be implemented in a transparent fashion over distributed data; in fact, I believe that IBM's CICS/ISC "data request shipping" feature does provide a measure of distribution independence for DL/I today. It is also not clear that distribution independence has anything to do with relational technology per se. Of course, I do agree that relational technology is the best basis for a distributed system, but that seems to me to be quite a separate point.

12. *Nonsubversion rule:* If the system provides a low-level (record-at-a-time) interface, then that interface cannot be used to subvert the system by (e.g.) bypassing a relational security or integrity constraint.

   While this may be a very desirable property of systems in practice, it does appear as if it was included in the list primarily in order to disqualify "born again" relational systems, i.e., systems—like IDMS/R and DATACOM/DB—that consist of a relational layer on top of an older, nonrelational DBMS. The low-level interface in such systems is certainly an Achilles heel, and it is legitimate to warn users of the potential dangers inherent in the existence of such an interface. But to make this requirement one of the basic "twelve rules," when there are many other candidate rules that are more genuinely relational, does not seem very objective.

Conclusion

Despite the many criticisms outlined in the foregoing, it is undeniable that Codd's "twelve rules" have had (and will probably continue to have) a major influence on the database marketplace. Furthermore, Codd has since incorporated versions of the rules into RM/V2 [12]. Thus, matters may already have gone too far; but it seems to me that it would be preferable to attempt to improve the rules before they become cast any further into concrete—improve them, that is, to the point where they are less arbitrary, better structured, and less open to criticism, and hence can serve as a fairer and more balanced basis for assessing systems. It also seems to me that a rating scheme could surely be found that is more scientific than the one proposed by Codd. In other words, a methodology for performing scientific, independent, and objective DBMS product evaluations is still sorely needed. Codd's twelve rules might form a basis from which such a methodology could be developed, but as they stand they are *not* satisfactory, in this writer's opinion.

16

A Critical Review of
the Relational Model
Version 2 (RM/V2)

ABSTRACT

Codd's 1990 definition of the relational model ("The Relational Model Version 2") is summarized and briefly criticized.

COMMENTS ON PUBLICATION

In the previous chapter, I examined Codd's 1985 definition of the relational model (i.e., "Version 1"), found it wanting in a number of respects, and proposed a reconstituted definition. In the present chapter, I turn my attention to Version 2.

Now, it goes without saying that the publication in 1990 of Codd's book on Version 2 (reference [3]) was an event of considerable importance in the database world, and one that was eagerly anticipated. When I was finally able to obtain a copy of the book, however, I regret to have to say

Previously unpublished.

that I found it quite disappointing in a number of respects. First, for a variety of reasons, it seemed to be quite difficult to read; second, I was surprised to see that there was almost nothing in it that was genuinely new; third (and much the most important, of course) I found that there was much that I disagreed with at the technical level—so much so, that I began to be seriously concerned about the impact the book might have if it were allowed to go unchallenged. Hence this review.

1. INTRODUCTION

The recent (1990) publication of Codd's book *The Relational Model For Database Management Version 2* [3] is almost by definition a highly signifi-cant event in the world of database management. As the originator of the relational model, on which virtually all modern DBMSs are based, Codd is clearly someone whose ideas deserve the courtesy of close and widespread attention. It is thus perhaps a little surprising to find that, to date, the book has received only one review in the literature so far as I am aware [25]. Moreover, what follows is not intended as a review of the book per se either (except incidentally). Rather, it is intended as a review of the ideas that the book propounds—namely, the Relational Model, Version 2 (which, follow-ing Codd, I hereinafter abbreviate to RM/V2).

Clearly, the first question we have to ask is: What exactly *is* RM/V2? It is a little difficult to answer this question in any very succinct manner (indeed, so far as I can tell, reference [3] does not even attempt to provide any kind of "one-liner" definition). But the following might help: RM/V2, whatever else it might be, is obviously meant as an extension (a compatible extension, of course) of Version 1 of the model (RM/V1). And the essential difference between the two is as follows: Whereas RM/V1 was intended as an abstract blueprint for one particular aspect of the total database prob-lem—essentially the user language aspect—RM/V2 is intended as an ab-stract blueprint for *the entire system*. Thus, where RM/V1 contained just three parts (structure, integrity, and manipulation), RM/V2 contains 18; and those 18 parts include not only the original three (of course), but also parts having to do with views, the catalog, authorization, naming, distrib-uted database, and various other aspects of database management. For ref-erence, here is a complete list of the 18 parts:

A	Authorization	F	Functions
B	Basic operators	I	Integrity
C	Catalog	J	Indicators
D	Principles of DBMS design	L	Principles of language design
E	Commands for the DBA	M	Manipulation

N	Naming	T	Data types
P	Protection	V	Views
Q	Qualifiers	X	Distributed database management
S	Structure	Z	Advanced operators

Within each of these parts, or rather *classes* as they are called in RM/V2, Codd defines a set of *features*. For example, the first feature in class A (authorization) is as follows:

> RA-1 (*Affirmative Basis*): "All authorization is granted on an affirmative basis; this means that users are explicitly *granted permission* to access parts of the database and parts of its description instead of being explicitly *denied access*" (emphasis as in the original).

Each feature has a label ("RA-1" in the example—"R" for relational and "A" for authorization), a name ("Affirmative Basis" in the example), and a prescriptive (or occasionally proscriptive) definition. RM/V2 includes a total of 333 such features, of which (according to Codd) 130 are "fundamental, and hence top priority," while the remainder are merely "basic" [sic].

As already mentioned, this review is meant to be a review of RM/V2 per se, not a review of the book that describes it. But the following table of contents from that book might be helpful in giving some indication of the book's scope and structure:

1. Introduction to RM/V2
2. Structure-oriented and data-oriented features
3. Domains as extended data types
4. The basic operators
5. The advanced operators
6. Naming
7. Commands for the DBA
8. Missing information
9. Response to technical criticisms regarding missing information
10. Qualifiers
11. Indicators
12. Query and manipulation
13. Integrity constraints
14. User-defined integrity constraints
15. Catalog

16. Views
17. View updatability
18. Authorization
19. Functions
20. Protection of investment
21. Principles of DBMS design
22. Principles of design for relational languages
23. Serious flaws in SQL
24. Distributed database management
25. More on distributed database management
26. Advantages of the relational approach
27. Present products and future improvements
28. Extending the relational model
29. Fundamental laws of database management
30. Claimed alternatives to the relational model

There are also two appendixes:

A. RM/V2 feature index
B. Exercises in logic and the theory of relations

Finally, there is a list of references and an index. Regarding the list of references, incidentally, one overall criticism that could be leveled at RM/V2 is that it pays comparatively little attention to (and often does not even acknowledge) the great deal of work that has been done by other workers in the field—work, that is, not on RM/V2 per se (of course not), but on every one of the problems that RM/V2 is intended to address. (Reference [25] makes the same point.) Specific instances of such omissions would be out of place at this juncture; examples will be given later in the body of this review.

And while we are on the subject of overall criticisms, there is another aspect of RM/V2 that I find a little disturbing—namely, its generally prescriptive tone. (Once again, reference [25] makes the same point.) Many of the specific ideas within RM/V2--for example, its approach to naming, features RN-1 through RN-14--are somewhat controversial, to say the least; in some cases they are surely wrong. And it does not seem appropriate to state categorically that the system must follow (for example) a particular naming scheme, when that scheme is demonstrably flawed and superior schemes have already been described in the literature (again, see later for more specifics). Even where the ideas are not wrong, or not controversial, it still seems undesirable to be too prescriptive, for fear of stifling invention.

2. GENERAL QUESTIONS

There are some obvious general questions that need to be raised and at least briefly discussed before we get into too much detail—namely:

- What is truly new in RM/V2?
- What is good about it?
- What is bad about it?
- What is its likely impact?

What Is Truly New?

By "new" here, I mean new compared with RM/V1 as defined by Codd in reference [2].* In the preface to his book [3], Codd states that the most important new features of RM/V2 are as follows (paraphrasing slightly):

- Extension of support for missing information from three- to four-valued logic (to deal with "inapplicable" as well as "unknown" information)
- Extended support for integrity constraints, especially "user-defined" constraints
- "A more detailed account of view updatability"
- Some "relatively new" DBMS and language design principles
- Details of the catalog
- Support for distributed database management
- A definition of "some of the fundamental laws" underlying the relational model

And a few more specific items might be added to the foregoing list—for example, there are some new relational operators, and certain previously existing ones have been redefined (see various discussions later). Referring back to the original question, however ("What is truly new?"), I would have to say that the answer is "Not very much!" Of the seven items in Codd's list above:

- The first *is* new, but I don't agree with it (see Section 4, later).
- The last is arguably new too, but is not really part of the model anyway (see Appendix A).
- The others may be new from the point of view of the relational model per se, but they are hardly new from the point of view of relational

---

*I have some criticisms of Codd's RM/V1 too, but this is not the place to air them. They are discussed in detail in reference [18].

technology in general (at least as that technology is perceived by most workers in the field). To be more specific:

(a) The area of integrity constraints has been previously addressed by many people. For instance, Eswaran and Chamberlin presented a statement of requirements for integrity support as far back as 1975 [21], and a more extensive and comprehensive set of requirements appeared in a recent paper of my own [13]. Furthermore, there are already a few products on the market—DEC's Rdb/VMS is a case in point—that go quite a long way toward supporting that "more extensive and comprehensive set of requirements."

(b) The area of view updating likewise has received considerable attention over the years, and a variety of results have been formally proved by, e.g., Dayal and Bernstein in 1982 [20] and Keller in 1985 [24]. Reference [10] (published in 1986) presented a set of informal algorithms very similar to those given by Codd.*

(c) The "DBMS design principles" are mainly just a set of miscellaneous features that many of today's relational DBMSs already support (e.g., feature RD-13, "Atomic Execution of Relational Commands"). The "language design principles" likewise are a set of miscellaneous features, some of them having to do with language design per se and some having to do with implementation (e.g., feature RL-2, "Compiling and Recompiling"). Once again, there is very little that is truly new, at least in concept, regarding these language features as such; it is true, however, that not all systems today support all the features, partly because most systems today support SQL (which fails to satisfy the requirements on numerous counts), and partly perhaps because some of the requirements are somewhat controversial (see later).

(d) Concerning the catalog: Comment seems superfluous.

(e) Finally, concerning distributed database: Again, research and development has been under way for many years; a good survey was published by Rothnie and Goodman as far back as 1977 [26]. Prototypes implementing many of the features identified by Codd (at least the good ones) have been operational since the early eighties. And I published a paper in 1987 (reference [15]) that identified many of the same principles that Codd includes in RM/V2.

---

*Except that it did not consider the union, intersection, and difference operations—but the extensions needed for those operations are essentially straightforward.

What Is Good?

I find it difficult to answer this question except in a rather general kind of way. Even if it is true (as claimed above) that there is little in RM/V2 that is truly new, it is certainly useful to have all of the material collected together in a single place; also, there is undoubtedly much food for thought in the 333 features, and there is unquestionably much wisdom scattered throughout the book. The 18 classes taken together do cover a large part of the database management problem (though there are some omissions—utility support might be an example—and there is some lack of orthogonality among the ones that are included). The emphasis on integrity is nice, and there is some recognition (though not enough, in my opinion) of the fact that systems these days need to have an open architecture—implying, among other things, that users need to be able to define their own data types and their own operators. Now read on . . .

What Is Bad?

I have to say that I do find much in RM/V2 that is bad. Here I will simply list some major areas of concern; more specific criticisms on these topics will appear in Section 4.

- Naming
- Domains and data types
- Operators
- Missing information support
- Orthogonality (or rather lack thereof)
- Distributed database support

In addition, I have a large number of criticisms at a more detailed level. Some of these criticisms will emerge later (in Section 3 especially).

What Is the Likely Impact?

Another difficult question. I certainly think that database professionals ought to read the book; vendors (meaning DBMS product designers and implementers) should *definitely* read it. But as indicated in Section 1, I do have a number of concerns. First, I am concerned about the prescriptive tone. Second, I am *very* concerned about those aspects I find to be bad (see above), such as the support for missing information. Third, I am also concerned about a lack of orthogonality in the requirements as stated;* unorthogonal, piecemeal statement of the requirements is likely to lead to unorthogonal, piecemeal DBMS and language designs and implementations. And, finally, I am concerned about the amount of "adhoc-ery" involved (to coin an ugly but convenient term). For all of these reasons, and more besides, I am concerned that the overall impact could be negative, not positive. Certainly it is desirable that everyone who reads the book—vendors especially—should do so very carefully, with a clear understanding that for many of its recommendations there do exist alternative approaches that are at least worthy of consideration.

To summarize: I have stated elsewhere [18] that I think it is crucially important to get the foundation—namely, RM/V1—right first before trying to build on that foundation to create any kind of "Version 2." RM/V2 does nothing to correct what I regard as mistakes in RM/V1 (some of them quite serious). If we are not careful, I think there is a real danger that we may be building houses on sand.

3. A SURVEY OF RM/V2

In this section I will try to give a more comprehensive survey of what is included in RM/V2. I will use Codd's own classification scheme as a basis for structuring the discussion. However, I will not attempt to follow any particularly logical sequence, but will simply present the classes alphabetically.

Authorization (Class A)

The authorization features consist essentially of a minor variation on what SQL already does today: They include (a) the use of views to hide information, plus (b) the GRANT and REVOKE operators (and GRANT includes the grant option), plus (c) a few miscellaneous features.† There is no mention of other aspects of authorization, nor of other security approaches or capabilities—for instance:

▪ User identification

---

*Despite the fact that two of Codd's "design principle" features for RM/V2 are, specifically, "Orthogonality in DBMS Design" (feature RD-6) and "Orthogonality in Language Design" (feature RL-8).

†E.g., "authorization can be conditioned by the [terminal] from which a user is operating" (feature RA-15). This requirement is an example of the lack of orthogonality mentioned earlier: If authorization constraints are specified by relational expressions (as they should be), and if a function is available that returns the ID of the terminal in use (as it should be), then this feature is logically redundant—there is no need to state it as an explicit requirement.

- Authentication (e.g., password checking)

- User group support

- CREATE and DROP PERMIT ("permits" are supported by at least one system today, namely INGRES, and I for one think them superior to the use of views for security purposes)

- Mandatory vs. discretionary authorization

- Flow controls

- Statistical or inference controls

- The Data Encryption Standard

- Public-key encryption schemes

- Etc.

Basic Operators (Class B)

The "basic operators" consist essentially of (a) the relational operators—natural join, etc.—of RM/V1 (including relational assignment), plus (b) a variety of INSERT, UPDATE, and DELETE operators, some of them with certain cascade effects.

Regarding the relational operators, RM/V2 unfortunately still treats restriction conditions that are simple comparisons (or combinations thereof) as somehow special, a distinction that I find unnecessary [18]. And while I am on the subject, I should note that RM/V2 extends the usual set of scalar comparison operators (equals, less than, etc.) to include the new operators *least greater than* ("L>"), *greatest less than* ("G>"), etc. An example of a query using such an operator might be "Find parts whose weight is the least greater than 10":

```
P WHERE P.WEIGHT L> 10
```

Here is a SQL version of this query:

```
SELECT  P.*
FROM    P
WHERE   P.WEIGHT =
      ( SELECT MIN ( P.WEIGHT )
        FROM    P
        WHERE  P.WEIGHT > 10 ) ;
```

One interesting aspect of these new comparison operators is that they are not scalar!—meaning that their arguments are not simple scalar values. The condition "P.WEIGHT L> 10" is not a simple restriction condition: It cannot be evaluated for a given row by examining just that row in isolation, as the SQL version of the query makes quite clear. These new operators thus violate Codd's own feature RZ-38, which requires (in part) that "the truth value of [such expressions] must be computable for each row using only [column values within] that row."

> *Aside:* An interesting sidelight on the "L>" (etc.) operators is the following: Suppose view V is defined using the SQL statement shown above. Then inserting a single row into table P or deleting a single row from table P or updating a single row in table P could change *the entire population* of view V "at a stroke." (Of course, the same is true for any view for which the view-defining condition is more complex than a simple restriction condition—e.g., a view that consists of those rows of table P with minimum WEIGHT, or maximum WEIGHT, etc.) *End of aside.*

Regarding the "cascade" operators (see, e.g., feature RB-36, "The Delete Operator with Cascaded Deletion"): First, I believe that CASCADE DELETE (and similar functions) should be specified declaratively, not procedurally;* second, it is entirely possible that different referential constraints involving the same primary key will require different treatment on DELETE (e.g., some might have DELETE CASCADES, others DELETE RESTRICTED), in which case the procedural operator makes no sense; third, Codd apparently ignores all of the work done on such matters by other people (see, e.g., reference [6]).

Catalog (Class C)

No surprises, and no comments.

Principles of DBMS Design (Class D)

A somewhat miscellaneous collection of features. To give some idea of the intent behind them, I will simply list the features by name:

1. Nonviolation of any fundamental law of mathematics
2. Under-the-covers representation and access
3. Sharp boundary [i.e., between logical and physical]
4. Concurrency independence
5. Protection against unauthorized long-term locks
6. Orthogonality in DBMS design
7. Domain-based index
8. Database statistics

---

*Though I might be persuaded that the declarative specification should be triggered only if the user uses the corresponding procedural operator, so that at least the user understands that cascading will (or might) occur.

9. Interrogation of statistics

10. Changing storage representation and access options

11. Automatic protection in case of malfunction

12. Automatic recovery in case of malfunction

13. Atomic execution of relational commands

14. Automatic archiving

15. Avoiding Cartesian product

16. Responsibility for encryption and decryption

A small comment regarding item number 4 here, "Concurrency independence": For some reason Codd discusses "intra-command" concurrency (which refers to the possibility of executing multiple portions of a single database request in parallel), also "inter-command" concurrency (which refers to the possibility of executing multiple database requests in parallel), but not *transaction* concurrency, which is surely the kind of concurrency most commonly found in systems today.

Commands for the DBA (Class E)

These commands (incidentally, I much prefer the term "operators," or— depending on the context—"statements") are basically the data definition operators (CREATE, ALTER, RENAME, and DROP operators for domains, base tables, and columns), plus UNLOAD and RELOAD operators, plus operators to create and drop indexes, plus some archival operators, etc.—plus a rather peculiar operator called CONTROL DUPLICATE ROWS (feature RE-20).

My only general comment on these "DBA commands" is that I do not think it is appropriate, in an abstract model of the kind that I assume RM/V2 is meant to be, to suggest that any "command" is only for the DBA, or only for anyone else for that matter. The question of who uses a particular feature is surely a question that lies outside the scope of the model per se.

Functions (Class F)

The set of required functions and operators includes:

- At least the usual scalar functions $+$, $-$, $*$, $/$, $**$, $|\,|$, and substring
- At least the usual aggregate functions COUNT, SUM, AVG, MAX, and MIN—with and without duplicate elimination*

---

*And, incidentally, with a suggested syntax that makes the same mistakes as SQL does regarding argument specifications (with respect to both argument scope and duplicate elimination).

Support for user-defined functions is also required.

Note: Codd unfortunately says that the required functions are "built into the DBMS." While such may indeed be the user's perception, I have argued elsewhere [17,18] that the functions should *not* actually be built into the DBMS per se; the DBMS should not truly need to "understand" those functions, it should only need to know how to invoke them.

Integrity (Class I)

Codd proposes support for "five types of integrity"—domain, entity, referential, column, and "user-defined." I do not have any major objections to this requirement, but I think a better (i.e., more systematic) classification scheme can be defined [13]—one that includes all the features that Codd discusses and more besides—and I also think that this is an area where credit should have been given to the very great deal of work that has been done by others (including vendors of commercially available products such as INGRES and Rdb/VMS). A couple of minor points: First, Codd does not permit "MAYBE qualifiers" to appear in integrity constraints, without offering any justification for this violation of orthogonality (of course, I am assuming for the moment that support for such qualifiers is desirable, which I do not in fact believe); second, throughout the discussion of constraints, *true* and *false* seem to be back to front (the text states that the "triggered action"—i.e., the specified response to an attempted integrity violation—is carried out if the constraint evaluates to *true;* surely it should be *false*).

Indicators (Class J)

Indicators are set to show that some exceptional situation has arisen during the execution of some operation. To give some idea of the scope of the proposed indicators, I will simply list them by name:

1. Empty relation
2. Empty divisor
3. Missing information
4. Nonexisting argument
5. Domain not declared
6. Domain check error
7. Column still exists
8. Duplicate row
9. Duplicate primary key

10. Nonredundant ordering

11. Catalog block

12. View not tuple-insertible

13. View not component-updatable

14. View not tuple-deletable

Space does not permit a detailed discussion of all of these indicators in detail. However, I will remark that the indicators class as a whole seems to be one that involves much "adhoc-ery." For example: Why a single "View not component-updatable" indicator instead of a set of distinct "Component not updatable" indicators? Why are the "Duplicate row" and "Duplicate primary key [value]" indicators set by LOAD but not INSERT? Why is the "Nonredundant ordering" indicator provided at all? (It is needed only if a query produces a result that involves essential ordering [1], which I thought was prohibited in RM/V1 [2], let alone RM/V2.*) Etc., etc.

Principles of Language Design (Class L)

As already noted in Section 2, the "language design principles" are basically a set of miscellaneous features, only some of which have to do with language design per se (the others have to do with implementation). None is truly new, in my opinion; however, some are certainly debatable. For example:

- "[Database] commands must be compilable separately from the host-language context in which they . . . appear. The DBMS must support the compilation of [database] commands, even if it also supports [interpretation] . . . the DBMS must support automatic recompilation of [database] commands whenever any change in access paths [etc.] invalidates the code developed by a previous compilation" (feature RL-2).

  I do not think it is appropriate, in an abstract model such as I assume RM/V2 is intended to be, to *require* a clear separation between database operations and host language—i.e., to bless the "embedded data sublanguage" approach—even if one happens to think that the sublanguage idea is a good one, which I do not [7]. And I do not think it is appropriate (again in an abstract model) to *require* that database operations be compiled, not interpreted, even though there may be good reasons to prefer compilation. Nor do I think it appropriate (again in an abstract model) to bless the System R approach of automatic recompilation, even though (again) it may be a good idea in many cases.

---

*It *is* prohibited in RM/V2--see features RS-1 and RM-5 and RM-16, and probably others.

- "[The relational language must be] more closely related to the relational calculus . . . than to the relational algebra" (feature RL-9).

  Very debatable!—even though I do prefer the calculus myself. The argument Codd gives to support this requirement, namely that it improves optimizability, is specious (see reference [23]).

- "There must be a single canonical form for every request . . ." (feature RL-12).

  While I am in sympathy with the objectives behind this requirement, I doubt whether it is achievable as stated.

- "Time-oriented conditions can be included in any condition specified in a [database] command . . ." (feature RL-16).

  Another example of lack of orthogonality in the requirements as stated. If time-oriented functions ("time now," "date today," etc.) are provided, as they obviously should be, then the feature is logically redundant—there is no need to state it as an explicit requirement.

Incidentally, it seems to me that if RM/V2 is to lay down a set of principles regarding language design, then it really ought to give some credit to, or at least pay some attention to, the achievements of the programming languages community over the last 30 years or so—especially since the most visible "achievement" of the database community in this regard, namely SQL (in all of its various forms), is in so many ways the prize example of how *not* to do it. See, e.g., reference [8].

Manipulation (Class M)

The manipulative class of features requires a "comprehensive data sublanguage" (note that this requirement was one of Codd's original "twelve rules" [2,19]), plus set-level INSERT, UPDATE, and DELETE operations, plus three- and four-valued logic support. It also includes (or reemphasizes):

(a) The need to support transactions (BEGIN, COMMIT, and ROLLBACK operations);

(b) The importance of closure;

(c) The importance of "dynamic mode" (e.g., the need to be able to create and drop tables without halting the system);

(d) The need for an appropriate interface to record-at-a-time languages such as COBOL;

(e) The importance of domain-constrained operators and "domain check override";

(f) "Library checkout and return" operators (intended as a primitive level of support for version control).

Regarding (a) here, Codd also requires a special kind of transaction—called a "catalog block"—for performing data definition operations; it is not really clear why two distinct transaction mechanisms are necessary (another example of lack of orthogonality?). Regarding (d), Codd goes out of his way to suggest that SQL-style cursors are *not* very satisfactory for the purpose, an opinion with which I concur. Regarding (e), I disagree with Codd's approach to this whole area (see Section 4). Likewise, I also disagree with his requirement for three- and four-valued logic support (again, see Section 4).

Naming (Class N)

Codd proposes a naming scheme for "domains and data types," relations and columns (including result relations and columns), "archived relations," functions, and integrity constraints (though oddly enough not security constraints*). And later he also proposes an extension of this scheme to be used in the distributed database context (class X).

As mentioned earlier, naming is one of the areas in which I have major concerns. I will therefore defer further comment on this subject until Section 4.

Protection (Class P)

"Protection" here means "protection of the user's investment." This class consists essentially of the physical data independence, logical data independence, integrity independence, and distribution independence features from Codd's original "twelve rules" [2,19]. No further comment.

Qualifiers (Class Q)

Qualifiers are *statement modifiers:* They are used within a statement "to alter some aspect of the execution of that [statement]." The available qualifiers are summarized below:

1. A-MAYBE: Converts the *inapplicable* truth value to *true.*
2. I-MAYBE: Converts the *unknown* truth value to *true.*
3. MAYBE: Logical OR of A- and I-maybe.
4. AR(x): Replaces "inapplicable" values by x during evaluation of some aggregate function.
5. IR(x): Replaces "unknown" values by x during evaluation of some aggregate function.

---

*This omission is presumably due to the fact that security constraints in RM/V2 are created by a SQL-style GRANT statement instead of by some kind of CREATE PERMIT operation.

6. ESR(*x*): Replaces empty relations by a relation containing the single tuple *x* during evaluation of some expression.

7. ORDER BY: Orders the result of a retrieval operation.

8. ONCE ONLY: (This qualifier applies only to some rather complex new operators called "T-joins," details of which are beyond the scope of this review. For more information, the reader is referred to Codd's book.)

9. DCO: "Domain check override." See Section 4.

10. EXCLUDE SIBLINGS: (Another complex one. This one has to do with the "cascade" update operations, in the case where multiple relations share a common primary key. Again, the reader is referred to Codd's book for more information.)

11. DOD: "Degree of duplication" (applies to projections and unions only). "For each row in the result, the DBMS calculates the number of occurrences of that row [that would have appeared in the result] if duplicate rows had been permitted. . . . This count is appended to each row in the actual result as . . . the *DOD column.*"

12. SAVE: Causes the result of a relational assignment to be saved in the database. (In RM/V2, relational assignment without this qualifier merely causes the expression on the right hand side of the assignment to be evaluated and the result to be saved, under a user-specified name, "in memory" [3].)

13. VALUE(*x*): Causes a column that is added to an existing base table (e.g., via APPEND COLUMN, feature RE-10) to be filled in every row with the value *x* instead of with a null. (*Note:* RM/V2 does not actually use the term "null." See later.)

The foregoing thumbnail sketches should be more than adequate to suggest that the "Qualifiers" class of features is rather ad hoc and not very orthogonal. To take two examples, more or less at random: First, given proper, orthogonal treatment for the aggregate functions (COUNT in particular), the "DOD" qualifier is totally redundant. Second, instead of an "IR(*x*)" qualifier—assuming for the sake of the discussion that we accept the idea that support for unknown-style "nulls" is desirable in the first place—surely it would be preferable to have a DB2-style VALUE function, or an ORACLE-style NVL function, or an INGRES-style IFNULL function (or whatever), and then to permit that function to be used completely orthogonally (i.e., to appear wherever a scalar literal of the appropriate type can appear).

Structure (Class S)

The only arguably new features in this class are those having to do with composite domains and composite columns (see below). The others are basically as expected—relations, columns, prohibition of duplicate rows,* prohibition of "positional concepts," primary and foreign keys, "domains as extended data types," representation of missing information by "marks," and so on. (Codd prefers to talk about "marks" instead of "nulls," partly in order to make it clear that in RM/V2 the representation of the fact that a piece of information is missing is not itself a value.)

Regarding composite domains and columns: I have to say that I find RM/V2 very muddled in this area. For instance: "The sequence in which the component columns are cited in [the declaration of the composite column] is part of the meaning of the [composite column]." So (A,B) and (B,A) are *different?* I thought there was a prohibition against "positional concepts"? And much worse: Reference [3] says that the expression "C θ D," where C and D are composite columns with components (C1,C2,C3) and (D1,D2,D3) respectively, is evaluated by performing "the sequence of tests C1 θ D1, then C2 θ D2, then C3 θ D3. The first test that fails causes the whole test to fail." According to this definition:

(1,4) = (1,5) is *false* (of course)

(1,4) ¬= (1,5) is *false*

(1,7) < (2,6) is *false*

(1,7) ¬< (2,6) is *false*

and an infinite number of similar absurdities. Note in particular that by these rules—using "¬" to mean NOT—the expressions "¬ (C θ D)" and "(C ¬θ D)" are not equivalent, in general!

Of course, if we limit our attention for the moment to composite columns, C and D say, with just two components each, the problem of assigning a meaning to the comparison "C θ D" is exactly the problem of assigning a meaning to the comparison "$z1$ θ $z2$" where $z1$ and $z2$ are complex numbers—and, of course, this latter comparison is defined only when θ is "equals" or "not equals."[†]

---

*Incidentally, I lost count of the number of times reference [3] told me that duplication was not permitted.

[†]In fairness, I should perhaps point out that Codd may not have intended his rule to apply to the case where θ is ¬= " (not equals). His book talks about "comparator[s] such as LESS THAN." It all depends what "such as" means, I suppose.

In any case, I believe that "complex domains" and "complex columns" per se should not be supported at all, as I have argued elsewhere [17,18].

Data Types (Class T)

RM/V2 requires certain specific "extended" data types (though apparently no specific *basic* data types?) to be built into the DBMS: calendar dates, clock times, and decimal currency. It also requires support for user-defined "extended" data types. Curiously, the discussion of data types nowhere mentions the necessary associated operators; instead, these are discussed elsewhere (in class F, functions), in a very divorced kind of manner. But a data type has no meaning without operators. In particular, the only significant distinction I can see between "decimal currency" and "decimal numbers" is that certain operators—e.g., multiply—might make sense for the latter but not for the former.* And a user-defined data type makes no sense at all without a corresponding set of user-defined operators.

Class T also includes two truly bizarre "FAO commands" (where FAO means "find all occurrences"). Here is an example from the book: "Find all occurrences of all city names that exist anywhere in the database . . . The result is a relation [with column names as follows]":

    (RELNAME, COLNAME, PK, VALUE)

PK here gives the column name(s) for the primary key of the relation identified by RELNAME, and VALUE gives a value for that primary key (i.e., a value that identifies a row that contains a city name in the column identified by COLNAME, presumably). Some questions: Where is the city name value in this relation? What is the primary key of this relation? What is the data type of that primary key? Does that primary key comply with the entity integrity rule? What is the data type for column VALUE? How does the user access columns PK and VALUE, given that (in general) they are composite, with an unknown (and variable) number of components? What about the case where columns PK and VALUE have no components (i.e., if the relation identified by RELNAME has a nullary primary key [27])? How could the FAO command be used to find all occurrences of "null"? What would the primary key of the result be in *that* case? Would *that* primary key comply with the entity integrity rule? Etc., etc., etc.

---

*RM/V2 actually requires decimal currency values to be represented as "nonnegative integers." Why *integers*?—surely "correct to two decimal places" would make more sense? And why *nonnegative*?—account balances, for example, might easily be negative.

Views (Class V)

RM/V2 requires proper support for views, including support for all retrieval operations and all theoretically possible update operations. The
book (i.e., reference [3]) gives some informal algorithms for the updating
case.* I support these requirements, of course; my only comment (already
mentioned earlier in this review) is that there is almost no acknowledgment
(except for a couple of throwaway remarks) of the large amount of work
done in this area by other researchers.

Distributed Database Management (Class X)

There seems to be little new here (although, again, there is very little acknowledgment of previous work, except for occasional scanty references to
the IBM R* prototype). But the tone (once again) is much too prescriptive:
A particular approach to the distributed database problem is *required,* an
approach that is at least partly debatable and is at least partly specified at
the wrong level of abstraction. And there are a few curious remarks and
claims—for example: ". . . it is a simple task to extend a local-only optimizer to handle the distributed case"; "all of the data residing at any site
X . . . can be treated by the users at site X in exactly the same way as if it
were . . . isolated from the rest of the network" (this objective is not fully
achievable [15]); "adoption of this assumption [of uniform value distribu-
tions in columns] is a significant step in the right direction" (i.e., toward
getting good statistics-based optimization); "there is every reason to believe
that the naming rules introduced here [for the distributed database environ-
ment] actually work and would satisfy most users' needs."

Advanced Operators (Class Z)

Here is a brief summary of the operators in this class.

1. FRAME: FRAME is basically an attack on the problem addressed in
   SQL by GROUP BY; however, the result of FRAME is another rela-
   tion, instead of the (conceptual) "set of relations" produced by
   GROUP BY. However, I see no need to apply FRAME without then

---

*The book does include one oddity regarding view updatability: In a discussion of the need to
retain the primary key of the underlying table in a projection view if that view is to be updatable, it says "[it would be possible to retain a candidate key instead of the primary key, but
RM/V2 does not allow for this case,] partly because the class of updatable views would not
be significantly enlarged in this way, and partly because *RM/V1 and RM/V2 do not require
all of the candidate keys for every base relation to be recorded in the catalog*" (emphasis
added).

immediately applying some further operation (probably an aggregate function) to the result. I would prefer a SUMMARIZE operator along the lines sketched in reference [18].

2. EXTEND: An ad hoc, incomplete, nonorthogonal approach to dynamically adding columns (possibly computed columns) to a relation. I would prefer an EXTEND operator along the lines sketched in reference [18].

3. SEMIJOIN: The semijoin of A with B is the regular (inner) join of A and B, projected back on to the columns of A. While this operator can sometimes be useful *internally,* I see no need to expose it to the user, or to include it in any version of the relational model. In other words, I think RM/V2 is at the wrong level of abstraction again.

4. OUTER JOIN: I assume the reader is familiar with this operator. I remark, however, that RM/V2 does not address the (very difficult) question of what kinds of "null" (or "mark") should be generated in the result. It does, however, address the baroque question of the interaction between "outer" operations and "maybe" operations; in fact, the "maybe" qualifier is *first discussed* in the context of the "outer" operations (reference [3], page 110), nearly 100 pages before it is explained.

5. OUTER UNION, OUTER INTERSECTION, OUTER DIFFERENCE: The definitions of these operations have (silently) been changed, but they are still—in my opinion—completely bizarre. I will not bother to give the new definitions here, which are in any case quite complex. For details, the reader is referred to Codd's book.

6. T-JOIN: ". . . the expected use of [the T-join operator]" is "for generating schedules" [3]. The operator is very complex, and I will not try to explain it here (Codd's explanation takes over 13 pages)—though I will mention that it basically seems to be a specific application of the new comparison operators "least greater than," etc., which I have already commented on in this review. Once again, for details the reader is referred to the source [3].

7. User-defined SELECT and JOIN: These names are inappropriate, and indeed misleading. What is really being proposed is the ability for users to define their own truth-valued functions. Orthogonality (if available) would then take care of the rest.

8. Recursive JOIN: Given a relation that represents an acyclic directed graph, this operator computes the transitive closure of that graph (slightly simplified explanation). The intent is to provide a basis for an attack on the bill-of-materials problem. Here I will only remark that,

while this operator is clearly necessary (and desirable), there is a lot more that needs to be done to address the bill-of-materials requirement fully [22].

Codd's class of "advanced operators" does not include Warden's SUMMARIZE and EXTEND (as already mentioned), nor any kind of generalized DIVIDE operator, nor a proper column RENAME operator [18]. I note also that Codd does not seem to give relational calculus versions or definitions for any of the new RM/V2 operators (in fact, reference [3] says very little about the relational calculus at all, in any context).

Summary

The only idea in all of the foregoing that is genuinely new, in the sense that I have never seen it discussed before in the literature, seems to be the set of new comparison operators ("least greater than," etc.). I think that's it! And even here, I find matters somewhat confused—first, because a comparison involving such an operator is not a restriction condition, as already pointed out; second, because there is a lack of orthogonality in the treatment of those operators; and third, because Codd himself says the operators are not new anyway but "well known"! (reference [3], page 123).

If the reader does not agree with the foregoing assessment, then I challenge him or her to point to a significant feature of RM/V2 that is [worthwhile and] not already described in some previously published book or paper.

By contrast, I do find numerous ideas in RM/V2 that are not new, or are muddled, or are just plain bad. Some important concerns are articulated in Section 4 immediately following.

4. MAJOR AREAS OF CONCERN

In this section I will briefly consider some serious problems with RM/V2. Space does not permit detailed elaboration of all of my concerns; in most cases, therefore, I will simply state my overriding objection(s) to Codd's proposal(s), and give some references to other papers that present alternative approaches.

Naming

Codd's proposed naming scheme is extremely ad hoc (to say the least), involves a number of arbitrary and dogmatic judgments, and includes some suggestions that are plainly wrong. The suggestion for naming columns in the result of a union, intersection, or difference operation (based on alphabetical ordering of names of operand columns) is weak—not to mention the fact that it is implementation- (i.e., alphabet-) dependent. The suggestion for naming columns in the result of a join or division operation is very bad (it violates closure). And the suggestion for naming columns that are the result of a scalar computation is grotesque; if taken literally, it would give the name "+.A", or possibly "+.A+", or possibly even "+.A+B" [sic], to the result of evaluating the expression "A + B"!* Furthermore, which one of these three names is actually assigned in any given situation is unpredictable, in general. (The reader is invited to meditate on the case of, e.g., a union of two relations involving such computed columns.) And there are further problems having to do with columns that are derived from literals (Codd's scheme does not address them), and with name uniqueness (Codd's scheme does not guarantee it), and with predictability (Codd's scheme does not guarantee it), and with "composite columns" (see earlier), and with the distributed database environment.

A naming scheme that is far better than Codd's—one that is closed, systematic, comprehensive, not ad hoc, etc.—is sketched in reference [28].

Data Types

I have explained elsewhere [11] what I think proper data type support should consist of. Codd's approach is again very ad hoc. A few quotes:

- "For each composite domain, of course, the sequence in which the [component] domains are specified is a vital part of the definition."

- "Note that a composite column is restricted to combining simple columns . . . I fail to see the practical need for [composite columns defined on composite columns]."

- (From a discussion of class I, integrity:) "One reason that C-type integrity [i.e., column integrity] is part of the relational model is that it makes it possible to avoid the needless complexities and proliferations of domains that are subsets of other domains."

- "When comparing (1) a computed value with a database value or (2) one computed value with another computed value . . . the DBMS merely checks that the *basic data types* are the same" (emphasis added). I have pointed out elsewhere [11] that this rule implies (among many other things) that the semantics of the two logically equivalent expressions

---

*Note the implication that "+" must be valid as a range variable name! (I am indebted to Hugh Darwen for this observation.)

```
P.WEIGHT > SP.QTY
```

and

```
P.WEIGHT - SP.QTY > 0
```

are different, which CANNOT be correct, or acceptable.

- ". . . the basic data type indicates whether arithmetic operators are applicable" (in the discussion of feature RE-3, CREATE DOMAIN). So the expression

```
P.WEIGHT * P.WEIGHT
```

is legal? Square weights?

Also, despite Codd's remarks on the subject (reference [3], page 44), I still do not understand the *real* difference between "basic" and "extended" data types. Nor do I think there is any, operationally speaking.* See reference [12] for further discussion of this question.

While we are on this general subject, I note too that the book includes a couple of rather fundamental questions for the reader—"What is the precise definition of a domain in the relational model?" (Exercise 2.2) and "Define the candidate key concept" (Exercise 2.5)—to which, so far as I could tell, the book does not provide any good answers. And Exercise 2.12 says: "Supply two reasons why the DBA should always control the introduction of new [data] types . . . to ensure that [their] values are atomic in meaning as well as atomic with respect to the DBMS." I would be very hard pressed to say exactly what this means, but the general intent seems to be that user-defined data types should not be allowed to be "of arbitrary complexity," a position that I do not agree with [11].

Finally, I categorically reject the "domain check override" idea, for reasons explained in reference [11].

Operators

I have no objection (of course) to extending the relational model to include new operators such as (e.g.) T-joins and recursive joins (though I reserve judgment on those particular operators per se). But I do think it is important to get the basic operators right first, and I do not think that RM/V2 has done this yet. See reference [18] for a discussion of what I would regard as a preferable set of basic operators.

---

*Though a fruitful analogy *might* be drawn between the system-defined vs. user-defined data types distinction on the one hand and the system-defined vs. user-defined relations distinction on the other—where by "system-defined relations" I mean basically the relations in the catalog.

Missing Information Support

I find everything to do with three-and four-valued logic support fundamentally misguided, and I categorically reject it [14]. Moreover, the chapter in Codd's book entitled "Response to Technical Criticisms Regarding Missing Information" does not properly respond to any of the really serious questions raised in reference [14]. (Incidentally, that chapter mentions "Date 1986" as a paper that criticizes the three-valued logic approach, but excludes that paper from the list of references—which makes it a little difficult for readers to study the arguments for themselves! For the record, "Date 1986" is the present review's reference [9]. But in any case, I now think the questions raised in reference [14] are much more serious.)

Orthogonality

I have mentioned my concerns in this area a couple of times already, and I will not repeat the details here. But I will offer this additional thought: If the principle of orthogonality had been applied to the statement of requirements in RM/V2, would there really have been a need for 333 distinct features?

Distributed Database Support

Again, I have already stated my overall objection in this area—namely, the combination of a controversial approach to the problem with an insistence on that approach being the one that must be followed. Codd ignores much of the work that has already been done on the distributed database problem, and his proposals are sometimes at the wrong level of abstraction. For instance: "The network [must contain] N copies ($N > 1$) of the global catalog, in the form of N small databases at N distinct sites" (feature RX-4); "The DBMS [must detect] intersite deadlocks" (feature RX-29); "The source code of application programs can contain local names, but these are converted by the DBMS . . . into global names. . . . It is this *globalized source code* that is retained in the system and remains unaffected by redeployment of the data, partly because it contains no local names" (reference [3], page 397).

5.   MISCELLANEOUS COMMENTS

In this section, I would like to offer a few miscellaneous comments—comments, that is, that do not properly belong in any of the previous sections of this review and yet I feel ought not to be lost entirely.

- First, regarding the question (already touched on several times) of levels of abstraction: It seems to me that there are quite a few features of RM/V2 that have no place in an abstract model. For example, there is much talk of indexes (of various kinds); there is a requirement that deleted data be archived "for seven days"; there is a requirement that data of type TIME be accurate to the second (no more and no less); there is a requirement that the system "avoid generating Cartesian products"; there is a requirement (as mentioned earlier) for compilation as opposed to interpretation and for an embedded sublanguage approach; the example (reference [3], page 26) of "several relations sharing a primary key" is surely of *stored* relations, not base relations or other relations that are visible to the user; the explanation of feature RS-13 (reference [3], page 39) talks about "bit boundaries." Many more examples could be given.

- There are several curious remarks in the book about join dependencies and fifth normal form [5]. First, feature RI-30 talks about join dependencies, and introduces a notation for them, in a way that simply makes no sense so far as I can see: "Column A is join dependent on columns B and C: R.A = R.B * R.C." Incidentally, in what sense is this a *feature* of the model anyway?*

    Codd then requires the catalog for a distributed database (but not, apparently, for a centralized database?) to contain definitions of relations *in fifth normal form* (emphasis added). But this requirement is unenforceable.† Of course, we could prohibit the specification of integrity constraints that happened to be join dependencies not implied by candidate keys (though I suspect that even this might be nontrivial to do, given the multiplicity of syntactic ways of stating such a constraint). But, of course:

    (a) Prohibiting such *specifications* does not mean that such constraints do not *exist*.

    (b) The twin objectives of Boyce-Codd normal form and "independent projections" can occasionally be in conflict [5], and so Boyce-Codd normal form (and hence, a fortiori, fifth normal form) is not even always desirable.

---

*The same question applies to "features" RI-28 and RI-29, which have to do with functional and multivalued dependencies respectively. Also, feature RI-28 says ". . . the DBMS assumes that all columns . . . are functionally dependent on the primary key, *unless otherwise declared*" (emphasis added). This remark is quite puzzling, given that (of course) *all* columns of a given relation are dependent on the primary key of that relation, always.

†Especially since, as pointed out earlier, "RM/V2 [does] not require all of the candidate keys for every base relation to be recorded in the catalog"!

- Reference [3] gives an example (page 270) that "clearly indicate[s] the need for the host language to be usable in programming the triggered action" (i.e., the action to be taken if an integrity constraint is violated—what I have referred to elsewhere as the *violation response* [13]). I would argue that what the example "clearly indicates" is, rather, that it was a mistake to separate the host language and the database language in the first place.

- In a very strange subsection entitled "Relating View Updatability to Normalization," we find the following: ". . . if a base relation T is the outer equijoin of two relations R and S that are more fundamental than T, but are not base relations themselves, R and S should nevertheless be described in the catalog . . . Such relations are . . . called *conceptual relations.*" I believe there is some confusion here.

- "Some excellent work on this transformation [of SQL queries involving nested subqueries to queries involving joins] has been done (Kim 1982, Ganski and Wong 1987)" (reference [3], page 380). While not at all wishing to discredit the referenced work, of course, I must point out that it does contain a number of errors, many of them having to do with three-valued logic; see references [4] and [16] for further discussion of this point.

- Reference [3] claims (page 81) that the union of two relations that have "the same" primary key also has "the same" primary key. This claim is false.

- Reference [3], page 183, first paragraph, apparently (and incredibly) suggests that it is acceptable to build logical inconsistencies into our databases and DBMSs . . . !

6. CONCLUSION

In the body of this review, I have necessarily had to concentrate on what seem to me to be the major problems with RM/V2. It seems to me that a number of those problems are very significant indeed, though I am of course open to discussion on such issues. But I certainly do not want the reader to think the list of problems is exhaustive; there are numerous additional items in reference [3] that give me cause for concern. Some of them are merely typographical (e.g., "L< =" instead of "L> =" on page 485 and elsewhere), but they could cause confusion; some are more serious (e.g., silent—and occasionally incompatible—changes in the definitions of DIVIDE, duplicates, outer union, entity integrity, and many other items); some are inconsistencies or contradictions (e.g., pages 247 and 248 contradict each other on the timing of "type E" integrity constraints); some are just wrong (e.g., the claim on page 338 that "this query could not be expressed as simply in SQL"). The reader is warned.

ACKNOWLEDGMENTS

I am grateful to Charley Bontempo, Hugh Darwen, and David McGoveran for their helpful comments on earlier drafts of this review.

REFERENCES AND BIBLIOGRAPHY

1. E. F. Codd and C. J. Date, "Interactive Support for Nonprogrammers: The Relational and Network Approaches," *Proc. 1974 ACM SIGMOD Workshop on Data Description, Access, and Control,* Ann Arbor, MI (May 1974).

2. E. F. Codd, "Is Your DBMS Really Relational?" (*Computerworld,* October 14th, 1985); "Does Your DBMS Run by the Rules?" (*Computerworld,* October 21st, 1985).

3. E. F. Codd, *The Relational Model for Database Management Version 2* (Reading, MA: Addison-Wesley, 1990).

4. C. J. Date, "Query Optimization," Chapter 18 of C. J. Date, *An Introduction to Database Systems: Volume I,* 5th edition (Reading, MA: Addison-Wesley, 1990).

5. C. J. Date, "Further Normalization," Chapter 21 of C. J. Date, *An Introduction to Database Systems: Volume I,* 5th edition (Reading, MA: Addison-Wesley, 1990).

6. C. J. Date, "Referential Integrity," *Proc. 7th International Conference on Very Large Data Bases,* Cannes, France (September 1981). Republished in slightly revised form in C. J. Date, *Relational Database: Selected Writings* (Reading, MA: Addison-Wesley, 1986).

7. C. J. Date, "An Introduction to the Unified Database Language (UDL)," in C. J. Date, *Relational Database: Selected Writings* (Reading, MA: Addison-Wesley, 1986).

8. C. J. Date, "Some Principles of Good Language Design," in C. J. Date, *Relational Database: Selected Writings* (Reading, MA: Addison-Wesley, 1986).

9. C. J. Date, "Null Values in Database Management," in C. J. Date, *Relational Database: Selected Writings* (Reading, MA: Addison-Wesley, 1986).

10. C. J. Date, "Updating Views," in C. J. Date, *Relational Database: Selected Writings* (Reading, MA: Addison-Wesley, 1986).

11. C. J. Date, "What Is a Domain?" in C. J. Date, *Relational Database Writings 1985-1989* (Reading, MA: Addison-Wesley, 1990).

12. C. J. Date, "User-Defined vs. Extended Data Types," Appendix A to "What Is a Domain?" in C. J. Date, *Relational Database Writings 1985-1989* (Reading, MA: Addison-Wesley, 1990).

13. C. J. Date, "A Contribution to the Study of Database Integrity," in C. J. Date, *Relational Database Writings 1985-1989* (Reading, MA: Addison-Wesley, 1990).

14. C. J. Date, "NOT Is Not "Not"! (Notes on Three-Valued Logic and Related Matters)," in C. J. Date, *Relational Database Writings 1985-1989* (Reading, MA: Addison-Wesley, 1990).

15. C. J. Date, "What Is a Distributed Database System?" in C. J. Date, *Relational Database Writings 1985-1989* (Reading, MA: Addison-Wesley, 1990).

16. C. J. Date, "EXISTS Is Not "Exists"! (Some Logical Flaws in SQL)," in C. J. Date, *Relational Database Writings 1985-1989* (Reading, MA: Addison-Wesley, 1990).

17. C. J. Date, "What Is a Relation?" (in this volume).

18. C. J. Date, "Notes Toward a Reconstituted Definition of The Relational Model Version 1 (RM/V1)" (in this volume).

19. C. J. Date, "An Assessment of Codd's Evaluation Scheme," Appendix D to "Notes Toward a Reconstituted Definition of the Relational Model Version 1 (RM/V1)" (in this volume).

20. Umeshwar Dayal and Philip A. Bernstein, "On the Correct Translation of Update Operations on Relational Views," *ACM Transactions on Database Systems* 7, No. 3 (September 1982).

21. K. P. Eswaran and D. D. Chamberlin, "Functional Specifications of a Subsystem for Data Base Integrity," *Proc. 1st International Conference on Very Large Data Bases,* Framingham, MA (September 1975).

22. Nathan Goodman, "Bill of Materials in Relational Database," *InfoDB* 5, No. 1 (Spring/Summer 1990).

23. P. A. V. Hall, "Optimisation of a Single Relational Expression in a Relational Data Base System," *IBM Journal of Research and Development* 20, No. 3 (May 1976).

24. Arthur M. Keller, "Algorithms for Translating View Updates to Database Updates for Views Involving Selections, Projections, and Joins," *Proc. 4th ACM SIGACT-SIGMOD Symposium on Principles of Database Systems,* Portland, OR (March 1985).

25. David McGoveran, "A Long Time Coming," *Database Programming and Design* 3, No. 9 (September 1990).

26. J. B. Rothnie, Jr., and N. Goodman, "A Survey of Research and Development in Distributed Database Management," *Proc. 3rd International Conference on Very Large Data Bases,* Tokyo, Japan (October 1977).

27. Andrew Warden, "Table_Dee and Table_Dum," in C. J. Date, *Relational Database Writings 1985-1989* (Reading, MA: Addison-Wesley, 1990).

28. Andrew Warden, "The Naming of Columns," in C. J. Date, *Relational Database Writings 1985-1989* (Reading, MA: Addison-Wesley, 1990).

APPENDIX A:
THE "FUNDAMENTAL LAWS" OF DATABASE MANAGEMENT

In Chapter 29 of his book, Codd introduces "some 20 principles with which any approach to database management should comply. . . . [These] fundamental laws are principles to which the relational model adheres." Now, I do not think Codd is claiming here that the laws were developed first, i.e., before the relational model was developed; certainly I never saw them in print before the publication of reference [3]. Indeed, it might be argued that the "laws" represent, as much as anything, features that happen to *characterize* the relational approach, rather than a set of formal underpinnings from which that approach was developed. But the idea of trying to identify such a set of laws, even if after the fact, is certainly an interesting one, and in this appendix I would like to examine it briefly.

As soon as Codd's book suggested the idea to me, I took a few minutes to jot down what seemed to me to be a reasonable set of such "fundamental laws." Here is the list I came up with:

- The DBMS must not forget anything it has been told to remember (i.e., data must not be lost)
- The DBMS must function from the user's point of view as an abstract machine
- That abstract machine must (of course) be formally and precisely defined
- Two specific corollaries of the previous point are that the behavior of the DBMS must be *predictable* and *repeatable*
- The higher the level of abstraction, the better (broadly speaking)
- It must not be necessary to go to a lower level of abstraction in order to explain the functioning of the abstract machine
- The abstract machine must possess certain specific features:
  - Parsimony (no unnecessary complexity)
  - Orthogonality
  - Closure
  - Identifiability (distinct objects are distinguishable)
  - Integrity is a property of the data

- Isolation (users can behave as if the database were private)
- Ownership (each piece of data belongs to some specific user)

Now, this list is certainly incomplete: It is the result of perhaps fifteen minutes' thought, and I make no great claims for it. Though it did occur to me as I was compiling it that most of the points applied equally well to programming languages, and that a study of the design of a well-conceived language (Algol 68 suggests itself) would probably turn up a few more "fundamental laws."

Here, by contrast, are the laws that Codd gives (with a few words of explanation in those cases that seem to warrant it):

1. Object identification
2. Objects identified in one way
3. Unrelated portions of a database ("if the database can be split into . . . unrelated parts without loss of information, . . . there [must exist] a simple and general algorithm . . . to make this split")
4. Community issues ("all database issues of concern to the community of users . . . should be . . . explicitly declared . . . and managed by the DBMS")
5. Three levels of concepts (logical, physical, and "psychological" issues should not be confused)
6. Same logical level of abstraction for all users
7. Self-contained logical level of abstraction (this is the same as my point that it should not be necessary to go to a lower level of abstraction in order to explain anything; but I think Codd violates this law himself in several places in RM/V2--e.g., in his explanation of T-joins)
8. Sharp separation (between logical and physical)
9. No iterative or recursive loops
10. Parts of the database interrelated by value comparing
11. Dynamic approach ("dynamic data definition," etc.)
12. Extent to which data should be typed ("types should be strict enough to capture some of the meaning of the data, but not so strict as to make the initially planned uses and applications the only viable ones")
13. Creating and dropping performance-oriented structures
14. Adjustments in the content of performance-oriented structures
15. Reexecutable commands
16. Prohibition of cursors *within the database* (emphasis in the original)
17. Protection against integrity loss

18. Recovery of integrity

19. Redistribution of data without damaging application programs

20. Semantic distinctiveness ("semantically distinct observations . . . must be represented distinctly to the users"; I am not really sure what this means, but Codd goes on to say that "The crucial question is: If the data were removed, would information be lost?")

Comparing the two lists, it seems to me that they are really at two different levels, with the first being the more abstract. Furthermore, it seems to me that the second is not even at a *uniform* level of abstraction. But I will stop here, leaving the question as a matter for the reader to judge.

THE PROBLEM OF
MISSING INFORMATION

```
SELECT  EMP#
FROM    EMP
WHERE   MAYBE ( DEPT# = 'D1' AND
                'D1' IN ( SELECT DEPT#
                          FROM    DEPT ) ) ;
```

Observe that the problem illustrated here is different in kind from that illustrated by Example 1 above. The problem in Example 1 was that "pure" three-valued logic does not recognize that the two references in the expression that evaluate to UNK are in fact two references to the same thing, and hence *must* refer to the same value. The problem in Example 2 is that treating UNK as *totally* unknown can also lead to wrong answers; it is necessary to take into account any additional knowledge that may be available in order to constrain the set of possible values that the UNK might stand for. Again, therefore, "pure" three-valued logic is not behaving in accordance with the way the real world behaves.

4. HOW GOOD IS YOUR INTUITION?

I will close with another example, based on the well-known suppliers-and-parts database (see Chapter 1, Appendix A), or rather a slight variation on that database; the only difference compared with the more familiar version is that table SP includes an additional column, SHIP#, which serves as the primary key for that table, and columns SP.S# and SP.P# do NOT have "NULLS NOT ALLOWED." Fig. 2 shows a set of sample values.

In reference [4], I posed the following problem: What does the following query mean? (*Note:* The query was deliberately expressed in terms of relational calculus instead of SQL for reasons beyond the scope of this article. They are explained in the original paper [4].)

```
S.SNAME WHERE NOT ( EXISTS SP ( SP.S# = S.S# AND SP.P# = 'P2' ) )
```

S

S#	SNAME	STATUS	CITY
S1	Smith	20	London
S2	Jones	10	Paris
S3	Blake	30	Paris
S4	Clark	20	UNK

SP

SHIP#	S#	P#	QTY
SHIP1	S1	P1	300
SHIP2	S2	P2	200
SHIP3	S3	UNK	400

P

P#	PNAME	COLOR	WEIGHT	CITY
P1	Nut	Red	12	London
P2	Bolt	Green	17	Paris

Fig. 2 The suppliers-and-parts database (variation)

Possible interpretations include at least all of the following:

(a) Find names of suppliers who do not supply part P2

(b) Find names of suppliers who are not known to supply part P2 (i.e., they *might* supply part P2, but the system does not know whether they do or not)

(c) Find names of suppliers who are known not to supply part P2 (i.e., they are *definitely* known not to supply part P2)

(d) Find names of suppliers who are either known not or not known to supply part P2 (this is the union of (b) and (c))

Reference [4] shows that the correct interpretation of the query is interpretation (c). (You should probably take the time to convince yourself that this is correct before continuing—it is certainly not obvious!) Now I would like to extend the example. Question: Which of the following expressions (if any) is equivalent to the one shown above?

```
S.SNAME WHERE NOT           ( S.S# IN ( SP.S# WHERE SP.P# = 'P2' ) )

S.SNAME WHERE NOT           ( S.S# IN ( SP.S# WHERE SP.P# = 'P2' ) )
        AND    NOT ( MAYBE ( S.S# IN ( SP.S# WHERE SP.P# = 'P2' ) ) )

S.SNAME WHERE NOT           ( S.S# IN ( SP.S# WHERE SP.P# = 'P2' ) )
        AND    NOT ( S.S# IN ( SP.S# WHERE MAYBE ( SP.P# = 'P2' ) ) )
```

The answer is given in Appendix A, and I defer further discussion to that appendix; here I will simply remark that close study of this example reveals further "psychological" difficulties over three-valued logic, this time having to do with the behavior of the IN operator.

5. CONCLUSION

This short note can be regarded as an appendix to reference [4]. It provides further evidence that three-valued logic is fraught with difficulties and traps for the unwary—the unwary implementer, that is, as well as the unwary user. Note that the problems are not merely problems with SQL; my objective has been to point out certain difficulties, not with SQL per se, but rather with some of the underlying ideas on which SQL is based (although in passing I will mention that SQL does manage to introduce some additional flaws of its own in this area—see reference [5]). Thus, it is still far from clear to me that three-valued logic is desirable as an approach to the missing information problem, or even that its implications are as yet fully understood.

ACKNOWLEDGMENTS

I am grateful to Nagraj Alur, Charley Bontempo, Hugh Darwen, Nat Goodman, and Colin White for several helpful discussions.

REFERENCES AND BIBLIOGRAPHY

1. E. F. Codd, "Extending the Database Relational Model to Capture More Meaning," *ACM Transactions on Database Systems* 4, No. 4 (December 1979).

2. E. F. Codd, "Missing Information (Applicable and Inapplicable) in Relational Databases," *ACM SIGMOD Record* 15, No. 4 (December 1986).

3. E. F. Codd, "More Commentary on Missing Information in Relational Databases (Applicable and Inapplicable Information)," *ACM SIGMOD Record* 16, No. 1 (March 1987).

4. C. J. Date, "NOT Is Not "Not"! (Notes on Three-Valued Logic and Related Matters)," in C. J. Date, *Relational Database Writings 1985–1989* (Reading, MA: Addison-Wesley, 1990).

5. C. J. Date, "EXISTS Is Not "Exists"! (Some Logical Flaws in SQL)," in C. J. Date, *Relational Database Writings 1985–1989* (Reading, MA: Addison-Wesley, 1990).

APPENDIX A:
ANSWERS TO EXERCISES

In the body of the paper (Section 4), I posed the following problem: Given (a slight variation on) the usual suppliers-and-parts database, which if any of the following expressions—

```
(a)  S.SNAME WHERE NOT             ( S.S# IN ( SP.S# WHERE SP.P# = 'P2' ) )

(b)  S.SNAME WHERE NOT             ( S.S# IN ( SP.S# WHERE SP.P# = 'P2' ) )
             AND    NOT ( MAYBE ( S.S# IN ( SP.S# WHERE SP.P# = 'P2' ) ) )

(c)  S.SNAME WHERE NOT             ( S.S# IN ( SP.S# WHERE SP.P# = 'P2' ) )
             AND    NOT ( S.S# IN ( SP.S# WHERE MAYBE ( SP.P# = 'P2' ) ) )
```

—is equivalent to the expression shown below ("Find names of suppliers who are known not to supply part P2")?

```
    S.SNAME WHERE NOT ( EXISTS SP ( SP.S# = S.S# AND SP.P# = 'P2' ) )
```

The correct answer is expression (c). Consideration of supplier S3 (refer back to Fig. 2 in the body of the paper) should help the reader to confirm this claim.

Note: The example does not illustrate the point, but observe that if x is UNK and X is nonempty, the expression "x IN X" evaluates to *unk.* Observe too that if X contains an UNK, then the expression "x IN X" always evaluates to either *true* or *unk,* never to *false,* regardless of the value of x.

298

18

Oh No
Not Nulls Again

ABSTRACT

This paper tells you more than you probably wanted to know about nulls.

COMMENTS ON PUBLICATION

The more you poke into it, the more difficulties—sometimes absurdities—you find in the realm of nulls (be they the nulls of three-valued logic in general or the nulls of SQL in particular). I wrote the paper that follows merely to document some of the difficulties and absurdities that I had encountered in my investigations. I make no claim that the points raised were previously null (sorry, I mean unknown), but most of them, at any rate, I have never seen documented anywhere else.

1. INTRODUCTION

This paper consists of a ragbag of miscellaneous points concerning nulls. I may be beating a dead horse, but it would be a shame not to record some

---

Previously unpublished.

of these items in a reasonably permanent manner, for purposes of reference if nothing else. Like an earlier paper of mine on the same general topic (reference [10]), this paper can be regarded as a kind of appendix to reference [7].

2.   THREE VALUED LOGIC VS. REALITY REVISITED

Reference [10] demonstrated the mismatch between three-valued logic and the real world. Here I would merely like to repeat the point and emphasize its seriousness. Codd himself quotes the following example of such a mismatch in reference [5] (pages 181–182). Consider the expression

```
( B < 66-1-1 ) OR ( B = 66-1-1 ) OR ( B > 66-1-1 )
```

This expression is intended to perform a comparison between some individual's date of birth *B* and the date "January 1st, 1966." In the real world, of course, the expression must evaluate to *true,* regardless of the value of *B.* In three-valued logic, however, if *B* happens to be UNK (the "value unknown" null), the expression evaluates to *unk* OR *unk* OR *unk,* i.e., to *unk* (the "unknown truth-value").

Codd goes on to say that "[The fact that the expression] as a whole evaluates to [*unk*] . . . is incorrect, but not traumatically incorrect. . . . [The incorrectness notwithstanding,] it is my opinion that . . . this is not a burning issue." But surely it is! I believe it was Wittgenstein who once said (and if he didn't, then he should have): "*All logical differences are big differences.*" In other words, once we know that the system is capable of producing the wrong answer to at least one query, all bets are off!—*every* answer produced by the system becomes suspect.

3.   THE RELATIONAL INFORMATION PRINCIPLE

Consider the following two quotations from writings by Codd:

- "*The information rule (Rule 1):* All information in a relational database is represented explicitly at the logical level . . . in exactly one way—by values in tables" (reference [4]).

- "[The A-mark] is treated *neither* as a value *nor* as a variable by the DBMS" (reference [5], page 173). ("A-mark" is Codd's term for the "value unknown" null, which I refer to as UNK.) In other words, the fact that (say) Joe's salary is unknown is represented in the database, not by a value, but rather by flagging the row-and-column slot that would normally hold such a value by an "A-mark"; and an A-mark, whatever else it may be, is definitely *not* a value in a table.

Is there not a conflict between these two statements? In other words, does not Codd's "A-mark" scheme violate his own Rule 1 for relational DBMSs?

4. DOMAIN CARDINALITY AND NULLS

Note: I am indebted to Hugh Darwen for drawing my attention to the first of the two points below.

- Let *D* be a domain with cardinality one, and let *C* be a column defined on *D*. Can *C* have NULLS (i.e., UNKs) ALLOWED? The answer must surely be "No"—"Yes" would be absurd (though whether the DBMS would be able to recognize the absurdity is probably a moot point).

- Next, let *D* be a domain with cardinality *N* greater than one, and let *C* be a column defined on *D*. If *C* has NULLS ALLOWED, any (UNK-style) null actually appearing in column *C* must stand for one of the *N* values in domain *D*. In other words, the value represented by the UNK in question is not *completely* unknown, and the interpretation of UNK as "value unknown" (meaning *totally* unknown) is really only an approximation to the truth. This fact has a number of consequences. For example, let columns *C1* and *C2* be defined on domains *D1* and *D2*, respectively, and let *D1* and *D2* be disjoint (meaning they have no values in common). Then the conditional expression "C1 = C2" should always evaluate to *false,* never to *unk,* even if the two comparands are both UNK. (I am assuming here that the system does permit cross-domain comparisons, of course [6].)

  More generally, of course, the possibility arises (once again) that the system will produce *wrong answers* to queries, since those answers will be based on an inaccurate model of reality.

5. EXPRESSION TRANSFORMATION

In reference [10], I pointed out that three-valued logic had certain implications for optimization. Specifically, certain identities in two-valued logic, which are important for purposes of expression transformation (and hence optimization), are no longer identities in three-valued logic. *Note:* By the term "identity" here, I mean a pair of expressions *A* and *B,* say, such that evaluating expression *A* produces the same result, unequivocally, as evaluating expression *B*—in symbols, $A \equiv B$.

It follows from the foregoing that extending a two-valued logic system to support three-valued logic—or, more generally, extending an *N*-valued logic system to support (*N*+1)-valued logic, for any *N* greater than 1--will probably be a nontrivial exercise. To repeat from reference [10]: "At best, such an extension is likely to require a certain amount of re-engineering of the existing system, since portions of the existing code are likely to be invalidated; at worst, it will introduce bugs" (i.e., if the re-engineering is not done, or is done incorrectly).

Here for the sake of reference is a representative list (it is certainly not exhaustive) of identities under two-valued logic that are no longer identities when we go to three-valued logic. In each case, the two expressions shown are equivalent under two-valued logic but not under three. The notation is intended to be obvious.

1. p AND NOT p *false*

2. p OR NOT p *true*

3. $x = x$ *true*

4. $x \neg= x$ *false*

5. $x < x$ *false*

6. $x < y$ OR $x = y$ OR $x > y$ *true*

7. $x = y$ AND $y = z$ $x = y$ AND $y = z$ AND $x = z$

8. $x < y$ AND $y < z$ $x < y$ AND $y < z$ AND $x < z$

9. $x - x$ 0

10. x / x 1   (Note 1)

11. $x + y > x$ *true* (Note 2)

12. X SUBSETOF X *true*

13. R JOIN R R (Note 3)

14. R INTERSECT S R JOIN S (Notes 3,4)

Note 1: Provided x is nonzero.

Note 2: Provided y is greater than zero.

Note 3: "JOIN" here means "natural join over columns with the same name."

Note 4: Provided R and S have identical column names.

6. AGGREGATE FUNCTIONS

Most DBMSs support the aggregate functions COUNT, SUM, AVG, MAX, and MIN. The question arises: What should these functions return if their argument happens to be an empty set? COUNT clearly should return zero, and I have argued elsewhere (reference [7]) that SUM should do likewise. Indeed, as Adrian Larner of IBM (UK) recently pointed out (in a private communication), an analogous problem arises in connexion with the "reduction" operation (/) of APL. The APL reduction operation reduces a specified aggregate (or vector, in APL terms) to a scalar value by repeatedly applying a specified *scalar* operation to the individual aggregate elements. Note that COUNT, SUM, MAX, and MIN (but not AVG) can all be thought of as special cases of reduction in this sense; the corresponding scalar operations are "add 1," "add next element," "greater than?" and "less than?" respectively.

The APL solution to the empty aggregate problem is to return the identity value for the relevant scalar operation. The rationale (and it is a good one) for this behavior is that it has the effect of preserving the equivalence

```
f ( f ( agg1 ), f ( agg2 ) )  ≡  f ( agg1, agg2 )
```

for all possible values of *agg1* and *agg2*—even if *agg1* or *agg2* evaluates to an empty set. (The symbol *f* here represents the aggregate function in question; the comma can be thought of as "list concatenation," or in SQL terms UNION ALL—i.e., union without duplicate elimination.) For example, if *f* is SUM and *agg1* is an empty set, we want the following equivalence to hold:

```
SUM ( SUM (), SUM ( agg2 ) )  ≡  SUM ( agg2 )
```

The left hand side here reduces to

```
SUM () + SUM ( agg2 )
```

from which it follows that SUM () should evaluate to zero.

A similar argument shows that MAX () should evaluate to "minus infinity" and MIN () to "plus infinity." Standard SQL does not support a PRODUCT operator, but if it did, then PRODUCT () should clearly evaluate to $+1$ (the relevant scalar operation is "multiply by next element"). What about AVG? Since AVG is not a "reduction-style" function, I would argue that the correct answer in this case is *undefined* (meaning that AVG () should raise an error, in the absence of any means for the user to instruct the system to do otherwise).

In SQL, however, SUM, AVG, MAX, and MIN of an empty set all return null ("value unknown"). As a consequence, certain expression transformations that ought to be valid are in fact not valid in SQL. (Note that these invalid transformations are in addition to the ones described in the previous section, which are invalid not because of the rules of SQL but rather because of the rules of three-valued logic per se.) Here is an example, based on the usual suppliers-and-parts database (see Chapter 1, Appendix A). The query is "Retrieve parts whose weight is greater than that of every Paris part."

First version (correct):

```
SELECT  P.*
FROM    P
WHERE   P.WEIGHT >ALL
      ( SELECT  P.WEIGHT
        FROM    P
        WHERE   P.CITY = 'Paris' ) ;
```

Transformed version:

```
SELECT  P.*
FROM    P
WHERE   P.WEIGHT >
      ( SELECT  MAX (P.WEIGHT)
        FROM    P
        WHERE   P.CITY = 'Paris' ) ;
```

These two expressions really ought to be equivalent; in the real world, if "$x > $ALL X" is *true,* then certainly "$x >$ MAX (X)" is *true,* and vice versa. (I assume here that the "real world" MAX function is defined as indicated above—i.e., it is defined in such a way as to preserve the validity of the transformation, even in the case where the argument X is an empty set.)

However, the transformation is certainly *not* valid in SQL. Suppose the argument is in fact empty—i.e., there are no parts in Paris at all. In the first formulation, then, the subquery returns an empty set; the expression in the WHERE clause of the outer SELECT thus evaluates to *true* for every part (check the definition of the $>$ALL operator if you don't believe this), and so every part is retrieved. In the second formulation, however, the subquery returns a null; the expression in the WHERE clause of the outer SELECT thus evaluates to *unk* for every part, and so no parts are retrieved at all.

The foregoing problem is discussed in more detail in references [1], [8], and [9].

7. THE EXISTS FUNCTION

This one also has to do with SQL specifically, rather than with three-valued logic in general. I have argued elsewhere (reference [8]) that EXISTS in SQL is logically flawed. I will not repeat the details here, but I will give one example, again based on suppliers-and-parts, in order to make another point. The query is "Retrieve parts whose weight is not equal to the weight of any Paris part"—or, more precisely, "Retrieve parts whose weight is *known* not to be equal to the weight of any Paris part."

First version (correct):

```
SELECT  P.*
FROM    P
WHERE   P.WEIGHT NOT IN
      ( SELECT  P.WEIGHT
        FROM    P
        WHERE   P.CITY = 'Paris' ) ;
```

Transformed version:

```
SELECT  P.*
FROM    P
WHERE   NOT EXISTS
      ( SELECT  Q.*
        FROM    P Q
        WHERE   Q.CITY = 'Paris'
        AND     Q.WEIGHT = P.WEIGHT ) ;
```

Again, these two expressions really ought to be equivalent, but in fact are not so in SQL. Suppose there is just one part in Paris, with a null weight. In the first formulation, then, the subquery returns a set containing just a null; the condition in the WHERE clause of the outer SELECT thus evaluates to *unk* for every part, and so no parts are retrieved at all. In the second formulation, the subquery returns an empty set; the EXISTS thus returns *false,* the NOT EXISTS returns *true,* and so every part is retrieved.

> *Aside:* After I first wrote the foregoing, I discovered there was yet another problem with this example. Suppose there are no parts in Paris at all, and suppose some other part, P*x* say, has a null weight. Then part P*x* should be retrieved (part P*x* does have some weight, even though we don't know what it is, and that weight is certainly different from the weight of "every" Paris part). According to reference [11], however, there is at least one product, namely ORACLE, in which the first formulation (the one involving NOT IN and a subquery) will *not* retrieve part P*x*. There is also at least one product, namely DB2, in which that formulation *will* retrieve part P*x* (again according to reference [11]). *End of aside.*

There is another point arising from this example that deserves more careful examination. When I talked just now about "a set that contains just a null," I was actually being rather sloppy. The set does *not* contain "just a null"; rather, it contains a single row, which in turn contains a single scalar component, which happens to be null. Some of the problems identified in reference [8] had to do, precisely, with the behavior of EXISTS in SQL when its argument is such a set; in such a case, EXISTS in SQL returns *true,* not *unk,* which is—at least arguably—counterintuitive. Let us take a closer look at what happens in such a situation.

- Strictly speaking, it is in fact correct for EXISTS to return *true;* there does exist a row in the argument set, after all. The problems arise because we naturally think of that row as being converted or "coerced" to the single scalar value that it contains. (This kind of coercion is exactly what happens when we invoke an aggregate function such as SUM, after all.) It is the lack of any such coercion that accounts for the counterintuitive behavior of EXISTS in SQL (but not for the *incorrect* behavior!—that is a separate problem, adequately discussed in reference [8]).

- Now suppose for the sake of discussion that the coercion *does* occur (since such coercion was clearly the intent behind the addition of EXISTS to the language in the first place). So the row containing a single null is converted to a null scalar. The next question is: What does that null denote? If it is a genuine UNK (meaning "value unknown"), then it is still correct for the EXISTS to return *true;* after all, a value does exist, we just don't know what it is.

- Suppose, by contrast, that the null is not a genuine UNK, but rather "undefined" (as it might be, for example, if the EXISTS argument is of the form "SELECT AVG . . ." and the argument to AVG is empty). Here it seems clearly wrong for the EXISTS to return *true.* However, the problem here is not really with EXISTS per se, but rather with AVG (see the discussion of aggregate functions earlier in this paper).

- Suppose the null is "not applicable" (as it might be, for example, if the EXISTS argument is of the form "SELECT COMMISSION FROM EMP . . ." and the EMP(s) in question is/are not in the Sales department). Here again it seems clearly wrong for the EXISTS to return *true.* However, the problem again is not really with EXISTS per se, but rather with SQL's semantic overloading of the null construct, which is used to bundle together far too many concepts that are semantically distinct (and thus ought to be operationally distinct also).

- Suppose the null is "nonexistent" (as it might be, for example, if the EXISTS argument is of the form "SELECT SOCSEC# FROM EMP . . ." and the EMP(s) in question does/do not have a social security number). The remarks of the previous paragraph apply to this case also.

- And similarly for other interpretations of "null." In other words, the culprit in this area is not exactly the SQL EXISTS function per se, but rather the semantic overloading of nulls in SQL (and in particular, in one case, SQL's incorrect treatment of aggregate functions).

8.   THE GROUP BY OPERATOR

Here is another oddity. Assume that table SP, the shipments table, contains rows for suppliers S1, S2, S3, and S4 (only), and consider the following queries:

```
1.   SELECT S#              2.   SELECT MAX (S#)
     FROM   SP                   FROM   SP
     WHERE  S# < 'S5'            WHERE  S# < 'S5'
     GROUP  BY S# ;              GROUP  BY S# ;

3.   SELECT DISTINCT S#     4.   SELECT MAX (S#)
     FROM   SP                   FROM   SP
     WHERE  S# < 'S5' ;          WHERE  S# < 'S5' ;

5.   SELECT S#              6.   SELECT MAX (S#)
     FROM   SP                   FROM   SP
     GROUP  BY S#                GROUP  BY S#
     HAVING S# < 'S5' ;          HAVING S# < 'S5' ;
```

The expression S# < 'S5' evaluates to *true* for every row of table SP, of course. A few moments' thought should serve to convince the reader that Queries 1, 2, 3, 5, and 6 are equivalent, inasmuch as they all produce the same result (namely the set of all four supplier numbers), and Query 4 produces just the single supplier number S4.

Now consider the following queries, which are the same as before except that the "<" has been replaced by ">" in every case.

```
1.   SELECT S#              2.   SELECT MAX (S#)
     FROM   SP                   FROM   SP
     WHERE  S# > 'S5'            WHERE  S# > 'S5'
     GROUP  BY S# ;              GROUP  BY S# ;

3.   SELECT DISTINCT S#     4.   SELECT MAX (S#)
     FROM   SP                   FROM   SP
     WHERE  S# > 'S5' ;          WHERE  S# > 'S5' ;

5.   SELECT S#              6.   SELECT MAX (S#)
     FROM   SP                   FROM   SP
     GROUP  BY S#                GROUP  BY S#
     HAVING S# > 'S5' ;          HAVING S# > 'S5' ;
```

This time, Queries 1, 3, and 5 all produce a table of zero rows —i.e., an empty table—but Queries 2, 4, and 6 produce a table of *one* row, containing a null! At least, this is what happens in ANSI standard SQL [2]. Here is a slight paraphrase of the relevant section of the standard (reference [2], page 56):

"If [the intermediate result to which the SELECT clause is to be applied] is a grouped table that has zero groups, then:

"(a) If some <value expression> in the <select list> is a <column specification>, then the result . . . is an empty table.

"(b) If every <value expression> in the <select list> is a <set function specification>, then the result . . . is a table having one row, in which the *n*th value is the result of the *n*th <set function specification> in the <select list>."

I leave it as an exercise for the reader to determine whether (or in what sense) the foregoing behavior can be regarded as correct. I would, however, like to point out one particularly bizarre implication of that behavior: If we extend, say, Query 2 above to include S# in the SELECT clause—

```
2.  SELECT MAX (S#), S#
    FROM    SP
    WHERE   S# > 'S5'
    GROUP   BY S# ;
```

—then the result, which was previously a one-row table, will now be an empty table instead! (According to the specifications of the SQL standard once again, that is.)

I should mention that at least one product, namely ORACLE, does *not* behave as just described. In ORACLE, only Query 4 produces a one-row result; all of the others produce an empty table. Who is correct here?— ORACLE? or the SQL standard? or neither? What do *you* think?

9. NOT TRUE, NOT FALSE, NOT UNKNOWN

Reference [7] (entitled "NOT is not Not!") demonstrates clearly that the logical operator NOT in three-valued logic is not the same thing as "not" in ordinary English. The argument (to repeat from that paper) goes as follows: Let *v* be a variable of type "truth value." The legal values of *v* are thus *true, false,* and *unk.* Then the statement "*v* is not *true*" means "*v* is either *false* or *unk*"; the statement "*v* is NOT *true*" means "*v* is *false*" (refer to the truth table for NOT).

As a rider to the foregoing problem (and in all probability in an attempt to *address* the foregoing problem), let me now observe that SQL2, the proposed follow-on to the existing SQL standard [3], includes a new construct called <boolean test>—a special form of <search condition>—with syntax as follows:

```
<boolean test>
    ::=  <boolean primary> [ IS [ NOT ] <truth value> ]

<boolean primary>
    ::=  <predicate> | ( <search condition> )
```

```
<truth value>
    ::=  TRUE | FALSE | UNKNOWN
```

The expression "*x* IS TRUE" (where *x* might be, for example, a simple comparison expression such as "*A* > *B*") evaluates to *true* if *x* evaluates to *true* and to *false* otherwise; and analogously for "IS FALSE" and "IS UNKNOWN", of course. (I remark in passing that (a) UNKNOWN here means *unk,* not UNK; (b) "IS UNKNOWN" corresponds to my MAYBE operator. See reference [7] if you require clarification of these remarks.)

The point I want to make here is that, according to reference [3], the expression (let us call it "Expression 1")

```
x IS NOT TRUE
```

is defined to be equivalent to the expression

```
NOT ( x IS TRUE )
```

(and analogously for "IS NOT FALSE" and "IS NOT UNKNOWN", of course).

Thus, if *x* is *true,* Expression 1 is *false,* and if *x* is *false* or *unk,* Expression 1 is *true.* So "IS NOT TRUE" means "IS FALSE OR UNKNOWN" (this is not meant to be valid syntax, of course). So "NOT" in "NOT TRUE" is not the NOT of three-valued logic, it is the "not" of ordinary English! (i.e., "NOT TRUE" here does not mean NOT "TRUE"). In other words, the situation in SQL2 is not "NOT is not Not" but rather "NOT is not NOT"! Do we *really* want to go any further down this crazy path?

10. CONCLUSION

Many of the anomalies described in this paper apply either directly or indirectly to SQL. If you have a SQL system available to you, you might be interested in trying out the various examples to see if your particular system actually behaves in the way I have described. I would be interested (though not particularly surprised) to hear of any discrepancies you might encounter. Please write to me care of Addison-Wesley Publishing Company, Reading, MA 01867. Thank you.

ACKNOWLEDGMENTS

The title of this article was taken from a private communication from Adrian Larner. I am also grateful to Hugh Darwen for his helpful comments on an earlier draft, and to Colin White for testing my SQL examples on his ORACLE system.

REFERENCES and BIBLIOGRAPHY

1. Nagraj Alur, "Nulls and DB2," *InfoDB* 4, No. 3 (Fall 1989).

2. American National Standards Institute, *Database Language SQL,* Document ANSI X3.135-1986.

3. ANSI X3H2 / ISO/IEC JTC1 SC21 WG3 Data Base Languages, (*ISO working draft) Database Language SQL2,* Document X3H2-90-264 (July 1990).

4. E. F. Codd, "Is Your DBMS Really Relational?" *Computerworld* (October 14th, 1985).

5. E. F. Codd, *The Relational Model for Database Management Version 2* (Reading, MA: Addison-Wesley, 1990).

6. C. J. Date, "What Is a Domain?" in C. J. Date, *Relational Database Writings 1985–1989* (Reading, MA: Addison-Wesley, 1990).

7. C. J. Date, "NOT Is Not "Not"! (Notes on Three-Valued Logic and Related Matters)," in C. J. Date, *Relational Database Writings 1985–1989* (Reading, MA: Addison-Wesley, 1990).

8. C. J. Date, "EXISTS Is Not "Exists"! (Some Logical Flaws in SQL)," in C. J. Date, *Relational Database Writings 1985–1989* (Reading, MA: Addison-Wesley, 1990).

9. C. J. Date, "SQL Dos and Don'ts," in C. J. Date, *Relational Database Writings 1985–1989* (Reading, MA: Addison-Wesley, 1990).

10. C. J. Date, "Three-Valued Logic and the Real World" (in this volume).

11. Rick F. van der Lans, "SQL Portability," *The Relational Journal* 2, No. 6 (December 1990/January 1991).

19

Watch Out for
Outer Join

ABSTRACT

An exploration of some of the subtleties of outer joins.

COMMENTS ON REPUBLICATION

I have written on the topic of outer join before [5], and the paper that follows can be regarded as a sequel to that earlier paper. I wrote it after carrying out an investigation into the outer join support provided in several different commercial products; I was frankly amazed at the number of ways vendors could get it wrong! It was quite clear that the subtleties of outer join, though surely not unknown, were nevertheless not at all widely appreciated. I therefore felt it would be a service to identify and explain those subtleties in a paper that could act as a "single source" reference for the material in the future.

Originally published (minus Appendix A) in *InfoDB* 5, No. 1 (Spring/Summer 1990). Reprinted by permission of Database Associates International.

1.   INTRODUCTION

I will begin by assuming that the reader is at least broadly familiar with both:

1. The outer join operation per se—including the fact that it comes in a variety of different flavors (left, right, and full outer θ-join, and left, right, and full outer natural join); and

2. The kinds of problems the outer join operation is intended to solve.

A discussion of such matters can be found in many places; see, e.g., reference [5]. Here I will content myself with a single example, based on a simplified version of the usual suppliers-and-parts database (see Chapter 1, Appendix A). Refer to Fig. 1.

The figure is meant to be interpreted as follows: Part (a) shows some sample values for the suppliers table (S) and the shipments table (SP); part (b) shows the regular (or *inner*) natural join of those two tables over supplier numbers (S#); and part (c) shows a corresponding *outer* natural join. As the figure indicates, the inner join "loses information" for suppliers who supply no parts (supplier S5, in the example), whereas the outer join "preserves" such information (indeed, this distinction is the whole point of outer join). Note that since every row in table SP necessarily has a matching row in table S (because SP.S# in table SP is a foreign key matching the

(a) S

S#	SNAME	STATUS	SCITY
S2	Jones	10	Paris
S5	Adams	30	Athens

SP

S#	P#	QTY
S2	P1	300
S2	P2	400

(b)   Regular (inner) natural join of S and SP over S#

S#	SNAME	STATUS	SCITY	P#	QTY
S2	Jones	10	Paris	P1	300
S2	Jones	10	Paris	P2	400

(c)   Left (also full) outer natural join of S with SP over S#

S#	SNAME	STATUS	SCITY	P#	QTY
S2	Jones	10	Paris	P1	300
S2	Jones	10	Paris	P2	400
S5	Adams	30	Athens	null	null

Fig. 1 Inner and outer natural joins (examples)

primary key S.S# of table S), the left and full outer natural joins are identical in this particular example and are as shown in part (c) of the figure; the right outer natural join, by contrast, degenerates to the inner natural join and thus is as shown in part (b) of the figure.

A few further preliminary remarks to close this introductory section:

- First, all discussions in what follows are framed in terms of SQL, for obvious reasons. But the points, or most of them anyway, do not apply just to SQL per se but rather are of wider applicability.

- Second, it is necessary—despite my many documented reservations regarding nulls and three-valued logic and related matters (see, e.g., references [7] and [8])—to assume throughout most of this paper that we are indeed operating within the three-valued logic framework. I will examine this aspect of the outer join problem in a little more detail toward the end of the paper. However, let me state right at the outset that it is not at all clear to me that outer join, as that term is usually understood, is really the operation that we need. But we are obviously not yet in a position to discuss this point in any detail.

- Last, the paper gives a number of examples, based on several commercially available DBMS products, of how *not* to do outer join. Please understand that those examples are not intended (or at least not primarily intended) as criticisms of the products in question—rather, they are intended merely to illustrate some of the many different ways in which it is possible to get outer join wrong. I certainly do not necessarily mean to imply that other products have got it right!

2.   WHY DO WE NEED SUPPORT FOR OUTER JOIN?

Even the most superficial consideration of what happens in the absence of such support is sufficient to provide an answer to this question. Here, for example, is the way the outer join of Fig. 1(c) would have to be expressed in DB2 (one product out of many that does not provide any direct support at all):

```
SELECT  S.S#, S.SNAME, S.STATUS, S.SCITY, SP.P#, SP.QTY
FROM    S, SP
WHERE   S.S# = SP.S#
UNION
SELECT  S.S#, S.SNAME, S.STATUS, S.SCITY, '     ', 0
FROM    S
WHERE   NOT EXISTS
        ( SELECT SP.S#
          FROM    SP
          WHERE   SP.S# = S.S# ) ;
```

Aside: DB2 does not permit the keyword NULL to appear as an element of a SELECT-list (neither does the SQL standard). In the example, therefore, we have to specify blanks and zeros, instead of nulls, for P# and QTY values for suppliers who supply no parts. *End of aside.*

The problems here are obvious: The query expression is complicated (it is much worse in more complex cases); it is error-prone (in general, the differences between a "genuine" outer join expression and some other expression that represents some quite different outer join, or some other result that is not an outer join at all, may be quite subtle); and there is little chance that the system optimizer will recognize that the user is actually trying to construct an outer join, and performance is thus likely to be poor. Furthermore, an analogous remark applies to the system's "view updatability analyzer": A view whose definition involves an outer join is sometimes (theoretically) updatable [6], which implies that the updatability analyzer, like the optimizer, needs to be able to recognize outer joins. (I am indebted to Hugh Darwen for this latter observation.)

Note: As the example suggests, the various outer join operations are not primitive—they can all be expressed in terms of existing operations of the relational algebra (for details, see reference [5]). But a user who wishes to formulate an outer join should not have to indulge in circumlocutions of the kind illustrated in the example.

3. WHY THIS PAPER?

My previous paper on this topic (reference [5]) was an attempt to explain the basic concepts of outer join, but it clearly failed in that attempt, or else was not widely seen—because the fact of the matter is that existing products have not done well in this area. Typically, either (a) they do not provide any direct support at all, or (b) they do provide some direct support, but only in a very limited set of special cases and only in a very ad hoc manner.

How have the products failed? Well, the body of this paper will give a number of answers to this question. For now, let me just remark that it is in fact quite difficult to extend SQL to do outer join "right." In order to explain why this is so, let me first remind the reader of the semantics of the basic SQL "SELECT-FROM-WHERE" construct (GROUP BY and HAVING and ORDER BY are irrelevant for the purposes of the present discussion). Conceptually, what happens is the following.

1. First, the *Cartesian product* of the tables listed in the FROM clause is computed.

2. Next, that Cartesian product is *restricted* to that subset of the rows that satisfy the "restriction condition" in the WHERE clause.

3. Finally, that restricted subset is *projected* over the columns named in the SELECT clause.

> *Aside:* For simplicity I ignore the point, here and throughout this paper, that a true projection always eliminates duplicate rows, whereas the SQL SELECT clause eliminates duplicate rows only if it is explicitly requested to do so by means of the operator DISTINCT. I also assume (usually) that the elements of the SELECT clause are indeed all column names; the explanation just given requires some slight refinement, which I ignore here for reasons of space, in order to be able to deal with arbitrary scalar expressions (as SQL in fact permits). Third, I also ignore the point that the condition in the WHERE clause is not necessarily a true restriction condition (i.e., it is not necessarily a condition that can be evaluated for a given row by examining just that row in isolation), because SQL allows it to include a subquery; once again, this simplification is justified because it does not materially affect the issue at hand. *End of aside.*

The foregoing conceptual evaluation algorithm works well for inner joins, because the inner θ-join is indeed a restriction of the Cartesian product, and furthermore the inner natural join is a projection of the inner equijoin. *Note:* "Equijoin" is what results when the "θ" in "θ-join" is taken to be "$=$". For simplicity, I will usually take θ to be "$=$" in what follows. The necessary extensions to handle the other comparison operators are essentially straightforward.

When we turn our attention to outer joins, however, the foregoing evaluation algorithm does NOT "work well" (in fact, it does not work at all). *This fact makes it virtually impossible to express outer joins in terms of ANY "simple" extension to the SELECT-FROM-WHERE construct* (and this is fundamentally why most of the products fail). There are several reasons for this state of affairs, but the basic point is that outer join possesses a number of Nasty Properties which together conspire to undermine the assumptions underlying the original evaluation algorithm. (Some might feel that "subtle" would be a better word than "nasty.") I will just state those properties here, for purposes of reference, and then go on to discuss them in more detail in the remainder of the paper.

1. Outer equijoin is not a restriction of Cartesian product
2. Restriction does not distribute over outer equijoin
3. "A $<$ = B" is not the same as "A $<$ B OR A $=$ B"
4. The comparison operators are not transitive
5. Outer natural join is not a projection of outer equijoin

Most of these properties can be discussed without any loss of generality in the context of two-table joins only. For reasons of simplicity, therefore, I will assume henceforth that all joins involve exactly two tables, barring any explicit statement to the contrary.

4.   WHAT DOES "SUPPORT" MEAN?

Before going any further, perhaps I should give some indication as to what I would regard as "good" outer join support (always assuming, of course, that we accept for the sake of argument that outer join per se is what we want to support in the first place; see the further discussion on this point toward the end of the paper). Briefly, I would want to see at least all of the following:

- Explicit "one-liner" outer join expressions: e.g.,

   S OUTER JOIN SP

   (where the syntax OUTER JOIN is intended to mean *outer natural join over columns with the same name*). *Note:* I first proposed a syntax somewhat along these lines in reference [5]. Such "one-liner" support is desirable for reasons of usability, analyzability, optimizability, etc.

- Support for:
  - Outer natural joins (much the most important case in practice)
  - Outer θ-joins (including outer equijoin in particular)
  - Left, right, and full versions for both of the above
  - Outer joins of any number of tables

- Generality (i.e., all possible outer joins handled, not just a ragbag of special cases)

- Ability for the user to control the representation of the fact that information is missing (see later)

   Let me now try to explain why it is not feasible to extend the SQL SELECT–FROM–WHERE construct in any straightforward manner to satisfy the foregoing requirements.

5.   WHY WE CANNOT "MERELY" EXTEND
THE WHERE CLAUSE (1)

The first "Nasty Property" is that outer equijoin is not a restriction of the Cartesian product of the tables in question. For an illustration, refer to Fig. 2, which shows (a) the Cartesian product of tables S and SP from Fig. 1

(a) Cartesian product of S and SP

SS#	SNAME	STATUS	SCITY	SPS#	P#	QTY
S2	Jones	10	Paris	S2	P1	300
S2	Jones	10	Paris	S2	P2	400
S5	Adams	30	Athens	S2	P1	300
S5	Adams	30	Athens	S2	P2	400

(b) Left (or full) outer equijoin of S with SP on S#

SS#	SNAME	STATUS	SCITY	SPS#	P#	QTY
S2	Jones	10	Paris	S2	P1	300
S2	Jones	10	Paris	S2	P2	400
S5	Adams	30	Athens	null	null	null

Fig. 2 Outer equijoin is not a restriction of Cartesian product

and (b) the left (equivalently, the full) outer equijoin of those same two tables over S#. To avoid confusion, I have renamed the two supplier number columns in the result tables as SS# and SPS#.

It follows from Nasty Property Number 1 that we cannot coherently expect to be able to express an outer equijoin by merely inventing some new kind of comparison operator (to be used in some new restriction condition), and then allowing that operator to appear in the WHERE clause. SYBASE and CA-UNIVERSE are examples of products that fail on this score. Here, for example, is the way that the outer join of Fig. 1(c) would be expressed in SYBASE:

```
SELECT  S.S#, S.SNAME, S.STATUS, S.SCITY, SP.P#, SP.QTY
FROM    S, SP
WHERE   S.S# *= SP.S# ;
```

Note the special comparison operator "*=" in the WHERE clause. (*Note:* CA-UNIVERSE uses "=?" in place of SYBASE's "*=".) According to reference [9], this operator means "include all rows from the first-named table in the join specification [i.e., table S, in the example] whether or not there is a match on the [joining] column in the [second-named] table."

Now, while it is undeniably true that this query is much more succinct than the DB2 "equivalent" shown earlier, and it is presumably true too that it produces the desired result, it is nevertheless also a fact that the technique illustrated will *not* handle the general case, and moreover it is not at all easy to state exactly which cases it will handle. And, since the result is not a restriction of the Cartesian product (i.e., the conceptual evaluation algorithm breaks down), how can the overall operation be explained to the user? (The "explanation" quoted above is not an explanation, in my opinion.) In fact, I defy anyone to produce a complete, precise, coherent, context-free explanation of the semantics of the expression "A *= B", for arbitrary A and B. (I hope it is obvious that such an explanation *can* be given for the more familiar expression "A = B".)

> *Aside:* There are a few minor points I ought to mention before continuing. First, in the interests of accuracy I should point out that (by virtue of the projection operation performed by the SELECT clause) the SYBASE query shown above actually produces a left outer *natural* join, not a left outer equijoin. However, this fact does not materially affect the discussion. Second, I hope I am not to blame for the SYBASE implementation! In my original paper (reference [5]), I used the notation "R [A *= B] S" to stand for the left outer equijoin of tables R and S on columns R.A and S.B. I also used "=*" and "*=*" analogously for the right and full outer equijoins. But there is a big difference between a mere notation that happens to involve the symbol "*=" and a formal syntax that actually attempts to use that symbol as an embedded operator! Finally, note that SYBASE supports "*=" and "=*" but not "*=*"—i.e., it does not support the full outer equijoin, but only the left and right versions. (As for CA-UNIVERSE, that product supports "=?" only, not "?=" or "?=?"—i.e., it supports the left outer equijoin only.) *End of aside.*

6. WHY WE CANNOT "MERELY" EXTEND THE WHERE CLAUSE (2)

The approach of inventing a new comparison operator and allowing that operator to appear in the WHERE clause also falls foul of Nasty Property Number 2—namely, that restriction does not distribute over outer equijoin. Informally, what this latter statement means is that the expressions

```
( R outer-equijoin S ) WHERE restriction-on-R
```

and

```
( R WHERE restriction-on-R ) outer-equijoin S
```

are not equivalent, in general. By way of example, consider the following SYBASE query (a slight extension of the previous example):

```
SELECT  S.S#, S.SNAME, S.STATUS, S.SCITY, SP.P#, SP.QTY
FROM    S, SP
WHERE   S.S# *= SP.S#
AND     SP.QTY < 1000 ;
```

This query has two potential interpretations, depending on whether the restriction condition "SP.QTY < 1000" is applied before or after the join condition "S.S# *= SP.S#". In terms of the sample data shown in Fig. 1 (in which it so happens that every QTY value is less than 1000), performing the restriction first gives a result containing rows for both supplier S2 and supplier S5; performing the join first gives a result containing rows for supplier S2 only (because after the join, the QTY for supplier S5 is given as null, and "null < 1000" does not evaluate to *true*).

So which interpretation is "correct"? And whichever it is, how can we formulate the other? (For the record, I note that SYBASE actually does the restriction first.)

The reader might like to meditate on the following examples (and an infinite number of others like them):

```
SELECT  S.S#, S.SNAME, S.STATUS, S.SCITY, SP.P#, SP.QTY
FROM    S, SP
WHERE   S.S# *= SP.S#
OR      SP.QTY < 1000 ;

SELECT  S.S#, S.SNAME, S.STATUS, S.SCITY, SP.P#, SP.QTY
FROM    S, SP
WHERE   S.S# *= SP.S#
AND     S.STATUS *= SP.QTY ;

SELECT  S.S#, S.SNAME, S.STATUS, S.SCITY, SP.P#, SP.QTY
FROM    S, SP
WHERE   S.S# *= SP.S#
AND     SP.S# *= S.S# ;

SELECT  S.S#, S.SNAME, S.STATUS, S.SCITY, SP.P#, SP.QTY
FROM    S, SP
WHERE   NOT ( S.S# *= SP.S# )
AND     SP.QTY < 1000 ;
```

The meanings of such queries are anybody's guess, in general.

Note: I do not particularly mean to pick on SYBASE here; analogous comments and criticisms apply to many other products also. For brevity, however, I will not usually bother henceforth to spell out such problems in so much detail for every individual product.

7.   HOW WE *MIGHT* EXTEND THE FROM CLAUSE

I have shown that the outer equijoin is not a restriction of the Cartesian product of the tables in question. However, it is a restriction of the Cartesian product of *augmented* versions of those tables—where by the term "augmented version" (of some table), I mean a table that contains all of the rows of the original table together with *an all-null row*.

Let us agree to use the notation "T +" to denote the augmented version of table T, and the notation "T1 TIMES T2" to denote the Cartesian product of tables T1 and T2. Then we can say, a little more precisely, that the left outer equijoin of T1 and T2 is a restriction of "T1 TIMES T2 +", the right outer equijoin is a restriction of "T1 + TIMES T2", and the full outer equijoin is a restriction of "T1 + TIMES T2 +".

The foregoing observations suggest that one possible approach to extending SQL to support outer equijoins would be to allow the FROM clause to refer to "augmented tables," and then to use the WHERE clause to express the restriction of the result of that FROM clause (namely, the Cartesian product of those augmented tables) that is needed to construct the desired outer join. And exactly such an approach was proposed by Chamberlin in reference [2]. This would be Chamberlin's formulation of the outer join of Fig. 1(c):

```
SELECT  S.S#, S.SNAME, S.STATUS, S.SCITY, XYZ.P#, XYZ.QTY
FROM    S, SP+ XYZ
WHERE   S.S# = XYZ.S#
OR      ( NOT EXISTS
            ( SELECT SP.S#
              FROM   SP
              WHERE  SP.S# = S.S# )
          AND XYZ.S# IS NULL ) ;
```

Note the need to introduce a range variable—XYZ in the example—in order to be able to refer to rows of the augmented version of table SP.

This approach certainly works, and it is not ad hoc. But it does suffer from a number of problems, of which perhaps the most significant is that it is very error-prone: It requires extremely careful use of range variables (the example in reference [2] in fact gets them wrong!), and it is not at all easy to get the restrictions in the WHERE clause right, even in simple cases such as the one illustrated. Moreover, the technique is intuitively difficult to apply, because there is no immediately obvious rule connecting the tables that need to be flagged with a plus sign and the tables for which information is to be preserved.

Note, incidentally, that the foregoing criticisms apply to all products that are based on the concept of flagging tables to be "augmented," including, for example, INFORMIX, ORACLE, and SQLBase (see below). Readers who are not convinced of the truth of these observations are recommended to try some examples for themselves (especially more complex examples, involving three or more tables).

A more comprehensive analysis of Chamberlin's approach, with additional examples, can be found in reference [5].

8. WHY WE CANNOT "MERELY" EXTEND THE FROM CLAUSE (1)

Given the fact that it is difficult to get the WHERE clause right in Chamberlin's approach—because the necessary restriction conditions rapidly become quite complex—it is tempting to try to find a way to extend the FROM clause to augment tables with all-null rows appropriately and to do the necessary "complex" restrictions automatically, without the user having to specify them explicitly. INFORMIX is an example of a product that has attempted such an approach. Here is how the outer join of Fig. 1(c) would be expressed in INFORMIX:

```
SELECT S.S#, S.SNAME, S.STATUS, S.SCITY, SP.P#, SP.QTY
FROM    S, OUTER SP
WHERE   S.S# = SP.S# ;
```

An immediate criticism of this syntax is that the result includes rows for which the condition in the WHERE clause does not evaluate to *true!* Another is that the reference to "SP" in the WHERE clause must presumably be taken to denote the *augmented version* of table SP, not table SP itself, and such syntactic trickery (punning on table names) does not seem to be a very sound basis on which to construct a formal language.

A rather more serious criticism is as follows. First, we must surely agree that, regardless of the sequence in which the individual clauses of the query are conceptually executed, the system must surely apply each one *in its entirety* before moving on to the next—for otherwise how can the semantics of individual clauses be defined? Yet the sequence in the example has to be as follows:

1. Augment table SP   (FROM clause)
2. Form the Cartesian product "S × SP+"   (FROM clause)
3. Apply join condition   (WHERE clause)
4. Apply "complex" restrictions   (FROM clause)

In fact, if the WHERE clause includes any "local" restrictions (such as "SP.QTY < 1000") that apply to just one of the FROM-tables, those local restrictions must presumably be applied either before Step 1 or after Step 4 in the foregoing sequence. Assuming for the sake of the discussion that it is before Step 1—I don't actually know what INFORMIX does—the overall execution sequence has to be:

1. Execute WHERE clause (certain portions)
2. Execute FROM clause (certain portions)

3. Execute WHERE clause (remaining portions)

4. Execute FROM clause (remaining portions)

And even if I have the sequence here wrong, the question remains: How can we express any other sequence? To repeat (or paraphrase) some of the criticisms I leveled at SYBASE earlier: This technique will definitely *not* handle the general case, nor is it easy to state exactly which cases it will handle. (Like SYBASE, INFORMIX supports left and right outer equi-joins, but not the full outer equijoin—at least one table in the FROM clause must not be marked OUTER.) And I have already indicated that it is at best difficult to explain the overall operation to the user. Reference [11] says: "The table which is marked by OUTER . . . will supply values . . . where there are values in the table which match the values in the [other] table, and otherwise will supply nulls." This is not an explanation, in my opinion. In fact, I defy anyone to produce a complete, precise, coherent, context-free explanation of the semantics of the expression "OUTER T" for arbitrary T.

I now turn my attention to ORACLE. *Note:* There is another product, namely SQLBase, whose outer join support is identical to that of ORACLE, as near as I can tell. For simplicity, I will limit my attention to ORACLE in what follows.

ORACLE's approach to the outer join problem is a kind of hybrid of Chamberlin's approach and INFORMIX's approach. It resembles Chamberlin's approach inasmuch as it also involves flagging tables to be "augmented" by means of a plus sign; and it resembles INFORMIX's approach inasmuch as it applies the "complex" restrictions automatically and implicitly. *Note:* The plus signs are actually specified in the WHERE clause, not the FROM clause, but this is nothing but a solecism; it is the FROM clause, not the WHERE clause, whose semantics are affected by those plus signs. (I will remark in passing, however, that this syntactic irregularity raises an additional problem of its own, which I will discuss in just a moment.)

Here then is ORACLE's version of the outer join of Fig. 1(c):

```
SELECT S.S#, S.SNAME, S.STATUS, S.SCITY, SP.P#, SP.QTY
FROM    S, SP
WHERE   S.S# = SP.S# (+) ;
```

All of the INFORMIX criticisms apply here also, *mutatis mutandis,* except (arguably) the criticism regarding the punning use of table names. First, the result includes rows for which the condition in the WHERE clause does not evaluate to *true.* Second, it is virtually impossible to explain exactly how queries are executed—in particular, the sequence of execution of the FROM and WHERE clauses is very unclear. (Reference [12] says: "Extra null columns will be created for the table with the (+) outer join operator and joined against all rows from the other table that would *not* have been returned in a normal join." This is not an explanation, in my opinion.) Third, whatever the sequence of execution actually is, there is no way to specify any different sequence. Fourth, the syntax will definitely not handle the completely general case, nor is it easy to state exactly which cases it will handle. (Like SYBASE and INFORMIX, ORACLE definitely does not support the full outer equijoin.) Finally, I defy anyone to produce a complete, precise, coherent, context-free explanation of the semantics of the expression "T.C(+)", for arbitrary T and C.

In addition to all of the foregoing, ORACLE suffers from an additional problem of its own, caused by the fact that the plus signs are specified in the WHERE clause instead of in the FROM clause, where they more logically belong. As a consequence of this fact, it is possible to include both "plussed" and "nonplussed" references to the same table in the same WHERE clause. Some examples:

```
SELECT  S.S#, S.SNAME, S.STATUS, S.SCITY, SP.P#, SP.QTY
FROM    S, SP
WHERE   S.S# = SP.S# (+)
AND     S.S# < SP.S# ;

SELECT  S.S#, S.SNAME, S.STATUS, S.SCITY, SP.P#, SP.QTY
FROM    S, SP
WHERE   S.S# = SP.S# (+)
OR      SP.QTY < 1000 ;

SELECT  S.S#, S.SNAME, S.STATUS, S.SCITY, SP.P#, SP.QTY
FROM    S, SP
WHERE   S.S# = SP.S# (+)
AND     S.STATUS = SP.QTY ;
```

I have no idea what these examples will produce.

9. WHY WE CANNOT "MERELY" EXTEND THE FROM CLAUSE (2)

The technique of flagging tables in the FROM clause and specifying the join condition in the WHERE clause as if it were a regular inner join (as in INFORMIX and—more or less—in ORACLE) suffers from another very serious drawback, thanks to Nasty Property Number 3: "A < = B" is not the same as "A < B OR A = B" (in the context of outer join). Consider the following two queries (expressed—for definiteness merely—in INFORMIX-style syntax):

```
SELECT S.S#, S.SNAME, S.STATUS, S.SCITY, SP.S#, SP.P#, SP.QTY
FROM    S, OUTER SP
WHERE   S.S# <= SP.S# ;

SELECT S.S#, S.SNAME, S.STATUS, S.SCITY, SP.S#, SP.P#, SP.QTY
FROM    S, OUTER SP
WHERE   S.S# < SP.S#
OR      S.S# = SP.S# ;
```

Given the sample data of Fig. 1(a), the first of these queries produces a result that happens to be identical to the outer equijoin of Fig. 2(b) (except for a slight difference in column headings). The second, however, produces a result that is the union of that outer equijoin with the left outer "less than"-join of the two tables. (At least, this is what it *should* do! I have not been able to test the query on an actual INFORMIX system.) In other words, the second query is (or ought to be) equivalent to the following:

```
SELECT S.S#, S.SNAME, S.STATUS, S.SCITY, SP.S#, SP.P#, SP.QTY
FROM    S, OUTER SP
WHERE   S.S# < SP.S#
UNION
SELECT S.S#, S.SNAME, S.STATUS, S.SCITY, SP.S#, SP.P#, SP.QTY
FROM    S, OUTER SP
WHERE   S.S# = SP.S# ;
```

And, of course, the two results are not the same: To be specific, the "union" result includes an additional row in which the supplier S# is S2 and the shipment S# is null.

So we see that the user has to wrestle here with a rather counterintuitive idea. The basic problem (loosely speaking) is that the union of the outer "less than"-join and the outer "equals"-join (i.e., equijoin) is not identical to the outer "less than or equals"-join (nor is there any reason why it should be), but the INFORMIX-style syntax strongly suggests that it is. (Perhaps I should add that the identity *is* valid if "outer" is replaced by "inner" throughout; i.e., the union of the inner "less than" and "equals" joins *is* identical to the inner "less than or equals" join. This fact probably serves only to compound the confusion.)

I remark in passing that the foregoing problem *ought* to apply to ORACLE as well as to INFORMIX; however, ORACLE (incorrectly, in my opinion) in fact treats "A < B OR A = B" as "A < = B" in this context!

Yet another criticism applies to the technique of flagging tables in the FROM clause and specifying the join condition in the WHERE clause. This one arises from Nasty Property Number 4: The comparison operators are not transitive. This property is a consequence of the fact that we are dealing with three-valued logic. For example, the statement

```
( A = B  AND  B = C )  implies  ( A = C )
```

(which is valid in conventional two-valued logic, of course) is *not* valid in three-valued logic. For instance, if A is 1 and B is null and C is 2, then the left-hand side evaluates to *unk* ("unknown"), but the right-hand side evaluates to *false*. And analogous remarks apply if we replace "=" by "<" throughout, or by ">" throughout, or if we leave the first "=" alone but replace the other two by ">", etc., etc. (The reader is referred to reference [8] for further discussion of such matters.)

The foregoing considerations become relevant when we examine outer joins of more than two tables. In reference [5], I considered the case of three tables, as follows:

```
S ( S#, SCITY )
P ( P#, PCITY )
J ( J#, JCITY )
```

(S means suppliers, P parts, and J projects). By examining a set of sample values, I showed that the expression "the outer equijoin of S, P, J on SCITY, PCITY, JCITY" was not well-defined. In fact, there are three distinct such outer equijoins, corresponding to the three distinct join conditions

```
SCITY = PCITY AND SCITY = JCITY
SCITY = PCITY AND PCITY = JCITY
SCITY = JCITY AND PCITY = JCITY
```

(Of course, these join conditions are distinct only in three-valued logic; they are all equivalent in two-valued logic.) It follows that anyone using a product that supports outer joins of more than two tables by "merely" flagging tables in the FROM clause and specifying the join condition in the WHERE clause needs to proceed with *extreme caution* in order to be certain that he or she is indeed formulating the outer join that is actually required.

> *Aside:* Interestingly, the foregoing problem does not occur with the outer *natural* join. As reference [5] shows, the expression "the outer natural join of S, P, J on SCITY, PCITY, JCITY" *is* well-defined. The reader is referred to reference [5] for the details. *End of aside.*

10.   HOW ABOUT A NEW PRESERVE CLAUSE?

By now the reader should be convinced that no "simple" extension to the FROM or WHERE clause can handle the outer join problem satisfactorily. So how about introducing some entirely new clause? In reference [5], I proposed a new PRESERVE clause (belonging both syntactically and semantically after the WHERE clause), whose effect was to "preserve" rows from the table(s) named in the clause that did not otherwise contribute to the result of evaluating the preceding FROM and WHERE clauses. A version of PRESERVE was implemented in Computer Associates' CA-DB product (previously known variously as Enterprise:DB, IDMS/SQL, and StellaR/ DB). Here is the CA-DB version of our running example (left outer natural join of S with SP over supplier numbers):

```
SELECT     S.S#, S.SNAME, S.STATUS, S.SCITY, SP.P#, SP.QTY
FROM       S, SP
WHERE      S.S# = SP.S#
PRESERVE S ;
```

The PRESERVE clause of reference [5] was adequate to handle left, right, and full outer θ-joins of *exactly two* tables. (The CA-DB implementation handles left and right outer θ-joins only, however, because it permits only one table to be named in the PRESERVE clause.) To deal with more than two tables, reference [5] also proposed the ability to include nested table-expressions in the FROM clause, together with a column renaming operator. (Indeed, I would argue very strongly that these latter capabilities are needed anyway for numerous other reasons [14,15].) Taken together, these facilities would be sufficient to deal with completely general outer θ- joins in a clean and systematic manner (and hence the CA-DB support is at least upward-compatible with such a clean and systematic implementation). However, the PRESERVE clause per se still does not provide a particularly elegant solution to the outer natural join problem,* thanks to Nasty Property Number 5.

11.   SO WHAT ABOUT OUTER *NATURAL* JOIN?

None of the approaches discussed so far in this paper is completely adequate to deal with the problem of outer natural join (i.e., the general, full, many-to-many case). The reason is that, as just indicated, the outer natural join is not a projection of the outer equijoin (Nasty Property Number 5). As a consequence, any language that is based—as SQL is—on taking projections (remember that the SQL SELECT clause really represents a projection operation) is awkward to extend to support outer natural join. This fact is unfortunate, since outer natural join is easily the most important case in practice.

By way of illustration, consider Fig. 3 (a revised version of Fig. 1, in which we assume for the sake of the example that SP.S# is *not* a foreign key matching S.S#, and hence that it is possible for a supplier number to appear in table SP that does not appear in table S). Part (a) of the figure gives a slightly revised set of sample values for the tables (S2 has been

---

*This remark is true in general, despite the fact that the CA-DB example shown above actually does produce an outer natural join.

(a) S   SP

S#	SNAME	STATUS	SCITY
S2	Jones	10	Paris
S5	Adams	30	Athens

S#	P#	QTY
S2	P1	300
S6	P2	400

(b) Full outer equijoin of S and SP on S#

SS#	SNAME	STATUS	SCITY	SPS#	P#	QTY
S2	Jones	10	Paris	S2	P1	300
S5	Adams	30	Athens	null	null	null
null	null	null	null	S6	P2	400

(c) Full outer natural join of S and SP over S#

S#	SNAME	STATUS	SCITY	P#	QTY
S2	Jones	10	Paris	P1	300
S5	Adams	30	Athens	null	null
S6	null	null	null	P2	400

Fig. 3 An illustration of Nasty Property Number 5

changed to S6 in one row of table SP); part (b) shows the outer equijoin
over supplier numbers; and part (c) shows the corresponding outer natural
join.

Here is one possible way of formulating a query for the outer natural
join of Fig. 3(c):

```
SELECT    S# = COALESCE ( S.S#, SP.S# ),
          S.SNAME, S.STATUS, S.SCITY, SP.P#, SP.QTY
FROM      S, SP
WHERE     S.S# = SP.S#
PRESERVE  S, SP ;
```

Explanation: First, the FROM, WHERE, and PRESERVE clauses together
construct the outer *equi*join of Fig. 3(b); the SELECT clause then derives
the outer natural join. The expression "S# = COALESCE (S.S#, SP.S#)"
is meant to be interpreted as follows. First, the COALESCE function (originally introduced in reference [5]) is rather like the VALUE function of DB2:
It returns a value equal to the value of its first nonnull argument, or null
if both of its arguments are null. Then the "S# =" portion of the expression assigns a name (S#) to the resulting column.

Thus we see that it is at least possible to use PRESERVE, plus certain
related facilities, to formulate outer natural joins. But the formulation is
hardly very succinct, and it is unfortunate, to say the least, that such a

commonly required operation should be so cumbersome to express. Of course, analogous remarks apply to *inner* joins in SQL also; in fact, as I have remarked elsewhere, the real reason that SQL is so hard to extend to support outer join is that it does not directly support inner join!

Which brings me (finally) to my preferred solution to this problem: Extend SQL to provide direct ("one-liner") support for inner join first; extending it to support outer join will then be almost trivial. I first proposed such an approach in reference [5], and I am glad to see that the SQL standards committees are in fact planning such an extension in their proposed follow-on to the existing SQL standard known as SQL2 [1]. Here is the SQL2 formulation of the outer natural join of Fig. 3(c):

```
SELECT *
FROM   S NATURAL FULL OUTER JOIN SP ;
```

Not quite as elegant as "S OUTER JOIN SP," perhaps, but a considerable improvement on most of what we have seen previously in this paper.

> *Aside:* I should mention that there are at least two vendors, namely Tandem and ShareBase, whose products do support (a subset of) the SQL2 proposal. For instance, Tandem's NonStop SQL product supports the construction of left outer θ-joins of two tables, where the left table of the two can in turn be a left outer θ-join of two tables (and so on, recursively). Outer natural joins are not directly supported, but of course they can easily be obtained in those cases where they do happen to be a projection of the corresponding outer equijoin. (*Exercise for the reader:* What is it exactly that characterizes such cases?) *End of aside.*

12. IS OUTER JOIN REALLY WHAT WE NEED?

I come now to the point that I touched on very briefly near the beginning of the paper: Is outer join really the right operator anyway? In my opinion, "outer join," as the operation is usually understood, is *too simplistic*, because of the well-known "nulls interpretation" problem [7,16]. The basic point is that there are numerous different reasons for generating nulls in the result of an outer join, and generating just a single ("value unknown") kind of null in every case is clearly not the appropriate thing to do in all cases.

Let us consider an example. Suppose we have the following tables:

```
EMP  ( EMP#, DEPT#, SALARY )
DEPT ( DEPT#, BUDGET )
PGMR ( EMP#, LANG )
```

PGMR ("programmer") is intended to represent a subtype table (if employee *Ex* is a programmer, *Ex* will appear in both the EMP and PGMR tables). All other aspects of the three tables are intended to be self-explanatory. Let us now consider some possible outer joins involving these three tables.

1. The left outer natural join of EMP with PGMR over EMP# will generate null LANG values for any employee who is not a programmer. Those nulls should clearly be of the "property does not apply" variety.

2. The left outer natural join of DEPT with EMP over DEPT# will generate null EMP# and SALARY values for any department that has no employees. The EMP# nulls are clearly* of the "value does not exist" variety. The SALARY nulls also mean "value does not exist," but they are at least arguably different from the EMP# nulls: Such a SALARY value does not exist *because a corresponding employee does not exist.*

3. The left outer natural join of EMP with DEPT over DEPT# will generate null DEPT# and BUDGET values for any employee who has an unknown department. The DEPT# nulls are thus clearly of the "value unknown" variety. The BUDGET nulls also mean "value unknown," but they are at least arguably different from the DEPT# nulls: Such a BUDGET value is unknown *because the corresponding department is unknown.*

4. Suppose that EMP.DEPT# is not a foreign key, and there exists at least one employee with a DEPT# value that does not appear in table DEPT. Then the left outer natural join of EMP with DEPT over DEPT# will generate a null BUDGET value for any such employee, but such a null seems to me to be different in kind yet again; it does not have the same meaning as any of the nulls mentioned in paragraphs 1, 2, and 3 above [16].

So suppose we now construct "the" full outer natural join of EMP and DEPT and PGMR. What kind of nulls should be generated? It looks as if the user is going to need to be able to specify that distinct kinds of null be generated *on an individual column-by-column basis.* And it is even conceivable that different kinds of null might need to be generated in *the same column* (in different rows, of course); suppose, for example, that some employees have an unknown department, others have a department that is not

---

*Well, maybe it is not so clear; it could certainly be argued that they are of the "value is the empty set" variety instead. And whether "value does not exist" and "value is the empty set" are the same kind of null or not is a separate question, beyond the scope of the present paper.

represented in the DEPT table, and still others have no department at all. What kind of nulls should be generated for the BUDGET column?

13. ARE NULLS REALLY WHAT WE NEED?

This is clearly the appropriate place to repeat my conviction that "nulls" per se—meaning the nulls of three- or higher-valued logic—are not what we want anyway [7,8]. I would prefer a DBMS that provides a (systematic) "DBA-defined default values" mechanism, and a version of outer join that generates such default values instead of nulls. All discussions in previous sections of this paper should thus be interpreted accordingly!

Reference [3] contains a specific proposal for a "default-generating" version of outer join that supports *only* certain many-to-one left (or right) outer natural joins. In terms of the example of the previous section, it would support Cases 1 (EMP with PGMR), 3 (EMP with DEPT), and 4 (likewise), but not Case 2 (DEPT with EMP). It would also not support our running example (left outer natural join of S with SP). The reader is referred to that paper for specific details of the proposal, also for a detailed justification of the apparent limitations. I will however give part of the justification here in order to allay the reader's curiosity somewhat.

The basic point is that outer join is not a good model of certain real world situations anyway. To return to Case 2 for a moment (left outer natural join of DEPT with EMP over DEPT#): As indicated in the previous section, this outer join should generate "value does not exist" nulls for EMP# and SALARY for any department that has no employees. Note, therefore, that if the result contains N rows for a given department Dx, it means that department Dx has N employees, *unless N is one*. In this latter case, it means *either* that department Dx has one employee *or* that it has no employees at all!

Let us examine this example a little more carefully. In general, a table of n columns can be thought of as an n-place *predicate* (i.e., a truth-valued function with n arguments), and the rows of that table can be thought of as *propositions,* i.e., assertions that certain combinations of values for the arguments (columns) make the predicate evaluate to *true.* For example, the appearance of the row (E1,D1,50K) in the EMP table is an assertion that the truth-valued function EMP (EMP#,DEPT#,SALARY) evaluates to *true* for the combination of argument values EMP# = E1, DEPT# = D1, and SALARY = 50K. In other words, the row (e,d,s) appears in the EMP table if and only if e is the employee number of some employee who works in department d and earns salary $s;$ this is the *criterion for membership* of a given row within the EMP table. It is what the EMP table "means."

What then is the "meaning" of the table produced by the outer join of

Case 2 (left outer natural join of DEPT with EMP over DEPT#)? The columns of that table are DEPT#, BUDGET, EMP#, and SALARY. What is the criterion of membership in this table for some candidate row (d,b,e,s)? It has to be something like the following:

> "There exists some department with department number *d* and budget *b,* and EITHER *e* is the employee number of some employee who works in that department and *s* is that employee's salary, OR that department has no employees at all and *e* is null and *s* is null."

This criterion of membership is not only difficult to state, it is quite difficult to understand as well. And any misunderstanding is likely to lead to incorrect queries and wrong answers out of the database (e.g., consider the difficulty already mentioned above that arises in connexion with counting the number of employees in each department).

For reasons such as the foregoing, some researchers are exploring alternative approaches to the outer join problem [10,13,16]. There is no space here to examine those approaches in any depth, but I wanted to alert the reader to the fact that the jury is still out on this issue. Outer join, or rather the problem that outer join is intended to address, is still partly a question in need of further research.

ACKNOWLEDGMENTS

I would like to thank Hugh Darwen, Nat Goodman, and Adrian Larner for numerous helpful discussions, and Hugh Darwen, Nat Goodman, and Colin White for their careful reviews of earlier drafts of this paper. I would also like to thank the following people for providing me with information regarding the indicated products: Valerie Anderson (SYBASE), Ron Landers (CA-UNIVERSE), David McGoveran (CA-DB and NonStop SQL), and Colin White (ORACLE, ShareBase, and SQLBase).

REFERENCES AND BIBLIOGRAPHY

1. ISO (International Organization for Standardization) / ANSI (American National Standards Institute, *(ISO working draft) Database Language SQL2,* Document ANSI X3H2-90-062 / ISO/IEC JTC1/SC21/WG3 DBL SEL-3a (February 1990).

2. Donald D. Chamberlin, "A Summary of User Experience with the SQL Data Sublanguage," *Proc. International Conference on Databases,* Aberdeen, Scotland, July 1980.

3. Hugh Darwen, "Outer Join with No Nulls and Fewer Tears" (in this volume).

4. C. J. Date, "Relational Algebra," Chapter 13 of C. J. Date, *An Introduction To Database Systems: Volume I,* 5th edition (Reading, MA: Addison-Wesley, 1990).

5. C. J. Date, "The Outer Join," in C. J. Date, *Relational Database: Selected Writings* (Reading, MA: Addison-Wesley, 1986).

6. C. J. Date, "Updating Views," in C. J. Date, *Relational Database: Selected Writings* (Reading, MA: Addison-Wesley, 1986).

7. C. J. Date, "NOT Is Not "Not"! (Notes on Three-Valued Logic and Related Matters)," in C. J. Date, *Relational Database Writings 1985–1989* (Reading, MA: Addison-Wesley, 1990).

8. C. J. Date, "Three-Valued Logic and the Real World" (in this volume).

9. Sandra L. Emerson, Marcy Darnovsky, and Judith S. Bowman, *The Practical SQL Handbook: Using Structured Query Language* (Reading, MA: Addison-Wesley, 1989).

10. Adrian Larner, "The Relational Model Twenty Years On." *Proc. 5th Annual Conf. of the UK Computer Measurement Group,* Glasgow, Scotland (UK Computer Measurement Group, Monarch House, 1A Herschel St., Slough, Berks. SL1 1SY, UK, May 1990).

11. Jonathan Leffler, *Using INFORMIX-SQL* (Reading, MA: Addison-Wesley, 1989).

12. ORACLE Corporation, *SQL Language Reference Manual* (ORACLE RDBMS Version 6.0 with the Transaction Processing Subsystem). Oracle Part No. 778–V6.0, October 1988.

13. Mark A. Roth, Henry F. Korth, and Abraham Silberschatz, "Extended Algebra and Calculus for Nested Relational Databases," *ACM Transactions on Database Systems* 13, No. 4 (December 1988).

14. Andrew Warden, "The Naming of Columns," in C. J. Date, *Relational Database Writings 1985–1989* (Reading, MA: Addison-Wesley, 1990).

15. Andrew Warden, "In Praise of Marriage," in C. J. Date, *Relational Database Writings 1985–1989* (Reading, MA: Addison-Wesley, 1990).

16. Andrew Warden, "Into the Unknown," in C. J. Date, *Relational Database Writings 1985–1989* (Reading, Mass, Addison-Wesley, 1990).

APPENDIX A:
IS OUTER NATURAL JOIN ASSOCIATIVE?

It is easy to see that inner natural join is associative—that is (using the keyword JOIN to represent inner natural join), the expressions (A JOIN B) JOIN C and A JOIN (B JOIN C) are always equivalent [4]. Outer natural join, by contrast, is not generally associative, as the following example demonstrates. *Note:* "Outer natural join" here means full outer natural join.

Example: Suppose we are given relations A, B, and C as shown:

A	X	Y
	1	2

B	X	Z
	0	3

C	Y	Z
	2	3

Using "*" to mean "full outer natural join (over columns with the same name)," and using question marks to represent nulls, we have:

(A * B) * C :

X	Y	Z
1	2	?
0	?	3
?	2	3

A * (B * C) :

X	Y	Z
0	2	3
1	2	?

On the other hand, in the special case where relations A, B, and C have just one "common column" and that is the column over which the joins are taken, then it can readily be seen that the operation *is* associative after all [5].

The associativity or otherwise of outer natural join is relevant, of course, to questions of language interface design and to questions of expression transformation and optimizability.

20

Outer Join with
No Nulls
and Fewer Tears

ABSTRACT

This paper is a companion piece to reference [5]. It proposes a concrete approach to the outer join problem.

COMMENTS ON REPUBLICATION

One of the reviewers of the original draft of the paper that became the previous chapter in this collection ("Watch Out for Outer Join") was Hugh Darwen, who immediately sat down and wrote the following as a companion piece to that earlier paper. I am grateful to Hugh for allowing me to include that companion piece here.

Originally published in *InfoDB* 5, No. 1 (Spring/Summer 1990). Reprinted by permission of Database Associates International.

1. INTRODUCTION

Reference [5] exposes some of the many snares and pitfalls that face would-be implementers of an outer join operator in relational query languages, and discusses some of the problems that arise in products in which such an operator has already been implemented. It strongly suggests that further research is still needed, and hints at a preference for an implementation that does not involve nulls. Here I suggest an operator, LEFT JOIN, that:

- Can be painlessly included in a relational algebra
- Is not a primitive operator in an algebra that includes Cartesian product (or, preferably, inner natural join), rename, restriction, projection, difference, and union operators [4]
- Always delivers a relation in first normal form
- Never generates nulls (neither does it accept them)
- Is constrained to a certain well-defined subset of the many varieties of outer join that can be distinguished

My suggestion is heavily based on an implementation made many years ago in a fairly princely [6] relational DBMS, Business System 12, that was available to users of IBM's European Bureau Service.

I also address the outer join requirements that may be considered as still outstanding even when LEFT JOIN is available.

2. LEFT JOIN

The operator I describe, LEFT JOIN, is intended for inclusion in a language based on the relational algebra, in which operands and results are all null-free relations (i.e., the concept of using nulls to represent "missing values" is not embraced at all). Furthermore, this language is based entirely on the traditional *two-valued* logic.

My definition espouses the so-called "marriage principle" of reference [7] (see also reference [4]), whereby "common columns" for joins and other dyadic operators are those that have *the same names*. The syntax is as follows:

    LEFT JOIN (*left, right, fill*)

Explanation:

1. The operands *left, right,* and *fill* are relation-valued expressions
2. Some candidate key of *right* is a subset of the common columns of *left* and *right*

3. The columns of *fill* must be precisely those columns of *right* that are not columns of *left*

4. The degrees of *left, right,* and *fill* are not otherwise constrained, and may even be zero [9]

5. The cardinality of *fill* must be exactly one*

Let *R* = LEFT JOIN (*A,B,C*). Then *R* is the **left outer natural join** of *A* with *B* (in that order), defined as follows. Each row of *R* consists of a row of *A* extended with values, for the noncommon columns of *B,* from either (a) the (unique) matching row of *B,* if such a matching row exists, or (b) the (unique) row of *C* otherwise. Every row in *A* has a corresponding row in *R*. Rows in *B* that have no matching row in *A* do not contribute to *R* (the very word LEFT implies that only the data of what would be the left operand in an infix notation is preserved, regardless of matches).

Some readers may find the following pseudoSQL version useful as an aid to understanding:

```
SELECT  all-cols-in-A, all-noncommon-cols-in-B
FROM    A, B
WHERE   common-cols-in-A = common-cols-in-B
UNION
SELECT  all-cols-in-A, all-cols-in-C
FROM    A, C
WHERE   NOT EXISTS
      ( SELECT *
        FROM   B
        WHERE  common-cols-in-A = common-cols-in-B ) ;
```

Note: It would be possible to incorporate LEFT JOIN into SQL in a more direct fashion, as is shown by the draft proposals for "SQL2" [1].

Points arising:

The heading (i.e., set of column names) of *R* is the union of the headings of *A* and *B*. Any candidate key of *A* is a candidate key of *R*. *R* is updatable to the extent that *A* is updatable, except that values in columns deriving from *B* may not be changed or specified on insert.

Point 2 under "Explanation" above assumes that all the candidate keys of any relation are known to the system. Reference [8] includes a set of rules for determining *primary* keys of derived relations (assuming that the primary keys of base relations are known), and those rules can easily be extended to support alternate keys as well [2].

---

*For this reason it might be better for *fill* to be represented by a tuple expression instead of by a relational expression.

LEFT JOIN directly supports all requirements for many-to-one left outer natural joins.

One-to-many right outer natural joins are trivially supported too, because of course the one-to-many *right* outer natural join of *A* with *B* (with fill *C*) is equivalent to the many-to-one *left* outer natural join of *B* with *A* (with fill *C*).

One-to-one full outer natural joins are indirectly supported, because "FULL JOIN (*A,B,Ca,Cb*)" can be expressed as UNION (LEFT JOIN (*A,B,Cb*), LEFT JOIN (*B,A,Ca*)).

One-to-many left, many-to-one right, and many-to-many outer natural joins are not supported.* Such joins are deprecated because of the dubious device of using a default value (or a null) to represent an empty set—for instance, a blank or empty string in EMP#, accompanied by values like 0 for SALARY, to show a department that has no employees. See reference [10] for further discussion of this problem when nulls are used instead of default values.

Outer joins that are not natural joins are not supported. Note that most such joins are generally of the deprecated many-to-many variety anyway.

The "fill table" *C* can be conveniently specified by "EXTENDing" the constant *nullary relation* TABLE_DEE (See references [4] and [9], respectively, for an explanation of EXTEND and TABLE_DEE). Alternatively, and even more conveniently, an operator such as GENERATE (i.e., EXTEND with TABLE_DEE as its implied operand) might be provided. Or the fill table could be some one-row base relation set up by the DBA, or it might, in really abstruse cases, be the one-row result of some nontrivial relational expression. In most cases, judicious specification of the fill table will give a result in which unmatched *A* rows can be guaranteed to be distinguishable from matched ones, if that is desired.

3. WHAT TO DO ABOUT THE OUTER JOINS NOT SUPPORTED BY LEFT JOIN

Consider the left outer natural join of DEPT (departments) with EMP (employees), not supported by LEFT JOIN because it is one-to-many.

As has already been stated, the commonly seen implementation, where an unmatched DEPT row is combined with a row of nulls or defaults to

---

*Some people find terms such as "many-to-one" somewhat confusing in this context. For instance, in the suppliers-and-parts database, shipments-to-suppliers (SP-to-S) is clearly many-to-one (many shipments have the same supplier); yet, if we form the natural join of these two relations, each shipment appears *once* and each supplier appears *many times* in the result (i.e., it is effectively the inverse of what the many-to-one terminology might suggest).

represent an employee-less department, is heavily suspect. The simple proposition represented by a regular row of this result is one expressing information about an **employee** and the department he or she works in. The proposition represented by one of the irregular rows is very different indeed, informing us about a **department** that no employees work in.

A relation is supposed to represent a single predicate, such that each of its rows supply values for the placeholders of that predicate. The single, disjunctive predicate that "covers" both of the simple propositions of the previous paragraph is extremely difficult to express. This lack of uniformity in the information represented by the rows of a many-to-many outer join is very likely to lead to traps for the unwary. For example, if SUSPECT is the left outer natural join of DEPT with EMP, consider the following apparently innocuous query:

```
SELECT DEPT#, COUNT(*)
FROM    SUSPECT
GROUP   BY DEPT# ;
```

The user had glanced at the contents of SUSPECT, seen that it was apparently all about employees working in departments, and had naturally wondered how many employees worked in each department. Unfortunately this query does not distinguish the empty departments from the singletons!

A correct way to express the required query involves the left outer natural join of DEPT with a *summary* of EMP. It is shown here in two steps, the first using SQL (slightly extended to allow derived columns to be named [6]), the second using the LEFT JOIN operator proposed above:

```
T1   :=   SELECT DEPT#, EMPCT = COUNT(*)
          FROM    EMP
          GROUP   BY DEPT# ;

ANS  :=   LEFT JOIN ( DEPT, T1, GENERATE ( EMPCT = 0 ) ) ;
```

DEPT# is a candidate key for T1, so the constraints we impose on the operands of LEFT JOIN are satisfied.

Note, incidentally, that this query cannot be expressed at all in current SQL *directly* (i.e., without using UNION)—not even in those dialects that do include some kind of outer join support*—owing to SQL's failure to support nested query expressions in the FROM clause [6].

The foregoing example demonstrates one case where LEFT JOIN really does deliver a thoroughly respectable relation as its result, where nulls are the very last thing you would want to appear (in EMPCT for unmatched

---

*Except possibly for those products, such as NonStop SQL and ShareBase, that have implemented a subset of the SQL2 proposals [1,5].

departments), and where the meaning of each column of the result (especially EMPCT, here) does not vary at all from row to row. But not all LEFT JOINs are so respectable (even if they are always many-to-one). Consider, for example, the LEFT JOIN of EMP with DEPT, where the fill table supplies (say) the value "Nameless" for LOCATION (a noncommon column in DEPT; we assume for the sake of the example that EMP.DEPT# is not a foreign key—i.e., there may be some department numbers in EMP that do not appear in DEPT). The intuitive, simple predicate for the result might lead us to conclude that, just as some employees work in a location called "London," so others work in a location called "Nameless." (It would be especially unfortunate in Tennessee, where there really is a location called "Nameless.")

Of course, I am touching here on the *interpretation* problem (i.e., what does it mean to say that a given piece of information is missing?). Space precludes detailed treatment of that problem here; further discussion can be found in reference [5].

To revert to table SUSPECT above: Perhaps it can reasonably be concluded from that example that the result of a one-to-many (and hence, a fortiori, many-to-many) outer join, whatever it is, is not safely treatable as a relation. After all, one of the fundamental properties of every relation is the existence of at least one **candidate key**. If we look at table (c) in Fig. 3 in reference [5], can we see a candidate key? There certainly is no **primary** key, for there is no column at all that does not permit nulls, except for column S#, and that column permits duplicates. I do not subscribe to the notion that nulls in primary key columns are acceptable in "derived tables" though not in "base tables," for I insist that "base table" is merely a degenerate case of "derived table".* Nor do I subscribe to the notion that nulls are acceptable in alternate keys, even if not in primary keys, for a candidate key that cannot be chosen to be the primary key is no "candidate"! But of course my objections to such "relations" go far deeper than that, and far deeper than there is time for here, and in any case I don't subscribe to nulls *at all* [10].

If the requirement for an operator to support one-to-many outer join remains, let that operator take relations as its operands, but deliver a result of some other type, such as **report**, not available to the operators of the relational algebra, but available to the operators that do things with reports. Analogs of relational projection and restriction might still be available, but certainly no grouping operator. And, by the way, you still don't need any beastly nulls, for reports don't have to have uniform rows.

---

*The term "derived table" (or relation) here refers to what is called an *expressible* relation elsewhere in this book.

Alternatively—and this is already a hot research topic—support **relation-valued domains** for columns [3]. Then some replacement for outer join could operate on DEPT and EMP to deliver a result with the columns of DEPT plus one extra, relation-valued column, containing, for each department, a **set** (which might be empty) of employee rows. What an incredible idea, to use an empty set, rather than a null, to represent an empty set!

ACKNOWLEDGMENTS

This paper was inspired by reference [5]—indeed, I wrote it from the outset as an intended companion to that paper—and I am indebted to the author of that paper, Chris Date, for many useful comments and suggestions.

REFERENCES AND BIBLIOGRAPHY

1. ISO (International Organization for Standardization) / ANSI (American National Standards Institute), *(ISO working draft) Database Language SQL2,* Document ANSI X3H2-90-062 / ISO/IEC JTC1/SC21/WG3 DBL SEL-3a (February 1990).

2. Hugh Darwen, "The Role of Functional Dependencies in Query Decomposition" (in this volume).

3. Hugh Darwen and C. J. Date, "Relation-Valued Attributes" (in this volume).

4. C. J. Date, "Relational Algebra," Chapter 13 of C. J. Date, *An Introduction to Database Systems: Volume I,* 5th edition (Reading, MA: Addison-Wesley, 1990).

5. C. J. Date, "Watch Out for Outer Join" (in this volume).

6. Andrew Warden, "The Naming Of Columns," in C. J. Date, *Relational Database Writings 1985-1989* (Reading, MA: Addison-Wesley, 1990).

7. Andrew Warden, "In Praise of Marriage," in C. J. Date, *Relational Database Writings 1985-1989* (Reading, MA: Addison-Wesley, 1990).

8. Andrew Warden, "The Keys of the Kingdom," in C. J. Date, *Relational Database Writings 1985-1989* (Reading, MA: Addison-Wesley, 1990).

9. Andrew Warden, "Table_Dee and Table_Dum," in C. J. Date, *Relational Database Writings 1985-1989* (Reading, MA: Addison-Wesley, 1990).

10. Andrew Warden, "Into the Unknown," in C. J. Date, *Relational Database Writings 1985-1989* (Reading, MA: Addison-Wesley, 1990).

21

The Default Values Approach to Missing Information

ABSTRACT

The so-called "default values" approach to representing and manipulating missing information is described in detail.

COMMENTS ON PUBLICATION

I have referred to "the default values approach" to dealing with missing information in other chapters in the present book (see especially Chapter 15) and elsewhere. But I have never spelled out in detail exactly what I meant by that phrase. I wrote the paper that follows to fill this gap. *Note:* I make no claim that the default values approach is pretty—in fact, in many ways it is quite ugly—but I certainly think it is preferable to the alternative (at least, the only currently available alternative), which is to support "nulls" and three-valued logic [2].

Previously unpublished.

Portions of this paper have previously appeared in somewhat different form in references [5] and [7], but the paper as a whole is new.

1. INTRODUCTION

I have explained in many places why I do not support the three-valued logic approach to missing information (see in particular reference [7]), and I have indicated that, in my opinion, an approach based on the *systematic* (I would like to emphasize that "systematic") use of default values seems preferable. The purpose of this paper is to explain in some detail what such an approach would look like. *Note:* The explanations that follow are basically an amplification and elaboration—and slight revision—of a scheme first described in outline in reference [5] and again, in slightly more detail, in reference [7].

The basic idea is simple, of course: We use real values ("default values") instead of "nulls" to represent the fact that some piece of data is missing, and we stay firmly in the world of traditional two-valued logic. For example, if we don't know Joe's salary, then we place some default value—obviously a value that cannot possibly represent an actual salary, say the value "minus one"—in the SALARY position within the row for employee Joe in the EMPLOYEES table. And we agree to interpret that special value to mean, precisely, that Joe's salary is not known.

Now, there is obviously more to it than I have just indicated. For instance, we would probably agree that the actual default values per se should not get hard-coded into programs, and so we need a way of referring to those values symbolically. Such refinements are the kind of thing I had in mind when I emphasized the word "systematic" in the first paragraph above, and they are, in essence, what the rest of this paper is all about. But before I go any further there is one other introductory point that I would like to stress—namely, that *the default values approach is the approach we use in the real world.* For example, if we have a form to fill out, say a census form, and we are unable to answer some question on that form for some reason, we typically respond with a blank value—or a dash, or "N/A," or a question mark, or a variety of other possible entries. And each of these possible entries is, precisely, a special value that is agreed by convention to bear a special interpretation.* What we most certainly do not

---

*An exactly analogous remark applies to reports. In a system that supports nulls, there has to be a means of displaying those nulls in reports. And, of course, what the system does is, precisely, to display them as some "special value that is agreed by convention to bear a special interpretation."

do in such a situation is respond with a (three-valued-logic-style) "null." *There is no such thing as a "null" in the real world.*

Essentially, therefore, I claim that the default values approach represents a systematic codification of real-world practice. The three-valued logic approach, by contrast, is a purely formal abstraction, one that I claim does not map in any straightforward manner to reality [10].

The remainder of this paper presents the default values approach in some detail: Section 2 considers data structure issues, Section 3 integrity issues, and Section 4 manipulative issues. In each case, the discussions are concerned with what support for the approach would look like in an "ideal" system, i.e., a DBMS specifically designed to include such support. Unfortunately, of course, DBMSs today have not been designed in such a manner; instead, they have been built on the assumption that SQL-style nulls (and all that such nulls entail) are the approach of choice.* It is an interesting—albeit rather frustrating—exercise to consider how, given one of today's SQL-based products such as DB2, a user (or rather DBA) might cleanly implement an appropriate default values scheme on top of that product.

Note: The bulk of the paper considers just one kind of missing information, namely information that is missing because *its value is not known.* If I say that Joe's salary is "missing" in this sense, I mean, of course, that Joe does have a salary, I just don't know what it is. I will use the symbol UNK (short for "value unknown") for this kind of missing information; I will *not* use the term "null," because that term carries too much undesirable baggage with it. (Though I remark that if we did retain the term, it would now be acceptable to refer to "null *values,*" because those nulls would indeed be values and would behave accordingly. In particular, the comparison "null = null" would now evaluate to *true,* not to *unk* [7].) Section 5 briefly considers what is involved in extending the default values scheme to deal with additional kinds of missing information.

2. STRUCTURAL ASPECTS

Note: The explanations of this section are deliberately couched in terms of columns rather than domains, because in principle a system could provide a useful level of support for default values without necessarily having to support domains as well, and of course few systems today provide anything

---

*I have pointed out elsewhere [8,11] that SQL-style nulls suffer from all of the problems of three-valued logic and more besides. In other words, I would not be a fan of SQL-style nulls even if I believed in three-valued logic per se.

much in the way of domain support at all. The ideas will require some slight refinement if domain support is provided. I do think as a general principle that different columns defined on the same domain should normally have the same default value, however; in particular, a primary key and any matching foreign keys should *certainly* have the same default value (see Section 3).

Here then are the relevant structural features.

- Associated with the declaration of each column of each base table is either an UNK clause specifying the UNK representation for that column, or else the specification UNKS NOT ALLOWED. For example:

```
CREATE TABLE S                                    /* suppliers */
     ( S#      ... UNKS NOT ALLOWED ,
       SNAME   ... UNK ( '   ' ) ,
       STATUS  ... UNK ( -1 ) ,
       CITY    ... UNK ( '???' ) ,
       PRIMARY KEY ( S# ) ) ;
```

The UNK value for a given column (if it exists) must be a value from the relevant domain; e.g., an UNK value of blanks would not be permitted for a DECIMAL column. *Note:* If a given column has neither an UNK clause nor UNKS NOT ALLOWED, it might be possible for the system to assume a "default UNK value"—e.g., blanks for string columns, zero for numeric columns. But this is purely a syntactic issue.

- For some columns it might be the case that every legal bit configuration is in fact a possible genuine (nonUNK) value of the column in question. It seems to me that such columns are likely to be quite rare in practice, however, and I therefore deliberately do not include any specific facilities for dealing with them here.* Instead, such cases will have to be handled by explicit, separate, user-controlled indicator columns (as with the host side of the interface in embedded SQL today).

- When a new row is inserted into a base table:

  (a) The user must supply a value for every column that has UNKS NOT ALLOWED;

  (b) For other columns, the system will supply the applicable UNK value if the user does not provide a value.

- When a new column is added to a base table:

---

*Such facilities could be defined, of course, but I am invoking The Principle of Cautious Design (see Chapter 2 of this book): I do not think at this time that the usefulness of those facilities would be sufficient to merit the increased complexity they would cause (complexity in the definition of the default values scheme per se, that is).

Or:

```
INSERT
INTO    P ( P#, CITY, WEIGHT, PNAME, COLOR )
VALUES ( 'P7', 'Athens', 24, UNK ( PNAME ), UNK ( COLOR ) ) ;
```

5. DISCUSSION

The advantages of the foregoing scheme compared to the three-valued logic approach include the following:

- It is intuitively easier to understand.

- It is also easier to implement.

- In fact, as pointed out in Section 1, it directly reflects the way we handle missing information in the real world.

- There are arguably fewer traps for the unwary.

- It is clearly extendable to other kinds of missing information, without the need to resort to four- or five- or . . . *N*-valued logic for arbitrary *N*. Of course, we would have to introduce additional keywords such as INAPP (inapplicable), UNDEF (undefined), etc., and corresponding functions IS_INAPP, IS_UNDEF, etc., but the extensions would not be conceptually difficult.

In reference [2], however, Codd argues strongly against the default value approach, on the grounds that it is unsystematic, misrepresents the semantics, and is a significant burden on DBAs and users (inasmuch as they have to choose and understand and manipulate the default values, possibly many different default values). My response to these arguments is as follows:

- I would agree that default values represent a significant burden on DBAs and users—but so too does three-valued logic, in my opinion (not to mention four- and five- . . . and *N*-valued logic), as references [5], [7], [8], [10], [11], and [13] surely demonstrate. The fact is, the missing information problem is a very complex problem, more complicated than I think anyone yet fully understands. A "solution" to that problem that is oversimplified is at least as dangerous as one that is inherently somewhat complex.

- Regarding the "unsystematic" claim: DBAs and users (and DBMSs, I might add) are always going to be able to use system facilities in an unsystematic manner, no matter how carefully defined those facilities might be. The default value approach is not totally unsystematic. At least the default values are explicitly made known to the system, and appropriate functions are provided to avoid the need for hardcoding those values into programs (in fact, users should normally not even know what the specific default values are). In fact, I would argue that the proposals of the present paper are more systematic in certain respects—certainly they are more orthogonal—than the "missing information" proposals of reference [2].

- As for the suggestion that default values "misrepresent the semantics": Exactly the same is true of the three-valued logic scheme, if it becomes necessary to deal with more than one kind of missing information. To repeat an argument from reference [7]: It is at least as dangerous (to my way of thinking) to represent, say, "not applicable" as "value unknown" as it is to represent, say, "value unknown" as "minus one"— possibly even more dangerous, in fact, because in the first case the user might be lulled into a false sense of security. Indeed, we can see exactly this kind of mistake in the design of the SQL language itself (in other words, system designers and implementers can make just the same kinds of mistakes as users). For example (as pointed out earlier in this paper), the fact that SQL regards the MAX of an empty set to be null (meaning "value unknown") is just plain wrong, in my opinion.

6.   DEFAULT VALUES IN DB2 AND THE SQL STANDARD

It is perhaps worth mentioning that IBM's DB2 product does include some default value support today [12]. However, that support is frankly not very much use; it simply provides a set of system-defined default values—basically zero for numbers, blanks for fixed length strings, the empty string for varying length strings, and a special "origin" value for dates and times (for details, see reference [12])—and then allows those values to be used instead of nulls on INSERT (i.e., if the user does not supply any other value for the relevant column). It does not provide any user-defined default values, nor does it provide anything along the lines of the UNK or IS_UNK or IF_UNK functions; furthermore, the default values it does provide are mostly much too precious to be used as UNKs (there is all the difference in the world between, e.g., a balance owing of UNK and a balance owing of zero!). Thus, if the DBA wishes to implement a default value scheme on top of DB2, with user-defined (or rather DBA-defined) UNK values, he or she will not receive much assistance from DB2 itself.*

---

*I note in passing that DB2 causes a slight problem with DATEs in this regard: Basically, every DATE value in a DB2 database is required to be a legal date; thus, e.g., a default value of 00/00/00 will not work.

For completeness, I should mention too that the SQL standard does also include some default value support, courtesy of the "Integrity Enhancement Feature" (IEF), which was incorporated into the standard in 1989. Moreover, those IEF default values (unlike DB2's) are user-defined, not system-defined (for details, see reference [4]). In terms of the proposals in the body of this paper, however, that IEF support addresses the requirements of the first two items in Section 2 only; in particular, there is still no support for the UNK or IS_UNK or IF_UNK functions. (The current SQL2 proposals [1] also include support for a SET DEFAULT referential integrity rule, which allows an UPDATE or DELETE operation on a row in a target table to set matching foreign key values to the applicable default value instead of to null.)

7. CONCLUSION

By way of conclusion, let me freely admit that the scheme described in this paper is not a particularly elegant approach to the missing information problem. However, I am very far from convinced that three-valued logic is any better—indeed, I believe quite strongly that it is significantly worse. In other words, I believe the whole area of missing information stands in need of considerable further research.

REFERENCES AND BIBLIOGRAPHY

1. ANSI X3H2 / ISO/IEC JTC1 SC21 WG3 Data Base Languages, *(ISO working draft) Database Language SQL2,* Document X3H2-90-264 (July 1990).

2. E. F. Codd, *The Relational Model for Database Management Version 2* (Reading, MA: Addison-Wesley, 1990).

3. Hugh Darwen, "Outer Join with No Nulls and Fewer Tears" (in this volume).

4. C. J. Date, *A Guide to the SQL Standard,* 2nd edition (Reading, MA: Addison-Wesley, 1989).

5. C. J. Date, "Null Values in Database Management," in C. J. Date, *Relational Database: Selected Writings* (Reading, MA: Addison-Wesley, 1986).

6. C. J. Date, "A Contribution to the Study of Database Integrity," in C. J. Date, *Relational Database Writings 1985-1989* (Reading, MA: Addison-Wesley, 1990).

7. C. J. Date, "NOT Is Not "Not"! (Notes on Three-Valued Logic and Related Matters," in C. J. Date, *Relational Database Writings 1985-1989* (Reading, MA: Addison-Wesley, 1990).

8. C. J. Date, "EXISTS Is Not "Exists"! (Some Logical Flaws in SQL)," in C. J. Date, *Relational Database Writings 1985-1989* (Reading, MA: Addison-Wesley, 1990).

9. C. J. Date, "Notes Toward a Reconstituted Definition of the Relational Model Version 1 (RM/V1)" (in this volume).

10. C. J. Date, "Three-Valued Logic and the Real World" (in this volume).

11. C. J. Date, "Oh No Not Nulls Again" (in this volume).

12. C. J. Date and Colin J. White, *A Guide to DB2,* 3rd edition (Reading, MA: Addison-Wesley, 1989).

13. Andrew Warden, "Into the Unknown," in C. J. Date, *Relational Database Writings 1985–1989* (Reading, MA: Addison-Wesley, 1990).

RELATIONAL VS. NONRELATIONAL SYSTEMS

22

Entity/Relationship Modeling and the Relational Model

ABSTRACT

An attempt to shed some light on "the great debate" between the entity/relationship and relational models.

COMMENTS ON REPUBLICATION

I wrote this article originally out of frustration at what seemed to me to be some very unproductive arguments between relational model and "E/R model" advocates. It seemed to me that in many cases the people involved were arguing at cross purposes, and indeed not communicating very much at all, owing to a lack of common interpretation of terms and a lack of understanding of objectives. I don't know that matters have improved much (if at all) since that time, but at least I found it helpful to articulate

Originally published in *InfoDB* 5, No. 2 (Summer 1990). Reprinted by permission of Database Associates International.

my own position on the subject. I hope the result may prove helpful to others too.

1. INTRODUCTION

A question that is often heard in some shape or form is "Will the entity/relationship (E/R) model take over from the relational model?" Certainly there are some who think it will. For example, here is a quote from the originator of the E/R model, Peter Chen: "Many people share my view that [the E/R model] will be the next wave in the DBMS field after the current relational wave is over" (from reference [2]). Equally certainly, there are many who do not agree with this position. E. F. Codd, for example, has written that ". . . companies intending to acquire a DBMS product should be concerned about the risk of investing in the E/R approach" (from reference [5]). The purpose of this article is to try to shed some light on this debate.

Note: For any readers whose professional expertise happens to lie in some realm other than that of database technology—especially for those who may be involved in logic or philosophy or artificial intelligence—I should make it clear that throughout this paper I use the term "model" to mean a database model specifically, and the terms "the real world" and "reality" to mean just those aspects of the real world or reality that we wish to capture in such a model. I make this remark because I do not wish to be accused of overclaiming when I say, for example, that the relational model is "a good formal model of the real world."

2. WHAT IS THE REAL ISSUE?

One of the biggest difficulties in attempting to get to grips with this subject is that the term "E/R model" does not have a single, precise definition, but rather is subject to numerous different (and occasionally conflicting) interpretations, of varying degrees of precision. The relational model, by contrast, is much more carefully defined, and relational model proponents (myself included) have not unnaturally focused on this point of difference as a basis for criticizing the E/R approach.

A second major criticism that is commonly leveled at the E/R model (again, by advocates of the relational model especially) is that there are no good objective criteria for distinguishing between an entity and a relationship, and hence that trying to make such a distinction is a source of unnecessary confusion and complexity. The relational model, of course, does not make any such distinction—entities and relationships are both represented in the same way, as tables.

In my opinion, however, the foregoing criticisms, while undeniably justified, have served to obscure the real issue. By concentrating on the two major points of difference just mentioned, the relational advocates have unwittingly reinforced the E/R model's claim to be seen as a viable alternative to the relational model! In other words, arguments that the relational model is superior to the E/R model on these two counts are made on the basis of a tacit assumption that the two models are in fact addressing the same problem. And I don't really think they are.

In fairness, I must immediately say that Chen's original intent *was* (at least in part) to address the same problem as the relational model, as a study of his first paper on the subject (reference [1]) will clearly show. But it is not in this area that the E/R approach has proved most useful, and it is not in this area that it has enjoyed its widest acceptance. Instead, of course, it has found its major practical application in the area of (logical) *database design*. The informal concepts "entity" and "relationship" are *useful*—at an intuitive level—as an aid to understanding what it is that needs to be represented in the database. I shall have more to say on this point in a moment.

It seems to me, therefore, that the E/R model and the relational model are both useful, and they both have a role to play. The issue (in my opinion) is thus not one of "E/R vs. relational"; rather, it is one of identifying what the respective roles of the two approaches are, and how they complement one another.

3. THE E/R MODEL AS AN INFORMAL FOUNDATION FOR THE RELATIONAL MODEL?

Database management is all about mapping the *informal* real world into some *formal* machine representation. Codd's very great contribution was that he developed a useful *formal* model—formal, and hence mechanizable, and hence usable as a basis for our computerized database systems.* But a formal model is only useful to the extent that it has some reasonable mapping to the *in*formal real world—i.e., to the extent that its formal constructs correspond in some reasonable way to relevant aspects of reality.

It follows, therefore, that although the relational model is of course an abstract theory, Codd could surely not have developed it without some regard for its meaning in real-world terms. On the contrary, he must surely have had something very close to the ideas of the E/R approach in mind as the intended interpretation. Indeed, Codd's own writings support this contention. In his very first paper on the subject (reference [3]), we find:

---

*Usable also as a basis for a vast amount of important database research, which the E/R model, whatever else its claims to fame might be, is not (in my opinion).

"The set of entities of a given entity type can be viewed as a relation, and we shall call such a relation an *entity type* relation. . . . The remaining relations . . . are between entity types and are . . . called *inter-entity relations*. . . . An essential property of every inter-entity relation is that [it includes at least two foreign keys that] either refer to distinct entity types or refer to a common entity type serving distinct roles."

Here Codd is clearly proposing that relations be used to model both "entities" and "relationships" (of arbitrary degree, incidentally, not just binary relationships). But—and it is a very big but—the point is that *relations are formal objects, and the relational model is a formal system.* The essence of Codd's contribution (to repeat) was that he found a good *formal* model of the real world. By contrast, of course, the E/R model is *not* (or, at least, not primarily) such a formal model.

4. DATABASE DESIGN

As indicated above, the E/R model has proved very useful in the area of database design. One of the principal reasons for its comparative success in this area, of course, is that the E/R model carries with it an associated diagramming technique—the well known "E/R diagrams"—which can be used to represent the logical structure of a database in an intuitively appealing manner. Thus, E/R ideas, and E/R diagrams, have a significant role to play in the construction of abstract (or logical) database designs; they provide a convenient basis for enabling the designer to get an intuitive grasp on the real world, and for enabling end users, DBAs, application analysts, and others all to communicate with one another.

In order to turn the abstract database design into something that can be used with some actual DBMS, of course, the informal E/R constructs have to be mapped into appropriate formal constructs. This is where the relational model comes in. The formal constructs of the relational model can be used in a variety of ways to represent the informal constructs of the abstract E/R design. Details of the process by which the E/R constructs are mapped to relational constructs are beyond the scope of this short note; numerous methodologies have been described in the literature (see, e.g., reference [6] or reference [8]).

5. IS THE E/R MODEL A DATA MODEL?

One issue I have skated over so far is the question of whether the E/R model is truly a data model at all, in the same sense that the relational model is a data model. In order to be able to discuss this question sensibly, we must obviously try to agree first on what we mean by the term "data model." The fact is, the term is used in the literature to denote two quite distinct concepts, at two quite different levels of abstraction (and it is this fact that accounts for much of the confusion that surrounds this issue). I will attempt to distinguish between the two levels by introducing the terms "Type 1" data model and "Type 2" data model, with definitions as follows:

- *Type 1:* A Type 1 data model is a formal system involving at least three components, namely a structural component, an integrity component, and a manipulative component. Those components can be *applied to* the problems of any specific enterprise or organization; *note carefully, however, that a Type 1 data model, in and of itself, has nothing to do with any such specific enterprise or organization.* The relational model is a Type 1 data model by this definition (not surprisingly, since the definition is essentially identical to the definition first given by Codd for the term "data model" in reference [4]).

- *Type 2:* A Type 2 data model, by contrast, is a model of some specific enterprise or organization; i.e., it is essentially just a *database design*. In other words, a Type 2 model takes the facilities provided by some Type 1 model and applies them to some specific problem. It can thus be regarded as *a specific application* of some Type 1 data model. *Note:* The term *data modeling,* frequently encountered in the literature, refers specifically to the activity of constructing what I am here calling a Type 2 data model.

The following analogy (based on a discussion in reference [7]) might help to clarify the distinction. A Type 1 model can be thought of as a *programming language*—albeit one that is a trifle abstract—whose constructs can be used to solve a wide variety of specific problems, but by themselves have no direct connexion with any such specific problem. (After all, a programming language also involves structural, integrity, and manipulative aspects. The difference is that a programming language also prescribes a specific syntax, whereas a data model does not.) If this analogy is accepted—i.e., if a Type 1 model is thought of as a programming language—then a Type 2 model can be thought of as a *specific program* written in that language! In other words, to repeat, a Type 2 model represents a specific application of some Type 1 model, an application that is intended to solve some specific problem.

Turning now to E/R modeling per se: The term "E/R modeling" is of course used to refer to the process of constructing a (more or less abstract) database design. (It is effectively synonymous with the term "data modeling" mentioned briefly above.) Therefore, an E/R model—not "the" E/R model, observe—is clearly a Type 2 model, not a Type 1 model, and hence is not a formal model in the same sense that the relational model is a formal model.

But what about *"the"* E/R model that underlies all of those Type 2 E/R models? Clearly it is a Type 1 model! As such, however, it does suffer from a certain lack of precision and formal definition (and here we come to some of the relational camp's objections to it, as briefly discussed earlier). Of course, there is no question that "the" Type 1 E/R model *could* be formalized and made more precise, if desired. There are basically two ways in which such a formalization could be carried out:

1. The first, less ambitious, approach was in fact attempted by Chen in his original paper (reference [1]). The most charitable interpretation of the result of that effort is that it is essentially just *a thin layer on top of the basic relational model*—the "thin layer" consisting of certain builtin integrity rules (actually foreign key rules) such as cascade delete.* Thus, the result is certainly not a *replacement* for the relational model. It might be thought of as a minor extension to the relational model.

2. The second approach would involve the definition of new formal "entity" and "relationship" objects, with corresponding formal operators and integrity rules. While various people have advocated such an approach, I feel bound to point out that it would necessarily result in something more complex than the relational model, and would elevate the arbitrary and logically unnecessary "entity vs. relationship" distinction to an undesirable level. Moreover, the added complexity would very likely prove a hindrance to formal reasoning and manipulation.†
   I conclude, therefore, that (again) the result would probably not be a serious competitor to the relational model as a formal basis on which to construct database products and theories.

6.   ENTITIES VS. RELATIONSHIPS

To pursue the point of the previous paragraph a little further: While I have already agreed that the "entity vs. relationship" distinction can be useful

---

*The formal objects and operators of Chen's model are essentially just the formal objects and operators of the relational model—except that the operators seem to be strictly less powerful than those of the relational model. For example, there is apparently no union and no explicit join. (I say "apparently," because reference [1] is actually not very clear on this point.)

†So we should apply Occam's Razor—which is strikingly apt here, incidentally: Its original formulation was "Entities should not be multiplied beyond necessity"!

from an informal point of view, it seems to me that any approach that insists on *formalizing* such a distinction is seriously flawed, because *the very same object* can quite legitimately be regarded as an entity by some users and a relationship by others. Consider the case of a marriage, for example:

- From one perspective, a marriage is clearly a relationship between two people (sample query: "Who was Elizabeth Taylor married to in 1975?").

- From another perspective, a marriage is equally clearly an entity in its own right (sample query: "How many marriages have been performed in this church since April?").

If the system insists on a formal "entity vs. relationship" distinction, then (at best) the two interpretations will be treated asymmetrically (i.e., "entity" queries and "relationship" queries will take quite different forms); at worst, one interpretation will not be supported at all (i.e., one class of query will be impossible to formulate).

As a further illustration of the point, consider the following statement from a tutorial on E/R-based database design in reference [8]: "It is common *initially* to represent some relationships as attributes [actually foreign keys] during conceptual schema design and then to convert these attributes into relationships as the design progresses and is better understood." But what happens if an attribute *becomes* a foreign key at some later time?— i.e., if the database evolves after it has already been in existence for some period of time?

There are obviously two possibilities: Either the subsequent conversion of such an attribute into a relationship will cause some disruption, or it will not. If it will, then, since (in general) *absolutely* any attribute might become a foreign key at some future time, the only safe way to design a database is to make everything a relationship right from the word go. In other words, databases should involve only relationships, no attributes at all! If on the other hand the conversion will *not* cause any disruption, then what is the point of treating attributes and relationships differently in the first place?

7. CONCLUSION

The debate over the relative merits of the E/R and relational models has raged for some considerable time, on some occasions productively, on others generating more heat than light. I hope the present article falls into the "light" and not the "heat" category.

ACKNOWLEDGMENTS

Portions of this article are based on certain sections from reference [6], and I am grateful to Addison-Wesley for allowing me to reuse the material in this fashion. I am also grateful to Nagraj Alur, Charley Bontempo, Chris Loosley, Colin White, and Paul Winsberg for their helpful comments on earlier drafts.

REFERENCES AND BIBLIOGRAPHY

1. Peter P. Chen, "The Entity/Relationship Model—Toward a Unified View of Data," *ACM Transactions on Database Systems* 1, No. 1 (March 1976).

2. Peter P. Chen, "The Entity/Relationship Approach to Database Definition," Interview in *Data Base Newsletter* 12, No. 5 (September/October 1984).

3. E. F. Codd, "Derivability, Redundancy, and Consistency of Relations Stored in Large Data Banks," IBM Research Report RJ599 (August 1969).

4. E. F. Codd, "Data Models in Database Management," Proc. Workshop on Data Abstraction, Databases, and Conceptual Modelling: *ACM SIGMOD Record* 11, No. 2 (February 1981).

5. E. F. Codd, "Claimed Alternatives to the Relational Model," *The Relational Journal for DB2 Users* 1, No. 1 (August/September 1989).

6. C. J. Date, *An Introduction to Database Systems: Volume I,* 5th edition (Reading, MA: Addison-Wesley, 1990).

7. C. J. Date, *An Introduction to Database Systems: Volume II* (Addison-Wesley, 1983).

8. Ramez Elmasri and Shamkant B. Navathe, *Fundamentals of Database Systems* (Reading, MA: Benjamin/Cummings, 1989).

23

Logic-Based
Database Systems:
A Tutorial Part I

ABSTRACT

A significant new trend has emerged within the database research community over the past few years. That trend is toward *database systems that are based on logic*. This is the first part of a three-part paper that attempts to explain what this fascinating, and potentially very significant, new field is all about.

COMMENTS ON REPUBLICATION

A version of this paper (all three parts) was previously published in my book *An Introduction to Database Systems: Volume I,* 5th edition (Addison-Wesley, 1990). However, I believe it is useful as a standalone tutorial on the topic; I also felt it worthwhile to include it in the present book because

Originally published (in somewhat different form) in my book *An Introduction to Database Systems: Volume I,* 5th edition (Addison-Wesley, 1990). Reprinted by permission.

I am conscious that people already owning the fourth edition of that earlier book might be reluctant—for obvious reasons—to invest in a copy of the fifth.

1. BACKGROUND

To repeat from the Abstract, a significant new trend has emerged within the database research community over the past few years—namely, a trend toward *database systems that are based on logic.* Expressions such as "logic database," "inferential DBMS," "expert DBMS," "deductive DBMS," "knowledge base," "knowledge base management system (KBMS)," "logic as a data model," "recursive query processing," etc., etc., are now frequently encountered in the research literature. But it is not always easy to relate such terms and the ideas they represent to familiar database terms and concepts, nor to understand the motivation underlying the research from a traditional database perspective. There is a clear need for an explanation of all of this activity in terms of conventional database ideas and principles. This three-part paper is an attempt to meet that need.

The aim, therefore, is to explain what logic-based database systems are all about from the viewpoint of someone who is familiar with database technology in general but not necessarily with logic per se. As each new idea from logic is introduced, I will try to explain it in conventional—i.e., relational—database terms, wherever possible or appropriate. *Note:* The reader is assumed to have some familiarity with the basic ideas of the relational model, which is of course directly based on logic. However, there is more to logic-based systems than just the conventional relational model, as we shall see.

The following broad topics will be covered:

1. Background and other preliminaries
2. Propositional calculus
3. Predicate calculus
4. Databases: the "proof-theoretic" view
5. Deductive DBMSs
6. Recursive query processing

The present part of the paper, Part I, is concerned just with items 1 and 2 from this list.

2. OVERVIEW

Research on the relationship between database theory and logic goes back at least to the late 1970s, if not earlier. However, the principal stimulus for the recent considerable expansion of interest in the subject seems to have been the publication in 1984 of a landmark paper by Raymond Reiter, "Towards a Logical Reconstruction of Relational Database Theory," which appeared in a book entitled *On Conceptual Modelling: Perspectives from Artificial Intelligence, Databases, and Programming Languages* (eds., Brodie, Mylopoulos, and Schmidt; Springer-Verlag, 1984). In that paper, Reiter characterized the traditional perception of database systems as *model-theoretic*—by which he meant, speaking very loosely, that:

(a) The database is seen as a set of explicit (i.e., base) relations, each containing a set of explicit tuples, and

(b) Executing a query can be regarded as evaluating some specified formula (i.e., truth-valued expression) over those explicit relations and tuples.*

Reiter then went on to argue that an alternative *proof-theoretic* view was possible, and indeed preferable in certain respects. In that alternative view—again speaking very loosely—the database is seen as a set of *axioms* ("ground" axioms, corresponding to tuples in base relations, plus certain "deductive" axioms, to be discussed), and executing a query is regarded as proving that some specified formula is a logical consequence of those axioms—in other words, proving that it is a theorem.

An example is in order. Consider the following query (expressed in relational calculus) against the usual suppliers-and-parts database (refer to Chapter 1, Appendix A):

```
SPX WHERE SPX.QTY > 250
```

Here SPX is a tuple variable ranging over the shipments relation SP. In the traditional (i.e., model-theoretic) approach, we examine the shipment (SPX) tuples one by one, evaluating the formula "SPX.QTY > 250" for each one in turn; the query result then consists of just those shipment tuples for which the formula evaluates to *true*. In the proof-theoretic approach, by contrast, we consider the shipment tuples (plus certain other items) as axioms of a certain "logical theory"; we then apply theorem-proving techniques to determine for which possible values of the variable SPX the formula "SPX.QTY > 250" is a logical consequence of those axioms within

---

*In the present context, I prefer to use the more formal terms "relation" and "tuple" rather than the informal terms "table" and "row." The reasons for this preference will become apparent in Parts II and III of the paper.

that theory. The query result then consists of just those particular values of SPX.

Of course, this example is extremely simple—so simple, in fact, that the reader may be having difficulty in seeing what the difference between the two perceptions really is. The point is, however, that the reasoning mechanism employed in the attempted proof (in the proof-theoretic approach) can of course be much more sophisticated than the simple example above is able to convey (indeed, it can handle certain problems that are beyond the capabilities of classical relational systems, as we shall see). Furthermore, the proof-theoretic approach carries with it an attractive set of additional features (the following list is based on one in Reiter's paper):

- *Representational uniformity:* It becomes possible to define a database language in which base data, "deductive axioms," queries, and integrity constraints are all represented in the same uniform way.

- *Operational uniformity:* Proof theory provides a basis for a unified attack on a variety of apparently distinct problems, including query optimization (especially semantic optimization), integrity constraint enforcement, database design (dependency theory), program correctness proofs, and other problems.

- *Semantic modeling:* Proof theory also provides a good basis on which to define various semantic modeling extensions, such as events, type hierarchies, and certain types of entity aggregation.

- *Extended application:* Finally, proof theory also provides a basis for dealing with certain issues that classical approaches have traditionally had difficulty with—for example, *disjunctive information* (e.g., "Supplier S5 supplies either part P1 or part P2, but it is not known which").

Deductive Axioms

This subsection provides a brief and preliminary explanation of the concept, referred to a couple of times above, of a *deductive axiom* (also known as a *rule of inference*). Basically, a deductive axiom is a rule by which, given certain facts, we are able to deduce additional facts. For example, given the facts "Anne is the mother of Betty" and "Betty is the mother of Celia," there is an obvious deductive axiom that allows us to deduce that Anne is the grandmother of Celia. To jump ahead of ourselves for a moment, therefore, we might imagine a "deductive DBMS" in which the two given facts are represented as tuples in a relation, as follows:

MOTHEROF	MOTHER	DAUGHTER
	Anne	Betty
	Betty	Celia

These two facts would represent the "ground axioms" for the system. Let us suppose also that the deductive axiom has been formally stated to the system somehow, e.g., as follows:

```
FORALL x FORALL y FORALL z
  ( IF    MOTHEROF      ( x, y )
    AND   MOTHEROF      ( y, z )
    THEN  GRANDMOTHEROF ( x, z ) ) ;
```

(hypothetical syntax). Now the system can apply the rule expressed in the deductive axiom to the data represented by the ground axioms (in a manner to be explained later) to deduce the result GRANDMOTHEROF(Anne,Celia). Thus, users can ask queries such as "Who is the grandmother of Celia?" or "Who are the granddaughters of Anne?"*

Let us now attempt to relate the foregoing ideas to traditional database concepts. In traditional terms, the deductive axiom can be thought of as a *view definition*—for example (SQL):

```
CREATE VIEW GRANDMOTHEROF ( GRANDMOTHER, GRANDDAUGHTER )
    AS SELECT M1.MOTHER, M2.DAUGHTER
       FROM   MOTHEROF M1, MOTHEROF M2
       WHERE  M1.DAUGHTER = M2.MOTHER ;
```

Queries such as the ones mentioned above can now be framed in terms of this view:

```
SELECT GRANDMOTHER
FROM   GRANDMOTHEROF
WHERE  GRANDDAUGHTER = 'Celia' ;

SELECT GRANDDAUGHTER
FROM   GRANDMOTHEROF
WHERE  GRANDMOTHER = 'Anne' ;
```

So far, therefore, all I have really done is presented a different syntax and different interpretation for material that is already basically familiar. However, I will show in Part III of this paper that there are in fact some significant differences (not illustrated by the simple examples above) between logic-based systems and more traditional DBMSs.

3. AN INTRODUCTION TO PROPOSITIONAL CALCULUS

I now proceed to present a very brief introduction to some of the basic ideas of logic. Propositional calculus is discussed in the present section; predicate calculus will be discussed in Part II of the paper. I remark immediately, however, that so far as we are concerned, propositional calculus is

---

*More precisely, they can ask the query "Who is Anne the grandmother of?" See Part II of this paper.

not all that important in itself; the major aim of the present section is really to pave the way for an understanding of predicate calculus. The aim of the discussions taken together is to provide a basis on which to build in the rest of the paper.

The reader is assumed to be familiar with the basic concepts of boolean algebra. Let me begin by stating a couple of boolean algebra laws that we will be needing later on.

- The distributive laws:

```
f AND ( g OR  h )  ≡  ( f AND g ) OR  ( f AND h )
f OR  ( g AND h )  ≡  ( f OR  g ) AND ( f OR  h )
```

- De Morgan's laws:

```
NOT ( f AND g )  ≡  NOT f OR  NOT g
NOT ( f OR  g )  ≡  NOT f AND NOT g
```

Now let us turn to logic per se. Logic can be succinctly defined as *a formal method of reasoning.* Because it is formal, it can be used to perform formal tasks, such as testing the validity of an argument by examining just the structure of that argument as a sequence of steps (i.e., without paying any attention to the meaning of those steps). In particular, of course, because it is formal, it can be mechanized—i.e., it can be programmed, and thus applied by the machine.

Propositional calculus and predicate calculus are two special cases of logic in general (in fact, the former is a subset of the latter). The term "calculus," in turn, is just a general term that refers to any system of symbolic computation; in the particular cases at hand, the kind of computation involved is the computation of the truth value (*true* or *false*) of certain formulas or expressions.*

Terms

Assume that we have some collection of objects, called *constants,* about which we can make statements of various kinds. In database parlance, these constants are the elements of the underlying domains. Then we define a *term* as a statement (involving such constants) that:

(a) Does not involve any quantifiers (EXISTS or FORALL), and

(b) Either does not involve any logical connectives (see below) or is contained in parentheses, and

(c) Evaluates to either *true* or *false.*

---

*We are concerned throughout this paper (all three parts) with two-valued logic only.

For example, "Supplier S1 is located in London" and "Supplier S2 is located in London" and "Supplier S1 supplies part P1" are all terms (they evaluate to *true, false,* and *true,* respectively, given the usual sample data values—see Chapter 1, Appendix A, Fig. 5). By contrast, "Supplier S1 supplies some part *p*" is not a term, because it contains a quantifier ("some part *p*").

Formulas

Next, we define the concept of a *formula.* Formulas of the propositional calculus—more generally, of the *predicate* calculus (see later)—are used in database systems to represent the conditional expression that defines the result of a query (among many other things).

```
formula
    ::=     term
          | NOT term
          | term AND formula
          | term OR formula
          | term ==> formula

term
    ::=     atomic-formula
          | ( formula )
```

Formulas are evaluated in accordance with the truth values of their constituent terms and the usual truth tables for the connectives. Points arising:

1. An "atomic formula" is a term that involves no connectives and is not contained in parentheses.

2. The symbol "==>" represents the *logical implication* connective. The expression $f \Longrightarrow g$ is defined to be logically equivalent to the expression NOT f OR g (it is sometimes written IF f THEN g).

3. We adopt the usual precedence rules for the connectives (NOT, then AND, then OR, then ==>) in order to allow us to reduce the number of parentheses that the grammar would otherwise require.

Rules of Inference

Now we come to the rules of inference for the propositional calculus. Many such rules exist. Each such rule is a statement of the form

$$\vdash \quad f \Longrightarrow g$$

(where the symbol $\vdash$ can be read as "It is always the case that"; note that we need some such symbol in order to be able to make "metastatements," i.e., statements about statements). Here are some examples of inference rules:

1. $\vdash$ (f AND g) ==> f

2. $\vdash$ f ==> (f OR g)

3. $\vdash$ ((f ==> g) AND (g ==> h)) ==> (f ==> h)

4. $\vdash$ (f AND (f ==> g)) ==> g

> *Aside:* This one is particularly important. It is called the *modus ponens* rule. Informally, it says that if *f* is true and *f* implies *g*, then *g* must be true as well. For example, given the fact that each of the following (a) and (b) is true—
>
> (a) I have no money;
>
> (b) If I have no money then I will have to wash dishes;
>
> —then we can infer that (c) is true as well:
>
> (c) I will have to wash dishes.
>
> *End of aside.*

5. $\vdash$ (f ==> (g ==> h)) ==> ((f AND g) ==> h)

6. $\vdash$ ((f OR g) AND (NOT g OR h)) ==> (f OR h)

> *Aside:* This is another particularly important one. It is known as the *resolution rule*. I will have more to say about it below and again in Part II of the paper. *End of aside.*

Proofs

We now have the necessary apparatus for dealing with formal proofs (in the context of the propositional calculus). The problem of proof is the problem of determining whether some given formula *g* (the *conclusion*) is a logical consequence of some given set of formulas *f1, f2, . . . , fn* (the *premises*)—in symbols:

```
f1, f2, ..., fn ⊢ g
```

(read as "*g* is deducible from *f1, f2, . . . , fn*"; observe the use of another "metastatement" symbol, $\vdash$). The basic method of proceeding is known as *forward chaining*. Forward chaining consists of applying the rules of inference repeatedly to the premises, and to formulas deduced from those premises, and to formulas deduced from those formulas, etc., etc., until the conclusion is deduced; in other words, the process "chains forward" from the premises to the conclusion. However, there are several variations on this basic theme:

1. *Adopting a premise:* If g is of the form $p \implies q$, adopt p as an additional premise and show that q is deducible from the given premises plus p.
2. *Backward chaining:* Instead of trying to prove $p \implies q$, prove the "contrapositive" NOT $q \implies$ NOT p.
3. *Reductio ad absurdum:* Instead of trying to prove $p \implies q$ directly, assume that p and NOT q are both true and derive a contradiction.
4. *Resolution:* This method uses the resolution inference rule (number 6 in the list shown earlier). I will discuss this technique in some detail, since it is of wide applicability (in particular, it generalizes to the case of predicate calculus also, as we will see in Part II).

Note first that the resolution rule is effectively a rule that allows us to *cancel subformulas;* that is, given the two formulas

    f OR g   and   NOT g OR h

we can derive the simplified formula

    f OR h

In particular, given f OR g and NOT g (i.e., taking h as true), we can derive f.

Observe, therefore, that the rule applies to a conjunction (AND) of two formulas, each of which is a disjunction (OR) of two formulas (in general). In order to apply the resolution rule, therefore, we proceed as follows. (To make our discussion a little more concrete, we explain the process in terms of a specific example.) Suppose we wish to determine whether the following putative proof is in fact valid:

    A ==> (B ==> C), NOT D OR A, B ⊢ D ==> C

(where A, B, C, and D are formulas). We start by adopting the negation of the conclusion as an additional premise, and then writing each premise on a separate line, as follows:

    A ==> (B ==> C)
    NOT D OR A
    B
    NOT (D ==> C)

Note that these four lines are implicitly all "ANDed" together. Next, we convert each individual line to *conjunctive normal form,* i.e., a form consisting of one or more formulas all ANDed together, each individual formula containing (possibly) NOTs and ORs but no ANDs. Of course, the second and third lines are already in this form. In order to convert the other two lines, we first eliminate all appearances of " ==> " (using the definition of that connective in terms of NOT and OR); we then apply the distributive laws and De Morgan's laws as necessary (see the beginning of this section). We also drop redundant parentheses and pairs of adjacent NOTs (which cancel out). The four lines become

```
NOT A OR NOT B OR C
NOT D OR A
B
D AND NOT C
```

Next, any line that includes any explicit ANDs we replace by a set of separate lines, one for each of the individual formulas ANDed together (dropping the ANDs in the process). In the example, this step applies to the fourth line only. The premises now look like this:

```
NOT A OR NOT B OR C
NOT D OR A
B
D
NOT C
```

Now we can start to apply the resolution rule. We choose a pair of lines that can be "resolved," i.e., a pair that contain (respectively) some particular formula and the negation of that formula. Let us choose the first two lines, which contain NOT A and A respectively, and resolve them, giving

```
NOT D OR NOT B OR C
B
D
NOT C
```

(*Note:* We also need to keep the two original lines, in general, but in this particular example they will not be needed any more.) Now we apply the rule again, again choosing the first two lines (resolving NOT B and B), giving

```
NOT D OR C
D
NOT C
```

We choose the first lines two again (NOT D and D):

```
C
NOT C
```

And once again (C and NOT C); the final result is the empty proposition (usually represented thus: []), which represents a contradiction. By reductio ad absurdum, therefore, the desired result is proved.

4. CLOSING REMARKS

This brings us to the end of Part I. In Part II, we will extend what we have learned regarding the propositional calculus to the predicate calculus, and build up from there to an explanation of what we mean by the "proof-theoretic" view of databases. In the meantime, readers might like to practice their skills in the propositional calculus by using the resolution method to see whether the following statements are valid:

(a) A ==> B, C ==> B, D ==> (A OR C), D $\vdash$ B

(b) (A ==> B) AND (C ==> D), (B ==> E AND D ==> F),
         NOT (E AND F), A ==> C $\vdash$ NOT A

(c) (A OR B) ==> D, D ==> NOT (E OR F),
         NOT (B AND C AND E) $\vdash$
                        NOT (G ==> NOT (C AND H))

For the record, (a) and (b) here are valid and (c) is not.

24

Logic-Based Database Systems: A Tutorial Part II

ABSTRACT

This is the second part of a three-part tutorial on the subject of logic and logic-based systems. Part I provided some background motivation and explained the propositional calculus; Part II now continues by discussing the predicate calculus and introducing the "proof-theoretic" view of a database. The sections are numbered from five to provide continuity with Part I.

COMMENTS ON REPUBLICATION

See the previous paper in this collection.

Originally published (in somewhat different form) in my book *An Introduction to Database Systems: Volume I,* 5th edition (Addison-Wesley, 1990). Reprinted by permission.

5. AN INTRODUCTION TO PREDICATE CALCULUS

The big difference between propositional calculus (discussed in Part I of this paper) and predicate calculus is that the latter allows formulas to contain quantifiers, which makes it very much more powerful and of very much wider applicability. For example, the statement "Supplier S1 supplies some part *p*" is not a legal formula in propositional calculus, but it is a legal formula in predicate calculus. Hence predicate calculus provides us with a basis for expressing queries such as "What parts are supplied by supplier S1?" or "Find suppliers who supply some part" or even "Find suppliers who do not supply any parts at all."

Predicates

A predicate is a *truth-valued function,* i.e., a function that, given appropriate arguments, returns either *true* or *false.* For example, ">" is a predicate; the expression ">(*x,y*)"—more conventionally written "*x* > *y*"—returns *true* if the value of *x* is greater than the value of *y* and *false* otherwise. A predicate that takes *n* arguments is called an *n*-place predicate. A proposition—or for that matter a formula—of the *propositional* calculus can be regarded as a zero-place predicate: It has no arguments and evaluates to either *true* or *false* unconditionally.

> *Aside:* It is common in database parlance to refer to an expression such as "*x* > 3" as a predicate. However, this usage is strictly incorrect—it is really the ">" that is the predicate, as just explained. If we think of that predicate as a function in the usual programming sense, then we can regard the expression "*x* > 3" as an *invocation* of that function, with the arguments *x* and 3. *End of aside.*

It is convenient to assume that the predicates "=", ">", "> =", etc., are builtin (i.e., they are part of the formal system we are defining) and that expressions using them can be written in the conventional manner, but of course users should be able to define their own additional predicates as well. Indeed, that is the whole point, as we will quickly see: The fact is, in database terms, a user-defined predicate is nothing more nor less than a user-defined *relation.* The suppliers relation S, for example, can be regarded as a predicate with four arguments (S#, SNAME, STATUS, and CITY). Furthermore, the expressions S(S1,Smith,20,London) and S(S6,Green,45,Rome) represent "instances" or invocations of that predicate that evaluate to *true* and *false* respectively (given the usual sample set of database values—once again, refer to Chapter 1, Appendix A, Fig. 5).

Well-Formed Formulas

The next step is to extend the definition of "formula." In order to avoid confusion with the formulas of the propositional calculus (which are actually a special case), we will now switch to the more specific term "well-formed formula" (WFF, pronounced "weff"). Here is a simplified syntax for WFFs:

```
wff   ::=   term
            NOT ( wff )
            ( wff ) AND ( wff )
            ( wff ) OR ( wff )
            ( wff ) ==> ( wff )
            EXISTS variable ( wff )
            FORALL variable ( wff )

term ::=   [ NOT ] predicate [ ( argument-commalist ) ]
```

Points arising:

1. A "term" is simply a possibly negated predicate instance. An "argument commalist" is a list of one or more arguments separated by commas. Each argument must be a constant, a variable, or a function reference, where each argument to a function reference in turn is a constant or variable or function reference. The argument commalist and enclosing parentheses are omitted for a zero-place predicate. *Note:* Functions are permitted in order to allow WFFs to include computational expressions such as "$+(x,y)$"—more conventionally written "$x + y$"—and so forth.

2. As in the propositional calculus, we adopt the usual precedence rules for the connectives (NOT, then AND, then OR, then ==>) in order to reduce the number of parentheses that the grammar would otherwise require.

3. The reader is assumed to be familiar with the quantifiers EXISTS and FORALL. Roughly speaking, however, EXISTS is an "iterated OR" and FORALL is an "iterated AND." As a consequence, De Morgan's laws can be generalized to apply to quantified WFFs, as follows:

```
NOT ( FORALL x ( f ) )   ≡   EXISTS x ( NOT ( f ) )
NOT ( EXISTS x ( f ) )   ≡   FORALL x ( NOT ( f ) )
```

4. Within a given WFF, each occurrence of a variable is either *free* or *bound*. An occurrence of a variable is bound if (a) it is the variable immediately following a quantifier (the "quantified variable") or (b) it is within the scope of a quantifier and has the same name as the applicable quantified variable. A variable occurrence is free if it is not bound.

5. A *closed* WFF is one that contains no free variable occurrences. An *open* WFF is one that is not closed.

Interpretations and Models

What do WFFs *mean?* In order to provide a formal answer to this question, we introduce the notion of *interpretation.* An interpretation of a WFF—or more generally of a set of WFFs—is defined as follows:

- First, we specify a *universe of discourse* over which the WFFs are to be interpreted. In other words, we specify a *mapping* between the permitted constants of the formal system (the domain values, in database terms) and objects in the "real world." Each individual constant corresponds to precisely one element in the universe of discourse.

- Second, we specify a meaning for each predicate in terms of objects in the universe of discourse.

- Third, we also specify a meaning for each function in terms of objects in the universe of discourse.

Then the interpretation consists of the combination of the universe of discourse, plus the mapping of individual constants to objects in that universe, plus the defined meanings for the predicates and functions with respect to that universe.

By way of example, let the universe of discourse be the set of integers $\{0,1,2,3,4,5\}$, let constants such as "2" correspond to elements of that universe in the obvious way, and let the predicate " > " be defined to have the usual "greater than" meaning. (We could also define functions such as " + ", " − ", etc., if desired.) Now we can assign a truth value to WFFs such as the following, as indicated:

```
2 > 1                    —true
2 > 3                    —false
EXISTS x ( x > 3 )       —true
FORALL x ( x > 3 )       —false
```

Note, however, that other interpretations are possible. For example, we might specify the universe of discourse to be a set of security classification levels, as follows:

destroy before reading	(level 5)
destroy after reading	(level 4)
top secret	(level 3)
secret	(level 2)
confidential	(level 1)
unclassified	(level 0)

The predicate ">" could now mean "more secure (i.e., higher classification) than."

Now, the reader will probably realize that the two possible interpretations just given are *isomorphic*—that is, it is possible to set up a one-to-one correspondence between them, and hence at a deep level the two interpretations are really one and the same. But it must be clearly understood that interpretations can exist that are genuinely different in kind. For example, we might once again take the universe of discourse to be the integers 0–5, but define the predicate ">" to mean *equality*. (Of course, we would probably cause a lot of confusion that way, but at least we would be within our rights to do so.) Now the first WFF above would evaluate to *false* instead of *true*.

Another point that must be clearly understood is that two interpretations might be genuinely different in the foregoing sense and yet give the same truth values for the given set of WFFs. This would be the case with the two different definitions of ">" in our example if the WFF "2 > 1" were omitted.

Note, incidentally, that all of the WFFs we have been discussing so far have been *closed* WFFs. The reason is that, given an interpretation, it is always possible to assign a truth value unambiguously to a closed WFF, but the truth value of an open WFF will depend on the values assigned to the free variables. For example, the open WFF

```
x > 3
```

is (obviously) *true* if the value of *x* is greater than 3 and *false* otherwise (whatever "greater than" and "3" mean in the interpretation).

Now we define a *model* of a WFF—or more generally of a set of (closed) WFFs—to be an interpretation for which all WFFs in the set are true. The two interpretations given above for the four WFFs

```
2 > 1
2 > 3
EXISTS x ( x > 2 )
FORALL x ( x > 2 )
```

in terms of the integers 0–5 were not models for those WFFs, because some of the WFFs evaluated to *false* under that interpretation. By contrast, the first interpretation (in which ">" was defined "properly") *would* have been a model for the set of WFFs

```
2 > 1
3 > 2
EXISTS x ( x > 2 )
FORALL x ( x > 2 OR NOT ( x > 2 ) )
```

Note finally that, since a given set of WFFs can admit of multiple interpretations in which all of the WFFs evaluate to *true,* it can therefore have multiple *models* (in general). Thus, a database can have multiple models (in general), since—in the model-theoretic view—a database is basically a set of WFFs (see later in this part of the paper).

Clausal Form

Just as any propositional calculus formula can be converted to conjunctive normal form, so any predicate calculus WFF can be converted to *clausal form,* which can be regarded as an extended version of conjunctive normal form. One motivation for making such a conversion is that (again) it allows us to apply the resolution rule in constructing or verifying proofs, as we will see later.

The conversion process proceeds as follows, in outline. We illustrate the steps by applying them to a sample WFF, namely

FORALL x (p (x) AND EXISTS y (FORALL z (q (y, z))))

Here *p* and *q* are predicates and *x, y,* and *z* are variables.

1. Eliminate "==>" symbols, using the definition of that connective in terms of NOT and OR. (In our example, of course, this first transformation has no effect.)

2. Use De Morgan's laws, plus the fact that two adjacent NOTs cancel out, to move NOTs so that they apply only to terms, not to general WFFs. (Again this particular transformation has no effect in our particular example.)

3. Convert the WFF to *prenex normal form* by moving all quantifiers to the front (systematically renaming variables if necessary):

FORALL x (EXISTS y (FORALL z (p (x) AND q (y, z))))

4. Note that an existentially quantified WFF such as

EXISTS v (r (v))

is equivalent to the WFF

r (a)

for some (unknown) constant *a;* that is, the original WFF asserts that some such *a* does exist, we just don't know its value. Likewise, a WFF such as

FORALL u (EXISTS v (s (u, v)))

is equivalent to the WFF

FORALL u (s (u, f (u)))

for some (unknown) function f of the universally quantified variable u. The constant a and the function f in these examples are known, respectively, as a *Skolem constant* and a *Skolem function,* after the Norwegian logician T. A. Skolem. (*Note:* A Skolem constant is really just a Skolem function with no arguments.) So the next step is to eliminate existential quantifiers by replacing the corresponding quantified variables by (arbitrary) Skolem functions of all universally quantified variables that precede the quantifier in question in the WFF:

```
FORALL x ( FORALL z ( p ( x ) AND q ( f ( x ), z ) ) )
```

5. All variables are now universally quantified. We can therefore adopt a convention by which all variables are *implicitly* universally quantified and so drop the explicit quantifiers:

```
p ( x ) AND q ( f ( x ), z )
```

6. Convert the WFF to conjunctive normal form, i.e., to a set of clauses all ANDed together, each clause involving possibly NOTs and ORs but no ANDs. In our example, the WFF is already in this form.

7. Write each clause on a separate line and drop the ANDs:

```
p ( x )
q ( f ( x ), z )
```

This is the clausal form equivalent of the original WFF.

Note: It follows from the foregoing procedure that the general form of a WFF in clausal form is a set of clauses, each on a line of its own, and each of the form

```
NOT A1 OR NOT A2 OR ... OR NOT Am OR B1 OR B2 OR ... OR Bn
```

where the A's and B's are all nonnegated terms. We can rewrite such a clause, if we like, as

```
A1 AND A2 AND ... AND Am  ==>  B1 OR B2 OR ... OR Bn
```

If there is at most one B ($n = 0$ or 1), the clause is called a *Horn clause* (after the logician Alfred Horn).

Using the Resolution Rule

Now we are in a position to see how a logic-based database system can deal with queries. We use the "grandmother" example from Part I of the paper. First, we have a predicate MOTHEROF, which takes two arguments, representing mother and daughter respectively, and we are given the following two terms (predicate instances):

1. MOTHEROF (Anne, Betty)

2. MOTHEROF (Betty, Celia)

We are also given the following WFF (the "deductive axiom," now rewritten in clausal form):

3. MOTHEROF (x, y) AND MOTHEROF (y, z) ==> GRANDMOTHEROF (x, z)

(note that this is a Horn clause). In order to simplify the application of the resolution rule, let us rewrite the clause to eliminate the " ==> " symbol:

4. NOT MOTHEROF (x, y) OR NOT MOTHEROF (y, z) OR
                                        GRANDMOTHEROF (x, z)

We now show how to prove that Anne is the grandmother of Celia—i.e., how to answer the query "Is Anne Celia's grandmother?" We begin by negating the conclusion that is to be proved and adopting it as an additional premise:

5. NOT GRANDMOTHEROF (Anne, Celia)

Now, to apply the resolution rule, we must systematically substitute values for variables in such a way that we can find two clauses that contain, respectively, a WFF and its negation. Such substitution is legitimate because the variables are all (implicitly) universally quantified, and hence individual (nonnegated) WFFs must be true for each and every legal combinations of values of their variables. *Note:* The process of finding a set of substitutions that make two clauses resolvable in this manner is known as *unification*.

To see how the foregoing works in the case at hand, observe first that lines 4 and 5 contain the terms GRANDMOTHEROF(x,z) and NOT GRANDMOTHEROF(Anne,Celia), respectively. So we substitute Anne for x and Celia for z in line 4 and resolve, to obtain

6. NOT MOTHEROF (Anne, y) OR NOT MOTHEROF (y, Celia)

Line 2 contains MOTHEROF(Betty,Celia). So we substitute Betty for y in line 6 and resolve, to obtain

7. NOT MOTHEROF (Anne, Betty)

Resolving line 7 and line 1, we obtain the empty clause []: Contradiction. Hence the answer to the original query is "Yes, Anne is Celia's grandmother."

What about the query "Who are the granddaughters of Anne?" Observe first of all that the system does not know about granddaughters, it only knows about grandmothers. We could add another deductive axiom to the effect that z is the granddaughter of x if and only if x is the grandmother of z (no males are allowed in this database). Alternatively, of course, we could rephrase the question as "Who is Anne the grandmother of?" Let us consider this latter formulation. The premises are (to repeat)

1. MOTHEROF (Anne, Betty)

2. MOTHEROF (Betty, Celia)

3. NOT MOTHEROF (x, y) OR NOT MOTHEROF (y, z) OR
   GRANDMOTHEROF (x, z)

We introduce a fourth premise, as follows:

4. NOT GRANDMOTHEROF (Anne, r) OR RESULT (r)

Intuitively, this says that either Anne is not the grandmother of anyone, or alternatively she is the grandmother of some person r. We wish to discover the identity of all such persons r, assuming they exist. We proceed as follows.

First, substitute Anne for x and r for z and resolve lines 4 and 3, to obtain

5. NOT MOTHEROF (Anne, y) OR NOT MOTHEROF (y, z) OR RESULT (z)

Next, substitute Betty for y and resolve lines 5 and 1, to obtain

6. NOT MOTHEROF (Betty, z) OR RESULT (z)

Now substitute Celia for z and resolve lines 6 and 2, to obtain

7. RESULT (Celia)

Hence Anne is the grandmother of Celia.

Note: If we had been given an additional term, as follows—

MOTHEROF (Betty, Delia)

—then we could have substituted Delia for z in the final step (instead of Celia) and obtained

RESULT (Delia)

The user expects to see both names in the result, of course. Thus, the system needs to apply the unification and resolution process exhaustively to generate *all possible* result values. Details of this refinement are beyond the scope of the present paper.

6. A PROOF-THEORETIC VIEW OF DATABASES

As explained under "Clausal form" above, a *clause* is an expression of the form

```
A1 AND A2 AND ... AND Am  ==>  B1 OR B2 OR ... OR Bn
```

where the A's and B's are all terms of the form

```
r ( x1, x2, ..., xt )
```

(here *r* is a predicate and *x1, x2, . . . , xt* are the arguments to that predicate). We now consider a couple of important special cases of this general construct.

1. *Case* 1: $m = 0, n = 1$

   In this case the clause can be simplified to just

   ```
   ==>  B1
   ```

   or in other words (dropping the implication symbol) to just

   ```
   r ( x1, x2, ..., xt )
   ```

   for some predicate *r* and some set of arguments *x1, x2, . . . , xt*. If the *x*'s are all constants, the clause represents a *ground axiom*—i.e., it is making a statement that is unequivocally true. In database terms, such a statement corresponds to a tuple of some relation *R*. The predicate *r* corresponds to the "meaning" of relation *R*. For example, in the suppliers-and-parts database, there is a relation called SP, the meaning of which is that the indicated supplier (S#) is supplying the indicated part (P#) in the indicated quantity (QTY). Note that this meaning corresponds to an open WFF, since it contains some free variables (S#, P#, and QTY). The tuple (S1,P1,300)—in which the arguments are all constants—is a ground axiom or closed WFF that asserts unequivocally that supplier S1 is supplying part P1 in a quantity of 300.

2. *Case* 2: $m > 0, n = 1$

   In this case the clause takes the form

   ```
   A1 AND A2 AND ... AND Am  ==>  B
   ```

   which can be regarded as a *deductive axiom;* it gives a (partial) definition of the predicate on the right-hand side in terms of those on the left (see the definition of the GRANDMOTHEROF predicate, earlier, for an example).

   Alternatively, such a clause might be regarded as defining an *integrity constraint*. Suppose for the sake of the example that the suppliers relation S contains only two attributes, S# and CITY. Then the clause

```
S ( s, c1 ) AND S ( s, c2 )  ==>  c1 = c2
```

expresses the constraint that CITY is functionally dependent on S#. Note the use of the builtin predicate "=" in this example.

As the foregoing discussions demonstrate, tuples in relations ("ground axioms"), derived relations ("deductive axioms"), and integrity constraints can all be regarded as special cases of the general *clause* construct. Let us now try to see how these ideas can lead to the "proof-theoretic" view of a database mentioned in Part I of this paper.

First, the traditional view of a database can be regarded as *model-theoretic*. By "traditional view" here, we simply mean a view in which the database is perceived as a collection of explicitly named relations (the base relations), each containing a set of explicit tuples, together with an explicit set of integrity constraints that those tuples are not allowed to violate. It is this perception that can be characterized as "model-theoretic," as we now explain.

- The underlying domains contain values or constants that are supposed to stand for certain objects in the "real world" (more precisely, in some *interpretation,* in the sense of that term explained under "Interpretations and models" earlier). They thus correspond to the universe of discourse.

- The base relations (more precisely, the base relation *headings*) represent a set of predicates or open WFFs that are to be interpreted over that universe. For example, the heading of relation SP represents the predicate "Supplier S# supplies part P# in quantity QTY."

- Each tuple in a given relation represents an instance of the corresponding predicate; i.e., it represents an assertion (a closed WFF—it contains no variables) that is unequivocally true in the universe of discourse.

- The integrity constraints are also closed WFFs, and they are interpreted over the same universe. Since the data does not (i.e., *must* not!) violate the constraints, these constraints represent assertions that are true as well.

- The tuples and the integrity constraints can together be regarded as the set of axioms defining a certain "logical theory" (loosely speaking, a "theory" in logic *is* a set of axioms). Since those axioms are all true in the interpretation, then by definition that interpretation is a model of that logical theory, in the sense of that term explained under "Interpretations and models" earlier. Note that, as pointed out in that section, the model might not be unique—that is, a given database might have multiple possible interpretations, all of which are equally valid from a logical standpoint.

In the model-theoretic view, therefore, the "meaning" of the database *is* the model, in the foregoing sense of the term "model." And since there are many possible models, there are many possible meanings (at least in principle).* Furthermore, query processing in the model-theoretic view is essentially a process of evaluating a certain open WFF to discover which values of the free variables in that WFF cause the WFF to evaluate to *true* within the model.

So much for the model-theoretic view. However, in order to be able to apply the rules of inference of the predicate (and propositional) calculus, it becomes necessary to adopt a different perspective, one in which the database is explicitly regarded as a certain logical theory, i.e., as a set of axioms. The "meaning" of the database then becomes, precisely, the collection of all true statements that can be deduced from the axioms using those axioms in all possible combinations—i.e., it is the set of *theorems* that can be proved from those axioms. This is the *proof-theoretic* view. In this view, query evaluation becomes a theorem-proving process (conceptually speaking, at any rate; in the interests of efficiency, however, the system is likely to use more conventional query processing techniques, as we will see in Part III of this paper).

Note: It follows from the foregoing paragraph that one difference between the model-theoretic and proof-theoretic views (intuitively speaking) is that, whereas a database can have many "meanings" in the model-theoretic view, it typically has precisely one "meaning" in the proof-theoretic view—except that (a) as pointed out earlier, that one meaning is really *the* canonical meaning in the model-theoretic case, and in any case (b) the remark to the effect that there is only one meaning in the proof-theoretic case ceases to be true, in general, if the database includes any negative axioms.

The axioms for a given database (proof-theoretic view) can be informally summarized as follows:

1. Ground axioms, corresponding to the tuples of the base relations. These axioms constitute what is sometimes called the *extensional database* (EDB).

2. A "completion axiom" for each relation, which states that no tuples of that relation exist other than those explicitly appearing in that relation. These axioms correspond to what is usually called the *Closed*

---

*However, if we assume that the database does not explicitly contain any negative information (e.g., an assertion of the form "NOT S#(S9)," meaning that S9 is not a supplier number), there will also be a "minimal" or *canonical* meaning, which is the logical intersection of all possible models. In this case, moreover, that canonical meaning will be the same as the meaning ascribed to the database under the proof-theoretic view, to be explained.

World Assumption (CWA), which states that omission of a certain tuple from a given relation implies that the assertion corresponding to that tuple is *false*. For example, the fact that the tuple (S6,Green,45,Rome) is not included in the suppliers relation S means that the statement "There exists a supplier S6 named Green with status 45 located in Rome" is *false*.

3. The "unique name" axiom, which states that every constant is distinguishable from all the rest (i.e., has a unique name).

4. The "domain closure" axiom, which states that no constants exist other than those in the database domains.

5. A set of axioms (essentially standard) to define the builtin predicate "=". These axioms are needed because the axioms in items 2, 3, and 4 above each make use of the equality predicate.

We conclude this section with a brief summary of the principal differences between the two perceptions (model-theoretic and proof-theoretic). First of all, it has to be said that from a purely pragmatic standpoint there might not be very much difference at all!—at least in terms of present-day systems. However:

▪ Items 2–5 in the list of axioms for the proof-theoretic view make explicit certain assumptions that are implicit in the notion of interpretation in the model-theoretic view. Stating assumptions explicitly is generally a good idea; furthermore, it is necessary to specify those additional axioms explicitly in order to be able to apply general proof techniques, such as the resolution method described earlier.

▪ Note that the list of axioms makes no mention of integrity constraints. The reason for that omission is that (in the proof-theoretic view) adding such constraints converts the system into a *deductive* DBMS. Deductive DBMSs will be discussed in Part III of this paper.

▪ The proof-theoretic view does enjoy a certain elegance that the model-theoretic view does not, inasmuch as it provides a uniform perception of several constructs that are usually thought of as more or less distinct: base data, queries, integrity constraints (the previous point notwithstanding), virtual data (etc.). As a consequence, the possibility arises of more uniform interfaces and more uniform implementations.

▪ The proof-theoretic view also provides a natural basis for treating certain problems that relational systems have traditionally always had difficulty with—disjunctive information (e.g., "Supplier S6 is located in either Paris or Rome"), the derivation of negative information (e.g., "Who is not a supplier?"), and recursive queries (see Part III of this paper)—though in this last case, at least, there is no reason in principle why a classical relational system could not be extended appropriately to deal with such queries (indeed, many proposals for doing so can be found in the literature). We will have more to say regarding such matters in Part III.

■ Finally, to quote from Reiter's original paper, the proof-theoretic view "provides a correct treatment of [extensions to] the relational model to incorporate more real world semantics" (including, to repeat from Part I of this paper, events, type hierarchies, and certain kinds of entity aggregation).

7. CLOSING REMARKS

This brings us to the end of Part II of the paper. In the next (and final) part, I will show how the ideas introduced in this part and its predecessor can be used as a basis for "deductive DBMSs." In particular, I will explain some of the ideas underlying *recursive query processing*. As in Part I, I close with a couple of exercises that readers might like to try:

1. Convert the following WFFs to clausal form:

(a) FORALL x (FORALL y (p (x, y) ⟹ EXISTS z (q (x, z))))

(b) EXISTS x (EXISTS y (p (x, y) ⟹ FORALL z (q (x, z))))

(c) EXISTS x (EXISTS y (p (x, y) ⟹ EXISTS z (q (x, z))))

2. The following is a fairly standard example of a "logic database":

```
MAN    ( Adam )
WOMAN  ( Eve )
MAN    ( Cain )
MAN    ( Abel )

PARENT ( Adam, Cain )
PARENT ( Adam, Abel )
PARENT ( Eve, Cain )
PARENT ( Eve, Cain )
PARENT ( Cain, Enoch )

PARENT ( x, y ) AND MAN ( x )   ⟹  FATHER ( x, y )
PARENT ( x, y ) AND WOMAN ( x ) ⟹  MOTHER ( x, y )

PARENT ( z, x ) AND PARENT ( z, y )  ⟹  SIBLING ( x, y )

SIBLING ( x, y ) AND MAN ( x )   ⟹  BROTHER ( x, y )

SIBLING ( x, y ) AND WOMAN ( x ) ⟹  SISTER ( x, y )
```

Use the resolution method to answer the following queries:

(a) Who is the mother of Cain?
(b) Who are Cain's siblings?
(c) Who are Cain's brothers?
(d) Who are Cain's sisters?

25

Logic-Based
Database Systems:
A Tutorial Part III

ABSTRACT

This is the third part of a three-part tutorial on the subject of logic and logic-based systems. Part I provided some background motivation and introduced the propositional calculus; Part II discussed the predicate calculus; and now Part III discusses "deductive DBMSs" and recursive query processing. The sections are numbered from eight to provide continuity with Part II.

COMMENTS ON REPUBLICATION

See the previous paper in this collection.

Originally published (in somewhat different form) in my book *An Introduction to Database Systems: Volume I,* 5th edition (Addison-Wesley, 1990). Reprinted by permission.

8. DEDUCTIVE DATABASE SYSTEMS

A *deductive DBMS* is a DBMS that supports the proof-theoretic view of a database, and in particular is capable of deducing additional facts from the "extensional database" (i.e., the base relations) by applying specified *deductive axioms* or *rules of inference* to those facts. The deductive axioms, together with the integrity constraints (discussed below), form what is sometimes called the "intensional database" (IDB), and the extensional database and the intensional database together constitute what is usually called the *deductive database* (not a very good term, since it is the DBMS, not the database, that carries out the deductions).

As just indicated, the deductive axioms form one part of the intensional database. The other part consists of additional axioms that represent integrity constraints (i.e., rules whose primary purpose is to constrain updates, though actually such rules can also be used in the deduction process to generate new facts).

Let us see what the familiar suppliers-and-parts database would look like in "deductive DBMS" form. First, there will be a set of ground axioms defining the legal domain values. *Note:* In what follows, we omit the (necessary) quotes surrounding string constants purely for reasons of readability.

```
S# ( S1 )      NAME ( Smith )    STATUS (  5 )    CITY ( London )
S# ( S2 )      NAME ( Jones )    STATUS ( 10 )    CITY ( Paris  )
S# ( S3 )      NAME ( Blake )    STATUS ( 15 )    CITY ( Rome   )
S# ( S4 )      NAME ( Clark )    etc.             CITY ( Athens )
S# ( S5 )      NAME ( Adams )                     etc.
S# ( S6 )      NAME ( White )
S# ( S7 )      NAME ( Nut   )
etc.           NAME ( Bolt  )
               NAME ( Screw )
               etc.

etc., etc., etc.
```

Next, there will be ground axioms for the tuples in the base relations:

```
S ( S1, Smith, 20, London )
S ( S2, Jones, 10, Paris  )
etc.

P ( P1, Nut, Red, 12, London )
etc.

SP ( S1, P1, 300 )
etc.
```

Note: We are not seriously suggesting that the extensional database will be populated by explicitly listing all of the ground axioms as indicated above; instead, of course, traditional data entry methods will be used. In other words, deductive DBMSs will typically apply their deductions to conventional databases that already exist and have been constructed in the conventional manner. Note, however, that it now becomes more important than ever that the extensional database not violate any of the declared integrity constraints!—because a database that does violate any such constraints represents (in logical terms) an inconsistent set of axioms, and it is well known that *absolutely any statement whatsoever* can be proved to be "true" from such a starting point (in other words, contradictions can be derived). For exactly the same reason, it is also important that the stated set of integrity constraints be consistent.

Now for the intensional database. Here are the domain constraints:

```
S ( s, sn, st, sc )  ==>  S# ( s ) AND
                          NAME ( sn ) AND
                          STATUS ( st ) AND
                          CITY ( sc )

P ( p, pn, pl, pw, pc )  ==>  P# ( p ) AND
                              NAME ( pn ) AND
                              COLOR ( pl ) AND
                              WEIGHT ( pw ) AND
     etc.                     CITY ( pc )
```

Primary key constraints:

```
S ( s, sn1, st1, sc1 ) AND S ( s, sn2, st2, sc2 )
                     ==>  sn1 = sn2 AND
                          st1 = st2 AND
                          sc1 = sc2
     etc.
```

Foreign key constraints:

```
SP ( s, p, q )  ==>  S ( s, sn, st, sc ) AND
                     P ( p, pn, pl, pw, pc ) AND
                     QTY ( q )
```

And so on. *Note:* We assume for the sake of the exposition that variables appearing on the right-hand side of the implication symbol and not on the left (*sn, st,* etc., in the example) are existentially quantified. (All others are universally quantified, as explained in Part II of this paper.) Technically, we need some Skolem functions; *sn,* for example, should really be replaced by (say) SN(*s*), where SN is a Skolem function.

Note, incidentally, that most of the constraints shown above are not pure "clauses" (in the sense of that term explained in Part II), because the right-hand side is not just a disjunction of simple terms.

Now let us add some more deductive axioms (analogous to view definitions in a conventional DBMS):

```
S ( s, sn, st, sc ) AND st > 15  ==>  GOOD_SUPPLIERS ( s, st, sc )

S ( sx, sxn, sxt, sc ) AND S ( sy, syn, syt, sc )
                                 ==>  SS_COLOCATED ( sx, sy )

S ( s, sn, st, c ) AND P ( p, pn, pl, pw, c )
                                 ==>  SP_COLOCATED ( s, p )
```

And so on.

In order to make the example a little more interesting, let us now extend the suppliers-and-parts database to incorporate a part structure relation, showing which parts *px* contain which parts *py* as immediate (i.e. first-level) components. First a constraint to show that *px* and *py* must both identify existing parts:

```
PART_STRUCTURE ( px, py )  ==>  P ( px, xn, xl, xw, xc ) AND
                                P ( py, yn, yl, yw, yc )
```

Some data values:

```
PART_STRUCTURE ( P1, P2 )
PART_STRUCTURE ( P1, P3 )
PART_STRUCTURE ( P2, P3 )
PART_STRUCTURE ( P2, P4 )
etc.
```

(In practice PART_STRUCTURE would probably also have a "quantity" argument, showing how many *py*'s it takes to make a *px,* but we ignore this refinement for simplicity.)

Now we can add a pair of deductive axioms to explain what it means for part *px* to contain part *py* as a component *at any level:*

```
PART_STRUCTURE ( px, py )  ==>  COMPONENTOF ( px, py )

PART_STRUCTURE ( px, pz )  AND  COMPONENTOF ( pz, py )
                           ==>  COMPONENTOF ( px, py )
```

In other words, part *py* is a component of part *px* (at any level) if it is either an immediate component of part *px* or an immediate component of some part *pz* that is in turn a component (at any level) of part *px*. Note that the second axiom here is recursive—it defines the COMPONENTOF predicate in terms of itself. Classical relational systems, by contrast, do not permit view definitions (or queries or integrity constraints or . . .) to be recursive in such a manner. This ability to support recursion is one of the most immediately obvious distinctions between deductive DBMSs and their classical counterparts—although, as mentioned in Part II of this paper, there is no fundamental reason why the classical relational algebra should not be extended to support an appropriate set of recursive operators.

We will have more to say regarding this recursive capability below.

Datalog

From the foregoing discussion, it should be clear that one of the most directly visible portions of a deductive DBMS will be a language in which the deductive axioms (usually called *rules*) can be formulated. The best known example of such a language is called (by analogy with Prolog) *Datalog*. We now present a brief discussion of Datalog. *Note:* The emphasis in Datalog is on its descriptive power, not its computational power (as was also the case with the original relational model, incidentally). The objective is to define a language that ultimately will have greater expressive power than conventional relational languages. As a consequence, the stress in Datalog (indeed, the stress throughout logic-based database systems in general) is very heavily on query, not update, though of course it is possible, and desirable, to extend the language to support update also (see later).

In its simplest form, Datalog supports the formulation of rules as simple Horn clauses without functions. In Part II, we defined a Horn clause to be a WFF of either of the following two forms:

```
A1 AND A2 AND ... AND An

A1 AND A2 AND ... AND An  ==>  B
```

(where the *A*'s and *B* are nonnegated predicate instances involving only constants and variables). Following the style of Prolog, however, Datalog actually writes the second of these the other way around:

```
B  <==  A1 AND A2 AND ... AND An
```

To be consistent with other publications in this area, therefore, we will do the same in what follows. In such a clause, *B* is the *rule head* (or conclusion) and the *A*'s are the rule body (or premises or *goal;* each individual *A* is a *subgoal*). For brevity, the ANDs are often replaced by commas. A *Datalog program* is a set of such clauses separated in some conventional manner— e.g., by semicolons (in this paper, however, we will not use semicolons but instead will follow the simple convention of starting each new clause on a new line). No meaning attaches to the order of the clauses within such a program.

Note, incidentally, that *the entire "deductive database"* can be regarded as a Datalog program in the foregoing sense. For example, we could take all of the axioms stated above for suppliers-and-parts (the ground axioms, the integrity constraints, and the deductive axioms), write them all in Datalog style, separate them by semicolons or by writing each one on a separate line, and the result would be a Datalog program. As noted earlier, however, the extensional part of the database will typically not be created in such a fashion, but rather in some more conventional manner. Thus, the primary purpose of Datalog is to support the formulation of deductive axioms specifically. As already pointed out, that function can be regarded as an extension of the view definition mechanism found in conventional relational DBMSs today.

Datalog can also be used as a query language (again, much like Prolog). For example, suppose we have been given the following Datalog definition of GOOD_SUPPLIERS:

```
GOOD_SUPPLIERS ( s, st, sc )  <=  S ( s, sn, st, sc ) AND st > 15
```

Here are some typical queries against GOOD_SUPPLIERS.

1. Find all good suppliers:

```
?  <=  GOOD_SUPPLIERS ( s, st, sc )
```

2. Find good suppliers in Paris:

```
?  <=  GOOD_SUPPLIERS ( s, st, Paris )
```

3. Is supplier S1 a good supplier?

```
?  <=  GOOD_SUPPLIERS ( S1, st, sc )
```

And so on. In other words, a query in Datalog consists of a special rule with a head of "?" and a body consisting of a single term that denotes the query result; the head "?" means (by convention) "Display."

It should be pointed out that, despite the fact that Datalog does support recursion, there are quite a few features of conventional relational languages that Datalog in its basic form does not support—scalar computational operations ("+", "−", etc.), aggregate operations (COUNT, SUM, etc.), set difference (because clauses cannot be negated), grouping, etc. It also does not support attribute naming (the significance of a predicate argument depends on its relative position), nor does it provide full domain support (i.e., full user-defined data type support). As noted earlier, it also does not provide any support for update operations, nor (as a special case of the latter) does it support the declarative specification of foreign key delete and update rules (DELETE CASCADES, etc.).

In order to address some of the foregoing shortcomings, a variety of extensions to basic Datalog have been proposed. Those extensions are intended to provide the following features, among others:

- *Negative premises*—for example:

```
SS_COLOCATED ( sx, sy )  <=  S ( sx, sxn, sxt, sc ) AND
                             S ( sy, syn, syt, sc ) AND
                             NOT ( sx = sy )
```

- *Scalar functions* (builtin and user-defined)—for example:

```
P_WT_IN_GRAMS ( p, pn, pl, pg, pc )  <==
            P ( p, pn, pl, pw, pc ) AND pg = pw * 454
```

In this example we have assumed that the builtin function "*" (multiplication) can be written in conventional infix notation. A more orthodox logic representation of the term following the AND would be "$= (pg,*(pw,454))$".

- *Aggregate functions and grouping.* Such operators are necessary in order to address (for example) what is sometimes called the *gross requirements* problem, which is the problem of finding, not only which parts *py* are components of some part *px* at any level, but also how many *py*'s (at all levels) it takes to make a *px*. (Naturally we are assuming here that relation PART_STRUCTURE includes a QTY attribute.)

- *Update operations.* One approach to meeting this obvious requirement—not the only one—is based on the observation that in basic Datalog, any predicate in a rule head must be nonnegated, and that every tuple generated by the rule can be regarded as being "inserted" into the result relation. A possible extension would thus be to allow negated predicates in a rule head and to treat the negation as requesting the *deletion* (of pertinent tuples).

- *NonHorn clauses in the rule body*—in other words, allow completely general WFFs in the definition of rules.

A survey of the foregoing extensions, with examples, can be found in the book *Relational Databases and Knowledge Bases,* by Georges Gardarin and Patrick Valduriez (Addison-Wesley, 1989). This book also discusses a variety of Datalog implementation techniques.

9. RECURSIVE QUERY PROCESSING

As indicated earlier, one of the most notable features of deductive database systems is their support for recursion (recursive rule definitions, and hence recursive queries also). As a consequence of this fact, the past few years have seen a great deal of research into techniques for implementing such recursion—indeed, just about every database conference since 1986 or so has included one or more papers on this subject. Since recursive query support represents a feature that typically has not existed in classical DBMSs, we discuss it briefly in the present section.

By way of example, we first repeat the recursive definition of the part structure relation (for brevity, however, we now abbreviate PART_STRUCTURE to PS and COMPONENTOF to COMP; we also convert the definition to Datalog form).

```
COMP ( px, py )  <==  PS ( px, py )

COMP ( px, py )  <==  PS ( px, pz ) AND COMP ( pz, py )
```

Here is a typical recursive query against this database ("Explode part P1"—i.e., find all components of part P1 to all levels):

```
?  <==  COMP ( P1, py )
```

To return to the definition per se: The second rule in that definition— i.e., the recursive rule—is said to be *linearly* recursive because the predicate in the rule head appears just once in the rule body. As a matter of fact, it would be possible to restate the definition in such a way that the recursion would not be linear:

```
COMP ( px, py )  <==  PS ( px, py )

COMP ( px, py )  <==  COMP ( px, pz ) AND COMP ( pz, py )
```

However, there is a general feeling that linear recursion represents "the interesting case," in the sense that most recursions that arise in practice are naturally linear, and furthermore there are known efficient techniques for dealing with the linear case. We therefore restrict our attention to linear recursion for the remainder of this paper.

Note: For completeness, we should point out that it is necessary to generalize the definition of "recursive rule" (and of linear recursion) to deal with more complex cases such as the following:

```
P ( x, y )  <==  Q ( x, z ) AND R ( z, y )

Q ( x, y )  <==  P ( x, z ) AND S ( z, y )
```

For brevity, however, we ignore such refinements here.

As in classical (nonrecursive) query processing, the overall problem of implementing a given recursive query can be divided into two subproblems, namely (1) transforming the original query into some equivalent but more efficient form and (2) actually executing the result of that transformation. The literature contains descriptions of a variety of attacks on both of these problems. An excellent survey, analysis, and comparison of published techniques (as of about 1988) can be found in the paper "An Amateur's Introduction to Recursive Query Processing Strategies," by F. Bancilhon and R. Ramakrishnan (Proc. ACM SIGMOD Conference, Washington D.C.,

May 1986). In the present section, we briefly discuss some of the simpler techniques. We will illustrate them by showing their application to the query "Explode part P1," using the following set of sample values for the PS relation:

PS	PX	PY
	P1	P2
	P1	P3
	P2	P3
	P2	P4
	P3	P5
	P4	P5
	P5	P6

Unification and Resolution

One possible approach, of course, is to use the standard Prolog techniques of unification and resolution, as described in Parts I and II of this paper. In the example, this approach works as follows. The first premises are the deductive axioms, which look like this in conjunctive normal form:

1. `NOT PS ( px, py ) OR COMP ( px, py )`

2. `NOT PS ( px, pz ) OR NOT COMP ( pz, py ) OR COMP ( px, py )`

We construct another premise from the desired conclusion:

3. `NOT COMP ( P1, py ) OR RESULT ( py )`

The ground axioms form the remaining premises. Consider, for example, the ground axiom

4. `PS ( P1, P2 )`

Substituting P1 for *px* and P2 for *py* in line 1, we can resolve lines 1 and 4 to yield

5. `COMP ( P1, P2 )`

Now substituting P2 for *py* in line 3 and resolving lines 3 and 5, we obtain

6. `RESULT ( P2 )`

So P2 is a component of P1. An exactly analogous argument will show that P3 is also a component of P1. Now, of course, we have the additional axioms COMP(P1,P2) and COMP(P1,P3); we can now apply the foregoing process recursively to determine the complete part explosion. The details are left as an exercise for the reader.

In practice, however, unification and resolution can be quite expensive in terms of performance. It will thus often be desirable to find some more efficient strategy. The remaining subsections below discuss some possible approaches to this problem.

Naive Evaluation

Naive evaluation is probably the simplest approach of all. As the name suggests, the algorithm is very simple-minded; it can most easily be explained (for our sample query) in terms of the following pseudocode.

```
COMP := PS ;
do until COMP reaches a "fixpoint" ;
   COMP := COMP UNION ( COMP ✕ PS ) ;
end ;
DISPLAY := COMP WHERE PX = 'P1' ;
```

Relations COMP and DISPLAY (like relation PS) each have two attributes, PX and PY. Loosely speaking, the algorithm works by repeatedly appending the join of relation PS and the current intermediate result until that intermediate result reaches a "fixpoint," i.e., until it ceases to grow. *Note:* The expression "COMP ✕ PS" is shorthand for "join COMP and PS over COMP.PY and PS.PX and project the result over COMP.PX and PS.PY."

Let us step through the algorithm with our sample set of data values. On the first iteration of the loop, the value of the expression COMP ✕ PS is as shown below on the left and the resulting value of COMP is as shown below on the right (with tuples added on this iteration flagged with an asterisk):

COMP ✕ PS	PX	PY
	P1	P3
	P1	P4
	P1	P5
	P2	P5
	P3	P6
	P4	P6

PS	PX	PY	
	P1	P2	
	P1	P3	
	P2	P3	
	P2	P4	
	P3	P5	
	P4	P5	
	P5	P6	
	P1	P4	★
	P1	P5	★
	P2	P5	★
	P3	P6	★
	P4	P6	★

After the second iteration, they look like this:

COMP ⋈ PS	PX	PY
	P1	P3
	P1	P4
	P1	P5
	P2	P5
	P3	P6
	P4	P6
	P1	P6

PS	PX	PY
	P1	P2
	P1	P3
	P2	P3
	P2	P4
	P3	P5
	P4	P5
	P5	P6
	P1	P4
	P1	P5
	P2	P5
	P3	P6
	P4	P6
	P1	P6	*

Note carefully that the computation of COMP ⋈ PS in this second step repeats the entire computation of COMP ⋈ PS from the first step but additionally computes some extra tuples (actually just one extra tuple—(P1,P6)—in the case at hand). This is one reason why the naive evaluation algorithm is not very intelligent.

On the third iteration (after more repeated computation), we get the following:

COMP ⋈ PS	PX	PY
	P1	P3
	P1	P4
	P1	P5
	P2	P5
	P3	P6
	P4	P6
	P1	P6
	P2	P6

PS	PX	PY
	P1	P2
	P1	P3
	P2	P3
	P2	P4
	P3	P5
	P4	P5
	P5	P6
	P1	P4
	P1	P5
	P2	P5
	P3	P6
	P4	P6
	P1	P6
	P2	P6	*

On the fourth iteration, the value of COMP ⋈ PS (after still more repeated computation) turns out to be the same as on the previous iteration; COMP has thus reached a fixpoint, and we exit from the loop. The final result is then computed as a restriction of COMP:

COMP	PX	PY
	P1	P2
	P1	P3
	P1	P4
	P1	P5
	P1	P6

Another inefficiency is now glaringly apparent: The algorithm has effectively computed the explosion for *every* part—in fact, it has computed the *transitive closure** of relation PS—and has then thrown everything away again except for the tuples actually wanted. In other words, again, a great deal of unnecessary work has been performed.

Note in conclusion that the naive evaluation technique can be regarded as an application of forward chaining: Starting from the extensional database (i.e., the actual data values), it applies the premises of the definition (i.e., the rule body) repeatedly until the desired result is obtained. In fact, the algorithm actually computes the *minimal model* for the Datalog program (see Part II of the paper).

Seminaive Evaluation

The first obvious improvement to the naive evaluation algorithm is to avoid repeating the computations of each step in the next step: *semi*naive evaluation. In other words, in each step we compute just the new tuples that need to be appended on this particular iteration. Again we explain the idea in terms of the "Explode part P1" example. Pseudocode:

```
NEW   := PS ;
COMP := NEW ;
do until NEW is empty ;
    NEW   := ( NEW ⋈ PS ) MINUS COMP ;
    COMP := COMP UNION NEW ;
end ;
DISPLAY := COMP WHERE PX = 'P1' ;
```

Let us again step through the algorithm. On initial entry into the loop, NEW and COMP are both identical to PS:

NEW	PX	PY		COMP	PX	PY
	P1	P2			P1	P2
	P1	P3			P1	P3
	P2	P3			P2	P3
	P2	P4			P2	P4
	P3	P5			P3	P5
	P4	P5			P4	P5
	P5	P6			P5	P6

At the end of the first iteration, they look like this:

---

*The transitive closure of a binary relation $R(X, Y)$ is a superset of R, defined as follows: The tuple (x,y) appears in the transitive closure of R if and only if it appears in R or there exists a sequence of values $z1, z2, \ldots, zn$ such that the tuples $(x,z1), (z1,z2), \ldots, (zn,y)$ all appear in R.

NEW	PX	PY
	P1	P4
	P1	P5
	P2	P5
	P3	P6
	P4	P6

COMP	PX	PY	
	P1	P2	
	P1	P3	
	P2	P3	
	P2	P4	
	P3	P5	
	P4	P5	
	P5	P6	
	P1	P4	*
	P1	P5	*
	P2	P5	*
	P3	P6	*
	P4	P6	*

COMP is the same as it was at this stage under naive evaluation, and NEW is just the new tuples that were added to COMP on this iteration; note in particular that NEW does *not* include the tuple (P1,P3) (compare the naive evaluation "equivalent").

At the end of the next iteration we have:

NEW	PX	PY
	P1	P6
	P2	P6

COMP	PX	PY	
	P1	P2	
	P1	P3	
	P2	P3	
	P2	P4	
	P3	P5	
	P4	P5	
	P5	P6	
	P1	P4	
	P1	P5	
	P2	P5	
	P3	P6	
	P4	P6	
	P1	P6	*
	P2	P6	*

The next iteration makes NEW empty, and so we leave the loop.

Static Filtering

Static filtering is a refinement on the basic idea from classical optimization theory of performing restrictions as early as possible. It can be regarded as an application of backward chaining, in that it effectively uses information from the query (the conclusion) to modify the rules (the premises). It is also referred to as *reducing the set of relevant facts,* in that it (again) uses information from the query to eliminate useless tuples in the extensional database right at the outset. The effect in terms of our example can be explained in terms of the following pseudocode:

```
NEW  := PS WHERE PX = 'P1' ;
COMP := NEW ;
do until NEW is empty ;
   NEW  := ( NEW ⋈ PS ) MINUS COMP ;
   COMP := COMP UNION NEW ;
end ;
DISPLAY := COMP ;
```

Once again we step through the algorithm. On initial entry into the loop, NEW and COMP are identical:

NEW	PX	PY
	P1	P2
	P1	P3

COMP	PX	PY
	P1	P2
	P1	P3

At the end of the first iteration, they look like this:

NEW	PX	PY
	P1	P4
	P1	P5

COMP	PX	PY	
	P1	P2	
	P1	P3	
	P1	P4	★
	P1	P5	★

At the end of the next iteration we have:

NEW	PX	PY
	P1	P6

COMP	PX	PY	
	P1	P2	
	P1	P3	
	P1	P4	
	P1	P5	
	P1	P6	★

The next iteration makes NEW empty, and so we leave the loop.

This concludes our brief introduction to recursive query processing strategies. Of course, many other approaches have been proposed in the literature, most of them considerably more sophisticated than the rather simple ones discussed above; however, there is insufficient space in a paper of this nature to cover all of the background material that is needed for a proper understanding of those approaches. The interested reader is referred to the paper by Bancilhon and Ramakrishnan already mentioned for additional information.

10. CLOSING REMARKS

This brings us to the end of our tutorial on the subject of database systems that are based on logic. The idea is still quite new, but looks very interesting. Several potential advantages were identified at various points in the paper. One further advantage, not mentioned explicitly in the body of the paper, is that logic could form the basis of a genuinely seamless integration between general-purpose programming languages and the database. In other words, instead of the embedded SQL approach supported by most DBMS products today—an approach that is not particularly elegant, to say the least—the system could provide a single logic-based language in which "data is data," regardless of whether it is kept in a shared database or local to the application. (Of course, there are a number of obstacles to be overcome before such a goal can be achieved, not the least of which is to demonstrate to the satisfaction of the DP community at large that logic is suitable as a basis for a general-purpose programming language in the first place.)

Quite apart from the foregoing possibility, it is certain that some applications, at least, will need Datalog-style access (or similar) to data stored in a shared database. The question thus arises: How exactly can such access be provided? There are two broad answers to this question, referred to generically as *loose coupling* and *tight coupling:*

- The loose coupling approach consists essentially of taking an existing DBMS and an existing logic programming language system and providing a call interface between the two. In such an approach, the user is definitely aware of the fact that there are two distinct systems involved—database operations (e.g., SQL statements) must be executed to retrieve data before logic operations (e.g., Prolog rules) can be applied to that data. (This approach certainly does *not* provide the "seamless integration" referred to above.)

- The tight coupling approach, by contrast, involves a proper integration of the DBMS and the logic programming system; in other words, the DBMS query language includes direct support for the logical inferencing operations (etc.). Thus, the user deals with one language, not two.

The pros and cons of the two approaches are obvious: Loose coupling is more straightforward to implement but is not so attractive from the user's point of view; conversely, tight coupling is harder to implement but is more attractive to the user. In addition, tight coupling is likely to perform better (the scope for logic query optimization is necessarily very limited in a loose coupling system). For obvious reasons, however, the first commercial products (a few do exist) are based on loose coupling.

In conclusion: This paper opened by mentioning a number of terms— "logic database," "inferential DBMS," "deductive DBMS," etc., etc.— that are often met with nowadays in the research literature (and indeed in vendor advertising and elsewhere). Let me therefore close it by providing (or attempting to provide) some definitions for those terms. The reader is warned, however, that there is not always a consensus on these matters, and different definitions can probably be found in other publications. Following are the definitions preferred by the present author.

- *Recursive query processing:* This is an easy one. Recursive query processing refers to the evaluation (and in particular the optimization) of queries whose definition is intrinsically recursive.

- *Knowledge base:* This term is sometimes used to mean what I called the *intensional database* in the discussion of deductive DBMSs—i.e., it consists of the *rules* (the integrity constraints and deductive axioms), as opposed to the base data, which constitutes the extensional database. But then other writers use "knowledge base" to mean the combination of both the intensional and extensional databases (see "deductive database" below)—except that (to quote from the book by Gardarin and Valduriez) "a knowledge base often includes complex objects [as well as] classical relations." Then again, the term has another, more specific meaning altogether in natural language systems. It is probably best to avoid the term entirely.

- *Knowledge:* Another easy one! Knowledge is what is in the knowledge base . . . (this definition thus reduces the problem of defining "knowledge" to a previously unsolved problem).

- *Knowledge base management system (KBMS):* The software that manages the knowledge base. The term is typically used as a synonym for deductive DBMS, q.v.

- *Deductive DBMS:* A DBMS that supports the proof-theoretic view of databases, and in particular is capable of deducing additional information from the extensional database by applying inferential (or deductive) rules that are stored in the intensional database. A deductive DBMS will almost certainly support recursive rules and so perform recursive query processing.

- *Deductive database:* (Deprecated term.) A database that is managed by a deductive DBMS.

- *Expert DBMS:* Synonym for deductive DBMS.

- *Expert database:* (Deprecated term.) A database that is managed by an expert DBMS.

- *Inferential DBMS:* Synonym for deductive DBMS.

- *Logic-based system:* Synonym for deductive DBMS.

- *Logic database:* (Deprecated term.) Synonym for deductive database.

- *Logic as a data model:* A data model consists of objects, integrity rules, and operators. In a deductive DBMS, the objects, integrity rules, and operators are all represented in the same uniform way, namely as axioms in a logic language such as Datalog; indeed, as explained earlier in this paper, a database in such a system can be regarded, precisely, as a logic program containing axioms of all three kinds. In such a system, therefore, we might legitimately say that the abstract data model for the system is logic itself.

ACKNOWLEDGMENTS

I am grateful to Charley Bontempo for his careful review of the earlier version of this material.

THE SQL LANGUAGE

26

An Overview of SQL2

ABSTRACT

This paper presents a brief overview of the currently proposed extensions to the official SQL standard known as SQL2.

COMMENTS ON REPUBLICATION

By the time this paper appears in print it will almost certainly be obsolete at the detail level—I have already revised it several times since it was first published, and I am sure it is still not in its final form. Nevertheless, I think it is still useful as a "first approximation" look at what is included in the proposed follow-on to the existing SQL standard called SQL2. After all, the "official" SQL2 working document is currently running at over 500 pages! So I hope the short paper that follows will at least serve its intended purpose, which is (as its title indicates) to provide an overview of the proposals.

An earlier version of this paper was originally published in *InfoDB* 4, No. 1 (Spring 1989). Another version also appeared (under the title "Future Extensions") in my book *A Guide to the SQL Standard,* 2nd edition (Addison-Wesley, 1989). Reprinted by permission of Addison-Wesley and Database Associates International.

413

1. INTRODUCTION

The ANSI and ISO SQL standards committees are currently at work on a proposed extended version of the existing SQL standard with the working title "SQL2." The purpose of this paper is to take a brief look at the SQL2 proposals. The reader is cautioned that the proposals *are* only proposals at this stage; they will undoubtedly change in a number of ways before they achieve official standard status (if they ever do). Nevertheless, it seems worthwhile to spend a little time to examine them now, if only because they do give some indication as to how the committees are currently thinking, and hence as to how the standard is likely to evolve over the next several years.

At the time of writing, it looks as if the proposals are likely to go for public review some time in 1991. Note, however, that they do represent a *major* extension to the existing standard, and hence a *major* (multi-year) implementation effort; any prospective implementation is likely to require rather careful staging. Indeed, the standards committees are proposing some such staging themselves; they are defining entry level, intermediate level, and full versions of the SQL2 language. Furthermore, the proposals are still somewhat fluid at the time of writing; hence, there does not seem to be a great deal of point in trying to be meticulously precise and detailed in trying to describe them at this time. The discussions that follow, therefore, deliberately do not go into a very great deal of detail.

Before we get into specifics, let me make a couple of general observations:

1. The proposed extensions (unlike the existing standard) do permit data definition operations such as CREATE TABLE to be executed from within an application program. As a consequence, the "schema definition language" of the existing standard is now totally redundant and could be discarded.

2. The proposed extensions, unlike the existing standard,* do include a full set of "embedded SQL" facilities—not only for the languages supported by the existing standard (COBOL, FORTRAN, Pascal, and PL/I) but also for Ada and C. As a consequence, the "module language" of the existing standard is now largely redundant and could probably be discarded also.

---

*After these words were first written, the American National Standards Institute (ANSI) approved a new, separate American National Standard, "Database Language Embedded SQL," which does define a set of embedded SQL facililties for the six host languages mentioned above.

The rest of this paper discusses certain aspects of the proposed extensions in more detail. Section 2 covers definitional aspects and Section 3 covers manipulative aspects. Section 4 is concerned with one specific (and rather important) aspect, namely *orthogonality*.

One last introductory point: I deliberately do not devote much space to explaining the underlying relational concepts (e.g., domains, θ-join, outer join, set intersection, etc.) that are being addressed by some of the proposed extensions. A tutorial on such material can be found in many places; see, e.g., my book *An Introduction to Database Systems: Volume I,* 5th edition (Addison-Wesley, 1990).

2. DEFINITIONAL EXTENSIONS

- Weak support* is provided for the relational concept of *domains.* Domains can be created and dropped (CREATE DOMAIN, DROP DOMAIN). Column definitions (in CREATE and ALTER TABLE) can specify a user-defined domain instead of one of the builtin data types such as INTEGER. Domains in SQL2 thus provide the ability to factor out scalar-level data type definitions. They also provide some support for "domain integrity" (i.e., the ability to specify an integrity constraint as part of the domain definition, to be satisfied by all columns defined on the domain). They do not provide:

  - Strong type checking on scalar comparisons (in particular, on joins)
  - Any ability to define valid operators for specified domains and to define the domain of the result of scalar expressions
  - Any "enumerated data type" support
  - Full user-defined data type support

- The following new builtin data types are supported:

VARCHAR	(varying length strings)
NCHAR	(national strings, fixed and varying length)
BIT	(bit strings, fixed and varying length)
DATE	(absolute dates)
TIME	(absolute times)
TIMESTAMP	(absolute timestamps)
INTERVAL	(date and time intervals)

- In addition to the "schema definition" operations in the current standard (CREATE SCHEMA, CREATE TABLE, CREATE VIEW, and

---

*The support is so weak, in fact, that some committee members attempted unsuccessfully to replace the term "domain" by the term "generic column," thereby leaving the door open for the provision of proper domain support at some future time.

GRANT [= create authorization]), the following "schema manipulation" operations are also supported:

```
DROP SCHEMA
DROP TABLE
DROP VIEW
REVOKE [= drop authorization]
ALTER TABLE [add/drop columns/constraints, replace defaults]
CREATE DOMAIN, DROP DOMAIN
CREATE ASSERTION, DROP ASSERTION
```

All schema definition and schema manipulation operations can be used from within an application program.

- Referential integrity support is extended to include explicit support for CASCADE, SET NULL, and SET DEFAULT rules and implicit support for a RESTRICT rule. All rules are supported for both UPDATE and DELETE. (Although this is not the place to go into details, it must be said that the SQL2 referential integrity proposals are unfortunately far more complex than they need to be, at least in their present form.)

- As suggested above by the appearance of CREATE and DROP ASSERTION in the list of "schema manipulation" operations, general integrity constraints (i.e., integrity constraints of arbitrary complexity, involving any number of tables) are supported. An unfortunate side-effect of this extension is that there is now a lot of redundancy in the language in this area:

  - "NOT NULL" constraints are a special case of single-column CHECK constraints
  - Single-column CHECK constraints are a special case of table-level CHECK constraints
  - Table-level CHECK constraints are a special case of general integrity constraints (i.e., assertions)

  Unique and primary key constraints can also be regarded as a special case of assertions; however, special-casing is desirable for these constraints, because they are so fundamental. FOREIGN KEY constraints would be a special case also, except that they include the ability to specify what the system is to do if an attempt is made to violate them—which CREATE ASSERTION, at least in its present form, does not.

3. MANIPULATIVE EXTENSIONS

- Several new scalar operators are supported—arithmetic, comparison, and component extraction operators for dates and times; a string concatenation operator (||); an operator to extract a substring from a given string (SUBSTRING); an operator to search for a substring in a given string (POSITION); an operator to return the length of a string (LENGTH); and so on.

- Manipulative statements generally are now defined to return an extensive set of feedback information if an exception occurs—not just an implementation-defined negative SQLCODE value as at present, but a SQL2–defined character string value in a special variable called SQLSTATE and a set of more detailed information in the "Diagnostics Area." The GET DIAGNOSTICS operation can be used to retrieve information from the Diagnostics Area. SQLCODE is now a "deprecated feature," meaning that it is a feature of the existing standard that is scheduled for removal at some future time. *Aside:* The only other "deprecated feature" at the time of writing is the ability to specify an integer instead of a column reference in an ORDER BY clause.

- A set of "schema information tables" (in effect, system-defined views of the system catalog) are supported. The schema information tables currently defined are as follows (the names should be more or less self-explanatory):

```
SCHEMATA, DOMAINS, TABLES, VIEWS, COLUMNS
TABLE_, COLUMN_, DOMAIN_PRIVILEGES
TABLE_, REF_, CHECK_CONSTRAINTS
ASSERTIONS
KEY_COLUMN_, VIEW_TABLE_, VIEW_COLUMN_USAGE
CONST_TABLE_, CONST_COLUMN_, COL_DOMAIN_USAGE
CHARACTER_SETS, COLLATING_SEQS, CHAR_TRANSLATIONS
SQL_LANGUAGES
```

- The ability to assign a name to a derived column is supported. Here are two examples:

```
SELECT X + Y AS Z
FROM    ...
 ...

SELECT T.Z + 1, ...
FROM    ( SELECT X + Y FROM ... ) AS T ( Z )
 ...
```

In the first example, the final result table—i.e., the table retrieved by the SELECT—has a single (derived) column called Z. In the second example, the table identified in the FROM clause of the outer SELECT is a (derived) table called T, with a single (derived) column called T.Z. *Note:* The second example also illustrates the point that the FROM clause can now include general table-expressions as well as simple table names. See further examples below and in Section 4.

- Scroll cursors are supported. A scroll cursor is an extended version of the existing cursor, a version for which not only "FETCH NEXT" but also "FETCH PRIOR" and other cursor movement operations are supported (note, however, that the table associated with such a cursor will be read-only). A cursor is defined to be a scroll cursor by the appearance of the key word SCROLL in the cursor definition. For example:

```
DECLARE X SCROLL CURSOR
    FOR SELECT ... etc.
```

The FETCH statement is extended to include a "fetch orientation" specification, as follows:

```
FETCH [ fetch-orientation ] cursor INTO target-commalist
```

where "fetch orientation" is one of the following:

```
NEXT
PRIOR
FIRST
LAST
ABSOLUTE scalar-expression
RELATIVE scalar-expression
```

(NEXT is the default, and is the only legal option if the cursor is not a scroll cursor). NEXT, PRIOR, FIRST, and LAST are self-explanatory. For the other two cases, let n be the result of evaluating the scalar expression (which must be of type exact numeric); n must not be zero. ABSOLUTE n moves the cursor to the nth row (counting backward from the end if n is negative). RELATIVE n moves the cursor to the nth row from the current position (again, counting backward if n is negative).

- A new kind of query expression, namely "joined table," is supported. Joined tables provide direct and explicit support for various kinds of join (in particular, natural join and outer join). Here is the syntax (slightly simplified):

```
table [ NATURAL ] [ INNER | LEFT | RIGHT | FULL ] JOIN table
                                    [ ON search-condition ]
```

LEFT, RIGHT, and FULL mean left, right, and full *outer* join, respectively; INNER (which is the default) means inner join. If NATURAL is specified, the appropriate natural join is computed *on the basis of common column names* (the ON clause must be omitted in this case); otherwise, the appropriate θ-join is computed (the ON clause must not be omitted in this case). Here is an example (based on the usual suppliers-and-parts database—refer to Chapter 1, Appendix A):

```
SELECT *
FROM ( S NATURAL LEFT JOIN SP )
```

The "SELECT * FROM" seems somewhat obtrusive, but is apparently required. More to the point, however, note that this example cannot be expressed *at all* in the existing standard. The best that can be done today is something along the following lines (note, however, that this expression produces blanks and zeros instead of nulls in its result):

```
SELECT S.SNO, S.SNAME, S.STATUS, S.CITY, SP.PNO, SP.QTY
FROM   S, SP
WHERE  S.SNO = SP.SNO

UNION

SELECT S.SNO, S.SNAME, S.STATUS, S.CITY, '       ', 0000000000
FROM   S
WHERE  NOT EXISTS
     ( SELECT *
       FROM   SP
       WHERE  SP.SNO = S.SNO )
```

Note: I use "SNO" to represent "supplier number" in the foregoing example instead of the more familiar "S#" because the character "#" is not valid as part of a regular identifier in the standard.

- Query expressions can also involve explicit INTERSECT and EXCEPT (difference) operators as well as the UNION operator. Like UNION, INTERSECT and EXCEPT can also include an ALL qualifier to specify that redundant duplicates are not to be eliminated. All three operators (UNION, INTERSECTION, and EXCEPT) also have a CORRESPONDING version to indicate that the operation is to be performed on the basis of common column names. Simplified syntax:

```
table  op  [ ALL ]  [ CORRESPONDING ]  table
```

where "op" is UNION or INTERSECT or EXCEPT. *Note:* Unfortunately, the two "tables" must be specified via SELECT-expressions, not just as simple table names. For example:

```
SELECT *
FROM    ( ( SELECT * FROM X )
            UNION
          ( SELECT * FROM Y ) )
  ...
```

An expression of the form

```
X UNION Y
```

would appear preferable!

- The ability to deactivate (and subsequently reactivate) individual integrity constraints is supported. For example, the statement

```
SET CONSTRAINTS CHECK47, CHECK82 DEFERRED
```

will cause checking of integrity constraints CHECK47 and CHECK82 to be suspended until such time as they are set IMMEDIATE again. This facility thus allows some integrity checking not to be done at the time of the relevant update operation, but rather to be deferred to some later time—e.g., to the end of the transaction.

- A new statement, SET TRANSACTION, allows the user to specify the transaction "status" (READ ONLY or READ WRITE) and transaction "isolation level" (0, 1, 2, or 3, corresponding respectively to what are usually known as "express read," "cursor stability," "repeatable read except for phantoms," and "repeatable read including phantoms"). Note, incidentally, that support for consistency levels less than 3 means that serializability can no longer be guaranteed and can therefore no longer be considered a requirement (it *is* a requirement in the existing standard).

- Temporary tables are supported. A temporary table is created via CREATE or DECLARE TEMPORARY TABLE. Such a table is totally private to the user who creates it; it does not need to be registered in the catalog or subjected to the usual recovery and concurrency controls (and associated overhead) that apply to other, more permanent tables. Temporary tables are destroyed automatically at the end of the user session in which they were created. (Exactly what constitutes a "session" is not defined, however.)

- "Dynamic SQL" is supported. Dynamic SQL provides the ability for an application to construct (and then execute) SQL statements dynamically, i.e., during application execution. Such a facility is extremely important in the construction of generalized applications. *Note* (for readers who may be familiar with the dynamic SQL facilities of DB2 or SQL/DS): The dynamic SQL facilities of SQL2 resemble those of SQL/DS—i.e., "extended" dynamic SQL—rather than those of DB2.

- Finally, SQL2 manipulative operations are much more *orthogonal* than the existing standard. As indicated in Section 1, this is such a significant point that we devote a separate section to it (Section 4 below).

4. ORTHOGONALITY

Standard SQL is not a very orthogonal language. Many of the detailed criticisms made by this writer in other publications (see, e.g., the paper "A Critique of the SQL Database Language" in the book *Relational Database:*

Selected Writings, Addison-Wesley, 1986) are essentially specific instances of this general—and very broad—complaint. Orthogonality means *independence:* A language is orthogonal if independent concepts are kept independent and are not mixed together in confusing ways. One example of *lack* of orthogonality (one among many, and one that unfortunately still applies to SQL2) is provided by the rule in existing SQL to the effect that the argument to an aggregate function such as SUM cannot be another aggregate function reference.

Orthogonality is desirable because the less orthogonal a language is, the more complicated it is and (paradoxically but simultaneously) the less powerful it is. "Orthogonal design maximizes expressive power while avoiding deleterious superfluities" (from A. van Wijngaarden et al., eds., *Revised Report on the Algorithmic Language Algol 68,* Springer-Verlag, 1976). As already indicated, SQL as currently defined is extremely deficient in this regard. SQL2 is somewhat better. I summarize below some of the major improvements (not all) in this general area.

■ Query expressions are no longer limited to appearing only in the context of a cursor definition. (*Note:* A query expression is basically the only context in which UNION can appear; essentially, a query expression in the existing standard consists of a set of SELECT-expressions all UNIONed together. Hence, UNION can be used only within a cursor definition in the existing standard.) In SQL2, by contrast, query expressions are permitted in all of the following contexts:

  ▪ Within DECLARE CURSOR (as in the existing standard)

  ▪ Within CREATE VIEW (i.e., as the view-defining expression)

  ▪ In a subquery (i.e., a subquery is now just a query expression in parentheses—except that in most contexts, the result of evaluating the subquery must still be a single-column table)

  ▪ Within INSERT (multiple-row format—i.e., INSERT . . . SELECT) to define the rows to be inserted

  ▪ In a "joined table" expression (see Section 3) to define one of the tables to be joined

  ▪ In a UNION (or INTERSECT or EXCEPT) expression to define one of the tables to be UNIONed (or . . .)

  ▪ Within a FROM clause (as a "derived table")

The last of these requires some additional explanation. The general syntax of the FROM clause is still

```
FROM table-reference-commalist
```

but "table reference" is now extended as follows (simplifying somewhat once again):

```
table-reference
   ::=   table [ [ AS ] ... See Section 3 ]
       | ( query-expression ) [ AS ... See Section 3 ]
       | joined-table
```

The first form is basically as in standard SQL today (except for the optional noiseword AS); the second and third forms introduce the idea that, instead of limiting the operands of FROM to be named tables, they can instead be *table-valued expressions*. For example:

```
SELECT MAX ( T.CITY )
FROM   ( SELECT S.CITY FROM S
         UNION
         SELECT P.CITY FROM P ) AS T ( CITY )
```

Note, however, that UNION (and INTERSECT and EXCEPT) are still illegal in a SELECT *statement* (i.e., a singleton SELECT).

Note: The foregoing extension, though desirable so far as it goes, still fails to recognize the basic point that a table name ought to be regarded as just a special case of a general table (or query) expression.

- The argument to a function that includes DISTINCT is no longer limited to being a column reference but can instead be any scalar expression.

- The restrictions on the number of times DISTINCT can appear within a given expression have been dropped.

- The restrictions regarding grouped views (e.g., a FROM clause that includes a reference to a grouped view cannot include any other table references) have been dropped. In fact, the term "grouped view" has been dropped entirely.

- To return to query expressions once again: Query expressions can be regarded as being at the top of the syntax tree. The following simplified explanation indicates how very much more orthogonal matters are in this area in SQL2.

  - A query expression is basically a collection of terms connected together by means of the operators UNION, and/or INTERSECT, and/or EXCEPT (each with or without ALL and with or without CORRESPONDING)

  - Each term in a query expression is either a query specification or a "table value expression"

- A query specification is basically just a SELECT–FROM–WHERE–GROUP BY–HAVING expression; a "table value expression" is basically just a list of one or more "row value expressions"
- A row value expression is basically a list of one or more scalar expressions
- A scalar expression (in addition to all of the obvious cases—arithmetic expressions, etc.) can be a subquery
- Finally, as explained earlier, a subquery is basically just a query expression in parentheses

One consequence of all of the above, incidentally, is that an UPDATE statement can update one value in the database from another in SQL2 (this is not possible in the existing standard).

5. CONCLUSION

We have taken a brief look at the currently proposed "SQL2" extensions to the existing standard. The standards committees are to be congratulated on addressing some important problems and providing some important functionality, though there are still some significant omissions (e.g., proper domain support, proper view operations, support for relational division, etc.). In particular, SQL2 is much more orthogonal than "SQL1." However, there are also some unfortunate hangovers from the past (e.g., duplicate rows, subqueries). The interested reader is encouraged to study the official SQL2 document and to be prepared to contribute to the public review process at the appropriate time (if it is not too late by the time this paper appears in print). For reference, the official SQL2 document is:

ANSI BSR X3.194-199*x*
Data Base Languages: *(ISO working draft) Database Language SQL2.*

It is obtainable for a fee ($75 US, $97.50 overseas) from

Global Engineering Documents Inc.
2805 McGaw Avenue
Irvine, CA 92714

27

Without Check Option

ABSTRACT

Arguments are advanced in support of the contention that views should never be without WITH CHECK OPTION.

COMMENTS ON PUBLICATION

In SQL, UPDATE and INSERT operations on views are not monitored to ensure that the newly inserted or updated row satisfies the view-defining condition unless the view definition includes the specification WITH CHECK OPTION. In the paper that follows, Hugh Darwen argues strongly that "*WITHOUT* CHECK OPTION" is very bad news—in effect, that WITH CHECK OPTION should always be specified. I agree with this position, but remark that both the current SQL standard and many existing SQL implementations cause difficulties in this regard.

- First, the standard says that WITH CHECK OPTION can be specified only if the view is updatable. Unfortunately, the standard's definition of which views *are* updatable is extremely limited. Thus, for example, view V might well be updatable theoretically, and might in fact be up-

Previously unpublished.

datable in some given product, and might even be updatable according
to the standard in some future version, and yet I am not strictly allowed
to specify WITH CHECK OPTION for it. (And when it does become
updatable in that future version of the standard, I will presumably have
to remember to go back and change my view definition.)

- Second, current SQL products suffer from numerous restrictions in this
  area. Some do not support WITH CHECK OPTION at all (SQL/400
  is an example). Some do support it, but not for all updatable views
  (DB2 is an example—in DB2, WITH CHECK OPTION cannot be
  specified if the view definition includes a subquery). In others, specifying WITH CHECK OPTION in itself changes the updatability of the
  view! (INGRES is an example—in INGRES, a view whose definition
  includes a WHERE clause will not accept INSERTs, nor UPDATEs
  that affect any column mentioned in that WHERE clause, if WITH
  CHECK OPTION is specified). And I would be very surprised if this
  were the end of the list of anomalies.

- Another problem that may well apply to some products (it applied to
  early releases of DB2, and it applies to the SQL standard also at the
  time of writing, although the problem is in the process of being fixed)
  is that WITH CHECK OPTION might not *inherit*. That is, an update
  to table V2, which is defined as a view of table V1, which is in turn
  defined as a view of table B, might be permitted to flout a WITH
  CHECK OPTION clause specified on V1.

I cannot help remarking too that it is strange to find so much attention
(on the part of the standards committees and the DBMS implementers) being devoted to an "integrity" feature (such as it is) for views, when an
analogous feature for base tables—which would be so much more important, both in theory and in practice [4]—has still, as yet, received comparatively little attention.

1. A SURPRISING EXAMPLE

You are a member of the personnel department, with responsibility for the
records of all the employees in departments D5 and D9. A new employee,
Jones, has just been recruited by the manager of department D5, and you
have to tell the database about this.

Your computer is already powered on and booted up, with various win-
dows and icons showing on its monitor screen. With a few deft shifts of
the mouse and clicks of its buttons, you soon have the familiar window
from which you operate your interactive sessions with your DBMS, and
you are in touch with the personnel database.

You press the function key that displays your catalog, wherein you see your table called EMP_D5_D9 and the fact that EMP_D5_D9 currently has 42 rows. "That's right," you think, "I have 19 in department D5 and 23 in department D9." Using the mouse again, you point at the catalog entry for EMP_D5_D9 and press the function key labeled "Form." This fires up yet another window, displaying the data entry form associated with EMP_D5_D9.

You type Jones's details into this form, and click the push-button labeled **Insert**. The DBMS expresses pleasure and gratitude at this, with the usual signal that you know means everything worked fine, all the database integrity checks have been passed, and the row for Jones is now in the database.

Now, it's a very slick frontend that you were provided with for this work. One of the things that has always been very helpful is that the window displaying the catalog is updated in "real time," as they say. Your eye, therefore, returns, as it always does in such circumstances, to the information displayed about EMP_D5_D9—in particular, to the "number of rows" window. Watching the 42 change to 43 takes only a split second, and it is always your final reassurance that you are doing everything right.

It doesn't change. It still says 42.

The pointer is still positioned on the **Insert** button of the window displaying your employee data entry form, so you click the mouse button again. This time the DBMS expresses displeasure. The alarm beeps, and a message pops up: *Row already exists in EMP_D5_D9.*

Now you wonder if you misread the original 42. It must really have been 41. Anyway, there's a quick and easy check to make sure. With Jones's details remaining safely in the data entry window, you click on the button labeled **Delete**, with the intention of watching the 42 change to 41, after which you will click **Insert** again and watch the row count rise back to 42.

But when you click on **Delete** there's another beep, and this time the popup message says *No such row in EMP_D5_D9.*

You call a few colleagues over and spend some time clicking alternately on the **Insert** and **Delete** buttons. The consequent alternation of the popup messages *Row already exists in EMP_D5_D9* and *No such row in EMP_D5_D9* is greeted with all-round hilarity and the usual jokes about the stupidity of computers.

You point at the catalog entry for EMP_D5_D9 and select *Display table* from a pulldown menu. The tabular display shows 42 rows, none of which is the one for Jones—the row that, according to one of the error messages, *already exists in EMP_D5_D9.*

Eventually somebody spots something very interesting in the window displaying the form in which you typed Jones's details. One of the boxes looks like this:

```
Department number:   D6
```

So you did make a mistake, for Jones's department is actually D5. You correct the error, but to no avail—the same two error messages continue to pop up, according to whether you click on **Insert** or **Delete**. The time has come to call in the database administrator, so you do that. The DBA asks for the experiment to be repeated, with tracing turned on, and the resulting log trace to be sent. Very soon after that, the DBA phones to say that the problem has been fixed and will never happen again.

2. THE EXPLANATION

Most readers will already know the explanation of all this, especially those who took note of the title of this chapter, but it's worth spelling out in detail, I think.

1. It all happened inside the Askew Wall.

2. Although you did not know it, EMP_D5_D9 was not a base table. It was a view, which the DBA had previously defined as follows:

```
CREATE VIEW EMP_D5_D9
     AS SELECT EMP#, ENAME, SALARY, JOB, DEPT#
        FROM    EMP
        WHERE   DEPT# IN ('D5','D9') ;
```

3. When you first inserted Jones, with the wrong department number D6, the DBMS seemed pleased and grateful because it had no trouble inserting that row into the underlying table EMP.

4. The number of rows in EMP_D5_D9 correctly remained 42. The inserted Jones wasn't in EMP_D5_D9, because EMP_D5_D9 expressly excludes employees in departments other than D5 and D9.

5. The error message *No such row in EMP_D5_D9* was correct. To delete the Jones row you needed access to one of the tables in which it did exist— either the underlying table EMP, or the view EMP_D6_D8 which the DBA had prepared for your colleague who is responsible for departments D6 and D8. But you did not know about either of those tables, and in any case you had been granted no authority to access them.

6. The error message *Row already exists in EMP_D5_D9* was incorrect. The error was not in the DBMS, and not in anything the DBA had

done. It was in the interface software supporting your data entry form. That software had noted the SQLCODE resulting from the attempted insert as the one meaning *unique constraint violation,* the "unique constraint" in question being the one implied by the declared primary key of EMP. The interface software wasn't sure that all its users would understand terms like "unique constraint" and "primary key," so chose the more intelligible (it thought) *Row already exists in . . .* , and completed the message with the name of the table that your form was designed for and against which all its SQL operations were therefore directed. It didn't occur to it that the error response to INSERT INTO EMP_D5_D9 might mean "row already exists *in EMP.*"

7. The DBA fixed the problem by executing the statement

```
UPDATE  EMP
SET     DEPT# = 'D5'
WHERE   ENAME = 'Jones'
AND     DEPT# = 'D6' ;
```

(having first checked that there were no other Joneses in department D6—but, of course, specifying the employee number in the WHERE clause would have been a safer and quicker alternative).

8. The DBA made sure the problem would never recur by issuing the following sequence of commands:

```
BEGIN WORK ;

DROP VIEW EMP_D5_D9 ;

CREATE VIEW EMP_D5_D9
    AS SELECT EMP#, ENAME, SALARY, JOB, DEPT#
       FROM   EMP
       WHERE  DEPT# IN ('D5','D9')
    WITH CHECK OPTION ;

GRANT ALL PRIVILEGES ON EMP_D5_D9 TO <you> ;

COMMIT WORK ;
```

Aside: Strange, is it not, that there is no ALTER VIEW operation, that would allow you to put the WITH CHECK OPTION option into a view definition that did not have it, or to drop it from one that did, or to change the view-defining expression without affecting the option? That is why the DBA had to bother with the above rigmarole, when a single, atomic operation should have been available for the job. And, should you note that wastes of time like the one in my scenario would have been rarer if the missing WITHOUT CHECK OPTION option had been supported,* such that WITH CHECK OPTION was the default option, I couldn't possibly disagree with you. *End of aside.*

3. FURTHER DISCUSSION

My scenario makes a strong case against what I call the WITHOUT CHECK OPTION option—that which is implied when you choose not to use the WITH CHECK OPTION option. If all views were treated as if they had been defined with the WITH CHECK OPTION option,† then mishaps like the one described above could never occur. I maintain that such should be the case, and I do so on the grounds that WITHOUT CHECK OPTION muddies the semantics of INSERT and UPDATE. Surely, if I insert a row R into a table T, then the new value of T includes the row R; if I update a table T, then the new value of T has exactly the same number of rows as the old value of T. Yet, with the WITHOUT CHECK OPTION option, these utterly intuitive observations cease to hold.

In view of this apparently very strong case, why is WITHOUT CHECK OPTION supported at all?

The first thing to note is that, if you really wanted to insert Jones with a DEPT# value of D6, you would necessarily have to *know* about that department, in the sense that you would have to know that D6 is a reasonable DEPT# value (i.e., such a department exists), and that D6 is the correct value to give in Jones's row. Is it reasonable for you to know all that and yet not to know of any table that is permitted to contain Jones's row? I think not. Either D6 should have been included in the IN list of the view definition the DBA set up for your use—because department D6 is one of the ones for which you are responsible—or you are somebody with the much bigger responsibility of overseeing the entire employee file. In either case, you would not use the table named EMP_D5_D9 as the target for the INSERT, and you would have no difficulty inserting the row into whichever table is appropriate to the purpose.

So we must look for the case where there might be some advantage in being able to insert a row with DEPT# D6 into base table EMP via a view such as EMP_D5_D9. And here I happily admit defeat, for I cannot think of any circumstance where such a facility would be particularly convenient,

---

*Many people think, as I do, that—as a matter of good language design—it should be possible to specify the WITHOUT CHECK OPTION option explicitly [5], even though it is the default. (Of course, I am assuming here that the option is supported in the first place, but the primary purpose of this paper is to argue that in fact it should *not* be supported.)

†The view updating algorithms presented in reference [3] effectively assume such a situation.

or desirable. Furthermore, while I acknowledge that there may be cases where a user who is permitted to insert is not permitted to delete, the case where permission to do both is granted but it is nevertheless sometimes impossible for a user to delete a row that was inserted by that very same user is a little hard to stomach. In fact, even worse, that poor user is not even able to *see* the inserted row!

What about UPDATE? When might it be especially convenient to update a row R in a table T such that, as a result of the update, R disappears from T just as though it had been deleted?

One answer lies, I think, in the scenario where you know that some employee is to be moved from one of your departments to department D6, but you do not yet know *which* employee. So you fire up a display of EMP_D5_D9 and browse through what you see, looking for the best candidate to move to department D6. When you have selected some employee, you type D6 over the displayed D5 (or D9) and click on **Update**. The DBMS expresses its pleasure and gratitude in response to this, and the row disappears from the display window (does it?).

Well, I do not deny the usefulness of such a capability, but I maintain that in your own mind you must have had a clear distinction between the view EMP_D5_D9 that you were browsing through and the underlying table EMP that you were updating. I therefore also maintain that you wouldn't really have objected to the slight inconvenience of setting up the form that way, allowing the browsed table to be different from the underlying target table for inserts, updates, and deletes.

Some might argue, contrariwise, that the WITHOUT CHECK OPTION option allows the foregoing requirement to be handled very conveniently by means of a *cursor,* using what the SQL standard calls a "positioned update" (i.e., UPDATE . . . WHERE CURRENT). If you have a cursor pointing to the row for the employee you wish to transfer to department D6, you do not have to go to the bother of identifying that row all over again by the values in one or more of its columns (probably its primary key columns). And I suppose there might possibly be a tiny performance advantage too, if the DBMS is not very intelligent.

Surely, however, the convenience advantage (and the performance advantage also, if there is one) could easily by obtained by means of a more flexible cursor mechanism, along the lines proposed in reference [2]. This is not the place to go into details, but if we suppose that the desired row has been found in EMP_D5_D9 and cursor D5_D9_CURSOR has been set to point to it, then an UPDATE of the form

```
UPDATE EMP       /* Not EMP_D5_D9, observe !!! */
SET    ...
WHERE  CURRENT OF D5_D9_CURSOR ;
```

ought to be legal. As it is, the Askew syntax for updating a table via a cursor requires that the table named in the UPDATE clause and the table named in the cursor declaration be identical—a curious rule, since it is logically unnecessary, and unnecessarily restrictive, and if broken provokes an annoying slap on the wrist in place of a user-friendly correction on the part of the system, and in an analogous context, namely FETCH, an analogous rule is not enforced. Thus, you are compelled (in the case at hand) to specify that your update is an update to EMP_D5_D9, even when it is no such thing!

4. A QUESTION OF INHERITANCE

In the foregoing sections I have argued that the WITHOUT CHECK OPTION option should *never* be used; in effect, I have criticized the Askew Wall for even providing such an option, and especially for making it the default (WITHOUT CHECK OPTION is what you get if you don't specify WITH CHECK OPTION explicitly). In this section and the next, I drive more nails into the coffin by pointing out some additional difficulties that the system makes for itself—not to mention the user—by supporting the WITHOUT CHECK OPTION option (albeit implicitly).

Consider once again the definition of view EMP_D5_D9:

```
CREATE VIEW EMP_D5_D9
    AS SELECT EMP#, ENAME, SALARY, JOB, DEPT#
       FROM    EMP
       WHERE   DEPT# IN ('D5','D9') ;
```

Now suppose that the underlying table EMP is not a base table but is instead another view, with definition as follows:

```
CREATE VIEW EMP
    AS SELECT EMP#, ENAME, SALARY, JOB, DEPT#
       FROM    EVERYBODY
       WHERE   JOB IN ('Programmer','Analyst') ;
```

Suppose further that the WITH CHECK OPTION option is specified for EMP_D5_D9 and not for EMP. What should happen if a row is inserted into EMP_D5_D9 that satisfies the WHERE-condition for EMP_D5_D9 but not that for EMP?—e.g.:

```
INSERT
INTO    EMP_D5_D9 ( EMP#, ENAME, SALARY, JOB, DEPT# )
VALUES            ( 'E4','Jones', 45K, 'Engineer','D5' ) ;
```

And what if WITH CHECK OPTION is specified for EMP and not for EMP_D5_D9? And would it make any difference if WITHOUT CHECK OPTION could be stated explicitly instead of implicitly?

Well, I am frankly not interested in what might be the official,* or correct, or best, or least bad answers to these questions, but I do note that they must be answered, and that means more work for the system, more words in the manual, more time needed to teach and learn the product, more opportunities for mistakes . . . and all for what?

5. JOIN VIEWS

Finally, here is an oddity that I find hilarious. Standard SQL does not yet support updatable joins of any kind, and nor do most current implementations. Nevertheless, here is a "join view" that the view updating pragmaticians would almost certainly deem to be updatable:

```
CREATE VIEW EMPDEPT
    AS SELECT *
       FROM   EMP E, DEPT D
       WHERE  E.DEPT# = D.DEPT# ;
```

EMPDEPT is a many-to-one (actually a foreign-to-primary-key) equijoin: EMP.DEPT# is a foreign key in the employee table EMP referencing the primary key DEPT.DEPT# of the department table DEPT. Note in particular that EMPDEPT contains two DEPT# columns. (I don't know how they would be differentiated, in the Askew Wall; that's a problem that is beyond the scope of the present discussion. I have discussed it in detail elsewhere—see reference [1].)

Now, admittedly it would have been more sensible to write an explicit SELECT-list, mentioning just one of the two identical DEPT# columns, but systems cannot rely on users always being sensible—perhaps our user, here, was really suffering from some of the other horrors I have written about, to be discovered inside the Askew Wall, and didn't want to have to write out the names of all the columns in EMP and DEPT, just to remove one of them.

Just suppose SQL did honor the updatability of view EMPDEPT, and the system did permit rows to be inserted into it. The normal treatment of insertion into such a many-to-one join is to split the inserted row into two components, a row for the "many" side of the join and a row for the "one" side. In the case at hand, the row for EMP (the "many" side) is simply inserted into EMP, and the row for DEPT (the "one" side) is inserted into DEPT unless it already exists, in which case nothing is done to

---

*The Draft International Standard for SQL2 [6] fixes the problem by allowing CASCADED or LOCAL to be specified with a view definition. Note the consequence—that omitting the WITH CHECK OPTION option no longer necessarily implies my WITHOUT CHECK OPTION option!

DEPT at all. Either way, the combined row will appear in the result of the join when the WHERE condition is reevaluated.

So far, so good. But what if the view definition is WITHOUT CHECK OPTION, and the inserted row has different values in the two DEPT# positions? Now *there's* a nice little conundrum for the poor system (never mind the user) to grapple with!

6.   CONCLUSION

In conclusion, I merely opine that the world would be a better place *without* WITHOUT CHECK OPTION.

REFERENCES AND BIBLIOGRAPHY

1. Hugh Darwen (writing as Andrew Warden), "In Praise of Marriage," in C. J. Date, *Relational Database Writings 1985–1989* (Reading, MA: Addison-Wesley, 1990).

2. C. J. Date, "An Introduction to the Unified Database Language (UDL)," in C. J. Date, *Relational Database: Selected Writings* (Reading, MA: Addison-Wesley, 1986).

3. C. J. Date, "Updating Views," in C. J. Date, *Relational Database: Selected Writings* (Reading, MA: Addison-Wesley, 1986).

4. C. J. Date, "A Contribution to the Study of Database Integrity," in C. J. Date, *Relational Database Writings 1985–1989* (Reading, MA: Addison-Wesley, 1990).

5. C. J. Date, "SQL Dos and Don'ts," in C. J. Date, *Relational Database Writings 1985–1989* (Reading, MA: Addison-Wesley, 1990).

6. ISO/IEC JTC1 (*Information Processing Systems*), DIS 9075:199x(E) *Database Language SQL2* (April 1991).

Here EMPLOYEE represents an entity supertype, and SALES represents a subtype of that supertype (every salesperson is an employee, but the converse is not true). So far as IEF is concerned, the EMPLOYEE relation is presumably now considered to be in 4NF whereas the previous version of that relation was not. The SALES relation is in 4NF also. (Note, however, that only one of those two relations EMPLOYEE and SALES actually represents an entity subtype—the statement that "Every 4NF collection of Attributes is a Subtype" notwithstanding.)

Now, I agree that replacing the original relation by two relations as suggested is a good idea. That is not the point at issue. What is at issue is the *terminology*—i.e., the suggestion that such a replacement can be regarded as a conversion to 4NF. In my opinion, this latter suggestion should be *firmly resisted,* for the following two reasons (at least, these are the principal reasons, though there are some additional minor reasons also):

1. It is demonstrably and unnecessarily confusing. As mentioned earlier in this note, the term "4NF" already has a well established and widely accepted meaning—namely, the meaning given it by Fagin.

2. *The IEF terminology would be wrong even if it predated Fagin's.* Fagin's use of the term "4NF" is logically correct because:

   (a) Fagin's 4NF implies BCNF, which implies 3NF, which implies 2NF (etc.). That is, if a relation is in Fagin's 4NF, then it is in BCNF; if a relation is in BCNF, then it is in 3NF; and so on. In other words, Fagin's 4NF is a logical next step in the progression 1NF–2NF–3NF–BCNF. By contrast, the IEF "4NF" does *not* imply any other level of normalization except first (1NF). It is not a logical next step at all.

   (b) In "classical" normalization (of which Fagin's 4NF is a part), the operation of replacing a relation that is in some given normal form by two or more relations in the next higher normal form—e.g., the operation of replacing a 2NF relation by two 3NF relations—is performed by means of the relational *projection* operator. In particular, the operation of replacing a BCNF relation by two 4NF relations (in Fagin's sense) is performed by means of projection. What is more, the operation of replacing a 4NF relation (in Fagin's sense) by relations in *fifth* normal form (5NF) is also performed by means of projection. (Note therefore that 4NF is not the end of the road. 5NF, however, is. But 5NF is beyond the scope of this short note.)

To sum up, classical normalization is, precisely, a process of taking projections. Furthermore, the process of recombining the results of those projections to recover the original relation is performed by means of the relational *join* operator (more accurately, the *natural* join operator); join is, in a sense, the inverse of projection.

In sharp contrast to the foregoing, the operation of replacing a relation by "4NF" relations in the IEF sense is *not* performed by taking projections, and the process of recombining those "4NF" relations to recover the original relation is *not* performed by taking a natural join. It follows that, whereas the IEF "4NF" might legitimately be regarded as a new normal form of some sort, it is a normal form that is *different in kind* from the classical normal forms. And, whatever else it may be, it is certainly not "fourth" in the sense that 3NF is "third" or 2NF is "second" (etc.).

> *Aside:* The operator that is used to obtain the IEF "4NF" is actually a *restriction/projection* combination, and the operator that is used to recover the original relation is *outer (natural) join*. For further discussion, see reference [5]. *End of aside.*

5. CONCLUSION

The concept of 4NF as defined by Fagin is useful. The concept of "4NF" as used in IEF is also useful. But they are not the same thing! So let's not use the same name for them. In particular, Fagin's use of the term 4NF has the prior claim, and furthermore has the virtue of being more logically correct; hence, Fagin's sense of the term is clearly the one to be preferred.

ACKNOWLEDGMENTS

The "4NF terminology" problem had been brought to my attention by several seminar attendees at different times, but it was not until Keri Healy of Seafirst Bank jogged my memory on the topic in mid 1989 that I got around to writing this short paper. My thanks also to Jim Adams of Nipsco and Doug Conley of Texas Instruments for their assistance; Doug in particular told me that TI has experienced some of the same confusions and has prepared a short explanatory note on the subject (which, however, I have not yet seen).

REFERENCES AND BIBLIOGRAPHY

1. R. F. Boyce, "Fourth Normal Form and Its Associated Decomposition Algorithm," *IBM Technical Disclosure Bulletin* 16, No. 1 (June 1973).

2. E. F. Codd, "Further Normalization of the Data Base Relational Model," in R. Rustin (ed.), *Data Base Systems,* Courant Computer Science Symposia Series 6 (Englewood Cliffs, NJ: Prentice-Hall, 1972).

3. E. F. Codd, "Recent Investigations into Relational Data Base Systems," *Proc. 1974 IFIP Congress,* Stockholm, Sweden (August 1974) and elsewhere.

4. C. J. Date, "Further Normalization," Chapter 21 of C. J. Date, *An Introduction to Database Systems: Volume I,* 5th edition (Reading, MA: Addison-Wesley, 1990).

5. C. J. Date, "A Practical Approach to Database Design," in C. J. Date, *Relational Database: Selected Writings* (Reading, MA: Addison-Wesley, 1986).

6. Ronald Fagin, "Multivalued Dependencies and a New Normal Form for Relational Databases," *ACM Transactions on Database Systems* 2, No. 3 (September 1977).

7. I. J. Heath, "Unacceptable File Operations in a Relational Data Base," *Proc. ACM SIGFIDET Workshop on Data Description, Access, and Control,* San Diego, CA (November 1971).

8. Texas Instruments, *A Guide to Information Engineering Using the IEF,* TI Part No. 2739 756-0001 (March 1988).

copies of a book; we are also not discussing the question of whether a new edition or a new printing—with or without corrections—constitutes a new book.

The ISBN consists basically of a ten-character identifier, made up as follows:

group code

publisher code

book number

check digit

However:

- Not all books have ISBNs. In particular, books published prior to 1970 do not. Such books are generally identified by a fake "ISBN" in which the first character is an X, and the remaining characters are "implementation-defined." But for the special case of British books published after 1967 (but prior to 1970), the first character is a zero and the rest of the ISBN is standard, since (a) zero is the group code for British books and (b) the ISBN is basically an extension of the British Standard Book Number as used since 1967.

- So long as the first character is not an X, all other characters except possibly the last must be numeric. The last character (the check digit) is either numeric or an X.

- The *group code* (beginning at character position one) is variable length.

- The *publisher code* is also variable length; furthermore, the algorithm for deciding the actual length depends on the group. By way of example, here are the rules for group zero:

If the publisher code begins with a value in the range:	*Then it is of length:*
0– 1	2
2–69	3
70–84	4
85–89	5
90–94	6
95–99	7

- The publisher code is "not quite unique" within its group. For example, "two small publishers might . . . be forced to share [the same code]" (quoting reference [1]).

- The remainder of the ISBN (excluding the check digit) is the "book number" (!).

- The tenth character is a check digit; the details of the formula by which the check digit is computed need not concern us here, but it is a base-11 computation, which means that the check digit might be an X (denoting ten).

- Note that the same book might have multiple ISBNs (e.g., if it is published by multiple publishers).

- Note too that the same book might exist in several versions (e.g., hardback, paperback, Book Club version, etc.). This is especially likely if the book is out of copyright (think of how many different versions there are of Shakespeare or Jane Austen). How many ISBNs?

4. CONCLUSION

Database professionals understand the dangers inherent in "intelligent keys." They should bring their expertise to bear on the problem of dissuading organizations from perpetrating (or perpetuating) the need for such keys.

ACKNOWLEDGMENTS

I am grateful to Charley Bontempo, Hugh Darwen, and Colin White for reviewing the first draft of this note.

REFERENCES AND BIBLIOGRAPHY

1. Geoff Lee, "Using the International Standard Book Number," *Computing* (June 15th, 1989).

2. C. J. Date, "Composite Keys" (in this volume).

With this design, when an order is first received, a row will be inserted into ORDER_RECEIVED, and the DBMS will perform a foreign key check on PROD#. When the order is subsequently filled (and a warehouse therefore selected), that row will be deleted from ORDER_RECEIVED and a corresponding row inserted into ORDER_FILLED, and the DBMS will perform a foreign key check on (PROD#,WHSE#). Note that this latter foreign key has NULLS NOT ALLOWED, so that the possibility of partly null foreign key values now no longer arises.

It might be objected that this design is excessively complex—in particular, that it involves excessive processing when an order is filled (a delete from one table and an insert into another, instead of a simple update)—and all of this complexity is caused by a mere desire on my part to conform to some piece of dogma ("Avoid partly null foreign key values"). But is the design truly that complex? Observe that:

1. There may well be additional items of information to record about received orders as opposed to filled orders (e.g., "scheduled delivery date"), or about filled orders as opposed to received orders (e.g., "actual delivery date"). Each such additional item lends weight to the argument in favor of the dual-table design.

2. Furthermore, it is far from clear that a delete followed by an insert is truly more complex than a "simple" update (though it might appear slightly more complex to the application programmer). In any case, there might be good reasons *not* to delete the ORDER_RECEIVED row after all (see the next point below).

3. Last but not least, the design permits the company to fill an order with a replacement product (represented by a different PROD#)—e.g., if the product ordered has been superseded by a new version—without losing information concerning the product that was originally ordered. The design also simplifies the process of filling an order in installments instead of all at once, should this prove necessary in some cases.

6.   DESIGN NUMBER 4

Design Number 4 is rather similar to Number 3, except that the two order tables are effectively joined into one:

```
ORDER ( ORDER#, RPROD#, FPROD#, WHSE#, ... )
       PRIMARY KEY ( ORDER# )
       FOREIGN KEY ( RPROD# ) REFERENCES PROD
                    NULLS NOT ALLOWED
       FOREIGN KEY ( FPROD#, WHSE# ) REFERENCES INV
                    NULLS ALLOWED
```

(Tables PROD, WHSE, and INV are as in Design Number 1.)

With this design, when an order is first received, a row will be inserted into ORDER with RPROD# identifying the product ordered and with FPROD# and WHSE# both set to null. When the order is subsequently filled, FPROD# and WHSE# will be set to identify the product shipped and the corresponding warehouse, respectively. The foreign key (FPROD#,WHSE#) does have NULLS ALLOWED, but every value of that foreign key will always be wholly null or wholly nonnull—there is now no need ever to have a value that is partly but not wholly null. *Note:* It may be necessary to maintain the additional (trivial) integrity constraint that within any given ORDER row, if FPROD# is nonnull, then it must be the same as RPROD#—or maybe not, if (as in Design Number 3) it is possible to fill an order with a product that is not the same as the one originally ordered.

As explained above, this design does avoid the problem of partly null foreign key values; however, it does not avoid the problem of conterminous referential paths.

7.   CONCLUSION

So which if any of the various designs described above is "the best"? At this point I am tempted to invoke The Principle of Cautious Design [3] and vote for Design Number 3. But I am open to persuasion in favor of some preferable alternative. Comments are invited.

ACKNOWLEDGMENTS

I would like to thank David Carrick for posing the original problem on which this paper is based. My thanks also to Hugh Darwen and Colin White for their comments on an earlier draft.

REFERENCES AND BIBLIOGRAPHY

1. C. J. Date, "Referential Integrity and Foreign Keys Part II: Further Considerations," in C. J. Date, *Relational Database Writings 1985–1989* (Reading, MA: Addison-Wesley, 1990).

2. C. J. Date, "Composite Keys" (in this volume).

3. C. J. Date, "The Principle of Cautious Design" (in this volume).